A HISTORY OF FRANCE

A History of France
H.E. MARSHALL

This edition published 2023
By Living Book Press
Copyright © Living Book Press, 2023

ISBN: 978-1-922950-79-6 (B&W Softcover Edition)
        978-1-922950-83-3 (B&W Hardcover Edition)
        978-1-922974-12-9 (Color Softcover Edition)
        978-1-922974-13-6 (Color Hardcover Edition)

First published in 1912.

All rights reserved. No part of this publication may be reproduced, stored in a retrieval system, or transmitted in any other form or means – electronic, mechanical, photocopying, recording or otherwise, without the prior permission of the copyright owner and the publisher or as provided by Australian law.

 A catalogue record for this book is available from the National Library of Australia

CONTENTS

1. HOW THE GAULS BENT THE PRIDE OF ROME — 1
2. HOW VERCINGETORIX DIED FOR HIS COUNTRY — 7
3. THE SAINTS OF FRANCE — 12
4. ATTILA, THE SCOURGE OF GOD — 16
5. THE STORY OF CLOVIS — 20
6. THE STORY OF THE SONS OF CLOVIS — 25
7. THE DO-NOTHING KINGS AND THE MAYORS OF THE PALACE — 29
8. CHARLES THE HAMMER — 33
9. THE STORY OF PEPIN THE SHORT — 36
10. CHARLEMAGNE—KING OF LOMBARDY — 40
11. CHARLEMAGNE—THE DEFEAT OF RONCESVALLES — 43
12. CHARLEMAGNE—THE EMPEROR OF THE WEST — 47
13. LOUIS I THE GOOD NATURED—THE FIELD OF LIES — 54
14. CHARLES THE BALD—THE WAR OF THE THREE BROTHERS — 58
15. LOUIS II THE STAMMERER AND HIS SONS — 62
16. CHARLES THE FAT—THE MEN OF PARIS DEFIED THE KINGS — 64
17. CHARLES III THE SIMPLE—HOW ROLLO DID HOMAGE — 69
18. HOW HUGH CAPET BECAME KING OF FRANCE — 74
19. HUGH CAPET—HOW THE BISHOP BETRAYED THE DUKE — 77
20. ROBERT I THE PIOUS—THE BEGGARS' KING — 79
21. HENRY I—THE PEACE OF GOD AND THE TRUCE OF GOD — 83
22. PHILIP I—HOW HAROLD THE SAXON PAID A VISIT — 85
23. PHILIP I—HOW DUKE WILLIAM SAILED TO ENGLAND — 91
24. PHILIP I—THE BATTLE OF HASTINGS — 95
25. PHILIP I—HOW PETER THE HERMIT PREACHED GOD'S WAR — 98
26. PHILIP I—THE FIRST WAR OF THE CROSS — 101
27. LOUIS VI THE FAT—THE PEOPLE OF LAON FOUGHT — 105
28. LOUIS VI THE FAT—THE KING OF FRANCE FOUGHT — 109
29. LOUIS VII—SECOND WAR OF THE CROSS — 112
30. LOUIS VII—A QUEEN OF FRANCE AND ENGLAND — 116
31. PHILIP II AUGUSTUS—HOW NORMANDY WAS LOST — 119
32. PHILIP II AUGUSTUS—WAR WITH THE ALBIGENSES — 123
33. PHILIP II AUGUSTUS AND LOUIS VIII—BOUVINES — 126
34. LOUIS THE SAINT—STORY OF HUGH DE LA MARCHE — 132
35. LOUIS THE SAINT—THE 'CROSS OF THE VOYAGE' — 137
36. LOUIS THE SAINT—THE KING'S LAST VOYAGE — 141
37. PHILIP III THE BOLD—STORY OF PETER THE BARBER — 143
38. PHILIP IV—KNIGHTS AND WEAVERS — 146
39. PHILIP IV—PRIDE OF ROME AND OF FRANCE — 150

40.	LOUIS X, PHILIP V, AND CHARLES IV—THE SALIC LAW	155
41.	PHILIP VI—WAR WITH FLEMISH MERCHANTS	157
42.	PHILIP VI OF VALOIS—BATTLE AND PLAGUE	164
43.	JOHN II THE GOOD—HOW THE KING QUARRELLED	168
44.	JOHN II THE GOOD—THE JACQUERIE	173
45.	JOHN II—STEPHEN WOULD HAVE BETRAYED PARIS	176
46.	CHARLES V THE WISE—A GREAT KNIGHT	179
47.	CHARLES V—HOW DU GUESCLIN FOUGHT	182
48.	CHARLES VI—THE MADNESS OF THE KING	185
49.	CHARLES VI—THE BATTLE OF AGINCOURT	189
50.	CHARLES VII—THE MAID OF ORLEANS	193
51.	CHARLES VII—THE END OF HUNDRED YEARS' WAR	197
52.	LOUIS XI—HOW THE KING FOUGHT WITH CHARLES	200
53.	LOUIS XI—THE TROUBLES OF THE DUCHESS MARY	204
54.	CHARLES VIII—DREAMS OF GLORY AND DOMINION	208
55.	LOUIS XII—THE KNIGHT WITHOUT FEAR	213
56.	LOUIS XII—THE BATTLE OF THE SPURS	216
57.	FRANCIS I—HOW BAYARD KNIGHTED THE KING	220
58.	FRANCIS I—HOW THE KING WAS TAKEN PRISONER	225
59.	HENRY II—THE DUKE OF GUISE DEFENDED METZ	229
60.	HENRY II— CALAIS ONCE MORE BECAME FRENCH	232
61.	FRANCIS II—THE RIOT OF AMBOISE	235
62.	CHARLES IX—HUGUENOT AND CATHOLIC	238
63.	CHARLES IX—THE MASSACRE OF ST. BARTHOLOMEW	243
64.	HENRY III—THE WAR OF THE THREE HENRIES	247
65.	HENRY IV THE GREAT—THE PROTESTANT KING	252
66.	HENRY IV—EDICT OF NANTES—FRANCE AT PEACE	257
67.	LOUIS XIII—THE REIGN OF FAVORITES	261
68.	LOUIS XIII—THE TAKING OF LA ROCHELLE	265
69.	LOUIS XIII—THE POWER OF THE CARDINAL KING	269
70.	LOUIS XIV—HOW A GREAT LADY BESIEGED ORLEANS	273
71.	LOUIS XIV—THE MAN IN THE IRON MASK	278
72.	LOUIS XIV—THE GRAND MONARCH	282
73.	LOUIS XIV—REVOCATION OF THE EDICT OF NANTES	286
74.	LOUIS XIV—THE WAR OF THE SPANISH SUCCESSION	291
75.	LOUIS XV—BUBBLE WEALTH	296
76.	LOUIS XV—THE WELL BELOVED	299
77.	LOUIS XVI—THE OATH OF THE TENNIS COURT	303
78.	LOUIS XVI—NOT REVOLT, BUT REVOLUTION	307
79.	LOUIS XVI—THE KING AND QUEEN WENT TO PARIS	311
80.	LOUIS XVI—FLIGHT	315
81.	LOUIS XVI—DEATH	320
82.	THE REPUBLIC—THE RED TERROR	325
83.	THE REPUBLIC—DIRECTORY, "LITTLE CORPORAL"	329
84.	THE REPUBLIC—CONSUALTE, GENERAL BONAPARTE	334
85.	THE EMPIRE—NAPOLEAN EMPORER AND KING	339

86.	NAPOLEON I—THE SUN OF AUSTERLITZ	346
87.	NAPOLEON I—A KING OF KINGS	352
88.	NAPOLEON I—THE HEART OF RUSSIA	357
89.	NAPOLEON I—FAREWELL TO FRANCE	361
90.	THE HUNDRED DAYS	364
91.	THE STORY OF THE EMPEROR WHO NEVER REIGNED	368
92.	LOUIS XVIII—WHITE TERROR AND HOLY ALLIANCE	371
93.	CHARLES X—THE REVOLUTION OF JULY	374
94.	LOUIS PHILIPPE—A REBEL PRINCESS	377
95.	LOUIS PHILIPPE—ADVENTURES OF A REBEL PRINCE	381
96.	LOUIS PHILIPPE—THE REVOLUTION OF FEBRUARY	384
97.	HOW A PRINCESS MADE A LAST STAND	387
98.	SECOND REPUBLIC—LOUIS NAPOLEON PRESIDENT	389
99.	THE SECOND EMPIRE—"THE CRIME OF DECEMBER"	391
100.	THE SECOND EMPIRE—NAPOLEON III A PRISONER	394
101.	THE THIRD REPUBLIC	397

CHAPTER 1

HOW THE GAULS BENT THE PRIDE OF ROME

ONE July day, long, long ago, under a blue and cloudless sky, a host of fierce, wild warriors passed through the sunny lands of Italy. These warriors were fair and tall. Their eyes were blue, their hair and moustaches long and rough. They were gaily dressed and gleamed with gold. The huge swords and shields which they carried were decorated with gold, gold collars were about their necks, gold bracelets upon their arms, and from their shoulders hung cloaks of brightly checked and striped cloth.

These warriors were the Gauls. As they passed onward the people of Italy fled before them in terror, and towns shut their gates against them. But the vast host swept on, leaving the people in peace. "We march to Rome!" they cried. "It is against the Romans alone that we fight; all others are our friends."

Onward the Gauls marched, seventy thousand strong But not until they were within twelve miles of Rome did they meet the Roman army. Here, where the little river Allier throws itself into the Tiber, a great battle took place.

Chanting a wild war song, the Gauls threw themselves upon the Romans, ere they had time to form in battle array. The Roman Legions could not stand against the onslaught. They broke, they fled. Many rushed into the river and found death there, many were slain before they reached it. A few fled even to Rome, carrying with them the news of defeat and slaughter, the news that the barbarians were at the very gates.

Wild despair seized the people of Rome. They knew not what to do. The city was filled with the sounds of mourning, with the weeping of children, with the cries of women wailing for their dead, while men rushed hither and thither in terror, forgetting even to shut the gates. Soon the streets were full of men, women, and children who fled, carrying with them what they held most precious, hiding in haste what they could not take.

But it was chiefly the old and the feeble who fled. Many of the young men remained and gathered together into the Capitol or citadel. This fortress rose above the town, and was very strong, for it was guarded on three sides by rocks which it was impossible to climb. It was surrounded, too, by high, thick walls. Here as much food as could be collected was hurriedly carried, and here the young men shut themselves in, resolving to die rather than yield.

Soon the city which had been noisy with sounds of grief and terror sank again into silence. The streets were empty and deserted, save for a few old men of noble birth who disdained to flee. These dressed themselves in their most splendid robes. Then each one, taking an ivory staff in his hand, seated himself in an ivory chair in the middle of his hall to await the coming of the enemy.

But not for three days after the battle did the Gauls arrive. For they had stayed to plunder the Roman baggage, to drink and carouse when, had they but known it, the gates of Rome stood open wide and all its treasures at their mercy. When at last they came, passed through these open gates, and into the deserted streets, the silence and the loneliness struck fear to the hearts of the rough soldiers of Gaul.

They clung together, moving warily, fearing a sudden attack from an unseen enemy. But presently gathering courage, they strayed through the open doors of the silent palaces. Here they saw, sitting motionless, old men with long white beards. Their faces were so noble, their dresses so splendid, that the Gauls were abashed.

Who and what were these silent figures? Were they gods? Were they statues? The wild barbarians dared not touch them. They dared hardly whisper in their presence. At length a Gaul more bold than his fellows put out his hand and stroked the long white beard of the silent Roman near him.

Instantly the old eyes flashed fire, the arm that had so often wielded a sword flew upward, and the Gaul fell to the ground stunned from the blow of the ivory staff.

It was a signal for slaughter. With wild cries the Gauls fell upon the old men, and slew them where they sat. Then through all the city they rushed, robbing and burning. But although the city with its palaces was at their mercy, the Gauls could not dislodge the Romans from their Capitol.

For seven months the siege went on, the Gauls hoping that hunger would force the Romans to yield. But instead of that, hunger and disease weakened the besiegers themselves. For in their first wild attack upon the city they had burned and destroyed much of the food it held. Now they had to suffer for their own ruthless waste. There was hunger, there was death both without and within the fortress.

At length one day a Gaul, passing beneath the rock upon which the Capitol was built, discovered a way by which one man at a time could climb to the top. He told his general of the discovery and led him to the spot.

That evening the general called his officers together. "We believed it impossible to climb the rock," he said, "but we have discovered a way. Where one man can go, an army can go."

Gladly and eagerly the Gauls set forth. The night was dark. One by o e they followed each other, clinging to roots and branches of trees and shrubs, finding a scanty foothold among rocks and boulders, till at length, after tremendous efforts, the foremost reached the top, arid crouched close beneath the bottom of the wall. Here the wall was low, for the rock was so steep that no attack from this side seemed possible. So secure, indeed, did the Romans feel that the sentinels were fast asleep. Even the lean, hungry dogs, which prowled about the citadel searching vainly for food, gave no warning.

Another and another man reached the top. The Gauls at length began to scale the wall, and lest the famished dogs should bark they threw some bread to them. The hungry creatures darted upon it and began to devour it greedily. All danger seemed over; the first by man was about to leap into the fortress, when suddenly a flock of geese, aroused by the smell of food, began to make a loud cackling and flapping of wings. These geese were held sacred to the goddess Juno, and so, although the garrison were starving, they had been spared.

Thus it was by a few geese that the Capitol was saved, for their loud cackling awakened the sleeping sentinels.

A soldier named Marcus Manlius was the first to awake. Seizing his weapons he called loudly to his comrades and rushed to meet the foe. With a blow of his spear he felled one Gaul to the ground, at the same time dashing his shield in the face of a second. Backward fell the Gaul upon his comrade behind, hurling him headlong down the cliff.

In a few minutes all the garrison were awake. With stones and spears they fell upon the besiegers, who, crashing one upon the other, were hurled pell mell down the cliff in utter rout. Of all those who had painfully struggled up the height but few regained the camp alive.

The Capitol was saved, but the siege went on; famine and pestilence

ONE BY ONE THE GAULS FOLLOWED EACH OTHER.

still did their work both within and without the walls. In vain the besieged looked for help.

No help came to them. They ate everything, even to the leather of their boots, suffering untold agonies of hunger. Still they would not give in.

Then the Gauls, well knowing that the garrison were starving, offered terms of peace. The Romans proudly refused, and to prove that they were not starving threw their last loaves of bread down among the enemy.

But at length even Roman pride could hold out no longer, and peace was signed. The Romans agreed to give the Gauls a large sum of money, and to provide them with food on their journey homeward. They also gave up some of the Roman territory and promised when they rebuilt the city to leave one gate forever open, in memory of the victory of the Gauls.

All the gold in the city was gathered to pay the ransom, but when it came to be weighed, it seemed not enough. Then the Romans fiercely accused the Gauls of treachery. "The weights are false," they cried.

In answer, the leader of the Gauls drew his sword and flung it into the scale, crying, "Woe to the vanquished!" It was as if he meant to show how impossible it was to outweigh the strength of his sword.

Stung by the taunt, many of the Romans wished to break off the peace and fight once more, this time till death. But the wiser among them said: "Let be. The shame lies not in giving more than we promised; it lies in giving at all. Let us suffer, in silence, insults which we can neither avoid nor avenge."

So the price was paid, the siege ended, and the Gauls marched away, leaving the Romans to rebuild their ruined city.

This siege of Rome took place nearly four hundred years before Christ, and it is perhaps the greatest feat accomplished by these ancient Gauls. And I have told you the story because the Gauls were the ancient inhabitants of France; but in those days the Gauls were a race, not a nation. They belonged to a race of people who were found not only in the country we now call France, but in Italy, Spain, and Portugal. They were to be found eastward as far as the isles of Greece and Asia Minor, northward almost to the shores of the Baltic, westward to the isles of Britain and of Scotia.

They were a wild and warlike people. Like the ancient dwellers in

Britain, they were Druids; they worshipped the sun and the stars and held the mistletoe to be sacred. Like the ancient Britons, many of them dyed their bodies blue. They wore their hair long. They were great talkers, loving to hear news and to listen to the tales of minstrels.

And for many a day after the taking of Rome there was told in the firelight the marvelous tale of how the Gauls had bent the pride of Rome.

CHAPTER 2

HOW VERCINGETORIX DIED FOR HIS COUNTRY

THE Gauls had stood at the gate of Rome. They had sacked and burned the city, and had forced the Romans to buy their freedom with gold. But Rome rose from the ashes, and took once more her proud, commanding position. Year by year the Romans grew stronger. Year by year they claimed more of the world for their own. Bit by bit they drove the Gauls out of Italy, out of Spain and Portugal. Then, in order to make their conquests safe and to secure a road from one peninsula to the other, the Romans took possession of the south of Gaul, that is the south of France. Thus the Gauls were shut out of both peninsulas, and were also cut off from the sea. And while the Romans pressed upon the Gauls from the south, wild tribes from the German Ocean and the Baltic pressed upon them from the north. Yet with two great foreign foes to fight, one on the north and one on the south, the Gauls were often at war within their own borders, and so less able to drive away outside foes.

Thus three hundred years and more went past, the Romans always growing stronger, the Gauls weaker. At length Julius Caesar came as Governor of the Roman province of Southern Gaul. He made up his mind not to be content with the south only, but to make the whole of Gaul a Roman province.

So the fight began. Caesar was one of the greatest soldiers and conquerors the world has ever seen. He marched over the country with unheard of swiftness, making roads and building bridges and ramparts wherever he passed. He crossed the wide, swift river Rhine upon a bridge, which had taken only ten days to build, in order utterly to subdue the wild tribes beyond it, who gave help to the Gauls. Next, finding that the Gauls were helped and encouraged by the people from the neighbouring island of Britain, he set sail and landed in Kent. Of that you will read in English history. A few weeks later he was once more in Gaul. So the great General worked and fought, striking a blow now here, now there, until the whole of Gaul was conquered.

When news of Cesar's conquests reached Rome, the people cried aloud in astonishment and admiration. It was the swiftness of Caesar's marches, the boldness and sureness with which he struck his blows that roused their wonder even more than his victories.

But Caesar's work was not done. The Gauls were beaten, but not subdued, and they rose in rebellion in 52 B. C. under a young noble named Vercingetorix. Vercingetorix really means merely commander-in-chief, but it is the only name for the young leader of Gaul that has come down to us. It was in the mountainous part of France that this rising took place, among the hills of Auvergne and in the Cevennes.

Caesar was in Rome when he heard of it, and although it was winter and the snow lay deep upon the Alps, he hastened back to Gaul. He had need of all his haste, for Vercingetorix, with a skill almost equal to Caesar's own, was gathering and drilling his troops. The different tribes of Gaul forgot their quarrels, and joined under their new leader to fight for the freedom of their country.

It was a last, brilliant struggle. The Gauls burned their towns and laid waste their country so that the Romans should find neither food nor shelter. They learned to make their camps in Roman fashion, they fought the Romans with their own weapons. Never before had Caesar met with so skillful and so obstinate an enemy. Battle after battle was fought.

At length, before the town of Gergovia, Caesar was defeated. He lost his sword and left seven hundred soldiers among the slain. Great was the joy among the Gauls. The all-conquering General had been defeated! Gaul they thought would once more be free. They praised their gods for the victory, and hung Caesar's sword in their temple. Long after, Caesar himself saw it there. But when his soldiers would have torn it from the place he smiled and said, "Let it remain; it is sacred."

Meanwhile Vercingetorix gathered his generals and spoke to them. "Now is the time," he said, "the hour of victory has come. The Romans are fleeing in all haste homeward. It is enough for the liberty of the moment; it is not enough for the peace in time to come. Soon they will return in greater force, and we shall never see the end of war. We cannot offer them battle direct, but we must harass their march, make them cast away their baggage so that they die from hunger and want, and flee from Gaul covered with shame."

When Vercingetorix had ceased speaking, a great shout went up from the leaders of the Gauls. With one voice they swore never more to see their homes, never more to greet their wives, children, and friends until they had twice crossed the enemies' line.

Next day the whole army of the Gauls set forth. But, although the soldiers were brave and their leader skillful, they had to fight against the greatest general in the world. They fought and lost. In a few days the Gauls found themselves shut in the city of Alesia, while Caesar and his legions lay around besieging them. Alesia was built upon a hill, in a very strong position, with two rivers flowing round the walls. Caesar saw that the position was so strong that he could not hope to carry it by storm. So he resolved to starve the Gauls into surrender. Quickly his soldiers set to work to dig a broad trench and build a high wall, so as to shut the city off from all outside help.

For thirty days and more the siege lasted. Then a mighty army, gathered from all parts of Gaul, appeared to help their starving comrades. There was a great battle in which the besieged Gauls took part, but it ended in a victory for Caesar. It was not a mere victory. It was the end of the struggle. The spirit of Gaul was crushed and broken.

Early on the morning after the battle Vercingetorix called together his counsellors. "I fought not for myself," he said, "but for Gaul. Yet I am the cause of this war, therefore I give myself up freely to the conqueror. Let his wrath fall on me, but let him spare my country."

Vercingetorix then put on his most splendid armor and jewels. He mounted his war-horse, the harness of which was gay with crimson and gold. Then the gates of Alesia were opened and he rode forth.

Before the gates Caesar sat in counsel. Vercingetorix on a splendid horse, his jewels and armor gleaming in the sunshine, rode quickly round the tribunal. Then vaulting from his horse he threw his sword and spear at Caesar's feet, and, without a sword, seated himself upon the steps of the throne.

Even the Roman soldiers were touched at the sight of this splendid hero who thus gave himself up for his country. Caesar alone remained cold and cruel. To him Vercingetorix was merely the man who had for one day robbed him of the name unconquerable. A few minutes he gazed at him in silent hatred, then he burst forth into a torrent of wrath. In silence Vercingetorix listened. Then at a sign from Caesar he was bound and led away.

Vercingetorix was sent to Rome a prisoner. There for six long years he lay in a dark and noisome dungeon. Then he was brought forth to

VERCINGETORIX THREW HIS SWORD AND SPEAR AT CAESARS FEET.

add glory to Caesar's triumph. And after having been led through the streets to be jeered at by the Roman multitude, his head was cut off at the foot of the Capitol, while upon its height Caesar knelt to the gods, giving thanks to them for his victories.

CHAPTER 3

THE SAINTS OF FRANCE

THUS, after eight years' fighting, there was peace in Home Gaul. The "Peace of Rome," it was proudly called.

It seems to us in reading history that the Romans brought only war. Yet, after a war of conquest was over, the Romans brought to the conquered people such peace as the world had never known before. The Gauls, as has been said, were found very widely spread throughout Europe. But it was Julius Caesar who first fixed the name of Gaul to that part of the continent which lies between the Alps and the Rhine, that part which is now divided into Belgium, Switzerland, Alsace, and France. For nearly five hundred years Gaul was under the rule of Rome, and during three hundred years of that time there was little fighting. For the attempts to rise against the conquerors were few and feeble.

And with the long peace came civilization. Gaul had had only small villages. Now aqueducts and roads were built, towns arose with fine buildings, streets and baths. Gauls fought side by side with Romans. They were given the rights of Roman citizens, and sat in the Roman senate. The old Gallic language disappeared before the Roman, and Latin became the language of all but the very ignorant and poor.

Following in the footsteps of civilization came Christianity. The story of Christ was first brought to Gaul, not from Rome, but from Greece. For long ages Greek merchants had traded along the shores of the Mediterranean. Marseilles was a Greek colony, and Greek merchants landed there and went far up the valley of the Rhone. And now they brought with them in their many comings and goings, not only merchandise, but the story of Christ. It was natural that the story of Christ should be brought by these merchants, for some of them came from places where St. Paul himself had preached and founded churches.

In Gaul, as in other lands, the coming of Christianity was hard. Those who believed in the new faith had to suffer terrible persecutions both from their fellow countrymen and from their Roman rulers. They were robbed of their liberty and their wealth. They were tortured, they were burned alive, thrown to wild beasts, and put to death in many cruel ways. It needed a courage of which we can form little idea to say, "I am a

Christian." And yet hundreds and thousands were found, weak women and children among them, who had the courage to say these words, and cling to their faith through the fiercest of tortures.

Among these early martyrs was St. Denis, of Paris. He, with six others, was sent from Rome to teach the Gauls about Christ. St. Denis became the first Bishop of Paris, and about 272, after a long and wearisome imprisonment, he died there for his faith. His head was cut off upon the hill Montmartre, which is said to have taken its name from this deed, Montmartre meaning "mount of the martyr." The body of St. Denis was thrown into the river Seine, but was recovered from it by a Christian lady, and buried not far from where it was found. After a time a chapel was built on the spot.

Later a great church and abbey arose there. St. Denis became the patron Saint of France, and his name is forever linked with the history of the country. "St. Denis " was the battle cry of French soldiers, just as "St. George" was the battle cry of English soldiers. It was over the high altar in St. Denis Abbey that the King's standard hung, except when he himself went to battle. It is in the Church of St. Denis that nearly all the kings of France lie buried.

But although St. Denis is the patron, St. Martin is the favorite, saint of France. St. Martin was born in Hungary, and his parents were heathen, his father being a soldier in the Roman army. Someone, perhaps his nurse, told Martin the story of Christ, and he longed to be a Christian. When quite a small boy he found his way to the Church, and there he was received as a scholar. He wanted to give himself up to a life of religion, but when he was fifteen the Emperor issued an order that all the sons of soldiers must become soldiers. So Martin was forced to join the army. In those days the life of a soldier was often rough and wild. But Martin lived so simply and quietly that his companions said he was more like a monk than a soldier. He kept only one slave, whom he treated as a friend and companion rather than as a servant. He astonished his equals by waiting upon himself and even lacing his own boots.

Martin was kind not only to his slave, but to everyone who was poor and unhappy. He gave away nearly everything that he possessed. One bitterly cold winter's day, as he was riding through the gates of Amiens with his companions, he met a poor beggar who was almost naked and shivering with cold. The wretched man begged of every one as he passed, but no one listened to him. Martin alone was filled with pity for the poor shivering creature. But he had already given away all that he had. The only thing which remained to him was his cloak. So, drawing his sword, he cut that in two, and gave half to the poor beggar.

Those around laughed at the figure Martin made, clad only in half a cloak; but he did not mind, for the beggar had gone away warm and comforted. That night, as Martin lay asleep, it seemed to him that Christ appeared with the half cloak wrapped round Him. 'Look well at my cloak, Martin," he said; "do you know it? >: Then, as he looked at it, Martin heard Christ say, "Martin who is yet only a learner has clothed me with this garment."

This vision made Martin very happy, for he remembered how when Christ was on earth he had said, "If ye did it unto them, ye did it unto me."

When he was eighteen Martin was baptized, and although he remained in the army, he was a soldier in little more than name, for there was no fighting. There came a time, however, when the Germans invaded Gaul, and the army was gathered to march against them. Then Martin asked to be allowed to leave the army. "I have served you faithfully," he said to the Emperor. "Permit me now to serve God. I am a soldier of Christ. I cannot fight."

"It is fear which makes you ask this," replied the Emperor; "you are afraid to face the enemy."

"Nay," said Martin, "it is not fear. Place me tomorrow in the front rank of the army, and, without arms or armor, but protected only by the Sign of the Cross, I will gladly march into the thickest of the fight."

To this the Emperor agreed. Meanwhile Martin was loaded with fetters so that he might not escape. But he had no need to keep his promise. There was no fighting, for that night the Germans sought for peace.

Martin was then allowed to leave the army, and he afterward led such a holy life that the people of Tours chose him for their Bishop. From that time forth he fought against idolatry. He took long journeys far into the country where Christianity was still unknown. His life was more than once in danger, for the fierce heathen in these wild and unknown parts of Gaul hated the new religion. They were angry because Martin cut down the sacred woods of the Druids, ruined the heathen temples, broke and burned their heathen images; and they would willingly have killed him.

Yet, though he waged war against idolatry, no one ever saw Martin angry or impatient. His heart was always full of kindliness and love, of peace and mercy.

By this time Christianity was no longer the despised and persecuted religion it had been. It had become the religion of the emperors, who treated Martin with great honor, and once when he was asked to dine with the Emperor, the Empress waited on him with her own hands, feeling herself greatly honored in the deed.

There are many stories told of miracles which Martin performed, and although we may not feel bound to believe all these, we may believe he was an unselfish, kindly man, simple in mind, tender of heart, who led a holy and useful life. He lived to a great age, and died peacefully, mourned by many friends.

CHAPTER 4

ATTILA, THE SCOURGE OF GOD

AS years went on, the power of the Romans grew less and less. They became less and less able to guard their wide provinces, to keep their many conquests. And as they grew weak the barbarians who lived along the borders of the vast Empire grew ever bolder and bolder.

Along the northern boundaries of Gaul lived the wild Germans. And now tribes of these, called Franks and Allemans, Goths and Vandals, would ever and again pour across the Rhine, break through the Roman wall, and waste the Roman province with fire and sword. Again and again they came, leaving death and destruction in their path. Again and again they were driven back. But still again they came. Other tribes came, not so much seeking plunder as seeking new homes. For they, in their turn, had been driven out by still fiercer tribes.

And thus after the long peace came a time of war and terror when all Gaul was wasted with fire and sword. Blackened ruins alone showed where fair cities had stood; a dreary waste, stretching as far as eye could reach, was all that was left of once smiling cornfields and vineyards.

Out of this confusion and desolation there arose three kingdoms, those of the Franks, the Visigoths, and the Burgundians. But before they could settle to peace, the land was once more swept by a fierce horde. This was the last and worst of all invasions by barbarians. For it was led by Attila the Hun, who gloried in the name of "Scourge of God."

Attila led his host, five hundred thousand strong, over the fairest fields of Gaul, leaving utter desolation and misery in his train, for it was his boast that grass never grew where his horse's hoofs had trod.

On and on he swept. His very name, which means something that is vast and awful, struck terror to the hearts of men. Yet this terrible creature was no giant. He was a little man like the Huns he led. He was little, but his shoulders were broad, his head large, and out of his swarthy face shone small piercing eyes which in anger flashed fire, giving to his whole appearance something proud and passionate.

He was a man born to terrify men and shake the world to its foundations. He spent his life in war for the love of war. He fought, not for love of conquest, but for the love of killing. He destroyed, not for the love of plunder, but for the love of destruction. The dress and armour of his followers glittered with gold and gems, the spoils of war, but Attila wore neither color nor ornament; his table was served with wooden cups and platters, and he ate nothing but raw meat.

Such was the ruler who dominated all the north of Europe from the Black Sea to the German Ocean, from the Danube to the Baltic. Vassal kings and princes served him humbly, they trembled at his frown, they feared his flashing eye, they sped to do his will at the slightest bidding.

Such was the conqueror who now marched triumphant through Gaul laying it in ashes. But at length his triumphant march was stopped at Orleans, where Gaul and Roman alike made a gallant stand against him. The Bishop of Orleans was a brave and wise man, and, as Attila marched upon the town, he sent to the Roman General Aetius begging for aid. "For five weeks," he said, "we can hold out. But if you do not come then, the wild beast will devour my flock."

Day by day the people of Orleans fought and prayed, encouraged by their brave Bishop. Day by day the savage hordes of Huns raged around the walls. They poured showers of arrows into the town, and were such splendid marksmen that a soldier hardly dared show himself upon the battlements. The defenders were brave and steadfast, but at length the walls shook beneath the battering rams of the heathen. There was no more food, and still no sign of help. All hope fled from the hearts of the people. Sobbing they crowded round their Bishop begging him to save them.

"Put your trust in God," he replied, "go, kneel to Him in prayer. Implore with tears the aid of the Lord, for He is an ever present help in trouble."

So all who could not fight knelt in the churches praying. And while they prayed the Bishop sent a secret messenger to the Roman General: "If you do not pome to-day, O my son," he said, "you will come too late."

Then the Bishop bade a servant go to the highest tower of the ramparts. "Go," he said, "look well, for perchance God in His mercy comes to our aid."

But the servant returned sadly. 'There is no one to be seen," he said.

"Yet pray with fervor," said the Bishop to the people, "for the Lord will deliver you this day." So the people continued in prayer.

"Go a second time," commanded the Bishop, "and look."

A second time the servant went and returned. "There is no one to be seen," he said again.

"Yet pray with all your hearts," said the Bishop, "for God will surely help you this day." So the people prayed aloud with groans and tears, making great supplication. "Go yet a third time," said the Bishop, "and look."

A third time the servant went and returned. "I see," he said, "a small cloud far in the distance."

"It is the aid of God," cried the Bishop.

And all the people cried with him, "It is the aid of God." Eagerly they rushed to the walls, and, as they watched, the small cloud came nearer and nearer, growing ever larger as it came. At last, lighted by the evening sunshine, they saw the flutter of both Roman and Gothic banners, the gleam of Roman and Gothic spears and shields. The legions of Rome under Aetius and the army of Theodoric, the King of the Visigoths, were marching together to help the besieged city.

Orleans was saved; and not only Orleans, but the whole of Gaul. Attila, fearing to meet the great army which was coming against him, marched away. But the Visigoths and Romans followed him, and on the plain near Chalons a great battle was fought. It was one of the most terrible battles fought in ancient times.

The day before the battle the Huns captured a Christian hermit. This man was thought by the peasants round to be a prophet. He was brought before Attila, who asked of him news of the coming battle.

"Thou art the Scourge of God," replied the hermit. "Thou art the hammer with which God Almighty strikes the world. But, when He pleases, God breaks the tools of His vengeance. He makes the sword to pass from one hand to another, according to His will. Know then that thou shalt be vanquished in thy battle with the Romans. Thus shalt thou learn that the strength that is in thee cometh not of this world."

But, nothing daunted, when morning came Attila gave battle. He made a speech to encourage his soldiers. "Myself will cast the first javelin," he said, "and if there be a man who stands still when Attila fights, that man dies the death."

It was a terrible battle, and when night fell sixty thousand dead lay upon the plain, among them Theodoric the King of the Visigoths. But Attila was defeated. Behind a rampart of his war chariots he sat like a lion at bay, and so fierce did he seem even in defeat that neither Roman, nor Goth, nor Gaul dare again attack him. So he retreated over the Rhine in safety.

This was the last victory of the Romans in Gaul and they won it by the help of half-savage Goths. Aetius has been called the last of all the Romans, and after this we hear no more of Roman power in Gaul. The land was divided hereafter into three kingdoms: that of the Visigoths on the West, that of the Burgundians on the East, and that of the Franks in the North.

It was the Franks who in the long run won the whole country and gave their name to it, for France is the kingdom of the Franks or Freemen. The Gaulo-Romans still lived in the land but the Franks were the conquerors and rulers. So I will now tell you something about these Franks and their Kings. But you must remember that just as in far-off times England was not all one kingdom neither was France all one kingdom. The France not all land possessed by the Franks was very small indeed compared with France, as we now know it. Even the Franks themselves were not all united under one King, but were divided into various tribes.

CHAPTER 5

THE STORY OF CLOVIS

WHILE the last of all the Romans was fighting against the Huns, there ruled over the Franks a King called Merovee, the Son of the Seas. After him the Kings who ruled over the Franks for nearly three hundred years were called Merovingians. When Merovee died, his son Childeric was made King. But after a time the Franks rebelled, and chased Childeric from the throne. The King took refuge in a far-off country, but before he fled he cut a coin in two, giving half to his faithful friend, Wiomad. "When I send you the half which I keep," said Wiomad, "you will know that you may safely return."

For eight years Childeric stayed in that far country. Then, at length, one day a messenger came who bore in his hand the half of a golden coin. By this Childeric knew that he might safely return home, which he gladly did. The Franks received him with joy, and once more he became their King. Once more he stood upon his shield, while his warriors raised him shoulder high, acclaiming him King with shouts and clashing of swords. For such was the custom of the Franks.

Childeric thought no more of the eight long years he had spent in that far country. But one day a lady came and stood at the palace door and knocked. When Childeric was told of it, he commanded that the strange lady should be led before him. And when she was brought, lo! it was Queen Basine, who had been kind to him in that far-off land. Childeric was filled with wonder.

'What has made you journey thus all alone from that far-off land?" he asked.

"I have come," replied Queen Basine,"because I know your worth and your courage. I have come to stay with you. Think not if I believed there was another even in these strange lands beyond the sea who could equal you that I would come to you. Nay, I should go to him."

When Childeric heard this he was overcome with joy, and made Queen Basine his wife.

Childeric and Basine had a son whose name was Clovis. When Childeric died, Clovis became King. He was then only fifteen years old, and he possessed none of the land which is now called France. His kingdom lay north of it, in what we now call Belgium. But when Clovis had reigned five years he began to wish to enlarge his kingdom, and he waged war against the tribes which surrounded him, and subdued them until a great part of the north of France was under his rule.

The people of Gaul against whom Clovis fought were Christians, but he and his Franks were heathen. So they destroyed the churches and robbed them of their treasures.

A story is told of how, after a battle at Soissons, the Frankish soldiers plundered the church. Among the spoil there was a vase of wonderful beauty. It was the greatest treasure the church possessed, so the Bishop sent to Clovis begging him to restore it. Although he was King, Clovis did not feel himself free to restore the vase. Therefore he replied to the messengers: "Follow me to Soissons where the booty is to be divided. If fate gives me the vase, I will return it to the Bishop."

When all the booty was gathered together, Clovis pointed to the vase. "I pray you, my brave soldiers," he said, "give me that vase as part of my share."

Those around him answered, "Great King, all that you see is yours. Do as you please with it."

Only one soldier was angry. Starting forward he cried in a loud voice, "You shall have nothing but what falls to you by lot." Then he raised his battle axe, and with one blow shattered the vase in pieces.

The King replied not a word, although his heart was full of rage. He sent another vase to the Bishop, but he could not forget that a soldier had set his wishes at naught, and deep in his heart anger slumbered.

A year passed. Then Clovis held a great review of his troops. All the soldiers passed before him, and at length came the man who had struck the vase. Clovis stopped him. "No one in all the army," he said, "has arms so badly kept as yours. Neither your lance, your sword, nor your axe is clean."

Saying that, Clovis seized the man's axe and threw it to the ground. The soldier stooped to pick it up, and as he did so the King raised his battle axe, and brought it crashing down.

"Even thus did you treat the vase of Soissons," cried Clovis, as the soldier fell dead at his feet. When his comrades saw the fate of the man who had dared to oppose the King's wishes, they were struck with fear.

It was some time after this that Clovis married the beautiful princess Clotilda. She was the niece of Gondebaud, King of Burgundy. Clotilda greatly feared her uncle, for he had slain her father, had thrown her mother into the river with a stone tied round her neck so that she was drowned, and seized the throne for himself. So when Clovis sent a messenger to her with a ring, begging her to be his wife, Clotilda gladly consented, although she was a Christian and Clovis was a heathen.

Gondebaud did not love his niece, and did not wish her to become a Queen. But Clovis was already so powerful that Gondebaud was afraid to refuse. So Clotilda set out in great state to the court of Clovis, riding in a litter and surrounded by a guard of honor. But hardly had Clotilda set out when Gondebaud was sorry that he had let her go, and he sent messengers after her to bring her back.

When Clotilda became aware of this she turned to the Franks who surrounded her. "If you wish that I shall reach your master," she said, "let me leave this litter. Put me on a horse, and let us gallop with all speed until we reach your borders; otherwise I shall never see your King."

So the Franks obeyed her, and put her upon a swift horse, and made great haste until they reached the court of Clovis. There Clotilda and Clovis were married with much pomp and state. Clovis was well pleased with the beauty and wisdom of his wife, and loved her dearly. But, although he allowed his children to be baptized, he would not himself become a Christian.

One day, however, when Clovis was fighting against the Allemans, his army began to lose. In vain he tried to rally his men, in vain he called upon his gods for help. The Allemans gained upon the Franks every moment. All seemed lost. Then in his despair Clovis raised his hands to heaven. "Jesus Christ," he cried, "Thou whom Clotilda believes to be the Son of God, Thou who, they say, grants help to those who are in danger, victory to those who believe in Thee, hear me. If Thou givest me to triumph over mine enemies, if Thou shewest me thy power, I will believe in Thee, and be baptized in Thy name. For I have called upon my own gods, and they are far from me. If they do not aid their faithful followers, it is that they are powerless."

Immediately the rout of the Allemans began. Their King was killed, and his soldiers yielding, became vassals of Clovis.

Then Clovis returned in peace to his own land, and told the Queen of the wonderful thing that had happened to him. She was greatly rejoiced and begged him at once to be baptized. But Clovis said "There is still one thing of which I must think. Will the people over whom I rule be willing to give up their gods? I will ask them."

So Clovis gathered his people together. But before he had spoken to them they cried out as with one voice: " Pious King, we will no longer worship gods of wood and stone. We are ready to obey the Everlasting God."

Then on Christmas Day, 496, there was a great and solemn ceremony at Rheims. The road from the palace to the church was hung with costly cloths, every house' was gay with banners and flowers. The clergy marched first, carrying golden crosses and jeweled banners, and singing hymns, as they marched. Behind them came the Bishop leading the King by the hand, then the Queen, and then the great crowd of people. The church itself was hung with rich cloths and silks, thousands of candles shone, and the scent of incense filled the stately building.

Amidst the glowing lights and colors Clovis and his followers sat gravely listening, while the Bishop taught them the story of Christ. He told them how the Lord of Heaven was despised and beaten and crucified. And at the sad story the heart of Clovis was touched with a kind of fierce pity. "Ah! had I been there with my Franks," he cried," I would have avenged Him."

Clovis was baptized first, and as the fierce warrior stood before him, clad no more in shining armor, but in a long white robe of peace, the aged Bishop murmured: "Bow thy head humbly, adore that which thou hast hitherto burned, burn that which thou hast hitherto adored." After Clovis, three thousand of his followers were baptized, and thus it was that Christianity came to the Franks.

But although Clovis became a Christian, he did not become gentle or peace-loving. God for him was still the God of battles. He still fought, until, by force or treachery, he had conquered all the lesser Frankish kings. The Burgundians and the Visigoths owned him as overlord, and even the wild Bretons of Armorica, whom the Romans had never been able really to conquer, paid him homage.

The Emperor of the East also honored him. He sent messengers to Clovis, giving him the titles and honor of Consul and Patrician. Then, like a Roman Emperor, he was clothed in a purple robe, and a golden crown was set upon his head. After this, mounting upon a splendid warhorse, he rode among the people, scattering gold and silver by the way. Henceforth Clovis called himself Clovis Augustus, and the common people looked upon him as the rightful heir to all the power and dignity of the Roman Caesars. After this, too, Clovis moved his court from Tours to Paris, as it was more in the center of his kingdom.

But although Clovis was thus in name a Christian and a Caesar he remained in his heart a true barbarian, and to the day of his death he was cunningly cruel and fierce.

He died in 511, having reigned thirty years, and was buried in Paris.

CHAPTER 6

THE STORY OF THE SONS OF CLOVIS

WHEN Clovis died, his four sons divided his kingdom. But after a time one of the sons, Clodomer, was killed in battle. He in his turn left three little sons, who, as they were too young to rule, went to live in Paris with their grandmother, Queen Clotilda.

But their uncle, King Childebert, seeing how much his mother loved her grandchildren, grew jealous of them. He sent secretly to his brother King Clotair saying: "Our mother keeps our brother's sons with her, and wishes to give them the whole of the kingdom. You must come to Paris quickly, so that we can take counsel together, and decide what we shall do with them. Either we must cut their hair like the rest of the people, or we must kill them and divide the kingdom of our brother equally between ourselves."

It seems strange to us that the choice should lie between cutting the little boys' hair and killing them. But among the Franks long hair was a sign of royalty. The King and his sons alone were allowed to wear their hair long; all the common people were obliged to cut theirs short. So Childebert knew that if he cut his little nephews' hair they could not be kings, for the Franks would not obey a common man with short hair.

When Clotair heard his brother's message, he was very glad and hastened to Paris. Childebert had mean time spread it abroad among the people that he and King Clotair were going to bring up the young princes so that they should one day be able to rule wisely. So now they sent to Queen Clotilda saying, "Send us the children and we will bring them up as befits princes."

When the Queen heard that she was greatly rejoiced. She called the children to her, dressed them in their best, gave them a little feast, and sent them away with many loving words. Her heart was heavy at parting from them, yet she said, "I shall feel that I have not altogether lost my son, if I see you succeed to his kingdom."

But as soon as the children came to their cruel uncles they were taken from their servants and shut up in prison. The servants, too, were put in prison. Then King Clotair and King Childebert sent a messenger to the Queen. In one hand he bore a naked sword, and in the other a pair of scissors.

When he came to the Queen, he showed them to her saying: "Oh, most glorious Queen! thy sons, our masters, desire to know how you would they should treat these children. Do you desire that they shall live with their hair cut, or do you desire that they shall die?"

When the Queen heard the cruel message, and saw the great, naked sword, she was filled with grief and despair. She covered her eyes, not daring to look at that sword, knowing for what it was meant. Yet she was shaken with anger, too, anger that any one should dare so to insult her darling children. To live disgraced! Nay, she thought, let them die as princes. So in her grief and anger, hardly knowing what she said, she cried out, "I would rather see them dead than shorn."

The messenger was a hard, cruel man who cared little for her grief, and ere she had time to repent of her hasty words he sped back to those who had sent him.

"You can go on," he said, "the Queen approves of what you have done. She wishes you to finish what you have begun."

At these words the two brothers were glad. They sent for the children, and when they came, Clotair at once took the eldest by the arm, and throwing him on the ground, killed him. Hearing his cries, his little brother, who was only seven years old, threw himself at Childebert's feet, clinging to his knees. "Help me, dear uncle," he cried; "do not let me be killed like my brother. Oh, save me!"

Then Childebert's heart was touched. With tears running down his face he begged Clotair to spare the child. "Dear brother," he said, "be generous. Grant me his life. I will give you anything you ask in return for it."

But such weakness only made Clotair the more angry. He turned upon his brother in terrible wrath. "Keep back," he cried, "or you shall surely die in place of the child. It was you who led me on. Now you would leave me to it alone. Is that the way you keep faith? Stand back, I say."

So Childebert, afraid of Clotair's anger, pushed the child away and Clotair seized and killed him as he had killed his brother.

But by this time the cries of the children had been heard, and some soldiers rushing in saved the third, who was named Clodoald. They carried him to a monastery outside Paris. There he grew up and spent his life in safety. When he died, he was made a saint, and the monastery was called by his name St. Clodoald or St. Cloud.

Meanwhile Clotair ordered the children's nurses and servants to be killed, and then he mounted upon his horse and rode away as if nothing had happened. For he was a cold, hard-hearted man, and thought nothing of having killed his little nephews. But Queen Clotilda was filled with grief. Sorrowfully she took the poor little bodies in her arms, and laid them on a bier. Then, with great and solemn pomp, with mournful chant and psalm, they were carried to the grave. All the people mourned with her, and wept for the death of the pretty, fair-haired princes; but none dared question the deeds of the two fierce Kings.

Clotair and Childebert then divided the kingdom of Clodomer, each taking a portion. But this was by no means the end of strife. The three brothers who remained were nearly always fighting with their neighbours, and they often quarrelled among themselves.

But, as the years went on, first one and then another died, till at length only Clotair was left. Then once more the kingdom of the Franks was united under one ruler. It was a much larger kingdom than Clovis had left. For each of the brothers had fought with the surrounding peoples, and each had added something to his kingdom.

Clotair was a cruel and vicious king, delighting in bloodshed. But he was punished by having a bad son called Chramme. Chramme was handsome and of great courage, but we are told in malice and disloyalty he had no equal, and that his heart was filled with so great cruelty that he destroyed the land which was his to keep and guard. At length Chramme rebelled against his father, and Clotair in great wrath gathered an army and marched to subdue him.

This savage old Frank was in name a Christian, and as he went into battle he prayed: "Great Lord God, look down from heaven. Judge according to the right and according to the judgement that Thou hast already given against Absalom when he also rebelled against his father David. I am, it seemeth, the second David."

Chramme was defeated and fled to the seashore where a ship was ready to take him, his wife, and children over the sea to safety. But, before they could embark, they were made prisoner by Clotair's soldiers.

When Clotair saw his son a captive, no pity filled his heart, but only savage wrath and desire for some fearful vengeance. So he ordered that Chramme and his wife and children should be bound and placed in a poor man's cottage hard by. This was done. Then the cottage was set on fire, and Chramme and all his family were burned to death.

So Clotair's vengeance was satisfied for the time. But afterward he began to repent of this horrid deed, and all his last years were made sorrowful by the thought of it. At last he died, worn out with his labours and his griefs, in 561, having reigned fifty years, but only for three years as sole King of the Franks.

CHAPTER 7

THE DO-NOTHING KINGS AND THE MAYORS OF THE PALACE

WHEN Clotair died, the kingdom was once more divided into four as at the death of Clovis. And thereupon there followed a time of wild disorder and misrule, when brother fought against brother, father against son. They fought both in open battle and in secret, by treachery, by poison, and by dagger. There is nothing fine or noble about these wars; they are full of horrible cruelty and mean tricks. They brought famine, plague, and desolation in their train. The poor, driven from their ruined homes, took refuge in woods and desert places. There they became a terror to travelers, for they attacked and robbed all who passed, so that it was dangerous to travel except in large companies. It was a time of misery and degradation.

"Do you see anything over that roof?" said the Bishop of Albi one day to a friend, pointing to the roof of the King's palace.

"I see a dove cote which the King has caused to be built," replied the friend. "Do you see anything else?"

"I see," said the Bishop with a deep sigh, "the sword of divine wrath hanging over that house."

At length Dagobert, the great-great-grandson of Clovis, came to me throne. In him the Franks found a better ruler. Under him the kingdom was once more united. He was a wise king and tried to rule well. Every day he sat upon his throne to do justice. And it mattered not to him who was rich and who was poor, they were all alike before him. He was kind and gentle toward those who were good, and very stern toward those who were bad. No King of the Franks had ever been loved as Dagobert.

In governing, Dagobert was very much helped by Pepin, the Mayor of the Palace. The Mayor of the Palace was at first merely chief of the royal household, but gradually he became more and more powerful. He led the army, helped the King to rule, and was, indeed, after the King, the chief man in the kingdom. We know nothing about Pepin's father, except that his name was Carloman. He is called sometimes Pepin of Landen, from the town in which he lived, sometimes Pepin the Old to distinguish him from other Pepins who came after him. It is well to remember his name, for he is the first of a family which came to great power.

There were wars during Dagobert's reign. But they were chiefly with outside enemies, so that, compared with the times that had gone before, the days in which Dagobert reigned were peaceful. He died in 638. When it was known, a noise of mourning and tears was heard throughout the palace, and the whole people wept bitterly for his loss.

Dagobert was the last of the great Merovingians. He is still remembered as the Great King Dagobert. The Kings who followed him were called the *Rois Faineants* or Do-nothing Kings. They very often came to the throne mere children. They all died young. They were crowned as kings, but that was all; the real power was in the hands of the Mayor of the Palace.

As year by year the Mayors grew stronger, the Kings grew weaker. They sat in their palaces, carefully tending their long fair hair, which was their sign of royalty, and looking on with mild blue eyes and vacant faces while the Mayors ruled. Or sometimes they went among the people in a chariot drawn by oxen whose soft brown eyes were scarcely more mild and vacant than those of the King they drew.

Meanwhile the land was full of strife. The fighting was chiefly between the East and the West. The land of the eastern Franks was called Austrasia, and from that we have to-day the kingdom of Austria. The land of the western Franks was called Neustria. The eastern Franks and the western Franks had each a King and at last there was a great battle between the two. The Austrasians were led by Pepin of Heristal, the grandson of Pepin the Old. The Neustrians were led by King Theodoric and his Mayor of the Palace, Bertaire.

It was a very great host which met upon the field of battle, for both sides had gathered all their might. At the last minute Pepin offered to make peace. But Bertaire was so sure of victory that he refused.

So Pepin made ready to fight. During the night, he gathered all his camp baggage together and set fire to it, so as to make the enemy believe that he was retreating. Then, in the gray light of early dawn, without noise of trumpet or of drum, he quietly took possession of a hill to the east of the Neustrian camp. He did this so that the sun's rays should be behind him, and shine in the eyes of the enemy.

Very early the Neustrians were astir. They looked across the plain to the spot where the night before the enemy had lain. Lo! the whole camp was wrapped in flame! At once the Neustrians decided that Pepin and his army were in flight. They prepared to pursue. But suddenly they became aware of the grim lines of silent warriors posted on the hill above them.

The battle began and was very long and desperate. But the great army of the Neustrians was badly armed and badly drilled. Dazzled by the sun, they threw themselves blindly on the enemy, and were broken against their wall of steel. King Theodoric and Bertaire fled, leaving on the field the best of their knights and nobles.

This battle of Tertry really marks the end of the Merovingians. Pepin of Heristal was henceforward the chief man in all France, and we may say that, from now onward, the family of Pepin reigned. But he still kept up the pretence of a king. The King Do-nothing was still led out on feast days to be shown to the people. Clothed in royal robes, a golden crown on his long fair hair, he sat upon a golden throne, and spoke the words he had been taught to say. Then he was led back to his palace, and carefully guarded in idleness until he was needed once more to play at royalty. And thus we read in the old chronicles of the history of France such sentences as the following: "At this time the glorious King Childebert died. He was a just man of pure memory. Of his deeds nothing is known, for history does not speak of them."

Pepin of Heristal ruled France wisely and well for twenty-seven years. But although he had put an end to civil war, he still fought many battles. He fought with all the heathen folk who lived around the borders of France. And wherever the armies of Pepin conquered, teachers of Christianity followed. For, by the power of the Cross, Pepin hoped to keep what he had won by the sword.

Pepin of Heristal died in 714, and once more France was plunged into civil war. For, shortly before Pepin died, his son Grimoald had been killed. He had left a little boy of six who was now declared ruler by Plectrude, Pepin's wife. Plectrude hoped really to govern until her grandson was old enough. But the proud nobles would not be ruled by a woman and a little boy, and they rebelled. After a fierce battle, Plectrude and her little grandson fled, and the nobles chose one of their number to be Mayor of the Palace.

But Pepin of Heristal had left another son called Charles. He was not Plectrude's son, but the son of another wife, and Plectrude hated him. She had shut him up in prison so that he might have no chance of ruling. But now, when all the country was full of war and wild confusion, came the news that Charles had escaped and was gathering an army. Many of the nobles who had served his father now joined Charles, and battle after battle was fought.

At first, fortune went against Charles; but his name means "the strong one." In battle after battle he beat his enemies, until, at length, he overcame them. Plectrude, who had taken refuge in Cologne, yielded now to Charles, and gave up to him all his father's treasures; thus Charles became King of France in all but name. For he, too, thought it needful to have a phantom king. He found a Merovingian somewhere no one knows where and set him upon the throne. To him was given the empty honor of the crown, while Charles held both sword and scepter.

CHAPTER 8
CHARLES THE HAMMER

AND now a new danger began to threaten France, to threaten, indeed, all Europe. About the year 570, a boy called Mohammed was born at Mecca. This boy, when he grew up, believed himself to be the last and greatest of the prophets. He taught a new religion which has since been called by his name. 'There is but one God, and Mohammed is his prophet,' he said, and he taught his followers that all the world must be brought to that faith by the sword.

So his followers set out to conquer the world, their book of faith in one hand, the sword in the other. Very quickly the new faith spread all over the East. Almost all the known world in Asia and Africa yielded to it; and then the Saracens, as we often call them, crossed the sea into Europe.

The Mohammedans first attacked and conquered all Spain. Then they turned their swords on France. Never since the time of Attila had there been such an invasion. Like the waves of a mighty ocean they rolled over the fair plains of France. They came with their wives and children and all their goods as if they meant to make France their home. And wherever they passed they slew the people, burned the churches, and destroyed the land. They were like hungry wolves among a flock of sheep.

It was against this vast horde that Charles now gathered all the strength of his army. From the farthest corners of his dominion he called men to fight for their faith. And they came from such distant countries that the mighty host which gathered together formed an European rather than a Frankish army.

It was near the town of Poitiers that the two armies met. There for seven days they lay opposite each other. On the one side were the tall, broad-shouldered men of the North, with fair faces and golden hair. They were clad in coats of steel, shining helmets covered their heads, and they carried long swords and heavy battle axes. On the other side were the brown-faced, dark-eyed men of the South, wearing white turbans and robes, mounted upon swift horses, and carrying small round shields and light spears and bows.

One by one the October days slid by. The Saracen horsemen dashed over the plain upon their prancing horses, raising clouds of dust, but never attacking the steel-clad warriors who watched them in silent waiting. At length one Sunday, toward the end of October, in the gray of morning, the Mohammedan call to prayer was heard. Soon the plain was covered with white-robed warriors praying for victory. When the prayer was over, the signal for battle was given.

"God is great! God is great!" they shouted as they dashed upon the enemy. But under the fearful onslaught the Franks stood unmoved. Again and again from the glittering wall of steel the white-robed warriors were thrown back like the foam of waves which beat upon a rocky shore. In vain the javelins and arrows of the Saracens rained upon the Christian host. "The Franks stood like a wall of iron as if frozen to blocks of ice," said a writer of the time. "They stood locked to one another like men of marble."

Twenty times the Mohammedans returned to the attack. Twenty times their furious charge was broken against the immovable wall, till hundreds lay dead upon the field, and riderless horses rushed madly over the plain.

Hour after hour the battle lasted. The sun had begun to sink toward the west when a great cry of distress rose from behind the Saracens. Part of the Frankish army had quietly crept round the enemy, and were now attacking the camp. Then Charles ordered the body of his troops, which had stood until now immovable as a wall of steel, to advance. And thus, taken on both sides, the Saracen army broke and fled in unutterable confusion. Night at last put an end to the slaughter and pursuit, and silence fell upon the field which, from dawn till dark, had rung with battle cries and clash of steel on steel.

When day dawned once more the Franks again made ready for battle. But all was still and silent in the gleaming white tents of the enemy. In vain the Franks listened and watched for any sign of life. None came. Then Charles sent a company of soldiers to discover what this might mean. Across the plain, strewn with thousands of dead, they rode, and at length reached the camp of the Saracens. One after another they entered the tents. Each one was empty. Not a living man was left in all the vast camp. In the night the Saracens had fled, taking only their horses and arms and leaving all their rich spoils and booty behind.

This battle of Poitiers, which was fought in 732, is one of the great battles of ancient times. For on it hung the fate of the Christian world. Between the infidel Saracens and the wild heathen people of the North there was only the empire of the Franks. Had Christianity been crushed out there, the fate of Europe would have been changed.

It was after this battle that Charles received the Charles surname of Martel or Hammer; "for as a hammer breaks iron and steel and all metals so he broke by his blows in battle all his enemies and all strange nations." The power of the Saracens was broken, but they were not utterly crushed. Charles fought them again and yet again, and in time they were driven out of France altogether.

Toward the end of his life Charles was greatly honored by the Pope Gregory III, who sent him many and great presents such as he had never before sent to any king. Among these were said to be the "Keys of the Holy Sepulchre," and the chains with which St. Peter was bound. The Pope called Charles the *Illustrious Viceroy of France*, and begged his help to drive the Lombards, who were attacking him, out of Italy.

"Our tears flow day and night from our eyes," he said, "when we see the Church forsaken on all sides by those of her children, from whom she most hoped for defence and protection. I implore your good-will before God that you may hasten to soothe our sorrows, or, at the least, to send us an answer in which we may rejoice." He offered, also, to make Charles Consul of Rome. This was, in fact, to make him Emperor of the West in place of the old, long-dead Caesars.

Charles the Hammer received the Pope's messengers with great honor, and sent them back to Rome laden with presents. But he himself never went to Italy to be made Emperor, and never fought the Lombards. For soon after this he fell ill and died. He was buried in the Church of St. Denis in Paris. Charles the Hammer had ruled for twenty-five years. He had vastly enlarged the borders of France, and left the kingdom in great peace and prosperity. A few years before he died the King Do-nothing had died. But so much of a pretence had he become that Charles did not think it worthwhile to crown another. So, in 741, when Charles the Hammer died, the throne was empty.

CHAPTER 9

THE STORY OF PEPIN THE SHORT

WHEN Charles the Hammer died, the kingdom was divided between his three sons, Carloman, Pepin, and Grippo. But Grippo was only about fifteen and otherwise unfit to rule, so Carloman and Pepin fought against him. And having conquered him they shut him up in prison, and divided his part of the kingdom between themselves. They then found a Merovingian and set him upon the throne, giving him the usual empty honors while they ruled.

There were many of the nobles, however, who would not quietly bow to the rule of Charles the Hammer's sons, and so there was much fighting. However, the two brothers were united, they fought side by side, and at length were victorious. But after six years of strife, when the realm seemed assured to him at last, Carloman became weary of it. Tired of war and bloodshed, tired of the struggle to keep a tumultuous people in check, he longed for peace and rest. So he laid aside forever his sword and armor, and giving up all the glories and troubles of ruling, he shaved his long fair hair, and putting on the robe of a monk, he retired into a monastery. There, praying in his little cell or pacing the quiet cloisters with his brother monks, he perhaps found the peace he longed for, after his life of warfare.

When Carloman went into a monastery, Pepin was left to rule alone. At last he was master of all France, and there was peace in the land. And now the time had come, he felt, in which to make himself not only master but King. So Pepin sent messengers to Rome to ask the Pope if the man who had the power, should not also have the name, of King. He begged the Pope to decide which ought really to be called King, he who lived without thought or danger in his palace, or he who bore all the cares of the kingdom on his shoulders.

And the Pope replied, "He who possesses the royal power ought also to enjoy the honors and title of royalty."

So Pepin was crowned King of the Franks with solemn ceremony. He was no longer merely the chosen chief of a band of warriors. He was not simply raised upon his shield high on the shoulders of his nobles and acclaimed King by the shouting of the people. Clad in splendid robes he knelt with his Queen on the steps of the altar. Countless candles gleamed, and the smoke of incense filled the church, while the Bishop placed the crown upon his head, and anointed him with holy oil.

Then King Pepin took an oath to help and protect his people. 'With all my power and all my knowledge I swear to each of you that I will keep justice and right, so that each of you render to me the honor due to me, and give me your help to preserve and defend the kingdom which I hold from God with faithfulness, with justice, and with right."

Thus a new race of Kings came to the throne. They are called the Carolingians, or sons of Charles. We do not know whether the name means sons of Charles the Hammer or sons of Carloman, who, you remember, was the father of Pepin the Old.

The last of the Merovingians was taken from his palace. His long fair hair, the last sign of his kingship, was cut off, and he was sent to end his days in a monastery. So the long pretense was over. It had endured for more than a hundred years.

Almost as soon as Pepin was crowned, he had to fight to defend his crown. For many nobles who were willing to obey him as Mayor of the Palace were not willing to obey him as King, although the difference seemed one of name only. But Pepin fought and conquered, and the nobles one by one yielded to him.

The Lombards were still threatening Rome, and now the Pope (not the same Pope as appealed to Charles the Hammer but another) resolved to cross the Alps, and beg in person for the help of the mighty King of the Franks.

The Pope was already looked upon with great reverence by the Christian world, and the French King was looked upon as the champion of the Christian Church. So when it became known that the Pope was coming to visit Pepin, crowds of people flocked from every side to do him honor. Pepin received the Pope with every mark of reverence.

With tears in his eyes, with ashes upon his head and clad in sackcloth, the great Pontiff threw himself before the soldier King to beg his help. Pepin promised help, and in return the Pope crowned him and anointed him again as King of the Franks, and made the nobles swear never to elect a King except from the family of Pepin. The Pope also gave Pepin the title of Patrician of Rome. This was really only an empty honor. It gave him no power in Rome.

Pepin faithfully kept his promise, and when he had defeated the Lombards, he restored to the Pope the land he had taken. It was after his return from this war that a story is told of Pepin which shows his wonderful strength and courage. He was called Pepin *le Bref*, or the Short, for he was a little man, but he was very strong and of marvelous courage.

It was told to him one day that his soldiers laughed at him because he was so little, so he made up his mind to teach them a lesson. In those days fights between wild beasts were the chief amusements of the people. They went to see a wild beast combat as we might go to a pantomime. So Pepin ordered a very fierce bull, which was so large that it made people afraid even to look at it, to be brought into the arena. Against this bull there was let loose the most ferocious lion that could be found.

The arena was filled with roaring and bellowing as the two fierce creatures met. With lowered horns and lashing tail the bull rushed at the lion. With a low growl the lion sprang at the bull, seized him by the throat, and brought him to the ground. The struggle was fearful. In breathless silence the people watched, glad to think there was a strong barrier between them and the fighting beasts.

Then Pepin spoke. "Go," he said to those around him, "go, tear the lion and the bull apart or kill them both."

The courtiers looked at each other in silence, their cheeks white with fear, their hearts cold with dread. Scarcely able to speak they stammered, "Lord Prince, there is no man under heaven who dare do such a deed."

Without a word Pepin rose from his throne, drew his sword, and jumped down into the arena. With one blow he cut off the lion's head, and with a second the null's. Then he put his sword back into the scabbard, and quietly returned to his seat.

"Does it seem to you now," he said, 'that I am fit to be your lord and master? Have you never heard how David as a boy vanquished the great Goliath? and how Alexander, in spite of his short stature, treated his generals?'

Then all his courtiers fell on their knees and prayed his forgiveness. 'We should be mad," they cried, "did we not acknowledge that you are born to be a leader of men."

At length, in 768, Pepin died and was buried in St. Denis. He had ruled France Tor eleven years as Mayor of the Palace, and for more than fifteen years as King. He was a great warrior King. But the fame of his father was so great, and the fame of the son who came after him was so great, that his own fame is almost lost sight of.

So true is this that, many years later, a King of France caused to be carved upon his tomb, "Pepin, the father of Charlemagne."

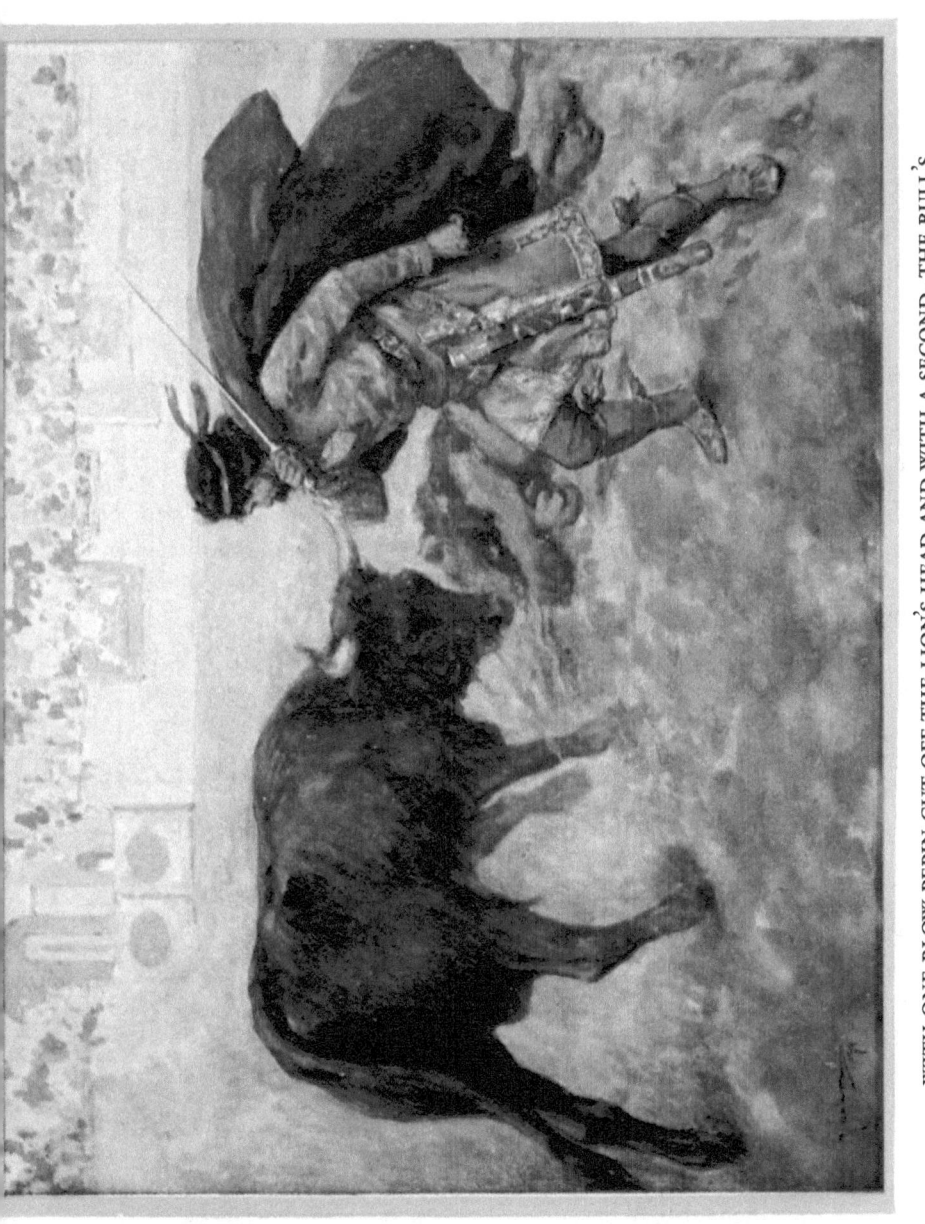

WITH ONE BLOW PEPIN CUT OFF THE LION'S HEAD AND WITH A SECOND, THE BULL'S.

CHAPTER 10

CHARLEMAGNE—KING OF LOMBARDY

WHEN Pepin died, his kingdom was once more divided between his two sons Charles and Carloman. Charles made for himself so great a name that he was called Carolus Magnus, or Charles the Great. The "magnus" has come to be looked upon as part of his name, and he is known to us as Charlemagne.

Very soon after their father's death the two brothers were crowned, Charlemagne at Noyon, Carloman at Soissons. Almost at once the two young Kings were plunged in wars, and almost at once it was seen that they could not agree with each other; and when, after little more than two years, Carloman died, Charlemagne quietly took possession of the whole kingdom. Carloman, it is true, had two sons, but they were only little boys. The idea that the son must succeed the father was by no means so settled as it is with us. The Franks, too, claimed the right of choosing their King, and when the choice lay between being governed by boys, and being governed by a wise and skillful soldier, the Franks chose the soldier.

During all his long reign Charlemagne had battles to fight. He fought with every people and tribe of the southwestern half of Europe, but his chief enemies were perhaps the Saxons. The Franks were themselves of the Saxon race, but they had become Christian, while the many tribes of the Saxons, who lived beyond the Rhine, were still heathen. That alone made them deadly enemies of Charlemagne, who did more than any King before him to spread Christianity over Europe.

Charlemagne began his conquests by marching into Germany and destroying a mysterious idol called Irmen's Column. For three days the Franks labored destroying this column and temple, amid fearful heat, beneath a blazing sun. The summer had been so hot that even the streams had run dry, and the Franks were weary with heat and thirst and scarcely able to work. Then, suddenly, it seemed a miracle happened. At mid-day the dried-up bed of a river all at once began to flow with water, so that every soldier in the army was able to quench his thirst. After this the Franks completely destroyed Irmen's Column and the sacred wood which surrounded it. Many of the Saxons then allowed themselves to be baptized, and taking strong hostages with him, Charlemagne marched away. But the Saxons were by no means subdued, and for thirty-three years Charlemagne had to fight them again and yet again.

Meanwhile he was called southward to help the Pope against the Lombards. With a great army he advanced to besiege the town of Pavia. The King of the Lombards, standing upon the ramparts with a friend, Ogger the Dane, watched him come.

At first they saw the huge engines of war in the distance. "Charlemagne is surely with this great army," said the King.

"No," replied Ogger.

Next came a great crowd of soldiers gathered from every corner of the Frankish kingdom.

"Surely Charlemagne comes in triumph in the midst of this great crowd," said the King.

"No, not yet. He will not come so soon," replied the Dane.

"What can we do, then?" said the King, who began to be afraid. "What can we do against him if he comes with so huge a company of warriors?"

"You will see what kind of man he is when he comes," said Ogger, "but as for what will be our lot I know naught."

While they thus talked, the main body of the troops appeared. They were old and tried soldiers who had already seen many victories under their great leader. At the sight of them the Lombard King was seized with fear. "Now of a certainty Charles comes," he cried.

"No," replied Ogger, "not yet."

Now followed in long and glittering array the Bishop:?, the Abbots, the Clerks of the Royal Chapel, and the Counts. As they came streaming on and on, their arms and ornaments glittering in the sunshine, the King of the Lombards covered his eyes. He could not bear to look upon the blaze and splendour.

'Let us go down," he cried. "Let us hide ourselves in the bosom of the earth far from the face and the fury of so terrible an enemy."

Ogger, the Dane, even although he knew of old the power and the strength of Charles, trembled also as the mighty host rolled on. But in answer to the King's outcry, he shook his head. 'When you see the very harvest in the field stricken with fear then you may know that Charles has arrived," he murmured.

Scarcely had he finished speaking when they saw in the west a dark cloud rising. It was Charlemagne, who came at last. He seemed to the trembling King a very man of iron. His head was covered with an iron helmet, his gauntlets were of iron, his breast and his broad shoulders were covered with an iron corselet. In his left hand he held a lance, in his right his mighty sword. His horse, too, was clad in armor, and all those who surrounded him, all the great men of the army, were clad like their leader. It seemed as if all the great plain was covered with men of iron.

"There," said Ogger, "there at length is the man you seek.' And as he gazed the heart of the King sank within him.

But in spite of Charlemagne's great army, in spite of the fear his great name carried to the hearts of his foes, Pavia did not give in. Other places all over the north of Italy yielded, but still Pavia held out.

Then at Easter Charlemagne left the camp and went to Rome, in order to keep the feast there. The Pope received him with every mark of honor. As he came near the city, vast crowds went out to meet him, grave senators in their robes of office, soldiers and priests carrying banners and crosses. And as he entered the city, children dressed in white and carrying branches of palm went before him singing songs of praise.

Upon the threshold of the great church of St. Peter, the Pope awaited Charlemagne. When the King reached the steps, he knelt down and kissed them. But the Pope raised him, kissed him upon the cheek, and, taking him by the hand, led him into the church. They were followed by all the Frankish nobles and the Roman monks and clerks who sang, "Blessed is he who cometh in the name of the Lord."

After the King and Pope had sworn faith and friendship to each other, Charlemagne returned once more to Pavia. The people there were now in great misery from hunger and disease. So at length they gave in.

Charlemagne took the King prisoner, added Lombardy to his empire, and set upon his own head the iron crown of the Lombards. This crown was a slender iron circlet, said to be made of one of the nails of the Cross. But the iron circlet was covered with gold and set with gems. The poor King who had last worn it was sent from one prison to another, until at length his head was shaved, and he was forced to become a monk, and spend the rest of his days in prayer and fasting.

While Charlemagne had been fighting in Lombardy, the Saxons had again risen, and he had no sooner returned from Italy than he had to set out against them. But we cannot follow Charlemagne in all his battles, for they were many and long. He went against the Saxons as it were with the sword of conquest in one hand and the water of baptism in the other. Those who would not yield to his sword he slew, and those w T ho yielded he baptized. It was by the might of his sword that he made these rough heathen bow to the Cross.

CHAPTER 11

CHARLEMAGNE—THE DEFEAT OF RONCESVALLES

BUT besides the Saxons there were other heathen foes to fight. All the way from Spain there came a man named Ibn-al-Arabi to beg the great King's help against the Saracens. Charlemagne remembered the deeds of his grandfather, Charles the Hammer, and promised Ibn-al-Arabi the help he sought. Ibn-al-Arabi on his side promised to open the gates of Saragossa to the Christian King.

So Charlemagne gathered a mighty host, and took his way toward Spain. He crossed the Pyrenees by the Valley of Roncesvalles and at first his march was one long triumph, the people submitting to him and giving him hostages of peace as he passed. It seemed as if the religion of Mohammed w T as doomed in Spain. But Ibn-al-Arabi either could not or would not fulfil his promise. The gate of Saragossa did not open to the Christian King, and the Arabs and Saracens, forgetting their quarrels among themselves, joined to resist the invader.

For this Charlemagne was not prepared. He could not face a siege of Saragossa. Food for his great army was already growing scarce, disease was thinning the ranks, besides which rumors that the wild Saxons had again risen reached him. Charlemagne resolved to give up the war. But he made the Saracens pay a large sum of money, and taking hostages with him to ensure the peace, he turned home again.

This was the first check in his triumphant career. It was a mere check, but, as the army journeyed back to France, so terrible a disaster fell upon it that all France was filled with woe and lamentation.

Slowly the great host wound along through the narrow pass homeward. Charlemagne led the main part of the army, while the rear was commanded by his nephew, Roland. In the rear-guard was all the baggage with much rich booty. The most tried soldiers were here, also many of the nobles. Charlemagne and his part of the army had safely reached the top of the pass and begun to descend the other side into France, when suddenly, to the ears of Roland and his host, there came the noise as of a great army advancing toward them.

"Sir Comrade," said Oliver, Roland's friend, "I believe that we shall have battle with the Saracens."

"God grant it," said Roland proudly, "we are here to fight for our King."

Then Oliver climbed to a height and looked backward. The sky was blue and the sun shone gloriously, and in the clear distance Oliver saw all the hosts of Spain. Helmets and bucklers inlaid with gold gleamed in the sunshine, pennons waved, and, rank behind rank, a forest of spears moved onward

Oliver's heart was filling with boding fear, and coming down from the hill he went to Roland. 'I have seen the heathen," he said, "with their lances and gleaming swords. Such an army was never seen before. Friend Roland, sound your horn so that Charlemagne may hear and return to help us."

For Roland carried a marvelous horn of ivory, the sound of which could be heard many miles afar. But Roland would not sound his horn. To ask for help seemed to his proud spirit a disgrace. Again and again Oliver begged it of him. Again and again he refused.

"I will not sound my horn," he said, "but I shall strike such blows with my good sword Durendal that you shall see it dyed red in the blood of the heathen."

And so the battle began. From the dark, tree-clad heights above, the enemy rushed upon the Franks in the narrow pass beneath. Rocks came crashing down, showers of arrows fell from unseen foes.

It was a terrible battle. Roland and Oliver and Archbishop Turpin fought as never heroes fought before, But the Franks were far outnumbered by their foes. Crushed together in the narrow valley, they fell man after man. Their heavy armor weighed them down, and their sharp swords and lances were useless against an enemy who rained darts and arrows on them at a distance.

The massacre was terrible. Hardly a Frankish soldier was left alive, when, late in the day, proud Roland did at length sound his horn. But it was too late. When the sun sank not one man of all the rear-guard was left. Night came and silence fell upon the valley broken only by the groans of the wounded and the sighs of the dying. For the victors fled as soon as the fight was done, carrying with them much rich spoil.

Roland was the last to fall, and ere he died he tried to break his trusty sword Durendal, so that it should not fall into the hands of the heathen. Again and again he dashed it against the hard rock. The steel, far from

PROUD ROLAND DID AT LENGTH SOUND HIS HORN.

breaking, showed neither scratch nor dint. Then, seeing he could by no means break his sword, Roland laid it beneath him, together with his ivory horn, and, turning his face to the enemy, he died.

Such was the combat of Roncesvalles of which, century after century, the poets of France have sung, until the story of Roland is to the Frenchman somewhat as the story of Arthur is to us. And you remember that when, three hundred years later, Duke William of Normandy came to our shores, his minstrel sang the Song of Roland as his soldiers marched against the English.

But I must tell you that much of the Song of Roland is a fairy tale. We know nothing really of the famous Roland of which it sings, except that he was Warden of the Marches of Brittany, and that he was killed in this battle. From history, too, we learn that the foes which fell upon Charlemagne's army were not treacherous Saracens, but Gascons and wild robber people who lived on the borders between France and Spain.

The Song of Roland tells us that when Roland at length sounded his horn Charlemagne heard it. Returning he pursued the Saracens and avenged the death of his favorite knight with fearful slaughter. But, that, too, is fairy tale. Charlemagne never returned to Spain, and the remembrance of his defeat there greatly darkened the joy of his later days. He could not help his soldiers at the time: he could not avenge them later. For as soon as the blow was struck, the enemy disappeared so quickly, and scattered themselves so widely among the forests that it was impossible to know where to attack them. To punish them would have meant a long and troublesome war. And Charlemagne had no soldiers to spare. For, knowing that their conqueror was far away, the Saxons had risen in rebellion once more, and were laying waste with fire and sword all the northern boundaries of his kingdom.

CHAPTER 12

CHARLEMAGNE—THE EMPEROR OF THE WEST

A Chieftain called Wittikind was now the leader of the Saxons. When other Saxons had yielded to Charlemagne, he had refused. Rather than accept the rule of a strange King and bow the knee to a strange God, he had fled and had taken refuge with the King of the Danes. Now he returned, and with words of fire he stirred the people to rebellion. Although he was a heathen he was wise and noble, and he loved his country and his freedom.

His words were so eloquent that the common people and the young nobles crowded to him. Many of them who had been baptized forsook the strange new faith, and turned again to their old gods.

Burning towns and churches, slaying men, women, and children, the Saxons advanced over the country. In a great battle the generals whom Charlemagne had sent against Wittikind were defeated with terrible slaughter. When Charlemagne heard of it he was filled with wrath. Thirsting for vengeance he gathered another army, and marched with all speed against the rebels. But the Saxons, hearing that the mighty warrior himself was coming against them, lost courage and gradually. Wittikind's army melted away. Finding himself thus left alone he once more took refuge with the Danes.

Then Charlemagne commanded the leaders of the Saxons to appear before him. Trembling they came. Very sternly he demanded to know the reason of their rebellion and who was their leader. "It was Wittikind," they replied.

Wittikind was beyond reach of Charlemagne's vengeance, but threatening to waste the country with fire and sword if he were not obeyed, he commanded that the chief of those who had helped in the rebellion should be given up to him. So four-thousand, five-hundred men were gathered together. Charlemagne condemned them to death, and in one day all their heads were cut off.

Charlemagne hoped by this fearful vengeance utterly to crush these people, and put an end forever to the rebellion; and for a little time,

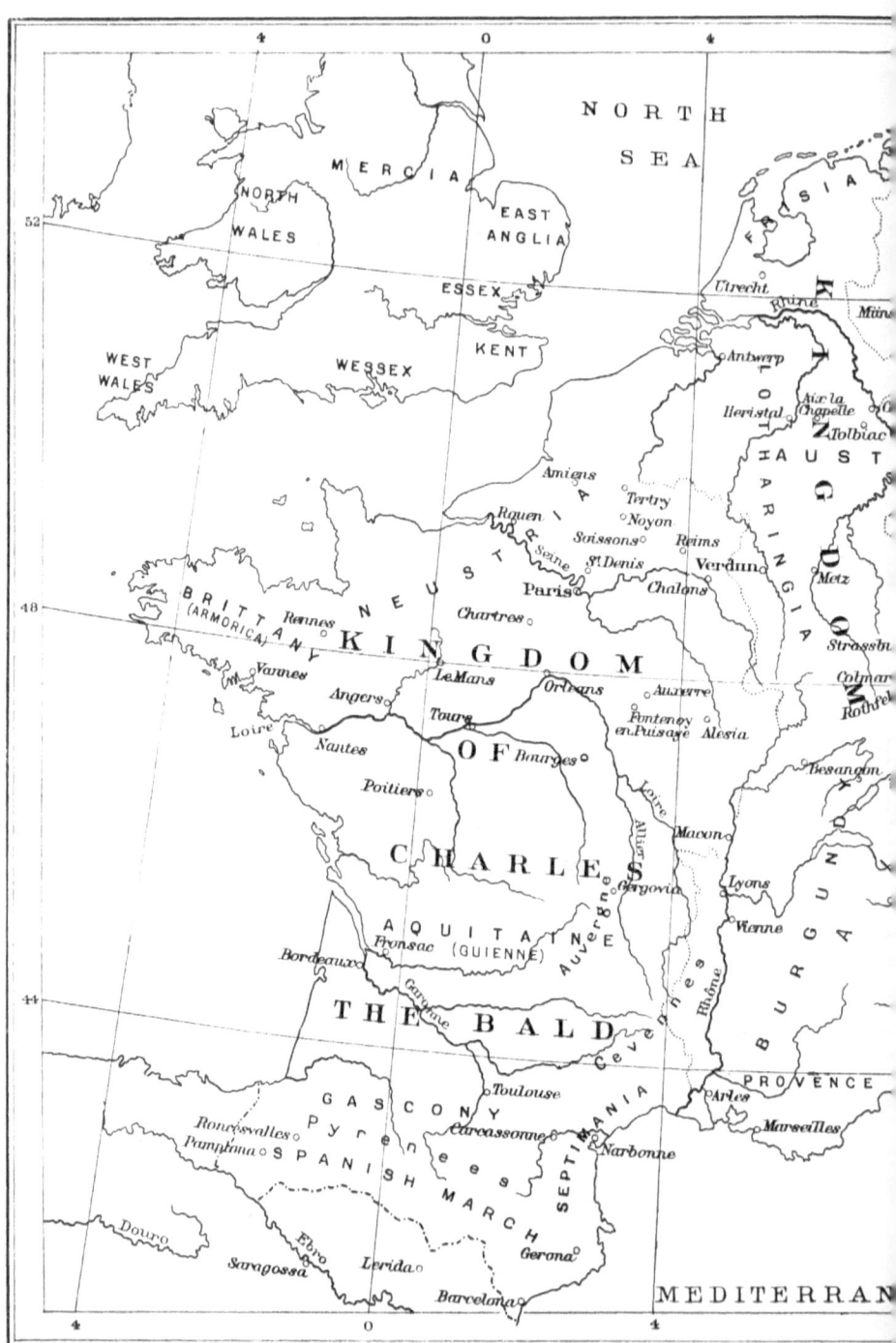

indeed, the country seemed quiet. But it was only the calm before the storm. Every Saxon heart was filled with rage, and every man who could carry a sword swore to avenge the blood of his comrades. Wittikind was recalled, and when spring came the fires of rebellion burst forth fiercer than ever. Churches were burned, altars were overthrown, priests killed, and the Saxons returned once more to their heathen gods.

Battle after battle was fought, time after time the Saxons were defeated, but never had they shown themselves so brave or so obstinate. Beaten, they still would not yield. The fight was stern and long. Each winter put an end to it, and Charlemagne returned to France. Each spring it was renewed.

Then one year Charlemagne made up his mind to spend the winter in Germany and utterly crush the rebellion. So all winter his soldiers marched forth, now here, now there, destroying and plundering. The Saxons had no rest or peace, and when spring came they were utterly worn out. They could fight no more, and the whole country yielded except the most northern part, where, beyond the Elbe, Wittikind, with a few faithful followers, still held out.

To Wittikind Charlemagne now sent messengers Wittikind promising him mercy if he would yield and be baptized. And the brave Saxon leader, weary of the long, hopeless struggle, gave in at last. His gods had not fought for him, he said. The God of Charlemagne was stronger, so he promised to serve Him.

The joy of Charlemagne was great. He received the beaten warrior with every mark of respect, loaded him with costly gifts, and stood as godfather to him when he was baptized. After this we hear no more of Wittikind, the Saxon. It is believed that he lived the rest of his life quietly, ruling his own estates, and that he died peacefully in some monastery.

With the baptism of Wittikind the resistance of the Saxons came to an end, and for seven years there was peace. This peace was looked upon with joy by the whole Christian world. Charlemagne sent a message to the Pope who rejoiced at the news, and ordered three days of prayer to mark the happy event. He also, it is interesting to know, sent a message to Offa, the King of Mercia, that is, one of the Kings of England, whom he called "the most powerful Prince of the Western Christians."

Like our own King Alfred, Charlemagne was not only a warrior but a law-giver. He took an interest in everything, however small, such as selling eggs and vegetables. Some of his laws seem to us very cruel, but in those rough days there was need of severe laws. A thief was punished the first time by the loss of an eye, the second time by the loss of his nose, and the third time by death.

The laws about religion were also severe. "If any man among the Saxons, being not yet baptized," says one, "shall hide himself and refuse to come to baptism, let him die the death." Another law shows us how ignorant the people still were. "No man may believe," it says, 'that he can pray to God in three languages only. For God is adored in all languages, and man is heard if he ask that which is right."

Besides making laws, Charlemagne founded schools and caused the people to be taught. For although the Romans had founded schools, these had all vanished in the wars and troublous times since the coming of the Franks. And in the time of Charlemagne there was hardly a school in the land. Charlemagne himself when he came to the throne could not even write his own name. One school was in the palace, and the King himself was one of the pupils. He learned both Latin and Greek, but he found it very difficult to learn to write. However, he tried hard and used to keep a pencil and tablets by his bed so that, if he woke in the night, he could spend his time trying to make his letters. But he was too old when he began to learn, and never succeeded in writing well.

Charlemagne gathered all the wisest men he could find to his court. There is a story told of how one day two Scotsmen came with some merchants to the shores of France. They were very learned men, and while the merchants sold their goods these learned men stood in The the market place and cried, "Who will buy knowledge? We are the merchants of knowledge. Who will buy knowledge?" But those who heard them took them for madmen. None wanted to buy knowledge. The Scotsmen, however, did not despair. All through France they journeyed. And in every market place they repeated their cry, "Who will buy knowledge? We are merchants of knowledge."

At length Charlemagne heard of those two men and commanded that they should be brought before him. "Is it true that you possess knowledge?" he asked them.

"Yes," they replied, "it is true, and we are ready to give it to any who seek it."

"What do you ask in return for it," asked the King.

"A house, and food, and clothes, and minds ready and willing to learn," they replied.

With great joy Charlemagne heard these words. He gladly promised the two men all they asked. One he kept in France, and one he sent to Italy, and both set up schools to which many scholars came.

Chief among the learned men whom Charlemagne gathered round him was Alcuin, an Englishman, the most learned man of his day. He was a great help to Charlemagne in his work of founding schools. These schools were not only for the sons of the nobles, but for the sons of all poor and honest men.

Charlemagne often used to inspect the schools himself and ask the children questions. One day he found that the young nobles had been idle and were unable to answer his questions. He was angry with them, and in a very severe voice, he threatened to give the appointments and posts about the court to the children of the poor, if the children of the nobles did not try to learn better.

After Charlemagne had subdued the Saxons, he still fought many battles with the surrounding peoples, but they were of less importance. The Northmen, indeed, began to be very troublesome. These wild sea robbers came in their ships to ravage the coasts of France even as far as the Mediterranean.

One day when Charlemagne was travelling through his kingdom, he arrived at a seaside place. There he found all the people watching some ships which were seen approaching. The people believed them to be merchants coming to trade. But Charlemagne's keen eyes saw that these were no peaceful merchants but Northern pirates.

So he turned to the people, saying, "These ships are not full of merchandise. They are full of cruel enemies."

At these words the Franks took to their ships and went out to meet the enemy. The Northmen, however, learning that the great King was there to fight against them, fled. So the danger passed. But Charlemagne stood a long time silently gazing out to sea, with tears in his eyes. No one dared to speak to him, or to ask the great warrior why he wept.

At length he turned to the people. ' Would you know why I weep?' he said. "It is not that I dread these miserable pirates; they cannot hurt me. But I weep to think of all the sorrow they will bring upon my people when I am no more with them."

Charlemagne had reached the height of his power. Once more he journeyed to Rome. Once more he was greeted with every mark of honor.

After the building of Constantinople, you remember, the great Roman

Empire had been split in two, and there had been one Emperor in the East and one in the West. But after the barbarians invaded Rome there had been no Emperor of the West. Now there was to be a new Emperor.

On Christmas Day of 800, all the people crowded to the great church of St. Peter to hear mass. The Pope stood by the altar, the King clad in splendid robes knelt on the steps. Suddenly the Pope raised a glittering crown high in his hands. Then stooping he placed it upon the head of Charlemagne. There was a moment of breathless silence, then the great vault rang and rang again with the shouts of the people. "To Charles Augustus crowned by God great and peace-giving Emperor of the Romans, life and victory."

Three times the cry rang out, while the Pope prostrated himself before the new Emperor.

And thus began what was to be known for many ages to come as the Holy Roman Empire.

The empire over which Charlemagne ruled was very vast. It stretched from the North Sea to the Danube, and from the Baltic to the Mediterranean. From his father he had inherited only a small part of what is now France. The rest he had conquered by the might of his sword.

As Emperor, Charlemagne ruled for fourteen years. During these years he still fought battles, but he employed himself too in framing laws and attending to the work of his schools. But at length, in 814, worn out with much fighting and weighed down by years, he died at his favorite palace of Aachen, or Aix-la-Chapelle. He was buried there in great splendour, clothed in his imperial robes, with a golden crown upon his head, a golden sword by his side, in his hands a golden testament and scepter.

CHAPTER 13

LOUIS I THE GOOD NATURED– THE FIELD OF LIES

WHEN Charlemagne died, his son Louis came to the throne. He was called in his own time Louis the Pious, and later writers of history gave him the name of *Debonnaire* or 'Good Natured'. And these two words describe him very well. He was a kindly and good man. But to govern his vast empire a stern ruler and skillful soldier was needed, and Louis was neither. He was a monk rather than a King. He was sad and grave, and no one ever saw him laugh. Indeed so grave was he that people even did not dare to laugh in his presence. He loved reading, but after a time he cared only to read the Bible.

Yet to begin with Louis ruled well. The death of Charlemagne was a signal for all the newly conquered peoples to rebel. But Louis put down the rebellions. Soon however other troubles began.

Keeping for himself the title of Emperor, Louis divided his kingdom among his sons, giving them each the title of King. This made his nephew Bernard, who thought he should have been given the kingdom of Italy, angry. So he rebelled and gathered an army to fight against the Emperor. False friends, however, persuaded Bernard to leave his army and come to Louis in order to make peace. He came, was seized, and at once imprisoned and condemned to have his eyes put out. This was done in such a savage way that two days later he died. The rebellion was at an end. But the remembrance of his cruelty to his nephew made Louis very unhappy. The more he thought about it, the more unhappy he became.

At last he felt that he could never find rest until he had openly confessed his sin and done penance for it. So all the nobles and priests were gathered together in a great church. It was the same church in which Wittikind the heathen had bowed his proud head to Christian baptism. Then, the people had crowded to see the strange sight of an Emperor standing godfather to a heathen rebel. Now, they crowded to it again, this time to see the stranger sight of a Xing humbling himself in sight of his subjects. And there, before the altar, with no crown upon his head, with no sign of royal state about him, but wearing the robe of a penitent, the King humbly confessed his sins and asked pardon.

Perhaps Louis's uneasy soul found rest after this penance, but it made many of his warriors angry. They saw in it only weakness. They thought that he who had bowed the knee before the priests was no longer worthy to lead the Frankish warriors. From this day many of them began to despise him secretly, and many became his open enemies. But his most bitter enemies were his own sons.

After Louis had divided his kingdom among his sons, another was born to him. He was the son of Louis's second wife, Judith, and was named Charles. It is interesting to remember that Judith was the daughter of Guelph, Count of Altorf. From this Guelph our own King George is descended.

Louis's three elder sons, Lothaire, Pepin, and Louis 70 the German were jealous of this newcomer. He was only a step-brother, and they thought he had no right to any part of the kingdom. But Louis the Good Natured loved this baby best of all his children.

Louis had already divided his kingdom among his sons. But he was always re-arranging these divisions. He did this no fewer than ten times during his life, and now, in order to give little Charles a kingdom, he took for him part of what he had already given to the elder brothers. This made the brothers so angry that they joined in rebellion.

They drove Louis from the throne, and then tried to make him become a monk. When he refused, they plotted to murder him.

Lothaire, the eldest son, meanwhile took the title of Emperor. But his two brothers soon grew jealous of his power, and they began to quarrel among themselves. Louis, however, had still some friends left, and they came to his aid. The brothers were then forced to set their father free and place him on the throne once more.

But soon the rebellion broke out again. The sons gathered one army, the father another, and marched to battle. They met upon a plain in Alsace called the Rothfeld or Field of Blood.

Day by day passed. Father and sons lay encamped over against each other, but no battle took place. The Pope who was with the army of the brothers came to the Emperor and tried to make peace. But good-natured Louis, who was ever ready to yield to persuasion, was now obstinate. He had a great army behind him, and he believed that he could conquer his rebel sons. He refused to make peace unless they gave themselves up and promised obedience to him.

Louis had at first a great army, but the smileless King did not know how to keep the love of his people. Noble after noble listened to the treacherous words of the rebel sons and carried his sword to the camp of the enemy. And once again, as many times through life, Louis showed his weak good-nature. When it was told him that many of his nobles were forsaking him, he sighed and said, "I would not that any man should die for me. Let them go to my sons."

At length one morning the Emperor woke to find his camp strangely silent. There was no clashing of armor, no stamp of horses, no sound of voices. All was still. So Louis went forth from his tent to see what this might mean. He found himself alone. In all the many tents which covered the wide plain there was not one man left. During the night the whole army had silently marched over to the enemy. Louis was left solitary save for his beautiful wife, Judith, and their little son Charles, who was now ten years old. Thus forsaken he felt that it was useless to resist longer, and, taking his wife and son by the hand, he slowly crossed the open space which divided his camp from that of his rebel sons.

When they saw their father come, the rebel sons rode toward him. Leaping from their horses they knelt before him as they met, with a show of humble obedience. The King kissed them, with his usual good nature, and they followed him to the camp, paying him every mark of outward respect. But it was all a mere show. Louis soon found that he was a prisoner.

From that day this bloodless battlefield was no longer called the Field of Blood, but the Lugenfeld or Field of Lies. For there those who had sworn to be faithful to their Emperor had proved false to him and to their oath.

Louis not only found himself a prisoner, but separated from his wife and favorite child. The beautiful Empress Judith was shut up in one place, her little son in another, he himself in yet a third. Again his sons tried hard to make him become a monk. They tormented him with falsehoods. Sometimes they told him that his wife was dead, sometimes that she had become a nun, or again that his beloved Charles had become a monk. And thus, torn from his kingdom, his wife, and his child, he became utterly broken down, and passed both day and night in tears and sorrow.

Yet in spite of all Louis steadily refused to give up the crown. He had, however, a gloomy sense of his sins. So once again he appeared before the people as a penitent. The Bishops and Abbots who were gathered to pass sentence upon him read a long list of his so-called crimes and pronounced him utterly unfit to rule. Once more Louis prostrated himself before the altar, confessing with tears that he had guided badly the kingdom which had been entrusted to him, and that he had broken up the great empire of his father, Charlemagne. Then his sword was taken from his side, he was bereft of his royal robes, and clad in the gray gown of a penitent, humbled and miserable, he was led back to his prison.

Louis had become a cause of sorrow for his friends, and a laughing stock for his enemies, and his son Lothaire once more took to himself the name of Emperor. But soon again the brothers began to quarrel amongst themselves. Two of them now sided with their father against Lothaire. Louis was taken from his prison, once more clothed in his royal robes, and set upon the throne by the very Bishops and Abbots who, a short time before, had declared him to be utterly unfit to rule.

Then it was Lothaire's turn to be humbled. He now knelt before the father whom he had imprisoned and insulted, and begged forgiveness. And good-natured Louis, sitting on a throne with his two "faithful" sons on either side of him, granted that forgiveness.

But among such turbulent spirits there could be no real peace. Again and again the brothers quarrelled, again and again they rebelled, and so passed five years of unrest. Then, in 840, the Emperor lay dying. He had but just returned from fighting a rebel son, Louis the German. The priests who knelt praying round the dying Emperor's bed begged forgiveness for him. "I pardon him," murmured Louis bitterly, "but say to him that he has brought my gray hairs with sorrow to the grave."

Yet, before the end, peace came to the troubled soul; bitterness was blotted out. With a smile at last upon his unsmiling face he died.

CHAPTER 14

CHARLES THE BALD—THE WAR OF THE THREE BROTHERS

LOUIS the Pious had, as you know, four sons, three who rebelled and one, the youngest, whom he loved very dearly. Pepin, one of Louis's rebellious sons, died before him, so that only three were left to succeed. To the eldest, Lothaire, he sent from his deathbed the crown and royal sword, begging him to be faithful to the Empress Judith and the young Charles. But Lothaire had no such desire. He had no love for his step-mother and brother, and he wished to have the whole Empire. So very soon war began.

This time, however, Louis the German took part with his young brother Charles against Lothaire. Both sides gathered their armies and at Fontenay-en-Puisaye they met in a terrible battle. At the last minute the two brothers sent to Lothaire offering to yield him much land and treasure and to make peace. But Lothaire would not listen. "I will have nothing but by the sword," he said. So at two o'clock on a fair June morning, when the first gray light crept up in the sky, the battle began. All day it raged, brother fighting against brother, kinsman against kinsman. The slaughter was awful, and when evening came the bravest and noblest of the Franks lay dead on the field.

The brothers had won, and Lothaire fled. But even the victors were sad over their victory, their loss was so great. They spent the next day burying the dead, and helping the wounded, friends and enemies, faithful and unfaithful, alike.

But although the battle of Fontenay was a terrible massacre it settled nothing. The war still went on. The next spring the two brothers, Louis and Charles, met near the town of Strasburg, and, in presence of their armies, took a solemn oath of friendship.

Now the soldiers of Louis were nearly all Saxons from beyond the Rhine, while the soldiers of Charles were Franks or Gaulo-Romans. They spoke different languages. The Saxons spoke the Teutonic language, which has since grown into German. The Franks spoke the Romance language, which was a mixture of Latin and Celtic and which has since grown into French.

So that all might understand the oath, Charles came to Louis's army and spoke in Teutonic, while Louis went to that of Charles and spoke in Romance.

Louis spoke first, because he was the elder. "For the love of God," he said, "and for the well being of our own and all other Christian peoples, from this day forward, in so much as God gives me to know and to do, I will aid my brother Charles in all things as I ought justly to aid my brother, provided that he do even so by me. And I will make no covenant with Lothaire which shall be harmful to this my brother Charles."

And when Louis had taken this oath the soldiers answered: "If Louis keeps the oath which he has sworn to his brother Charles, and if Charles my lord breaks his, if I cannot turn him from it neither will I lend him any aid, neither I nor any that be with me."

Louis having taken the oath Charles did the same, and afterward the two brothers spent some days in feasting and knightly games. Then they marched together against Lothaire. He, seeing that his brothers being united he could not hope to conquer them, became anxious for peace. To this Louis and Charles agreed, and a treaty of peace was signed at Verdun in 843.

By this treaty Lothaire kept the title of Emperor and the kingdom of Italy. Louis had the German states, and Charles most of what is now France. Thus the mighty Empire which Charlemagne had spent his life in welding together was again broken up, and three distinct kingdoms were carved out of it. The boundaries, of course, wTere not quite what they are to-day, and for hundreds of years they remained unsettled, one country growing larger and another smaller as the kings and peoples fought and wrested the land from each other. Still out of Charlemagne's great Empire we have now the beginnings of Germany, France, and Italy.

But it is the history of France only that we will follow at present. And it is well to remember that in the Oath of Strasburg we see the beginnings of the French language as in the treaty of Verdun we see the beginnings of the France of to-day; and we might say that Charles was the first King of France. This Charles was surnamed *le Chauve*, or the Bald, not because he was really bald, but because he had not the flowing locks which were the pride and glory of the Frankish Kings. It is interesting also to remember that his daughter Judith married Ethelwulf, the Anglo-Saxon King, and was thus the step-mother of our great Alfred.

Although, after this treaty of Verdun, the quarrels of the brothers seemed settled, there was little peace for Charles. In different parts of the kingdom rebels rose calling themselves kings and fighting against their liege lord. But the worst enemies were the wild, heathen Northmen.

Ever since the days when Charlemagne had wept to see them attack his shores they had grown bolder and bolder. While the princes had been taken up by their own quarrels, those wild sea robbers had descended upon the unprotected shores. They did not come to settle, but merely to plunder and to burn. They came suddenly, and went again as suddenly. When the storms raged, when the waves dashed high, and the wind whistled and screamed so that other people fled for shelter, the Northmen rejoiced. Then they spread their sails and made their light ships dance over the billows. Up the rivers they sailed to towns far inland. There they robbed and burned the churches, slew the people, or carried them away captive.

Charles, finding himself too weak to fight these fierce people, paid them gold to go away. This was the worst thing he could have done. For the Northmen took the gold and went away. But they returned again the next year in the hope of getting more.

There was one man however who fought the Northmen bravely. He was Robert le Fort or Robert the Strong, Count of Anjou. For five years he kept these sea robbers in check, but at last he met his death fighting against them, as you shall hear.

A party of about four hundred Northmen, led by the famous Sea King Hastings, came sailing up the Loire, and marched to attack the town of Le Mans. Robert the Strong hearing of it marched to meet them. But he was too late. When he reached Le Mans the town was already in flames, and the robbers fled with their booty. Robert at once pursued them, and the Northmen, seeing themselves hard pressed, took refuge in a village church, which was large and strongly built. When Robert and his men reached the church it was evening. Seeing how strongly built it was they did not try to storm it, but pitched their tents around it in order to be ready to attack the Northmen next morning.

The day had been very hot, and Robert was weary with marching and fighting. So now, feeling that the enemy were safely shut up till morning, he went to his tent and took off his helmet and coat of mail, in order to rest.

He had hardly done so when there was a loud noise. Uttering their fearful battle cries the Northmen rushed from their shelter, and threw themselves upon the Franks. Seizing his sword, and without waiting to put on helmet or armor, Robert rushed forth. Springing to arms, his men followed him and quickly drove back the Northmen. But Robert the Strong was too reckless. He pursued the Northmen too far. And even in the moment of victory he was slain. He fell dead upon the steps of the church, struck to the heart by the spear of a Northman.

Having lost their leader the Franks had no more heart to fight. So the Northmen regained their ships in triumph and sailed on up the Loire, leaving, as was their wont, desolation and ruin in their track.

The nobles, finding little help from their King against these wild freebooters, now began to build strong castles and fortresses all over the country to protect themselves and their goods against their ravages. The poor people, glad of the shelter, built their huts near these great castles, and paid a small sum of money yearly, or promised help in war in return for protection. This made the nobles very much more powerful than they had been. Soon the whole country was covered with castles and estates over which the nobles ruled like kings, making laws and waging war as it pleased them, and owning the King merely as "over-lord." But this was only exchanging one evil for another. For by the lawless wars of these lawless nobles the whole land was filled with misery and bloodshed, and the state of the people became truly wretched.

Charles saw how this growing power of the nobles weakened his power, and again and again he forbade castles to be built, or towns to be fortified without his leave. But the nobles did not listen to him. He was too feeble a ruler to force men to obey him, and in the end he was obliged to allow what he could not hinder.

Charles could not keep peace within the land he possessed, nor protect it from outside foes. Yet he was greedy of more. So when his brother, the Emperor, and his son after him died, he hurried to Rome and had himself crowned Emperor. He quarrelled with his brother, Louis the German, with whom he had sworn everlasting friendship. And when Louis died he continued the quarrel with his nephews, for he hoped once again to unite under his scepter all the vast Empire of Charlemagne. It was while fighting against one of the sons of Louis the German that Charles met his death in 877. He became ill and died of fever in a wretched hut among the Alps near the Mont Cenis pass. It was a miserable end to a miserable reign of thirty-seven years.

CHAPTER 15

LOUIS II THE STAMMERER AND HIS SONS

CHARLES the Bald was succeeded by his son, Louis *le Begue*, or the Stammerer. He was weak in health and weak in will, but his reign was so short that it is hard to know whether or not he added anything to the misery into which the realm had fallen.

The misery could hardly have been greater. The people were wearied with constant wars. Hunger, poverty, and sickness were abroad in the land. The nobles fought among themselves, the Northmen ravaged all the western shores, the Saracens attacked the south, from Italy and Germany the sons of Louis the German threatened their cousin.

The whole country was full of wars and troubles, when the Stammerer died in 879, after scarcely eighteen months' reign. He was succeeded by his two young sons, Louis and Carloman. Louis was eighteen, Carloman only fourteen. Unlike the other Carolingian princes they loved each other and did not quarrel over the division of the kingdom. They were courageous and warlike, but they were mere boys and could do little to stem the troubles of the time.

Louis indeed built a castle of wood as protection against the Northmen. But it became a fortress for them, rather than a defence for the Franks. For, badly supported by his vassals, Louis could find no one to hold the castle for him.

After two years of troubled reign Louis died suddenly from an accident while out riding. Carloman then ruled alone. He too fought the Northmen, sometimes defeating them, sometimes being defeated by them. But for want of soldiers, and want of agreement among his nobles, he was never able to drive them out. At length, weary of the struggle, he made a treaty with them, and having received a great sum of money the Northmen promised to go away, and not return for twelve years.

A few days after this Carloman went hunting. He was chasing a wild boar when it suddenly turned and attacked him savagely. Seeing that the King's life was in danger, a comrade rode quickly forward and struck at the boar with his spear. But in his eagerness he aimed badly. His spear slipped, and instead of killing the boar it pierced the King in the thigh.

The wound was a very bad one, and in these days doctors were not skillful. In a few days it was seen that the young King must die. He faced death bravely. He knew that his comrade had meant to help and not to hurt him. But he knew, too, that, if the truth were told, the people would kill the brave man, perhaps in some cruel fashion, for having caused their King's death. Carloman did not wish an innocent man to suffer. So he hid the real cause of his wound, and told those around him that his leg had been torn by the tusks of the boar. He died in 884, having reigned four years in all.

Neither Louis nor Carloman had any sons and the heir to the throne was their little step-brother Charles, who was not yet five years old. But this was no time in which to give the ruling of the state into the hands of a helpless child, so the nobles chose the Emperor Charles le Gros, or the Fat, to be their King.

Charles the Fat was the youngest son of Louis the German. He was already Emperor and King of Italy and Germany. So now once again all the realm of Charlemagne was united under one scepter. But Charles was a very different ruler from his great-grandfather, Charlemagne. He was fat and lazy, treacherous and cruel, neither a soldier nor a statesman.

CHAPTER 16

CHARLES THE FAT—HOW THE MEN OF PARIS DEFIED THE SEA KINGS

AS soon as the Northmen heard of the death of Carloman they returned. From far and near the sea robbers came. Never before had they gathered in such numbers as now. The Franks stood aghast as they saw the dragon-headed vessels sail up their rivers.

"Have you not been paid?" they asked. "Have you not promised to keep away for twelve years?"

"Nay," replied the Northmen, "it was with Carloman we made our bargain. Carloman is dead, we are free from our oath. If the new King would make a bargain with us let him pay us more gold."

Up the river Seine they sailed, ship upon ship, large and small, to the number of seven hundred. They attacked and took town after town, growing ever bolder and more insolent as they advanced.

At length they reached Paris. For miles the river was black with vessels bringing an army of thirty thousand heathen against the fair city.

But here in Paris the bravest of the Franks had gathered led by Eudes, Count of Paris, son of Robert the Strong, who in his day alone had held the Normans in check. With him was the fighting Bishop Gozlin. And here the Northmen were stopped in their triumphal course.

Finding Paris so strongly guarded, Siegfried the Sea King demanded to be brought before the Bishop.

"Gozlin," he said, "take pity on yourself and your followers. If you do not wish to perish allow us to pass through Paris. If you do this, we promise to preserve you and Eudes and all your goods from harm."

But Gozlin answered, 'This city has been given into our care by Charles our Emperor. He has given it to us, not to bring ruin on our Empire, but to insure peace. If by chance this city had been given unto you to guard would you have yielded it to the enemy?'

"Nay, had I done so I should perish by the sword," replied Siegfried. "Nevertheless, if you will not yield what I ask, as soon as the sun rises we shall begin our attack."

So saying he departed. Gozlin would not yield, and Siegfried kept his

THE DRAGON-HEADED VESSELS SAILED UP THE RIVERS.

word. Day had hardly dawned when the Northmen attacked the tower which guarded the bridge across the Seine. All day the fight lasted. Arrows rained upon the brave defenders. They on their side poured burning oil and melted lead upon the enemy, so that to escape being burned many of the Northmen threw themselves into the river and were drowned. Night at last put an end to the fight.

Next morning it began again. All day it raged as fiercely as before. Then, seeing that Paris was not to be taken by assault, the Northmen resolved to starve the people into surrender. So a long siege began.

While the Northmen lay encamped around the walls, the people of Paris suffered all the horrors of hunger and disease. Not a day passed without some fighting, and every day the number of the brave defenders grew smaller. Still they fought on and hoped on.

Message after message was sent to the Emperor begging for aid, but no aid came. Still encouraged by their brave Bishop the people held out. Then one sad day the Bishop died. Without the walls of Paris there was rejoicing, within wailing and tears. It seemed as if with the gallant Bishop hope too had died. Then at last Count Eudes decided to go himself to seek aid from the Emperor. Disguised as a Northman he left Paris in secret, and passed safely through the camp of the enemy.

Eudes left the city in charge of Ebles, a nephew of the dead Bishop. He guided the people gallantly while their brave Count was absent, and kept hope alive in their hearts until one morning Eudes, surrounded by soldiers, appeared upon the height beyond the walls. The people of Paris saw him and rejoiced.

The Northmen too saw him and made ready to fight, and prevent him entering the city. But Eudes put spurs to his horse, and drawing his sword, he dashed forward, cutting his way through the enemy. To right and left his sword flashed again and again, and many a heathen warrior fell dead in his tracks. Followed fast by his men Eudes reached the gates. As he came near Ebles threw them open wide, and Eudes dashed through. Then turning he and his followers beat back with great slaughter the heathen host who pursued them.

Great was the joy within the walls at the return of the hero. Greater still was the joy at the news that the Emperor was fast approaching with help.

But Charles the Fat was slow to move. For many, many long days and nights the people looked in vain for the Emperor and his army.

At last they came. The slopes of Montmartre were white with their tents, the glitter of their spears was like the stars at night, and the hearts of the brave defenders rejoiced. Now, at length, the Northmen would be utterly defeated.

The French watched eagerly from the walls of Paris ready to join in the fight as soon as the Emperor gave the signal. But day by day passed. No trumpet sounded to battle, no war cry was heard. The soldiers of the Emperor lay idle, their banners fluttering lazily by their tents. Then suddenly one day the people of Paris learned that the Emperor had made a treaty with the enemy. He had given the Northmen leave to go to spend the winter in the part of France called Burgundy, and pillage there at will. This he did because the Burgundians had rebelled against him. It was an easy way, he thought, of getting rid of the Northmen and punishing the rebels at the same time.

When the people of Paris heard of this shameful treaty, they were filled with anger. All their suffering had been in vain. They had endured month after month of misery, in order to prevent the Northmen getting farther into the country. Now the Emperor was giving them free leave to pass to the very heart of it, there to plunder and burn at will.

But the people of Paris would not consent to this bargain. They refused to allow the Northmen's ships to pass up the river, and manned the walls, and fought as sturdily as at the beginning of the siege. The Northmen, however, were now determined to reach the rich lands of Burgundy. So, seeing that they could in no way pass the city by river, they took their boats out of the water, carried them more than two miles overland, and launched them again above the city, well out of reach of the French arrows and slings.

So the great siege of Paris ended. The city had been saved. It seemed at first as if only the city had been saved, and as if the rest of France was to be given over to the Northmen. But it was really not so. For the fame of the siege spread abroad in the kingdom, and the French took heart. If one city could keep the Northmen at bay for a whole year why should not others? they asked. It was plain then that the Northmen might be conquered, they said.

Charles the Fat did not reign long after his cowardly treaty with the Northmen. His people had grown tired of his sloth, and, in 887, they drove him from the throne, and chose another Emperor. He made no resistance. He who had been one day ruler of a vast empire found himself the next a lonely beggar. He was so old and fat that he could not move without help; his mind, too, was giving way. He was an object for pity rather than anger. But in his weakness and distress he found no friend. Forsaken by every one, in danger of starving, he was obliged to beg his bread until he died a few months later. He had reigned in France three years, but the French had such a contempt for him that they do not count him among their Kings. Charles the Bald is Charles II and Charles the Simple, of whom we shall hear later on, is Charles III. The Emperor Charles the Fat is passed over.

CHAPTER 17

CHARLES III THE SIMPLE—HOW ROLLO THE SEA KING DID HOMAGE TO THE KING OF FRANCE

WHEN Charles the Fat was deposed, the great Empire of Charlemagne was at an end forever. Never again have France, Italy, and Germany been united under one ruler. The Germans chose another Emperor, and the French, remembering how bravely Eudes had led the siege of Paris, chose him for their King. He was crowned with great rejoicing. But the gallant young King had no easy task, for France was all torn and desolate with civil war, and five other princes at least set themselves up as kings of different parts.

Besides this, some of the nobles took Charles the young son of Louis the Stammerer and crowned him King. You remember that he had been passed over before because he was too young to rule, and Charles the Fat had been chosen instead. He was now fourteen, still too young to rule, but by placing him on the throne some of the turbulent nobles hoped to win great power for themselves. For Charles was young and gay, and seemed so easy to lead that he is called Charles the Simple.

So Eudes had to fight for his crown. But he was wise as well as brave and kingly; he remembered that, although he was the chosen of the people, the father of Charles had been his king. So he put an end to the quarrel by giving Charles part of the kingdom and promising to him the rest when he died.

And brave, wise Eudes had not long to live. Soon he became very ill. Feeling that he was about to die he called his nobles around him, and begged them to keep faith with Charles. Then, on New Year's Day, 898, he closed his eyes forever, having reigned for ten years. He was buried in St. Denis among the Merovingians and Carolingians who had gone before him.

Eudes was the first of a new race of kings who were to sit upon the throne of France for many generations. But in the meantime the Carolingians were restored. For three days after Eudes's death Charles the Simple was crowned once more.

The country was still torn by civil war, still desolated King by the Northmen. Their chief leader was now called Rollo. He was a hardy old sea-king, taller and stronger than any of his followers, fierce and pitiless as a hungry wolf. He laid waste the land and filled it with tears and mourning till at length Charles, weary of the strife, made a treaty with him.

By this treaty Rollo was to be given the King's daughter Gisella for his wife, and the dukedom of all that part of France which we now call Normandy. In return for this, Rollo was to promise to become a Christian, to cease from ravaging the land, and become the subject of King Charles. To all this Rollo agreed, but he asked for still more land. For Normandy was the part of France which had suffered most from the attacks of the Northmen, and was now little more than a desert waste. So to it Charles added the part of France called Brittany. Brittany was really not his to give, for the Bretons had never owned the rule of the French Kings, but Hollo was satisfied, and so peace was made.

Then, upon an appointed day, there was a great meeting between Hollo and the King. Charles came with all his knights and nobles and Bishops. Hollo with all his best warriors. Charles with his crown upon his head sat upon his throne, while Rollo knelt before him and placed his hands between the King's hands and swore to be his man.

It was hard for the proud sea-king to bend his knee to another, or to put his hand within the hand of another in token of subjection. Rollo, however, knelt and repeated the words as the Bishops bade him. But that was not enough.

"You must now kiss the King's foot," they said.

Rollo started up in anger, "Never, by heaven!" he cried, his blue eyes flashing.

"But you must," said the Bishops. "It is the custom that whoever receives such a gift from the King must kiss his foot."

"Nay, never will I kiss the foot of any man," said Rollo.

But the Bishops still insisted.

"Then let one of my warriors perform it for me," said Rollo.

And to this the Bishops were fain to consent, for it was plain the proud sea-king would never stoop to kiss the foot of Charles.

So one of the Northmen warriors was called forward. But he had little liking for the act which seemed to him beneath the dignity of a freeman. He was told to kneel, but he had no mind to kneel. Stooping, he roughly lifted the King's foot to the level of his mouth, and Charles the Simple fell off his throne backward amid the rude laughter of the Northmen.

In this way Hollo the Northman became Duke of Normandy, and he and his followers took possession of the land and settled there. They forgot their far-off homes, and took France for their home, and the French language for their language. So now we will call them no more Northmen, but Normans, which is the name by which we know them best.

Hollo kept his word and was baptized. Robert, Count of France, brother of brave Eudes, was his godfather and gave him the new Christian name of Robert. But he is best known by his heathen name of Rollo.

Seeing their leader baptized, many of his warriors followed his example, and became Christians also. Then Rollo, the wild sea-king, settled down and became a wise and peaceful ruler. He rebuilt the churches and towns which before he had ruined. He made good laws, and saw that they were kept. Theft especially was punished so severely that it was almost unknown. No man had need of locks and bolts; ploughs and carts were left in the fields at night, flocks and herds might be shepherdless yet safe. The people said that even gold and jewels might be left upon the highway, and no man would touch them.

One day the Duke thought he would put this to the test. He had been hunting, and at mid-day he and his companions sat down to rest and dine by a lake. And as, after the meal, they sat at ease drinking, and sheltering from the heat of the mid-day sun, it may be the talk fell upon the people, and the laws, and the peace which had come to the land. Rollo lay upon the grass in the shade of a mighty oak tree, and as he listened to the talk he looked up through the green branches and smiled. Then rising he unclasped the golden bracelets from his arms, and hung them upon the branches of the tree. And there he left them.

Hollo and his companions returned to the chase; the sound of the hunting horns and the baying of dogs died away in the distance. The glade by the lake was deserted once more. Only on the tree, like some strange fruit, there hung the glittering jewels. Huntsmen and husbandmen, travelers and pilgrims, passing that way saw them there, but no one touched them. In rain and sunshine, in summer and winter, they hung unharmed, so that when three long years had passed and Rollo returned to the spot, he found his bracelets still upon the branches where he had set them. And ever after the lake was called Roumare, or lake of Rollo.

But while Rollo the Duke was ruling well, Charles the King was showing more and more that he was unable to rule. He allowed himself to be led by a favorite called Haganon, who was a clever soldier, but of humble birth. It made the great nobles angry that they could only reach the King through this common man. And the more power the King allowed to him, the more insolent he became. Once many of the nobles and people of high estate came to see the King. But for four days they stood without his door waiting in vain to see him. For Haganon was with Charles, and he would neither come out to speak with the nobles nor send them any message. So they went away very angry saying, "Haganon will soon be King, or else Charles will be brought as low as Haganon."

At length the King and nobles all gathered to a great council at Soissons. As Charles sat upon his throne in all his royal state, one noble after another advanced before him, holding in his hand his rod of office. Each one as he reached the throne broke his rod, and cast the pieces at the King's feet. "We reject you, O Charles!" they cried; "we will no longer have you as lord and master, for you are but a King of a coward's heart."

Then one by one they turned to go, till at length the King was left sitting in state upon his throne, utterly alone.

The nobles then chose Robert, Count of Paris, to be their King. He was an old man, the brother of brave Eudes. Some of the people, however, still clung to Charles. So there was civil war once more. But Robert was never really King, for, in the battle that followed, Charles indeed was defeated, but Robert was killed.

Robert, however, had a son named Hugh. He might now have been King had he wished. But he refused. He chose rather to be simply Duke of France than take the more glorious and more dangerous title of King. The nobles therefore chose Robert's son-in-law Raoul, and crowned mm as King. King

After the battle in which Robert had been killed Charles had fled. But he was soon taken prisoner by the treachery of Count Herbert, one of the greatest of his nobles. This noble sent a messenger to Charles saying that he was not pleased with the choice of Raoul for King, and promising to set Charles upon the throne again.

Simple Charles believed this, and with his few remaining followers set out for the Count's castle. The traitor received the poor King with great state. He knelt to him, and when his son refused to follow his example he gave him a box on the ear saying, "Learn not to stand when you receive your King."

For one day Charles was surrounded with homage. Then Count

Herbert sent away his few followers, saying that the King had no more need of them. They went, and Charles at once found himself in prison.

Then his Queen Elgiva fled to England with her little son Louis and took refuge at the court of Athelstane. For Athelstane was her brother.

Charles remained a prisoner for the rest of his life. Once or twice, indeed, when the nobles, wanting to force King Raoul to do as they wished, they brought the poor old King out of his prison, clothed him in fine clothes and threatened to place him upon the throne again. But as soon as they got what they wanted, Charles was sent back again to prison, and there he died.

CHAPTER 18

HOW HUGH CAPET BECAME KING OF FRANCE

RAOUL was not a great King, and Hugh, Duke of France, was by this time far the most powerful man in the country, being indeed called Hugh the Great. So when Raoul died in 936, leaving no son, Hugh might again have been King, but he again refused. He thought it was wiser to allow some one else to have the appearance of power, while he had it in reality. So instead of becoming King himself he sent over the sea to England for Louis, the young son of Charles the Simple. Louis was now a boy of sixteen, and Hugh hoped he would be easily led, as his father had been.

Louis-d'outre-mer, or Louis-from-over-the-Sea as he was called, came and was greeted by the nobles with great joy. But it was soon seen that he was by no means like his father. Although still so young, he was clever, and of a proud and headstrong will. He determined to rule himself, and not be a mere King of show. This was by no means what Hugh wanted. From being Louis's friend he became his enemy, and soon France was once more torn by civil war.

The young King made a brave fight, but all his courage was useless against the skill and wisdom of Hugh, who took and held him prisoner for a year. He was only set free after he had yielded the town of Laon to the Duke. This was almost the last possession remaining to the unhappy King, and with the loss of it his power sank to a mere shadow. Then he appealed for help to the Pope and to the Emperor of Germany, and at last Hugh was forced to make peace with him. He came to the King, once more put his hands between the King's hands, and promised to be his faithful vassal.

But even after this there was no real peace in the land, and all the reign of Louis-from-over-the-Sea was spent in fighting his nobles. For eighteen years he struggled on, then one day while chasing a wolf he was thrown from his horse and died.

Louis-from-over-the-Sea left two sons, the eldest of which, Lothaire, was only thirteen. And for a third time the crown was offered to Hugh,

Duke of France. For a third time he refused it, and Lothaire was crowned. Two years later Hugh died, but his son, also named Hugh, succeeded him as Duke. He, like his father, was of great power. "Lothaire is King in name," said a writer of the time, "Hugh is King in fact."

King Lothaire reigned for thirty-two years in troublous times. He was succeeded by his son Louis V, who is called Louis Do Nothing. Perhaps the name was undeserved, for he had scarcely time to do anything, as his reign lasted little more than a year. In 987 he had a fall from his horse and died. He left no son and with him ended the great Carolingian line, although Louis Do Nothing had an uncle, Charles of Lorraine. He was the younger brother of King Lothaire, and according to our ideas he was heir to the throne. But in those far-off and warlike times these ideas had not yet become fixed. The great nobles had grown very powerful. Most of them did not want to have Charles to reign over them, for he was a vassal of the German Emperor, and had married a lady beneath him in birth. So they resolved to choose a King from among themselves.

At the time of Louis's death it happened that many of the nobles were met together in council. Among them was the powerful Bishop named Adalberon, and of course Duke Hugh. They began to talk of who should be King. Then the Bishop rose in his place and stood beside the Duke.

"It seems to me," he said, "that we ought to put off for some time the choosing of our King so that each one of us may think over it carefully. Then on an appointed day let us again meet together to choose our leader. Will you swear to me and to our noble Duke to do naught in the matter until that day?"

To this all those gathered there agreed. They put their hands between the hands of the Duke and swore to keep faith. And when they had fixed the time at which they should meet again they separated and went to their own homes.

Meanwhile Charles of Lorraine came to the Bishop and sought his help. "All the world knows, reverend father," he said, "that I ought to succeed to my brother and my nephew. Why should I be cast out of my inheritance? I am a man, and have birth, and courage, and all that is needed in a King."

But the Bishop had no wish to help Charles and answered him in a few words.

'You have always made friends with low, wicked folk," he said. "Even now you will not give them up. How can you expect to reach the throne in company with such men, and by the help of such men?"

"I cannot forsake my friends," replied Charles. "I hope to win others."

"I can do nothing without the consent of the nobles," said the Bishop, as he turned coldly away.

Very sadly, with no hope of the throne, Charles went back to Lorraine, which he held as vassal of the German Emperor.

At the time appointed the nobles met again together. Again the Bishop spoke. "It is true Charles has his followers," he said. "But we must set on the throne one who is not merely noble of birth, but noble in mind. Charles has so far forgotten himself as to have no shame in serving a stranger king. He has married a wife taken from the rank of his vassals. How is it possible that you should bend the knee to her as Queen? Think well. If you wish to bring unhappiness on our land, make Charles King. If you wish happiness for it, choose Hugh, the illustrious Duke."

When the Bishop had finished speaking, all the nobles cried out with one consent, "Let Hugh, the great Duke, be King.

Thus a new line of Kings came to the throne of France, a line which was to hold it for eight hundred years.

At once Hugh was crowned, and, in order to make his kingdom more sure, the new King asked the Archbishop to crown his son Robert as King and successor. At first the Archbishop said it was impossible to crown two kings in one year. But after a little he yielded. So with great ceremony Robert, son of Hugh, was crowned.

But although Hugh was careful thus to make sure that his son would reign after him it is said that he himself never wore the crown except upon the day of his coronation. It is hard to tell why he refused to wear his crown. Whatever the reason may have been, some people say that he received his surname Capet because of this, from the Latin word caput, a head, his being a head without covering. Others say that he received the name because he had a large head, or because he wore a chape or cope. Still others say that Capet was already a family name in the time of his father, Hugh the Great, In any case, the name clung to the family, and the whole line of Kings is known as the Capetians.

CHAPTER 19

HUGH CAPET—HOW THE BISHOP BETRAYED THE DUKE OF LORRAINE

ALTHOUGH most of the nobles had chosen Hugh as King, all had not done so, and some would not acknowledge his right to reign. We hear of one proud noble who overran the country round him and called himself Count of it, caring nothing for Hugh. The King, angry that his authority should be thus set at naught, sent for the noble.

'Who made you Count?" he asked.

"Who made you King?" quickly answered the insolent lord. And Hugh had no reply to make, for well he knew that his power was but small. Well he knew that he sat upon the throne by the favor of even such haughty and turbulent nobles as he who now defied him.

So long as Charles of Lorraine lived and claimed a right to the throne, Hugh could not feel safe. So the rivals fought. But Charles was hard to beat, and it was by treachery that in the end he was overcome.

The traitor was named Ascelin, he was a Bishop, and he and Charles had once been friends. But they had quarrelled, and Charles had driven the Bishop into exile. Now, however, having agreed with Hugh to betray him, Ascelin pretended to make friends once more, and while he laid his wicked plans the Bishop went to stay with Charles. So it fell out that one night as they sat at supper Charles took a golden cup full of wine, and holding it toward the Bishop said: "Drink in token of your faith to me. But if you mean not to keep faith, drink not lest you would be classed with the traitor Judas."

Falsely smiling, Ascelin replied, "I will take the cup and willingly drink all it contains."

"You must say," cried Charles, "'and I will keep faith.'"

The Bishop took the golden cup and drank to the last drop. Then setting it down empty he cried, "I will keep faith, or I will perish as did Judas."

The evening passed in talk and laughter, the false Bishop being among the gayest of the company. At length the feast was over and all lay down to rest, save the traitor. He alone waked. For he felt that now the time had come to carry out his wicked plans.

So when every one was asleep Ascelin crept softly to the bedside of Charles. Cautiously he stole his sword and dagger, and those of the knights near him.

Then going to the sentinel at the door Ascelin ordered him to go quickly and gather his followers. The man hesitated.

"Go," said the Bishop, "I will guard the door till you return." So the man went.

As soon as the sentinel had gone, Ascelin placed himself in the middle of the doorway, holding his sword ready beneath his robe in case of attack.

Soon all his followers were gathered round the Bishop. They entered the room where Charles was sleeping, and he awakening from a heavy sleep found himself surrounded by armed men. He leaped from his bed, at the same time putting out his hand to seize his sword. It was not there.

"What means this?" he cried, as his eyes fell on the cruel face of the crafty Bishop.

"Once you forced me into exile," replied Ascelin, "now it is my turn. Now I will hunt you forth. I am a free man, but you will be in bondage to others."

"O Bishop," cried Charles bitterly, "I ask you have you no remembrance of last night's supper? Was your oath last night a lie?"

So saying Charles dashed in blind rage at the traitor. and taken But he had no sword. He was powerless. Armed soldiers closed in upon him. They seized him, and throwing him back on his bed held him there. In a few moments he was bound and cast prisoner into a darksome dungeon. There after a few months he died, and so Hugh was free from his greatest rival.

CHAPTER 20

ROBERT I THE PIOUS—THE BEGGARS' KING

HUGH died in 996 and was succeeded by his son, Robert the Pious. He was tall and handsome, with soft eyes and a kindly mouth. As his surname tells us, he was very religious, and spent much of his time in praying. He wrote poetry, too, and played upon the lute. He was so fond of music that often, dressed in his royal robes and with his crown upon his head, he would go into the Cathedral and lead the choir and sing among the monks. A gentle, kindly man with winning ways and generous heart, he was little suited to be a King in those rough times.

But although Robert was so good, and although he gave a great deal of money to the Church, the Pope was angry with him and threatened to excommunicate him. The Pope did this because Robert had married his own cousin, which the Pope said was wicked. Robert loved his wife, and refused to give her up. But at length the people became afraid of the anger of the Pope. They all fled from the King, who was left at last with only two servants. Even they served him in fear, burning everything he had touched, and cleansing by fire the metal cups and plates he used. So at length King Robert yielded to the Pope, and put away his beautiful wife Bertha.

A few years later he married another lady named Constance, the daughter of the Count of Toulouse. She was beautiful and frivolous, with a sharp tongue and proud manners. She brought to her husband's gloomy court a merry train of courtiers and troubadors.

The grave monks who surrounded King Robert were shocked at the gay life these courtiers led, shocked at the strange clothes and bright colors they wore. For they cut their hair short, shaved their beards, and wore ridiculous shoes, curled up at the toes. It seemed to the sober people of Northern France that men who could dress in such a strange manner could not fail to be wicked. And yet, sad to say, some of the people began to copy these frivolous fashions which the Southerners had brought among them. And although the priests told them that they were thus yielding to the wiles of the Evil One, many of them still kept to their wicked ways, shaving their beards, cutting their hair, and wearing ridiculous dresses and shoes.

But while the Queen and her courtiers lived a gay life, spending money carelessly on all sorts of splendor, there was much misery in the land. Many of the people had not enough to eat and the country swarmed with beggars.

Robert was so sorry for the poor and helpless that he gave nearly all he had in charity. Beggars followed him everywhere, even into his palace, and when he had no more money to give he pretended not to notice when some of them stole, and they grew so greedy and so bold that they stole even the ornaments of his dress. This made the haughty Queen very angry, so Robert did his best to hide his deeds of charity from her. Many a time he gave a poor beggar money or food with the warning, "Beware lest the Queen see thee." It is told how one day when he sat at dinner a poor man placed himself at his feet, and was fed by the King under the table by stealth. As the beggar sat crouching beneath the table he saw a beautiful golden ornament hanging from the King's robe; so, taking his knife, he cut it off and then hurried away.

When the company rose from the table the Queen noticed that the precious ornament was gone. She was very angry and cried out sharply, "Oh, my good lord, what enemy has stolen your beautiful golden ornament?"

"Oh," replied the King, "no one has stolen it. Please God, it will be of more use to him who took it than to us." And quite unconcerned the King went away with a smiling face to say his prayers.

But even in church Robert was not free from beggars. One day while he knelt in prayer a robber cut the golden fringe from his robe. He had cut half of it off when the King noticed him.

"That will do, go away now," said he gently. "You have taken enough, perhaps some one else has more need of the rest than you have."

These stories show us into what dreadful poverty the constant wars and terrible misrule had brought many of the people. Indeed, the lives of the poor were so hard and bitter that in many places throughout France they rose in rebellion. In Normandy especially there was great discontent.

"The nobles," said the peasants, "do us nothing but evil. With them we have neither gain nor profit from our labors. Every day they take our cattle for forced service. Then there are old taxes and new taxes, and pleas without end. There are so many bailiffs and sergeants that we have not an hour of peace. Every day they harry us, take our goods, and hunt us from our land. There is no protection for us against the nobles and their servants. No oath binds them.

"Why should we let ourselves be treated thus? Are we not men as they are? It is only courage that we need. Let us bind ourselves together by an oath, and swear to help each other. If they want to fight, have we not thirty or forty peasants for every one of their knights? Have we not peasants who are young and both ready and willing to fight with axe and club, with bow and arrow, and even with stones if they have no other weapons?

"Let us resist the knights. Then we shall be free to cut down trees, hunt game, and fish as we like. Then we shall do as we will in field, and stream, and wood."

In this way the peasants talked in their secret meetings. But these meetings became known to the nobles. One day, when the chief leaders were met together, a large body of armed men burst in upon them. The poor peasants, who were half naked and badly armed, could do nothing against soldiers clad in steel, and armed with sword, and spear, and battle axe.

All the leaders were taken prisoners. Some of them were put to death in cruel fashion, some had their eyes put out, their hands and feet cut off, and were then sent home to their villages that the sight of their dreadful sufferings might strike fear into the hearts of their fellows. After this, seeing the dreadful punishment which had overcome their leaders, the rest of the peasants gave up their plotting, and with despair in their hearts, returned to their ploughs.

Yet we can hardly believe that Robert made the misery of the poor any lighter by allowing them to steal. This was simple weakness rather than goodness, and although he was so lenient to the thieves and beggars who surrounded him, his religion made him very cruel in other ways. In his reign began the persecution of the Jews, which lasted during many centuries.

At this time many people had begun to make pilgrimages to the Holy Land. The Caliph, the heathen ruler of the land, became angry at this, for he hated all Christians, and he destroyed the Church of the Holy Sepulchre at Jerusalem. This filled the whole Christian world with anger. They believed in their anger that the Jews, who were to be found in every country in Europe, had written to the Caliph and encouraged him to do the deed. So in punishment the Jews were hunted from their homes, robbed, ill-treated, and killed. Yet hunted and ill-treated though they were, they always returned. They were not allowed to possess land, but they had money and learning. They were the doctors, and the bankers and the chief merchants of the time. Indeed the people could not get on without them.

But although the people were thus obliged to bear with the Jews, they insulted and humiliated them cruelly, and many ceremonies were invented for this purpose alone. On Easter Day, for instance, a Jew was obliged to come to church to receive a blow on the head from a Christian. The person whom the Bishop most wished to skillful was given the right to strike the blow. Once, it is said, a noble hit so hard that he knocked the Jew's brains out, and he fell to the ground dead.

But it was not only Jews who were persecuted. It was now that Christians first began to kill each other for the love of God. In Orleans some one began to teach Christianity not as the priests taught it. This filled King Robert and his monks with horror. Such an evil must be crushed out at once. So the heretics were taken prisoners, tried, and condemned to be burned to death.

Not far from the city a great bonfire was built. As the heretics came out of the church where they had been condemned, the Queen stood in the porch to watch. At the head of the procession marched a priest who had once been her confessor. Seeing him thus among the heretics the haughty Queen was filled with anger, and springing forward she struck him in the face with her staff so that he lost the sight of one eye.

The heretic priest bore this blow calmly. The procession did not pause, and the thirteen men marched slowly on singing hymns, until they reached the place where they were to die. This was the beginning in France of persecutions in the name of religion. In years to come many cruel things were to be done in the same cause.

The last days of Robert the Pious were made bitter by the conduct of his sons. They, encouraged by their willful, haughty mother, rebelled against the weak and kindly King. And Robert saw himself, like so many of the Carolingians, obliged to march to battle against his own sons. But peace was made at length, and very soon after, in 1031, Robert died. When it was known that he was dead the land was filled with sorrow and wailing. A crowd of poor widows and orphans surrounded the palace weeping aloud, beating their breasts, and praying. "O dear God," they cried, "why do you so afflict us? You have taken our father from us, and we are left desolate."

CHAPTER 21

HENRY I—THE PEACE OF GOD AND THE TRUCE OF GOD

ROBERT the Pious was succeeded by his son, Henry I. He did not come to the throne in peace, for turbulent Queen Constance wanted the throne for her youngest son, Robert. So in his name she fought against her son Henry. But Queen Constance was defeated and died soon after.

Henry was even a weaker King than Robert had been. He did nothing to try to make his people better or happier. Indeed, the power of the King had gradually grown so weak that it was now far less than that of some of the great nobles who in name were vassals to the crown. Far more powerful than the King, for instance, was Robert of Normandy, the descendant of Duke Rollo. He was so great that he was called Robert the Magnificent, or sometimes, because of his wickedness, Robert the Devil. It was he more than any other who helped Henry to conquer Queen Constance. But he made the King pay for his help by giving him yet more land, and thus making him yet more powerful.

During the reign of Henry the misery of the people increased. For there was famine in the land. For three years the harvests failed. The sky was overcast with clouds, the rain hardly ceased. The corn seed rotted in the sodden earth, while weeds grew apace. The little grain which sprouted was destroyed by blight; so that it became so dear that men paid large sums for a handful of mouldy wheat.

Rich and poor alike were attacked by awful hunger, for money could not buy what none had to sell. Rich and poor alike grew gaunt and pale. They devoured the wild birds and beasts, and when there were no more they ate the bark of trees and the weeds that grew in the streams. They mixed a kind of white clay with what little they had of flour or bran and made bread of that. But the pangs of hunger were so cruel that some were even driven to the horror of eating human flesh. The people died in hundreds, in thousands. They fell by the wayside and in the fields, in such numbers that it was impossible to bury them all, and the wolves devoured them, and their bones lay whitening the earth.

No words can tell the misery and the horror and pain of this time.

But at length it came to an end. The sky cleared, the rain ceased, and once more waving fields of golden corn covered the land.

During this time of fearful suffering the pride of the great had been softened. They felt that the famine had been sent by God as a punishment for their sins. And now that it was over the priests and Bishops prayed for a time of repentance and peace. Then the nobles met together with the Bishops and agreed to keep peace everywhere throughout the realm. It was commanded that whoever broke the peace should be despoiled of his goods and suffer dire punishments. For the breaker of the peace there should be no sanctuary. Even if he were found upon the very steps of the altar he should not escape the punishment of his crime.

Everywhere throughout the land the Bishops gathered the people together to hear the blessed news. It was received with joy both by great and small. The people listened to the voice of the priests as to the voice of God. For every heart was still shaken by the memory of the past misery. In every heart there lurked the dread lest some misfortune should prevent them from enjoying the promise of the golden harvest.

When the Bishops had spoken and told their good news, they raised their crosses to heaven crying, "Peace, peace, peace!" And the people stretching up their hands answered with one voice, "Peace, peace, peace!" Thus was a compact made between the people of France and God on high. And it was called the Peace of God.

The Peace of God was a glorious ideal. But it was too sublime, too splendid. It was impossible to hold to it in those rough times when war was the pastime of the great, the trade of half the world. The Peace of God was broken again and yet again.

Then, seeing that war could not be done away with altogether, some of the peoples of France made a new law. This was that from Wednesday evening till Monday morning there should be no fighting, and that during the weeks of Lent and Advent there should be no fighting at all. During Lent and Advent it was also forbidden to build castles, to make weapons, or to drill soldiers, or, indeed, do anything in connection with war.

This was called the Truce of God. It was perhaps never quite thoroughly kept, but it at least put a stop to a great deal of fighting. So although Henry I was a poor weak King and did little for his people, we have to remember that it was during his reign that men's hearts were moved to pity, so that they tried to lessen the misery of the people by such acts as the Peace of God and the Truce of God.

CHAPTER 22

PHILIP I—HOW HAROLD THE SAXON PAID A VISIT TO DUKE WILLIAM

WHEN Henry died in 1060 he was succeeded by his son Philip I. Philip was only a little boy of seven, and, of course, could not really rule, so the country was governed by a regent. But when Philip was about fourteen the regent died and after that the King himself ruled. He was not a good King; he was idle and pleasure-loving, and in his long reign of forty-eight years did nothing which makes him worthy of being remembered. The deeds of his great vassal, the Duke of Normandy, were of far more importance than the King's, both to France and to England.

While Robert was still on the throne the Duke of Normandy, Robert the Devil, made up his mind to go to the Holy Land in order to atone for his many sins. Before he set forth he called his vassals and barons together to tell them of his intentions. They begged him not to go, seeing his land would be open to great dangers and troubles if left without a lord.

"By my faith," replied Robert, "I will not leave you lordless. I have a young son who, please God, will grow great and strong. Take him, I pray you, for your lord. I make him my heir from this day forth of all Normandy."

This young son was called William and he was only eight years old. But the barons promised to take him for their lord, and swore to be true to him. So Robert set out on his pilgrimage. He never came home again, but died in that far-off land.

The Barons had sworn to be faithful to their young lord, but hardly had Robert gone when they began to revolt. It was with difficulty that Duke Alain of Brittany, who had been left as regent, could prevent the dukedom from being torn from William.

Meanwhile William was growing up. He was very willful, and had a quick, violent temper. But he was so handsome and high spirited that every one admired him. When he played games with his companions he took the leading parts and made the others obey him. He was the judge in their mock trials, the general in their sham fights.

Soon he began to understand what the real fighting meant which was always going on around him. In his child's heart thus there awakened the strength and wisdom of a man, and he tried to gain the love and trust of his father's nobles so that they might give up their quarrels and be true to him as their Duke.

Among the nobles who surrounded William there was a handsome, fair-haired man with gentle, winning manners. This was his cousin, Prince Edward of England. Duke William's aunt, Princess Emma, had married King Ethelred of England, and when he was driven from his throne by the Danes, she and her sons took refuge at the Court of Normandy. For nearly thirty years Edward lived in Normandy. He loved the country and the people and the language and all his Norman relations. So although Edward was much older than his cousin William, and although they were very different from each other, they were good friends.

When Edward was at length called back to England to become King, William was just fifteen. And when the cousins said good-bye to each other they hoped to meet again, although in those days people seldom went journeys unless it was for war or a pilgrimage.

The year that his cousin went away, William insisted on being made a knight. So for the first time he was dressed in full armor, a sword was girt to his side, golden spurs were fastened to his heels. Then, without touching the stirrups, he vaulted into the saddle of his prancing war horse, and galloped up and down in front of an eager, admiring crowd of servants and vassals. For Duke William, with all his fierce tempers and willful ways, made his servants and his neighbors love him dearly.

This day upon which William first put on the arms of a knight was a day of rejoicing for his faithful barons, and a day of dread for his enemies. For it was said that in all France there was no knight who could so well guide a horse and wield a sword or spear.

Now with a firm hand William proved that he meant to be master in his own land, and he "beat down with the sword heads that were too high." The nobles who had at first opposed him knew that they had found a master, and now tried how they could prove to him their firm faith and respect.

Nine years after Edward became King of England William went to pay him a visit. When he reached England he might still have believed himself to be in Normandy, For he found Norman soldiers and sailors, Norman priests and courtiers, everywhere. For Edward, because of his love for them, had surrounded himself with Normans, and Norman French was the language of his court.

Edward greeted his cousin with affection. He entertained him with great splendor, and, when he went away, loaded him with presents of rich arms, splendid horses, hounds, and falcons, and whatever other good and fair gifts he could find that become a man of high degree. It is even said that Edward so far forgot his duty to his people as to promise his crown to his cousin. But of that we cannot be sure.

But whether Edward promised the crown to William or not, William desired to have it.

A few years after this Harold Godwin, the greatest and wisest prince in England, asked King Edward to give him leave to go to Normandy. He wanted to bring home his youngest brother and his nephew who were exiled in France and in the power of Duke William.

Edward was unwilling that Harold should go. "I will not forbid you," he said. "But if you go it will be without my wish. For your journey will surely bring misfortune upon yourself and upon our country. I know Duke William and his crafty spirit. He hates you and will grant you nothing unless he sees some great advantage therein."

Harold, however, was full of a generous wish to free his brother and nephew. He was full of confidence and for himself he feared nothing. So taking with him his hounds and falcons, as if he were but going a-hunting for pleasure, he set out gaily.

But it was already late in the year, and the sea was rough. A great storm arose, and, after being tossed bout by the angry winds and waves, Harold's ship was at length thrown a wreck upon the shores of France.

In those days little help or kindness was shown to those who were shipwrecked. They and their goods were looked upon as lawful prizes. So now Harold and his followers found themselves taken prisoners, with no hope of being released until some one should pay a ransom for them.

As soon as Duke William heard that this great enemy of the Normans was a captive, he paid the ransom, and Harold was sent to the court of the Norman Duke.

William received Harold with a great show of friendliness. He told him that he might at once return to England, but begged him to remain at least a few days as his guest.

Harold well knew that he was in the power of the Duke, and that this show of friendliness hid craft and guile. So he consented to stay. He could do little else. Then followed a gay time. William treated Harold as a brother and equal. He made him a knight of the great Norman order.

Then from one castle to another they went, taking part in tournaments and knightly games. Everywhere Harold was received with the greatest skillful, and all the time he shared a tent with Duke William, and ate from the same table.

Then, as war was almost as much a game as a tournament, William asked Harold and his companions to "try their new spurs" by going with him to fight the Bretons. So Harold went to fight against the Bretons.

As Duke William returned from the war, he and Harold rode side by side, chatting and telling stories. One day William began to tell of the days when Edward had lived in Normandy.

'When Edward and I," he said, "lived like brothers under the same roof, he promised that if ever he became King of England he would make me his heir. I would that you, Harold, would aid me to make this promise sure. And be certain that if by your aid I gain the kingdom whatever you ask of me shall be granted."

At this Harold knew not what to say. He murmured some vague words which William took eagerly as a promise.

"Ah," he cried, "since you will aid me this must you do. You must strengthen the castle of Dover. You must sink in it a well of fresh water. And when I send, you must deliver it over to my soldiers. In return you shall marry my daughter, the fair Adela, and your sister shall marry one of my lords."

What could Harold do? He felt himself in the power of the wily Norman. So once more he murmured vague words of consent. He hoped in this way to buy his freedom and be allowed to return home. He hoped that God would forgive him the falsehood which was wrung from him.

But Duke William was not content with a vague promise. So he called together a great council of all the knights and nobles of Normandy. He also bade his priests and Bishops bring, from all the country round, bones and relics of saints. So many were brought that they filled a large chest. This was placed in the middle of the council chamber and covered with a cloth of gold.

When the day was come upon which the great meeting was called, William set himself upon his throne. He was dressed in splendid robes, a circle of gold and gems was upon his head, and a drawn sword in his hand. Around him stood a crowd of Norman lords and barons. Alone among them stood the Saxon Harold.

"Harold," said William, "I require you now, before these noble lords,

HAROLD'S HANDS TREMBLED AS HE LAID THEM UPON THE LITTLE CASKETS.

to make sure by oath the promises that you have given to me. You must swear to me now, upon holy relics, that, after the death of King Edward, you will aid me to the kingdom of England, that you will marry my daughter Adela, and that you will send your sister to me so that she may be married to one of my nobles."

Again Harold was surprised and troubled. It was one thing to make a vague promise which he did not feel bound to keep. It was quite a different matter to swear solemnly on the relics of saints and martyrs. For in those days to break a promise so sworn was counted a deadly sin. On the cover of cloth of gold two small caskets were laid. With slow, unwilling steps Harold drew near to them. They were very small. After all, he thought, an oath sworn upon such small relics might not be very binding. To break such an oath might not be very wicked. Yet as he stood there he shuddered. His hands trembled as he laid them upon the little caskets, and in a low and troubled voice swore his oath.

As the last words died away all the nobles cried out, "God grant it."

Harold knelt to kiss the caskets. Then, as he rose from his knees, at a sign from Duke William, the cover was removed from the chest.

Of a sudden Harold saw upon what holy relics he had sworn. As he gazed upon the pile he shuddered and turned pale. How was it possible, he asked himself, to break such an oath and yet save his soul.

William had now got all he wanted from his captive guest and he allowed him to go home. He rode with Harold to the seashore, kissed him upon either cheek, and bade him be faithful to his oath. Then, greatly rejoicing, he turned homeward again.

CHAPTER 23

PHILIP I—HOW DUKE WILLIAM SAILED TO ENGLAND

A year or so after Harold's unhappy visit to Normandy King Edward died. But Harold did not keep his oath, and he himself was crowned King of England.

One of the many Normans who lived in England then took ship to France, and made all speed to the Court of Normandy to tell William the news.

When the messenger arrived at Rouen he found William out hunting. The Duke stood with his bow in his hand, surrounded by knights and pages.

"My lord Duke," said the messenger, "I have news to give you." And when William had drawn a little aside from his followers he told his news.

"Edward of England is dead," he said.

"Ah!" exclaimed the Duke.

"And Harold Godwinson is crowned King in his stead."

Then the Duke's face flushed red with anger. He choked with rage. A while he stood clasping and unclasping the rich cloak that fell from his shoulders. He spoke to no man, and no man durst speak to him.

In silent wrath he turned back to his palace. There in the hall he threw himself down on a bench, covering his face with his mantle.

Long time he remained thus, for none dared to speak to him. But his courtiers whispered together.

"What ails the Duke?" they said. "Why makes he such evil cheer?"

At length one who was his familiar friend entered the hall. Straight to the Duke he went.

"Sire," he said, "do not hide the news from us. For soon the people in the streets will know how Harold has taken the kingdom. Bestir yourself and be avenged. Send to him and demand the kingdom, and if he will not yield it cross the sea and take it from him."

So William called the messenger to him. "Go," he said, "tell Harold Godwinson that I, William, Duke of Normandy, send to remind him of the oath which he has sworn by his mouth and with his hand upon good and holy relics. Tell him that I send to claim the crown and throne of England."

So in all haste the messenger departed, and came to Harold as he sat upon his throne among his nobles. Harold listened to the messenger, then he proudly answered: "Go tell William of Normandy that the crown of England is not mine to take and give at pleasure."

But William meant to be King of England. And when he heard Harold's reply he at once made up his mind to cross the sea and fight for the crown. So he gathered all his lords together and asked them to go with him. But many were afraid.

"Sire," said some, "we fear the sea. We are not bound to serve beyond it."

"These English are a great and strong people," said others. "They will kill us and what the better shall we be? It is well for you, for if you conquer them, you will rule all the fair, broad lands. But what will it profit us?"

So Duke William took each of the great lords aside and spoke to them one by one. If they would aid him, he promised them land in England, besides money and rich spoil. So one by one the barons yielded and promised to go with him.

Duke William also sent to the Pope to tell him that Harold had broken his oath sworn upon holy relics. At this news the Pope was angry. He was angry too with the English, because they had ceased to pay a tax called Peter's Pence, which he claimed from them. So he excommunicated Harold and all who held to him. He also sent to William his blessing, a silken banner, and a fair and precious ring in which, beneath a diamond, there was enclosed one of St. Peter's hairs.

Meanwhile, at the mouth of the Dive, William was gathering a huge army of men and ships. For he sent into all parts of France telling how Harold had broken his oath and lied to him, and offering to every tall and stout man who would serve him with spear and bow, money, and great plunder, and fair, broad lands. So from far and near, from north and south, the people flocked to him. Some were great knights and nobles, some were plain serving men. Some asked for money, some for plunder, and some for castles and broad, fair lands. And to all Duke William gave ready promises.

In every port in Normandy the sound of hammer and saw was heard as ships and boats were built, masts were reared, and sails were stretched. In every town throughout the country the clang of hammer on anvil was heard as smiths and armorers made swords and lances and coats of mail.

And all the roads were thronged and busy with merchants and messengers who carried food and wine and arms to the ships. Never before had such an army and fleet been seen in Normandy.

At length all was ready. But the weather was bad, and for a month and more the ships lay waiting for a fair wind. Then the soldiers as they lay idle began to grumble amongst themselves.

"Mad and foolish is he who seeks to possess himself of another's kingdom," they said "God is angry with such, and shows His anger by denying us a fair wind."

When he saw the discontent of his soldiers, the Duke, too, grew anxious. But at length a fair wind blew. One September morning the sun rose in splendor. Soon all the camp was astir. Joyfully the men flocked to the ships. All day there were trumpet calls and noise of shouting. Then, as the afternoon sun sloped to the west, the great fleet sailed out into the open sea, and a shout of joy went up from sixty thousand throats.

The Duke's ship, the *Mora*, led the way. It was a splendid sight. The sails were colored, and upon them were painted the three lions of Normandy. Upon the prow there was carved a golden boy, with a bent bow in his hand, leaning forward as if eager to reach the English shore. From the mast-head fluttered the banner sent by the Pope, and there too gleamed a huge lantern as a guide to all the fleet.

The *Mora* sailed much faster than the other ships, and when morning dawned it was alone upon the empty sea.

Duke William then ordered the master of his ship to cast anchor and sent a sailor to the mast-head to look if there were any ships in the distance.

The sailor went and returned. "I see only the sea and the sky," he said.

Nothing daunted, William ordered a good breakfast to be served to all on board, with plenty of strong spiced wine. When breakfast was over the sailor was again sent to the mast-head. Shading his keen eyes with his hand from the bright morning light he gazed for a minute or two in silence. There was an anxious, breathless pause. Then with a shout he cried, "I see four ships!"

A third time the sailor was sent to the mast-head. This time he had no need to look long. "I see such a number of ships," he cried, "so close together that their masts seem like a moving forest."

Then anxious hope was turned into joy, and followed by the whole of his great fleet, Duke William sailed on and landed at Pevensey without hindrance. For there was no one to guard the shores, for King Harold was far away in York fighting another enemy.

As Duke William leaped eagerly ashore he stumbled and fell. At once a murmur arose from all around. "Ah," they cried, "what an evil sign is this?"

But Duke William sprang up quickly, and showing his hands full of turf, "By heaven!" he cried, "I have seized England with my two hands."

Then one of his men sprang forward, and tearing a handful of thatch from a cottage, ran with it to the Duke. "Sire," he cried, "of this land I give you an earnest. Without doubt the country is yours."

"In God's name I accept it," said the Duke.

CHAPTER 24

PHILIP I—THE BATTLE OF HASTINGS

SOON to King Harold far in the North there came a panting messenger. "The Normans," he cried, "the Normans, they have come! They have landed at Hastings. They will wrest your land from you if you hasten not to meet them."

"Sorry am I," said Harold, "that I was not there to meet them. It is a sad mischance. Had I been there we might have prevented them landing and driven them backward into the sea. But it is the will of God. I could not be everywhere at once."

With all speed Harold marched southward, and in a few days' time the English and the Normans faced each other in battle array.

The night before the battle the Norman soldiers prayed and confessed their sins to the priests, and those who had no priest near confessed to each other. The English, on the other hand, drank and sang and made a great noise.

When day dawned, the Duke took his stand upon a little hill with all his nobles around him. To them he spoke.

"I love and thank you all," he said, "who have crossed the sea for me and come with me to this far land. It grieves me that I cannot now give to you such thanks as are your due. But when I can I will, and what I have shall be yours. If I conquer, you will conquer. If I win lands, you shall win lands. These English have done much ill to our people and to our ancestors, and if God so please, we will avenge them. When we have conquered them we will take their gold and silver and the wealth which they have in plenty, and their manors, which are rich. We shall conquer them with ease, for in all the wide world there is not so fair an army nor such proved men and vassals as are here gathered together."

Then all the nobles cried out, "You will not see one coward; none here will fear to die for love of you, if need be."

"I thank you well," the Duke answered. "Remember to strike hard. There will be no safety in flight. The English will never love or spare the Normans. Felons they were, felons they are. False they were, and false they ever will be. Shew no pity for them, for they will shew none to you."

Much more the Duke spoke, until at length a noble rode forward, all clad in steel from top to toe. "Sire," he cried, "we tarry too long. Let us arm ourselves for battle."

Then as the battle was about to begin Taillefer the minstrel rode toward the Duke mounted on a swift horse.

"A boon, sire," he cried. "I pray you let me strike the first blow in this battle."

And the Duke answered, "I grant it."

Then Taillefer put his horse to the gallop, and singing as he went the Song of Roland and his knights and how he died at Roncesvalles, he dashed against the English.

His sword flashed in the morning light. It flashed and fell, and an Englishman lay dead. Still singing, Taillefer rode on while the army behind him took up the song and the air was full of the music of men's voices. Again the sword flashed, again an Englishman lay dead. But the enemy closed round the valiant minstrel. He fell beneath a sword stroke, and the sound of his singing was stilled forever.

Loud rose the shouts of battle, and over the dead body of the minstrel the Normans rushed on the foe.

From nine in the morning till three in the afternoon the battle swayed this way and that. Both sides fought so well that no one could tell which would win.

The English were posted on a hill and surrounded by a strong wooden fence. Again and again the Normans charged against the solid mass in vain. Once the noise went abroad in the army that the Duke was killed, and, their hearts failing them, they would have fled.

But the Duke, taking off his helmet, rode up and down among the soldiers crying, "I am here! Look at me! See, I live, and by God's help will conquer!"

So the Normans took heart again and fought on.

Then William ordered his archers to shoot upward so that their arrows should fall upon the heads of the English within their fence. In this way many of the English were wounded, and the King was pierced in the eye. But in spite of the pain he still fought on, encouraging his men.

But at length the English guard was broken through. Then round the King, with his standard floating above him, a last stern fight was fought. The English fought like heroes, but man after man went down. And when at length night fell, the King and all the nobles of his house lay dead on the field, and his splendid standard which had fluttered in such brave defiance against the foe, now all torn and bloodstained, drooped mournfully above the tent of the Norman conqueror.

So ended one of England's saddest days.

But it was scarcely a day less sad for France. For, by the swords of Frenchmen, the crown of England had been won for William of Normandy, a vassal of the King of France. By their swords Frenchmen had made a vassal greater than their King, and France paid dearly for it. It brought upon France a hundred years of war and some of her darkest hours; it brought eight hundred years of jealous hate between two peoples who might have been kindly neighbors.

And now we must leave William the Conqueror. For the story of what he did after the battle of Hastings, and of how he was crowned King of England, belongs more to English than to French history.

CHAPTER 25

PHILIP I—HOW PETER THE HERMIT PREACHED GOD'S WAR

PHILIP the First was still only a boy when his great vassal became King of England. He was a grown man when thirty years later another great war took place. This was the First Crusade, or War of the Cross.

In that far country called Palestine Jesus Christ was born, lived, and died. And when the story of Christ was spread abroad in Europe the thoughts of the people turned lovingly to that far-off land. Many longed to see the holy places, and from very early times Christians began to make journeys to Palestine. These people were called pilgrims, from the Latin word *peregrinum*, meaning one that comes from a far land, and their journeys were called pilgrimages.

As years went on, more and more pilgrims went to the Holy Land, although the journey was difficult and dangerous, and many of them were robbed of all they had long before they reached the end of it. Many others were killed upon the way. But even if pilgrims reached Palestine in safety their troubles were not over. For the country was in the hands of Turks and Mohammedans, who hated the Christians. So when after many perils the pilgrims arrived at Jerusalem they found the gates of the holy city shut against them. They were not allowed to enter until they had paid a large sum of money. As many were penniless, having been robbed of all they possessed on the way, they were obliged to remain without. Hungry and in rags they wandered round the city walls, vainly awaiting leave to enter. Many of them died there without ever seeing the Holy Sepulchre and other sacred places they had come to visit.

The pilgrims found all this hard to bear. But even harder to bear were the insults to their religion. The churches which they built were again and again destroyed. They were again and again robbed of their treasures. Even while mass was being said, wild mobs would rush in, scattering the terrified congregation. With rude laughter and insults they would hurl the sacred vessels and candlesticks to the ground, sit on the altar, beat the priests, and tear their vestments.

Pilgrims who returned home told of all that they had seen and suffered until, throughout all Europe, people grieved at the sorrows of the pilgrims, and the desolation of the holy places.

At length a Frenchman named Peter the Hermit went upon a pilgrimage to the Holy Land. He was an almost mean-looking, thin little man, but in his lean face his piercing eyes shone with courage and zeal. They were the eyes of a dreamer and a martyr; they burned with the light of the great soul which lived in his mean little body.

When Peter saw all the misery which had fallen upon the Holy Land, his heart was filled with sorrow and anger. He longed to do something to save the City of his Lord from degradation. Then one night as he prayed in the church he fell asleep. And as he slept it seemed to him that Christ appeared standing before him.

"Rise, Peter," He said, "and haste thee. It is time to cleanse the holy places and to help my servants. I shall be with thee."

Full of the glory of his vision Peter rose and made haste to depart. Taking with him a letter from the head of the Church of Jerusalem to the Pope, he set forth on his long and dangerous journey and landed safely in Italy.

The Pope received Peter gladly and gladly promised to help him. So to preach the Holy War to all Europe Peter set forth. From town to town he went, from province to province. He rode upon a mule, and carried a crucifix in his hand. He was clad in a rough woolen shirt tied about his waist with a cord. Over it hung a coarse cloak which fell to his heels. His head, arms, and feet were bare.

In every town and village through which he passed, Peter called the people together and preached to them. Sometimes he spoke by the wayside, sometimes in the market places, sometimes in the churches. The place mattered not to him so that the people heard.

Peter the Hermit told of all the cruelties he had seen, of the desecrations of the holy places, of the sorrows of God's people. He spoke with such fire that every heart was touched. Sobs and groans burst from the crowd, and the people pressed eagerly round him, offering him gold and silver and all manner of gifts to help the great cause.

But it was not until Peter reached France that the wildest enthusiasm burst forth. At the town of Clermont so many people gathered to hear him that the country round was covered with tents, for there was no room in the town for the crowds who came. The Pope, too, came to the meeting. Peter spoke first and as he spoke his voice shook, and tears ran down his cheeks. When he ceased the Pope spoke.

"Hath not Christ said," he cried, "that whoso forsaketh houses, or brethren, or sister, or father, or mother, or wife, or children, or land, for My name's sake, shall receive an hundredfold and shall inherit everlasting life?' Then forget your quarrels among yourselves. Take the road to the Holy Sepulchre, and wrest the land from the hands of the enemies of God."

As the Pope spoke, all the people cried, "God wills it! God wills it!" Again and again the cry rang out mingled with sobs. At length the Pope held up his hand as if to ask for silence. Then again he spoke.

"Christ Himself hath said," he cried, "'Where two or three are gathered together in My name there am I in the midst of them.' Truly He hath been in our midst this day and hath put into your mouths these words. Then let them be your battle cry, and when you march against the foe shout, 'God wills it! God wills it!'"

Once again the air was rent with the cry, "God wills it! God wills it!" Then hundreds and thousands crowded round Peter eager to receive the red cross which was to mark them as soldiers of Christ. And thus France, which had seen God's Peace and God's Truce, now saw God's War declared.

CHAPTER 26
PHILIP I—THE FIRST WAR OF THE CROSS

FROM all parts of Europe people crowded to France to take the cross. When men met who could not understand each other's language, they crossed their fingers to show that they wished to take part in the Holy War. High and low, rich and poor, young and old, all joined. Nearly all the great princes set forth, followed by their vassals; so private wars quarrels ceased as if by magic.

But the nobles and princes took a long time to get ready, and many of the poor who had no preparations to make grew impatient. So in the spring of 1096 a great mob of people set out. It could not be called an army, for part of it was made up of women and children and old and feeble men. And as they were nearly all poor most of the men who were strong and able to fight had no arms. The host was led by Peter the Hermit and Gauthier Have-nothing, a poor knight. They started off eagerly, but the way was long. Soon the children grew weary of it, and whenever they came to a town they would cry out, "Is this not Jerusalem?" And the mothers would reply sadly, "No, not yet."

These poor pilgrims had made no preparations for their long journey. They had no food and no money to buy it. So they stole from the people of the countries through which they passed. This made the people angry, and they fought the Crusaders. Many were killed and many died by the way and only a small number reached Asia Minor, still a long, long way from Palestine. Here most of them were killed by the Turks, others were sold into slavery, and few, if any, of the immense host which had set out reached Palestine.

Meanwhile the great lords gathered an army of a hundred thousand knights and nobles, and six hundred thousand foot soldiers. From all parts they came, and meeting at Constantinople, crossed over into Asia Minor. Here they were met by Peter the Hermit and a miserable remainder of his once great host. The nobles were filled with pity for him and treated him with much kindness.: But he whose burning words had stirred men's hearts and made them set forth upon this Holy War was henceforth of little importance.

The second army of the Crusade was more fortunate than the first.

But it was only after terrible sufferings, after plague and famine and battles and sieges, after the shedding of much blood and the loss of many lives, that the Crusaders at length saw Jerusalem.

As they neared the Holy City their hearts beat eagerly. At length they climbed the last hill which separated them from it. They reached the top. Suddenly they saw Jerusalem unrolled before them. From the front ranks a great shout went up, "Jerusalem! Jerusalem!" By rank after rank the cry was taken up, "Jerusalem! Jerusalem!" It echoed down the valleys until those far in the rear heard the joyful sound. Tears coursed down the cheeks of the rough soldiers as they gazed. Some knelt in prayer, some bent to kiss the ground which Christ perchance had trod, others stood with arms outstretched toward the holy place, while sobs burst from them. Then once again as from one voice went up the mighty shout, "God wills it! God wills it!"

But Jerusalem was still to win. It was strongly held The siege by the Turks, and the Crusaders began to besiege it at once. But they had no battering rams or engines with which to break down the walls. So day after day the siege lasted, and the suffering among the Crusaders grew great. They were weary with long marching and fighting, and now disease attacked them. The burning sun of summer blazed down upon them. The streams were dried up, and they began to suffer all the horrors of thirst.

Every day the suffering grew worse. The sun shone like a ball of red fire, the sky was pitilessly cloudless. Night brought no coolness, dawn no refreshing dew. The strongest warriors lay idle in their tents, the weak died. Even the horses suffered. For the grass was all burned up. Gaunt and drooping, they had scarcely strength to carry their masters to battle, and the sound of the war trumpets no longer stirred them.

But at length the Crusaders found some wood and began to make huge battering rams, and upon a day fixed they made a great assault upon the walls.

The Crusaders attacked with fury, with equal fury the defenders resisted. Boiling oil and lead were poured from the walls. Stones, javelins, and arrows flew thick and fast. At dawn the fight began, and only night put an end to the slaughter.

Jerusalem was not yet taken, and the Crusaders returned to their tents full of sorrow. Next day the fight began again, with double fury. The Christians, maddened by the sneers of the unbelievers, who taunted them with adoring a God who could not help them, fought desperately.

At length a breach was made in the walls. At length the Crusaders poured into the town, and Jerusalem echoed with the cry, "God wills it! God wills it!" The Saracens fled, the Christians pursued. Jerusalem held no place of safety for the unbelievers. No prayer for mercy was of avail. In the streets, in the houses, in the mosques, men, women, and children were slain until the streets ran red with blood and were piled high with the dead. Then the fury of the Christians was stayed. Then they laid down their arms and armor, put off their blood-stained garments, and clad themselves in pilgrims' robes. With bare feet and bowed heads, singing hymns and sobbing with joy, they went to visit the sacred places.

Thus, three years after the army set out, was Jerusalem taken. But to keep what they had conquered the Crusaders felt that they must have a ruler. So, a few days later, they met together and chose as king Godfrey of Bouillon, one of the bravest of the nobles who had taken part in the Crusade.

But although Godfrey accepted the skillful, he refused to be called king or to wear a crown. "I cannot wear a crown of gold," he said, "in the town where the Savior of the world wore a crown of thorns." So he was called the Defender and Baron of the Holy Sepulchre.

Very soon most of the Crusaders turned home again, leaving but a little company of three hundred to guard their conquests. Those who remained behind said adieu to their comrades with sad hearts. "Never forget your brothers whom you have left in exile," they said. "Send us soldiers to fight the heathen." Those who went promised with tears to send help quickly. But, alas, fifty years passed before any help came to the little Christian kingdom in that far-off land.

Among those who returned home was Peter the Hermit. We hear little more of him, and he ended his days quietly in a monastery. But his work was done. He had awakened to life a wonderful religious zeal which burned for more than a hundred years, changing the whole life of Europe.

The Crusaders did not succeed. Jerusalem, held for a short time, fell again into the hands of the Saracens. But in other ways they did much good. While the great lords were fighting for the Cross, their countries at home kept peace. Thus the poor men and women who stayed at home could sow and reap and weave in quiet. Their lives became happier and better, trade grew, and merchants prospered. Many men, too, who had followed their lords to battle as slaves returned as freemen. Thus, seeking Jerusalem, they found liberty.

France suffered much and gained much through the Crusades, and they were given by one of the writers of the time the proud name of "God's works by French hands." For it was in France that they began. It was under French leaders that the first army set out.

CHAPTER 27

LOUIS VI THE FAT—HOW THE PEOPLE OF LAON FOUGHT FOR FREEDOM

PHILIP I took little interest in the Crusade or in anything else. He died in 1108 and was succeeded by his son, Louis VI.

Philip was the last of the Do-nothing Kings of the Capetian line. Louis who came after him was young and gay, a soldier and a ruler. When he was young he was called Louis the Fighter, or Louis the Wide awake. But as he grew older he became very stout and so was called Louis *le gros*, or the Fat, and by that name he is best known in history.

When Louis came to the throne, many of the great barons were lawless and turbulent. They rode about the country fighting and robbing at will. They attacked merchants on the roads and held them prisoner until they paid large sums of money. They ground down the peasants, making them pay whatever they liked. They knew no law but their own will; they obeyed no ruler.

Louis spent the first years of his reign in quelling these lawless barons. And it was by the help of the people that he succeeded. The Crusades had given many of them new ideas of freedom, and taught them to use sword and spear. Many of them, too, had grown rich. It was they who suffered most from the lawlessness of the nobles, and so they willingly helped Louis against their oppressors. This union of the King and peasants against the nobles is one of the wonderful things of Louis the Fat's reign.

The people soon began to find out their power and they bound themselves together into communes or brotherhoods. "Commune," says a writer of the time, "is a new and very bad word. And this is the meaning of the word—men shall not pay the rent they owe to their lords more than once a year. If they commit any fault they shall be free on paying a fine fixed by law. And as for other taxes which custom lays upon slaves they shall go free."

When once a town had won the right of commune the people in it were no longer the slaves or serfs of the lord. Sometimes a town won the right easily, for many nobles had returned from Palestine poor. So they were glad to sell these liberties to their vassals for gold. But sometimes the people fought for them. Sometimes, in return for the help the people gave him, Louis granted charters of freedom to their towns.

Louis did not found the communes. They founded themselves. It was the people themselves who rose against oppression, and it is to Louis's skillful that he did not crush them. And therefore he lives in the hearts of Frenchmen as the soldier King who protected the poor and curbed the cruel oppression of the nobles.

The city of Laon was one which fought for its freedom. The lord of the city was a Bishop, and he ruled very badly. He was more a soldier than a priest, and both greedy and cruel. He loaded the people with taxes and tortured or killed any who opposed him.

The people grew more and more weary of his rule. At length, once when he was away, they begged the nobles who governed for him to sell to them for a large sum of money the rights of commune. This the nobles did, thinking it an easy way of growing rich.

The joy in the city of Laon was great. But when the Bishop returned he was very angry. However, when the people offered him still more money, he allowed his anger to cool and promised to give up all his rights over the town. Then, so that nothing should be lacking to make sure their freedom, the people sent messengers to Paris with rich presents for the King, begging him to sign their charter of freedom.

This he did and everything seemed well with the commune of Laon. But soon the Bishop and nobles had spent all the money given them by the people, and they began to repent of their bargain. They resolved at length to persuade the King to take away the charter he had given. So the Bishop invited the King to come to spend Easter at Laon.

The King came, and as soon as he arrived the Bishop began to talk to him and persuade him to take away the charter. But at first the King refused. For the towns people had been warned of the Bishop's wicked plans, and they offered to give the King four hundred pounds in silver if he would refuse to do what the Bishop asked.

When the Bishop learned this, however, he offered the King seven hundred pounds in silver. He did not possess the money, but he made up his mind to grind it out of the townsfolk as soon as the King had taken away their charter, and he could once more tax them as he liked.

The King wanted money, and he yielded. The Bishop absolved him from his oath, and also absolved himself with solemn ceremony. Then heralds were sent out into the market-place to declare to all the people that their charter with the great royal seal of which they were so proud was of no more use; that their magistrates must cease from office; that they must give up the seal and banner of the town, and no longer sound the bell in the belfry.

When the people heard the proclamation they were filled with fear and anger. They crowded into the streets uttering cries of rage and vows of vengeance. There arose such a tumult that when the King heard the noise he was afraid of what he had done. He took refuge that night in the Bishop's palace, which was very strongly fortified. The next morning before the day dawned he fled away without waiting to keep the feast of Easter for which he had come.

All that day a stillness as of death rested upon the town. The streets remained empty. Inns, shops, and workshops were closed and silent. It was as if the people mourned the death of some great and loved friend.

Then the news went forth that they were to be taxed, taxed to the uttermost so that the King might have the money promised to him. With cruel laughter the Bishop said, "You paid great sums to have your commune set up. You shall pay as great to have it destroyed."

Anger and fear drove the people mad. Forty of them banded themselves together and swore to put the Bishop to death. The Bishop was warned of the plot, but he laughed scornfully. "Fie then!" he cried, "shall I perish by the hands of such people?" Yet he ordered his servants to wear arms under their robes.

For three days the town was in a state of riot and disorder. Several houses were attacked and plundered. But when the Bishop heard of it he laughed.

"What do you suppose these good people will do with their riots? If my black man John pulled the nose of the bravest of them he would not dare to grumble. I have forced them to give up their commune. I have no fear but I shall be able to rule them."

Next day, however, as the Bishop sat in his palace he heard great cries of "The commune, the commune!" It was the signal of revolt. Bands of townsfolk, armed with swords, lances, hatchets, and all kinds of weapons, rushed into the cathedral and from there to the Bishop's palace.

At the first sound of the revolt the nobles hurried to help the Bishop. But they were slaughtered by the angry people, who soon spread all over the palace seeking the Bishop. "Where is the traitor, the villain?" they shouted.

The Bishop meanwhile, having changed clothes with one of his servants, ran to the cellar and hid himself in a barrel.

But no place was safe from the fury of the mob. He was found, dragged from the barrel by the hair of the head, and hurled out into the street, while the townsfolk beat him pitilessly. He fell upon his knees crying aloud for mercy, promising them money, freedom, everything.

But there was no pity or mercy in those angry hearts. "You would keep your promise as you kept it before," they answered, and blow after blow fell upon him till he died. Then, despoiled of his jewels and stripped of his clothes, his body was cast aside into a street corner. And all who went by flung mud and stones, insults and curses, at the mangled remains of what was once their Bishop.

But as soon as the townspeople had satisfied their vengeance they began to be afraid of the King's anger. Panic seized them. In their fear they begged one of the nobles of the neighborhood called Thomas of Marle to protect them.

This Thomas was a fierce and brutal knight. Horrible stories were told of the deeds he did in his castle, of how he attacked and tortured travelers and merchants. But the townsfolk felt they must have some protection against the King, and Thomas seemed the best man from whom to ask it. For it was well known he had no love for Louis the Fat, who tried to curb the power of all unruly barons.

So the townsfolk went to Thomas of Marie.

"I cannot hold your town against the King," said he; "but if you will come to my castle I will defend you there as best I may."

These words struck terror to the hearts of the people of Laon. How was it possible to trust themselves in that fearful castle, full of dark and horrible dungeons of which they had heard such awful stories? But there seemed no help for it, so they went.

As soon as it was known that the people of Laon had left their city unprotected, all the people from the towns round about came in bands and began to plunder it, so that the state of the city was more miserable than ever. Many of the leaders of the revolt were hanged, others were banished, the whole countryside was in arms. At length the King, whose broken word had been the cause of all the misery, came with an army. He attacked Thomas in his castle, and after long resistance it was taken. A new Bishop was appointed and Laon sank once more into a state of slavery. But the people still kept the memory of the freedom they had once possessed, and sixteen years later they received a new charter, which again the King sealed with his great seal.

CHAPTER 28

LOUIS VI THE FAT—HOW THE KING OF FRANCE FOUGHT HIS VASSAL, THE KING OF ENGLAND

FORCING the barons to bow to the will of the King was the great work of Louis's reign. From one end of his kingdom to another he fought them.

"The King has long hands," said one of his advisers. And so the barons found to their cost.

But Louis had another great enemy to fight. This was Henry I, King of England and Duke of Normandy. Louis and Henry had once been friends. But when Henry became King and wrested the Dukedom of Normandy from his brother Robert, Louis found in him a rival. A vassal who wore a crown and who was far more rich and powerful than his sovereign lord was a dangerous vassal.

When Henry seized the Dukedom of Normandy, the Norman lords and barons were not all united in accepting him as their Duke. Many would rather have had Robert or his son William. Louis took the part of these, and so, for twenty years and more, there was almost constant war between lord and vassal.

The battles that were fought were not always very deadly, but the country was wasted and many castles and villages were laid in ruins.

Once when they were fighting for a castle it is said Louis offered to settle the quarrel in single combat with Henry. The two armies lay opposite each other on either side of a river. The only way of crossing was by a wooden bridge which was so frail and rotten that it could hardly bear the weight of one man. Upon this shaking bridge Louis challenged Henry to fight.

"Nay," replied Henry, "my legs are not steady enough for such bravado. I will not risk thus losing a castle which would be of exceeding use to me. When I see my sovereign lord of France in a place where I can defend myself I shall not flee."

One of the chief battles was fought at Bremule. In this about nine hundred knights took part. It was more like a great tournament than a battle. Shouting their war cries the knights dashed at each other, lance in rest. When their lances were shivered, they fought with swords. But it was a courteous, knightly game. The King of England indeed as he fought received a mighty blow on the head which, but for the strength of his helmet, had stretched him lifeless on the plain. But for the most part the knights fought not to slay, but to show their skill and to take prisoners.

The day went ill with the French. Knight after knight was taken prisoner.

"Alas, Sire," cried one of Louis's knights, "eighty of our knights who were in the van of the army are no more to be seen. The enemy overmatches us in strength and numbers. Our best knights are taken, our men give way everywhere. Flee, my lord, ere all is lost."

So Louis turned and fled, and his knights scattered to right and left. The French King lost the battle, his banner, and his horse. Many of his knights were taken prisoners, but only three men were killed.

Yet this almost bloodless battle was a severe defeat for Louis. He burned with wrath against Henry, and did everything in his power to get the better of him, but without success. For another year the war went on. Then at length the two Kings made peace and Henry's son William paid homage to Louis as his liege lord. Then father and son set sail for their own land.

But, alas! for England and for France; the White Ship in which Prince William sailed went down and the prince was drowned. It was a great sorrow for Henry and for England. It was a great misfortune for France. For now the heir to the English throne was Matilda, Henry's daughter, who for her second husband had married Geoffrey Plantagenet of Anjou. Thus a still greater part of France was added to the crown of England, and the King of England became yet more powerful against his lord the King of France.

Louis was a true soldier King and his sword was seldom at rest. It was during his reign that the oriflamme first came into use. It was the banner of the Abbey of St. Denis and in time became the royal standard. Each time the King went to war he took the banner from its place beside the high altar. Each time he returned in triumph it was hung there again. The oriflamme was a piece of flame-colored silk, the ends being slit into points like a swallow's tail. It was ornamented with green tassels and mounted on a golden lance. The word means golden flame. It was so called because it looked like a flickering tongue of fire as it fluttered in the wind at the head of the army.

Even when Louis became so stout that he could hardly move he still longed to fight. "Ah," he groaned, "what a miserable life is ours. We never have strength and knowledge at one time. Had I *known* when I was young, if I *could* now that I am old, I would have conquered empires."

But at length, after his life of war and strife, the soldier King lay dying. Then all his thoughts turned to holy things. He bade his servants stretch sackcloth upon the floor, sprinkle ashes on it in the form of a cross, and lay him upon it. There, clad in the robe of a monk, he folded his hands, and made his peace with God.

CHAPTER 29

LOUIS VII THE YOUNG—THE SECOND WAR OF THE CROSS

A month before Louis VI died, his son, Louis the Young, had set forth with great pomp on a journey to Aquitaine,. there to marry the beautiful Princess Eleanor. The marriage took place, and Louis was crowned Duke of Aquitaine, bringing thus to the crown of France lands over which his ancestors had never ruled. Then the young bride and bridegroom journeyed homeward. But on the way a messenger of sorrow met them. "The King is dead," he said. "Long live the King."

Thus in 1137, at the age of seventeen, Louis the Young came to the throne. Although he reigned for forty-three years he kept his name, the Young. For all his life he remained simple and lacking in wisdom. He was idle and pleasure loving, and held with but feeble hands the sword which his father had left him. But in the beginning of his reign Louis had wise counsellors; the chief of these was the Abbot Suger.

Suger was of the people. His father was a poor workman, yet, in this time when the common people were despised and down-trodden, he became great. He did not look like a great man. He was very small, thin, and sickly. But in spite of his ill health he was always at work. He knew men and how to deal with them, he loved peace, and he loved his country and King. He was indeed one of the finest of French statesmen, because he worked for the country that he loved, not to make himself powerful. Suger was Abbot of St. Denis, and toward the end of Louis VII's reign he rose to great power in the state.

Now that Louis VII reigned, his power was greater even than it had been. For the new King was weak and idle, and had little desire to rule.

But Louis was passionate as well as idle, and he soon had a quarrel with the Pope. The Popes had for a long time claimed the right of appointing what Bishops they chose in any Christian country. The Kings of France, on the other hand, had denied the right, and claimed that they alone should appoint Bishops in France.

Now the Pope appointed an Archbishop to the See of Bourges. At this the King was very angry and he appointed another. "Never," he cried, "so long as I live shall the Pope's Archbishop enter the city of Bourges."

"Tut, tut," said the Pope, "the King is a child. He needs teaching. We must stop him of these bad habits."

So he laid the land where Louis dwelt or through which he passed under an interdict. Wherever the King came the church bells ceased to ring. Night or morning no prayers were said, the dead were hurried silently to the grave without chant or prayer. There were no weddings, no baptisms. When the King passed on, the bells rang out once more and prayers and chants were heard.

For a time Louis bore this, but at length war broke out.

One of Louis's vassals, the Count of Champagne, sided with the Pope. This made Louis very angry.

"Are your own lands not large enough to give you work to do?" he asked in wrath. "Attend to what is yours and leave me to govern my kingdom as I will."

But the count still took the part of the Pope and gave shelter to his Archbishop. Then Louis marched through his land, fighting and slaying. Neither man, woman, nor child did he spare in his wrath. Villages and towns went up in flames. Among them was the town of Vitry. It was mostly built of wood and once the fire was begun it leaped from house to house until the whole town was wrapped in flames. The people fled for safety to the church. That too caught fire. Amid the roar of flames and the crackle of burning wood cries of agony rang out. They reached the ears of the King. At the thought of these helpless peasants, caught in such a trap, given over to such a fearful death, all the anger faded out of his childlike heart. He called upon his men to save the church, to save their fellows. But all their efforts were in vain. The roof fell in, the walls crashed together, and the cry of agony was stilled. Thirteen hundred men, women, and children had perished in the flames.

Louis could not blot out from his eyes the memory of that awful sight. He could not shut out from his ears Louis' the cry of despairing agony he had heard. His will was broken, the Pope had his way, and his Archbishop took possession of Bourges.

Not long after this, news came from Palestine that the Turks were once more in arms against the Christians. They had taken a town and killed all the Christians in it.

Louis's heart was stirred at the news. Here he thought was the way of peace. He would take the Cross, he would fight for the Sepulchre of his Lord, and so find rest for his troubled conscience, and take from his soul the burden of Vitry the burned.

But Suger the Wise tried to dissuade him. The King's place was in his own country, he said, ruling his own people. Another great man, however, the Abbot Bernard, encouraged Louis to go. So again there was much stir throughout the land. Meetings were held and the Cross was preached.

It was St. Bernard now who, like Peter the Hermit fifty years before, preached the Crusade. To a great gathering at the town of Vezelai the people came in such crowds that neither castle nor market-place could hold them. So out on the hillside beyond the town the King's throne was raised. There he sat dressed in his royal robes, with his crown upon his head. At his side sat his Queen, while St. Bernard stood to speak to the people. He spoke to them with such burning words that all hearts were touched. He bade them remember their fathers who had conquered Jerusalem, whose names were written in heaven.

"Then why stay ye, oh, noble knights? God the eternal and living hath charged me to say to you that He will punish those who do not fight His enemies. To arms then! Let all the Christian world resound with the words of the prophet, 'Woe to him who dyeth not his sword in blood.'"

Almost before St. Bernard had finished speaking his words were drowned in cries of, "The Cross! the Cross!"

Then the King, first of all the throng, knelt and received the Cross from St. Bernard. Next the Queen knelt. Upon her splendid, jeweled dress the sacred sign was fastened. Following the King and Queen, noble after noble pressed forward all eager for the Cross. And although a great number had been made ready there were not enough. But St. Bernard would not turn one willing helper away. Quickly slipping off the robes he wore, he tore them into shreds and of them made crosses to give to the eager people.

Then through all France went St. Bernard preaching the Crusade. People thronged to him from far and near, and the towns and villages were emptied of men. "I have opened my mouth and I have spoken," he wrote to the Pope, "and the number of the Crusaders may no more be counted. The towns and castles are deserted. You will hardly find one man to seven women. Everywhere one sees widows and orphans whose husbands and fathers are yet among the living."

Not content with preaching the Crusade in France, St. Bernard passed into Germany. There too his burning words roused the people. The Emperor himself took the Cross and thousands of his subjects followed him.

It was King Louis who first thought of the Crusade. It was St. Bernard who made it. Now the people clamored that he should be their leader. But he refused. He remembered too well the fate of Peter the Hermit. "Who am I," he said, "that I should form camps and march at the head of an army? Nothing is further from my office. Even if I lacked not the strength, I have not the knowledge." So the Crusaders chose another leader, for although Louis joined the Crusade he did not go as commander-in-chief.

But now it was asked who was to rule the kingdom in the absence of the King? "Here be two swords," said St. Bernard, pointing to Suger and a count; "they be enough."

But the count refused the difficult task. Suger too at first refused. The burden seemed to him too great. The Pope himself, however, added his entreaties to those of others. So Suger yielded, feeling that he could not refuse what the Pope asked.

CHAPTER 30

LOUIS VII THE YOUNG—HOW A QUEEN OF FRANCE BECAME QUEEN OF ENGLAND

THE Crusade took a long time to prepare. But at length the armies set off, the German first, the French second. After many adventures the French reached Constantinople and passed over into Asia Minor, where they expected to join the Germans. But there they were met with the terrible news that the German army had been attacked and destroyed by the Turks. Utterly crushed and spiritless, the Emperor came to greet Louis with his few remaining followers. With tears in his eyes Louis received him.

"My lord King," said the Emperor sadly, "I will separate from you no more. We will encamp wherever seems best to you. I only ask that my followers and yours may keep together."

This was a terrible beginning, but even now the misfortunes of the Crusaders were by no means over. Disaster after disaster befell them. They were beaten by the Turks, their ranks were thinned by sickness and disease. Many died of hunger and weariness. Many more were taken captive. It was with but a miserable remnant of his once great army that Louis reached Jerusalem. But such as they were the Christians greeted them with joy. As he came near, King Baldwin III, followed by many Christians, came out to meet him, singing, as they re-entered the city, "Blessed is he that cometh in the name of the Lord."

After visiting all the holy places, the Crusaders turned their thoughts to war once more. For so far they had done nothing to free the Holy Land from the Turks. They decided now to besiege Damascus.

But even in this the Crusaders did not succeed. Finding the difficulties greater than they thought, they gave up the siege and returned to Jerusalem. Angry and ashamed, the Emperor now went home, and one by one the great nobles followed. But Louis could not bring himself to leave the Holy Land, having done nothing to deliver it. He could not bring himself to own that the Crusade had been an utter failure. So month by month he lingered almost alone.

As one by one the few who had lived through all the terrible sufferings reached France they told their sorry tale. Then long and bitter was the cry of woe that arose. For there was hardly a family high or low which had not lost some loved one. They had been promised victory, and, behold! there was only death and bitterness. So the land was filled with the sound of weeping as the women mourned for the fathers, brothers, husbands, and sons they would see no more. In their pain they cursed the great Abbot who had sent them forth, and the King who had led them. But St. Bernard felt no repentance for what he had done; he believed it to be right, and he meekly bowed his head to the storm. "Curse me," he said; "it is well that men should curse me rather than God."

But Suger, who had never wished Louis to go, sent messenger after messenger begging him to come home. But Louis ever refused. At length Suger wrote to him very urgently.

"Dear King and lord," he said, "I must cause you to hear the voice of your whole kingdom. Why do you stay far from us? The barons and lords of the kingdom have returned, yet you remain among heathen folk. The disturbers of the peace have returned, and you who should defend your subjects remain in a strange land. Of what do you think, my lord, when you leave thus the sheep at the mercy of the wolves?"

Then at last Louis returned. He had been away more than two years, and he found that during that time Suger had well and truly ruled his kingdom. Unlike many kings, Louis at least was grateful. He called Suger "The father of his country," and, bearing that proud title, Suger very gladly laid down the heavy burden of state and went back to his Abbey of St. Denis. Here in little more than a year he died.

Then Louis, having lost his wise counsellor, knew not how to rule. He made mistake after mistake. One of the first mistakes he made was to divorce his wife. At first Louis had loved his wife very dearly. But out in the Holy Land they had quarrelled. Eleanor grew to despise her husband and say she had married a monk with a sword in mistake for a King. Suger tried hard to make the angry husband and wife forgive each other, but in vain. He died, and the next year the King and Queen were divorced.

Eleanor, you remember, was very wealthy. She brought fair and broad lands to the kingdom of France. But the Queen of France had now again become only the Duchess of Aquitaine, and all these broad, fair lands were lost to the crown.

Eleanor was beautiful as well as wealthy, and many great lords and princes were eager to marry her. Like a princess in a fairy tale, she fled from one and another who had vowed to marry her whether she would or no. But there was one among them she could not escape. This was Henry Plantagenet, Duke of Normandy and of Anjou. Young, handsome, splendid, he married beautiful Eleanor, who was thirteen years older than himself.

Stephen was still upon the throne of England, but Henry claimed it. Too late Louis saw the danger to France if the King of England should also be lord of half of France. As over-lord he forbade Henry to marry Eleanor. But Henry laughed at the King of France and went his own way. A few years later Stephen died, and Henry became King of England. Henry was also Duke of Normandy, Count of Anjou, Duke of Aquitaine, and indeed over-lord of half of France. At twenty-two he was the most powerful ruler in Europe, far more powerful than Louis, his over-lord and enemy.

To the end of his days Louis fought with his clever, wily enemy, Henry. When Henry quarreled with Thomas a Becket, Louis took the Archbishop's part, received him with every skillful, and fought the King of England. When Henry's sons rebelled against their father, Louis encouraged them and helped them. In every way he showed himself a bitter enemy to the King of England.

CHAPTER 31

PHILIP II AUGUSTUS—HOW NORMANDY WAS LOST TO ENGLAND

LOUIS died in 1180 and was succeeded by his son Philip II, also Augustus, because he was born in August. He was only fifteen when he came to the throne, and many of the proud nobles thought that as they had now only a child to deal with they might go their own way. But Philip soon showed that he was already a man in thought, and meant to rule, not only as a King, but as a great King.

One day a courtier saw him standing in deep thought, gnawing dreamily at a little green twig. "I would give my best horse if any one would tell me of what the King is thinking," he said.

Another courtier then boldly went up to the King. "Sire," he said, "we would know of what it is you think so deeply."

"I am wondering," answered Philip, looking at him gravely, "whether God will grant grace unto me or unto one of my heirs to raise France to the height at which she stood in the time of Charlemagne."

And that was what Philip held ever in his thoughts, to make France great.

Philip spent the first years of his reign fighting his unruly barons. And, strange to say, his father's greatest enemy, Henry II of England, not only made peace with him, but even helped him to settle his quarrels. For Henry was growing old; his heart was wrung by the rebelliousness of his own sons. They were his chief enemies, and he had enough to do to guard his kingdom against them without trying to wrest land from the French King.

But peace was not possible for long between the two countries. Philip soon began to plot with Henry's sons against their father. With Richard Coeur de Lion especially he made great friends. They were like brothers; they did everything together, ate at the same table, and slept in the same bed. This friendship made Henry very uneasy, and soon again there was war. But Henry was afraid of being betrayed by his son Richard, and he begged for peace.

So the English and the French met under the shadow of a great elm near the town of Gisors. The elm stood at cross roads upon the boundary between French and Norman land. It was so vast that many people could find shelter under its branches. The trunk was so thick that four men with outstretched arms could not span its girth. Many times French and English had met beneath its branches, and it was called the Elm of Conference. The King of England was very proud of this tree, and had been heard to say: "Even as this tree can never be torn from the green grass which surrounds it, so can the French never tear from me what I possess. When I lose this tree, I shall lose all the land."

One January day, under the leafless, wide-spreading branches of this elm, the two Kings met, the one old and worn, the other young and vigorous, both keen and wily. They could not agree. Sharp words were said on either side. But as they wrangled, slowly there advanced to them a company of people. First marched a cross-bearer, behind him came two Bishops, and again behind them a crowd of knights clad in white surcoats marked with a red cross.

As the procession came the angry Kings fell silent. Then in the silence one of the Bishops stood forth. He had a message to give. He told in moving words how once again the Holy Land had fallen into the hands of the heathen, how Jerusalem was taken and the King a prisoner. Eight Kings had sat upon the throne of Jerusalem, all of them Frenchmen. Surely France would fight once again for the City of the Lord. Surely French knights would avenge their brother knights who had laid down their lives in that far land for the love of Christ.

As the Bishop finished speaking, the cry broke out, "The Cross! the Cross!"

Hastily Henry rose and kneeling before the Bishop took the first Cross from his hands.

"Ah," cried the French barons, "do the Plantagenet colors always go before the French?" and there began a struggle as to who should take the Cross first. Presently the uproar was quieted, and Philip and Richard Coeur de Lion took the Cross together.

Many knights and nobles followed them, the Frenchmen taking a red cross and the Englishmen a white. After this the two Kings settled their quarrels, they gave each other the kiss of peace, and swore friendship which was to last forever. In memory of this meeting they raised a Cross, founded a church and gave the place the name of Holy Meadow. Then each went home to make preparations for the Crusade.

But, long ere they were ready to set out, quarrels burst forth, and Henry and Philip were once more at war. Then Philip in wrath cut down the mighty elm, swearing by all the saints of France that never more should parliament be held beneath its branches.

Thus the two Kings went on, now fighting, now making peace, Richard taking part with Philip against his father, until at length the old King Henry died a broken-hearted man. Richard Coeur de Lion was then at once crowned King of England, and soon afterward set out for the Holy Land with his friend Philip.

The German Emperor had also joined the Crusade, and he was the first to set out. He had already reached Asia Minor, gained one victory, and died. Before he died, the Emperor begged his young son to carry his bones to Palestine and bury them there. But most of his barons had lost interest in the Crusade and turned back. So it was a mournful little band, led by a boy and carrying a bier, that went on.

While this sad little army was wending its way through the deserts of Asia Minor, Philip and Richard were putting off time quarrelling and fighting tournaments in Sicily. The Christians in Palestine who had begun to besiege St. Jean d'Acre awaited their coming eagerly. At length they arrived, Philip first, then Richard. For these dear friends had found it best to part, and now when they met again there were constant bickerings and quarrels.

After a long siege St. Jean d'Acre was taken. Then Philip, feeling he had now done all that he need in fulfillment of his vow, returned home.

Richard was unwilling that he should go. He knew the danger there would be to his French lands from his clever, scheming rival. So, before he went, Philip swore a solemn oath that he would do no hurt to King Richard, his land, or his people. But even as he sailed homeward, wicked thoughts filled his mind and, landing in Italy, he asked the Pope to set him free from his oath.

The Pope refused and, very ill pleased, Philip went on his way.

In little more than a year, however, Philip heard what to him was joyful news. He heard that returning homeward Richard had been taken and was now held prisoner by the Emperor of Germany.

In all haste he wrote to the Emperor, "Keep him safe, for the world will never be at peace so long as such a disturber is abroad."

Philip then made friends with Richard's bad brother, John Lackland, and they arranged to divide between them all Richard's possessions.

The Emperor was powerful. But even he could not long keep the

King of England in prison. Before a year was gone he wrote to Philip and to John: "Look to yourselves. The devil is unchained. I could not do otherwise."

Richard was free. He pardoned his brother John. He fought with Philip till five years later he was killed by a chance arrow at the siege of Chalus, as you will read in English history.

John Lackland at once claimed the throne of England and all Richard's French possessions. But Philip took the part of little Prince Arthur, who was John's nephew and had perhaps more right to the throne. Philip hoped in this way to win back for France all the French land held by the King of England. For Arthur was only a child and could not really rule. Philip ordered John to give up all his French possessions to Prince Arthur. But John paid little heed to this order. Instead he took his nephew prisoner. Then, one dark night, he murdered him and threw his dead body into the Seine.

John thought he had thus made safe his claim to England and to Normandy. He was never more mistaken. All France rose against him. Town after town, fortress after fortress, were conquered by the French. Meanwhile John sat in his castle at Rouen drinking and feasting and caring little what happened to his kingdom.

Messengers came to him once and again. "Sire," they said, "the King of France has overrun all your land. Many and many a castle has been taken. He leads your vassals captive. He does as he will with all that is yours."

"Let him," replied King John. "Some day with one blow I will win back what he is now taking from me bit by bit."

But soon the soldiers of Philip reached almost to the walls of Rouen, the capital of Normandy. Then John fled to England. The people of Rouen, however, were faithful to their duke. They begged Philip to give them thirty days' truce so that they might get help. If, within that time, John did not help them, they promised to surrender. Philip granted the truce, and messengers set out for England. They found John playing at chess. He listened gloomily to what they had to say, but answered not a word until the game was finished. Then he spoke.

"I cannot help you," he said. "Do the best you can for yourselves."

So the messengers returned, and when the thirty days were over the flag with the red lions of Normandy was hauled down and the blue flag of France, sewn with golden fleur-de-lis, floated out upon the breeze.

Thus after three hundred years the duchy of Normandy came back to the crown of France.

CHAPTER 32

PHILIP II AUGUSTUS—THE WAR WITH THE ALBIGENSES

PHILIP as over-lord now called upon John as his vassal to appear before the peers of France and answer for his crimes. John from the safe distance of England sent a Bishop as his messenger to the King of France. "The King of England will willingly come," said the messenger. "He will show all obedience in the matter. But safe conduct must he have."

"Let him come in peace and surety," said the King.

"Yea, and go again so also?" asked the Bishop.

"If so the peers allow it," said the King.

Then the messenger begged Philip to grant John safe conduct both going and returning. But the King was wroth.

"No, by all the saints of France!" he cried. "He shall not go again unless he prove him innocent and the peers will it."

"But, my lord King," replied the messenger, "the Duke of Normandy cannot come if the King of England come not too, since the Duke and the King are one and the same person. The barons of England would never permit it. And the King, even if he were willing, would stand in danger of imprisonment and death. That you know well."

"How now, my lord Bishop?" cried Philip. "It is well known my vassal, the Duke of Normandy, took possession of England by force. And so, prithee, if a vassal increase in honor and power shall his over-lord lose his rights? Nay, never!"

So the messenger, finding that he could not by any means get a promise of safe conduct from Philip, departed home again. And John, fearing the French King, refused to come at his bidding.

Then, although he would not come to hear his sentence, the peers of France declared him guilty of treason and of murder and condemned him to lose all his lands in France, and to be put to death. But of course no French lords could really condemn the King of England to death. So the sentence was idle and empty. But Philip was powerful enough to keep possession of all John's French lands, which made his kingdom twice as large as it had been.

While Philip had been thus fighting at home to enlarge his kingdom, Frenchmen had been founding a French Empire in the East. In 1202 a fourth Crusade set out. This time the Crusaders were nearly all Frenchmen. But they never reached Palestine. They turned aside and besieged Constantinople instead, which at this time was still the capital of the Greek Empire.

They took Constantinople and divided the Greek Empire amongst themselves. Baldwin of Flanders was made Emperor, other great nobles were made kings and dukes, and thus a New France was founded upon the very outposts of Europe. But these robber knights were not strong enough to keep their conquests and in sixty years this new empire ruled by Frenchmen passed away. It had never been anything but a burden and hindrance to France.

Hardly was this Crusade over when another began. This one, however, did not set out to fight the Saracens, but Frenchmen gathered to fight Frenchmen. At this time, as you know, nearly all Christians belonged to the Church of Rome and the Pope claimed power over every Christian land. But in the south of France some people had begun to draw away from the Church of Rome. These people did not believe that the Pope could do no wrong, and they preached against a great many things which were taught by the Church. This was called heresy, which really means that these people began to think for themselves, for heresy comes from a Greek word meaning to choose or go one's own way.

At first there were very few of these heretics, but their number grew and grew until there were very many. They were called by different names, but among the chief were the Albigenses, so called from the town of Albi.

When the Pope saw how the heretics were increasing he was angry. He sent monks to preach to them and when they would not listen to the monks he tried the Inquisition. This was a new and terrible court before which the heretics were brought. If they would not confess they, were tortured and many were burned to death.

But even the Inquisition could not crush out the heresy. So the Pope next preached a Crusade against the heretics. They were worse than Saracens, he said, and he promised to give their lands to all good Christians who would help him to punish them.

Many knights and barons eager for war, eager for plunder, flocked to his banner. King Philip did nothing.

"Tell my lord Pope," he said to his messenger, "that I have upon my flanks to great and terrible lions. The one is the German Emperor, the other John, King of England. Both labor with all their strength to cast trouble into the realm of France. How does he think then that I can leave my kingdom, either I or my son? It is enough that I give my barons leave to march against these disturbers of the Faith."

Again and again the Pope urged King Philip to fight for the Faith. But the King stood firm. He was no lover of heretics, but neither did he love fighting for fighting's sake. He fought to strengthen and enlarge his kingdom.

"It is impossible," he said, "to raise and keep two armies, the one to defend my country against the King of England, the other to fight the Albigenses. Let my lord Pope supply the money and the soldiers; then we shall see."

But though the King did not help the Pope, many of his nobles did, and a great army was gathered. Their leader was Simon de Montfort. He was the father of that Simon de Montfort who became so great in English history. He was a brave man, a splendid soldier and fearless leader. He loved his men and thought for them, and they in return loved him and followed him gladly. To his enemies he was pitiless. Now he believed that he was fighting God's battle, that the Albigenses were God's enemies, and he had no mercy for them.

With such a leader it was no wonder that the war was cruel and pitiless. No mercy was shown to prisoners. When a town was taken, the people were all put to death, often in cruel ways. Once the question was asked, "How shall we know true believers from heretics?'[1]

"Kill them all," was the answer; "the Lord will know His own."

This cruel war lasted fifteen years. The Pope who preached it, Simon who led, and Philip who looked on, were all dead before it ended. It began as a war of religion; it ended as a war against the nobles of southern France. For the Pope had promised the lands they might conquer to the Crusaders as a reward. Philip was little pleased that the Pope should thus give away lands which belonged to his vassals. So unjust did he deem the war that, although eager to enlarge his kingdom, he refused to take possession of the conquered states when they were offered to him. Five years later, however, the offer was again made to his son. This time it was accepted, and thus more land was added to France.

CHAPTER 33

PHILIP II AUGUSTUS AND LOUIS VIII—THE BATTLE OF BOUVINES

MEANWHILE Philip had to do with the two "great and terrible lions" upon his flanks. John of England at length roused himself from his cowardly idleness and determined to make a fight for his French possessions. He agreed with the German Emperor that they should both attack France at the same time. So John, gathering a great army, landed at La Rochelle, while the German Emperor with some English troops marched upon the north of France.

Philip sent his son Louis to meet John. He himself marched northward to meet the Germans and their English allies. At Bouvines a great battle was fought. Before he went to battle Philip ordered mass to be said, When it was done he asked that bread and wine should be brought. Taking a piece of bread he dipped it into the wine and ate it.

Then turning to those around him he said: "I pray you, my good friends, that you eat and drink with me in remembrance or the Apostles who ate with our Lord, And if there be any among you who has evil thought or treachery in his heart let him come not near."

Then one of the lords came and took a piece of bread and dipping it in the wine said, "Sire, you shall see this day whether I be a traitor or no."

After him another and another of the knights pressed forward till there was such a great crowd round the table that it was hard to get near it.

When the King saw this he was greatly rejoiced and said to his barons: "My lords, you are my men and I am your King. Such as I am, I love you much. And I pray you keep this day my honor and yours. And if you see that the crown better befits one of you than me I will give it up willingly."

When the barons heard the King speak so they wept. "Sire," they said, "God guard us. We desire no other King than you. Now ride boldly against your enemies, for we are ready to die with you."

And not only were the knights and their vassals ready to die for the King; the common people and the citizens too were ready, and from almost every commune men flocked to his standard.

The German Emperor also made ready for battle. He called his knights together and spoke to them.

"It is against Philip himself and against him alone," he said, "that we must fight. He it is who must be slain first, for he alone is our enemy in all things. When he is dead, then you will conquer his whole kingdom and divide it among you as you will."

At the first sounds of battle Philip entered into a small chapel near and said a short prayer. Then he leaped upon his great war horse as gaily as if going to a wedding or a feast. "To arms! barons, to arms!" he cried, and darted forward amid a blare of trumpets.

On the French side the men of Soissons were the first to attack. But the knights against whom they charged disdained to fight with common men and they stood still. At length one of them, shouting "Death to the French!" rushed forward. The others followed and a terrible fight took place. Men and horses were mingled in wild confusion, the air was full of sounds of clashing armor, the clang of sword and steel, shouts of battle, cries of pain. Amid it all rode a gallant knight who cried with a clear and happy voice, "Remember your ladies!" To him it was but a tournament. Such was the reckless bravery of those days.

Above the roar of battle there rose from the French ranks the sound of singing. For behind the King marched his chaplain and another priest chanting psalms. "Deliver me, O Lord, from mine enemies. I flee unto Thee to hide me."

They sang as lustily as they could, but tears ran down their cheeks and sobs mingled with their singing. "And of Thy mercy cut off mine enemies, and destroy all them that afflict my soul."

The German knights had not forgotten the words of their Emperor. They fought their way to the King of France, they surrounded him and dragged him from his horse. As he lay on the ground helpless it seemed as if he would be trodden to death by horses' hoofs. Blow after blow fell upon him. But his armor was true and trusty, and he struggled to his feet, almost unhurt, although a lance head was sticking in his gorget.

His standard bearer waved high the golden oriflamme and shouted, "Help! To the King! Help!" Quickly his knights rushed to his aid and the Germans were scattered. The King leaped once more upon his horse and dashed into the fight.

The Emperor too was in danger. Twice one of the French knights had him by the neck. Twice he escaped by the swiftness of his horse. Then

PHILIP DARTED FORWARD AMID A BLARE OF TRUMPETS.

his horse being wounded suddenly reared and turning round fled away.

"You will see his face no more this day," said Philip, looking after the fleeing Emperor. And he was right. The Emperor's horse stumbled and fell. Quickly leaping on to another he fled far from the field.

Still the fight went on. But at length it ended in a great victory for the French. Yet so sure had the Emperor been of victory that in his camp four cart loads of ropes were found which had been brought to bind French prisoners. The French now made use of them to bind their foes.

Philip's return to Paris was a march of triumph. In every town and village through which he passed the bells were rung, and services of thanksgiving were held. The houses were hung with silks and flags, and wreathed in flowers. Flowers and green branches were strewn upon the streets, which were filled with a rejoicing multitude. In Paris never had such feasting been seen. The people came out to greet their King with shouts and songs of joy. Night was made as bright as day with hundreds of torches. For a week the city rejoiced.

And France might well rejoice, for the battle of Bouvines marked its birth as a nation. The victory was not the King's alone. It was the victory of the nation, the victory of the King, nobles, and people, all fighting for one end and that end, not the crushing of some revolted barons, but the freeing of their own land from foreign foes. France was awake.

While France was rejoicing, John of England fled homeward a beaten, angry, man, and he too found a nation awake. England was awake, and English barons, fighting for the English people, made him sign the Great Charter. Thus the true national life of France and of England began at the same time. Yet from this point the two countries went different ways. Step by step England went toward freedom. Step by step France went toward an absolute monarchy.

But, as you know, John did not keep the promises made by the Great Charter, and war began. Then English men sent to France offering the crown of England to Louis, the son of Philip. For Louis had married John's niece, and that seemed to some of the English to give him a title to the throne.

It was a splendid offer. Philip seemed to see the dream of his boyhood coming true. France would be great as in the days of Charlemagne. But the Pope forbade Philip to help the revolted Englishmen against their King.

"The kingdom of England," replied Philip, "has never been in the gift of Saint Peter. It never will be. The throne is vacant since John was condemned by our court as having forfeited it by the murder of Arthur."

But all the same, not wishing to offend the Pope, Philip forbade his son to go.

"Sire," replied Louis, "I am your liegeman for the fief you have given me on this side of the water. But it does not belong to you to decide about the kingdom of England. I beg you not to oppose me, for I will fight for my wife's heritage till death if need be."

So Louis went. Secretly his father helped him with money and gave him his blessing. Openly he pretended to forbid him.

Louis landed in England. The barons did homage, the kingdom seemed sure. Then John died. And with the death of John everything changed. The anger of the barons died away. Their hearts went out to John's son, little nine-year-old Henry. He had done no harm; why should they hate him? They forsook Louis and crowned Henry, and, bitterly disappointed, Louis returned to France.

Six years later, in 1223, Philip died. He was a soldier and a statesman, but he seldom fought for the mere love of fighting. He had doubled the size of France, yet he was not, ruthless, for he had loved justice and peace.

On his deathbed he begged his son Louis to do good justice to the people, and above all to protect the poor and the little against the insolent and the proud.

Louis, the new King of France, was a grown man, thirty-six years old, when he came to the throne. To make sure of the crown the Capetian princes had always been crowned during the lives of their fathers. Louis VIII was the first who was not so crowned. The kingdom was so sure and safe now that there was no need. Besides, Louis seemed to have a double claim to the throne, for his mother was a descendant of Charlemagne. It pleased the French people to think that with Louis VIII they returned to the family of Charles the Great. There is little to tell of Louis VIII's reign, for it lasted only three years. It was but a continuation of that of his great father.

Yet, although his reign was but a continuation of his father's, Louis was by no means great like Philip Augustus. An old writer said of him that his chief fame lay in being the son of a great father, and the father of a great son. Indeed, had it not been for his beautiful wife, Blanche of Castile, he might have proved himself a mere Do-nothing King. But she was proud and beautiful, had a firm will and high courage, and knew well how to rule, and greatly aided her husband.

Like his father, Louis fought with the English, for hardly was he seated on the throne when Henry sent messengers to him asking him to restore all the lands which Philip had conquered. The Pope too asked him to restore them.

"Not an inch of the land which my father left me in dying shall be given back to the English," replied Louis.

But Henry would not meekly give in to this and he made war. It did him no good, however. He only lost some more of the very little remaining to him of his French possessions.

The war against the Albigenses too went on, and in this, unlike his father, Louis took part. He besieged and took the town of Avignon. It only remained to besiege and take Toulouse to subdue the whole of the South. But the year was far advanced, so Louis turned northward, meaning to spend the winter in Paris and return in the spring to take Toulouse. But on his way north he became ill and died.

CHAPTER 34

LOUIS THE SAINT—THE STORY OF HUGH DE LA MARCHE

LOUIS was succeeded by his son, also called Louis, who was only twelve. He was a beautiful, gentle boy, with big blue eyes and long fair hair. He was too young to rule, and his mother, Queen Blanche, became Regent.

That a woman should rule France was in those far-off days an unheard-of thing. It made many of the great nobles angry. It would be easy to fight a child and a woman they thought, and many of them rebelled.

Queen Blanche was a Spaniard and a stranger in the land. She had no relations near her to give her aid. But her beauty and wisdom won many friends for her. She was warned now that the nobles had risen and with her son she fled to Paris. But when they had got some way they dared go no further lest they should be taken prisoner. So the Queen sent to the citizens of Paris asking for aid. And the citizens came forth in great numbers and led the King safely into Paris. All the way on both sides the road was lined with people armed and unarmed. And as the King passed they cheered him and prayed God to bless him and defend him from all his enemies and give him a long life and a happy one.

Years after when Louis had grown to be a man he loved to recall that day.

For five years the struggle with the barons went on. But by degrees they learned to bow to the firm rule of Queen Blanche and, when he grew old enough, to that of Louis. When Louis was nineteen he was declared of age, and although his fair, gentle face made him look like a girl, he soon proved himself a valiant soldier and firm ruler and made his barons obey him. But it was not only his own vassals whom Louis had to fight. He had also to fight his old enemy, the King of England.

When Louis's younger brother was twenty-one he made him Count of Poitou and held a grand court to which all the vassals of Poitou came to do homage to their new lord. Now, although thirty-five years had passed since Philip Augustus had conquered Poitou, no treaty had been signed to make his conquest sure, and Richard of Cornwall, the brother of Henry III, still called himself the Earl of Poitou. The barons had been quite pleased at this. They had paid homage to neither King, and had done much as they liked. Now many of them paid homage but unwillingly to the new count.

Among the most powerful of these was Hugh Count de la Marche. His wife was Isabella, the widow of John Lackland. She was a very proud woman. She had been the wife of one King, she was the mother of another. She could not bear the thought that she was now merely the wife of a simple count, and he vassal to another count.

After he had done homage, Hugh de la Marche found his proud wife Isabella given over to tears and anger. He tried to comfort her, but she cried out in passionate wrath against him.

"Ah, you do not see!" she cried: "three days did I wait on the good pleasure of your King and your Queen at Poitiers. And they scorned me. When I came into the room where they sat, they did not call me to them or make me sit down. They did it of purpose to make me appear vile in the eyes of others. Neither when I came in nor when I went out did they rise even a little, thus flouting me. Ah, you must have seen it yourself!"

Isabella looked very beautiful as she spoke, her eyes flashing, and her cheeks glowing with anger, her words broken by sobs.

"I can hardly speak of it," she moaned, "so full am I of sorrow and of shame. It is worse to bear even than the loss of our land which the French have torn so unworthily from us. I shall die of it if by God's grace I do not make them repent. I would that they too were desolate; that they too were reft of their lands. I will do all to make them so or die in the attempt."

When the count saw his wife's tears and anger he was greatly moved. "Lady," he said, "command me. I will do all that man can. You know that right well," and with many and great oaths he swore to it. And so as the new Count of Poitou sat one day ready to receive the homage of his vassals he saw Hugh Count de la Marche come riding upon a horse with his wife behind him. Around him were his vassals and men at arms. An insolent smile was on his face.

Before his over-lord Count Hugh paused. "Sir Count," he said, "in a moment of weakness and great forgetfulness I did homage to you. But I swear to you from this hour that I will never be your liegeman. For you are not my true lord, having basely stolen this land from my stepson,

Richard, Earl of Cornwall. You will not confess it, so I come here to fling the truth in your teeth."

Having thus spoken, Hugh de la Marche, swollen with pride and insolence, put spurs to his horse and rode away at a gallop with his wife and all his men at arms. Then, as he left the town, as a parting insult he ordered his men to set fire to the house in which he had been lodged. He watched it blaze and roar, and as the fierce light lit up the darkening sky, he turned and sped away to his own castle.

Right wrathful was the Count of Poitou and bitterly did he complain to his brother, King Louis, of the outrage done to him by his rebel vassal. So the King called the peers together. "What think you," he asked of them, "should be done to a vassal who would hold his land without doing homage to his over-lord?!"

"Sire," they replied, "the over-lord must then take the fief back into his own keeping."

"By my name," cried Louis, "the Count de la Marche doth claim thus to hold land which has been a fief of France since the days of the great King Clovis, who conquered all Aquitaine from the King Alaric, a pagan without faith or creed."

And having thus spoken the King gathered horse and foot and marched against Hugh de la Marche. Splendidly armed knights with their followers flocked to him from every side, like rivers flowing to the sea, until he had a great army. As they advanced they took castle after castle and laid the walls even with the ground.

Meanwhile Hugh, afraid of what he had done, strengthened his castles and armed his men and sent to the King of England begging for help. "Bring me but some money," he said, "for I have soldiers enough and to spare." "As if," says an old writer, "the King of England were a banker or huckster rather than a King and a noble leader and commander of knights."

The King of England was eager to go. Not so his barons. Again and again had they given him money and help for this need or that, and never one bit the better was the kingdom. They were no longer minded to be despoiled of their money to no advantage. But at length, by craft and by force, Henry III gathered a great sum of money and with knights and men crossed the sea to France.

Near the Castle of Taillebourg the two armies met. The King of England lay on one side of the river, the King of France on the other.

Early in the morning King Henry rose and looked forth upon the camp of the French. As he gazed his heart sank within him. Rank upon rank stretched the white tents as far as the eye could see. It was like a great city. What were his handful of men against this host?

Wrathfully he turned to his stepfather. "How now, my lord and father," he cried, "where are your promises? When we were in England you promised us many times by frequent messengers that you would gather a force for us which could stand against the French King without fear. You told us only to trouble ourselves about money."

"Thus did I never," cried Count Hugh.

"You did," interrupted Richard of Cornwall, "and I have here and now your letters thereon."

"They were never written nor signed by me," muttered the count.

"What," said the King in great astonishment, "what is this I hear from you, my father? Have you not sent to me, aye again and again, begging me to hasten? Where are now your promises?"

Then the count swore a dreadful oath. "This was never done by me," he cried. "Blame none but your mother, my wife. She has done it unknown to me." And so with many and strange oaths he swore to it.

Meanwhile the French had advanced and fighting had begun. Then Earl Richard, seeing that his brother the King was in great danger of being taken prisoner, put off his armor. And taking a flag of truce in his hand he went toward the French camp.

King Louis received him with great honor, and granted him a truce until the next day.

"My lord earl, my lord earl," he said, "I have granted you this truce to last to-day and to-night so that you may think of what is best to be done in the A truce future. For night brings counsel with it."

In all haste the earl returned to the King of England. Quietly he whispered in his ear, "Haste, haste, let us get from this place, for we are in danger of being taken prisoner."

They took a hasty meal. Then each gathered his goods together, and when night fell the King, mounted on a swift horse, sped away and did not spare either whip or spur. He was soon followed by the whole army, not without danger both to horses and men. For many of the men were dinnerless and the horses were wearied.

At the Castle of Saintes the English drew rein. As soon as the truce was over, the French followed them and a battle was fought. The two sides rushed upon each other, one crying "Montjoie! Montjoie!" the other "King's men! King's men!"

It was a fierce fight. In the narrow lanes, with vineyards stretching on either side, men fought hand to hand while the July sun streamed down upon them. The English fought desperately, but they were far outnumbered by the French and they fled before them.

King Henry fled nor drew rein until he reached the city of Blaye. He cared little for the rest of his army or whether they followed him or no. They did follow him in such haste that all the way was strewn with wounded and dying men.

This battle ended the war. Hugh de la Marche, seeing it useless to fight longer, yielded to King Louis. With his wife and three sons he humbly knelt before him begging forgiveness with tears.

Many of the English then asked the French King's leave to pass to their homes. When Louis heard it he was glad. "Let them go free," he said; "let them pass through my land without hindrance, never, I hope, to return."

So the English took their way in peace through France. But neither did they nor their King escape the scorn and laughter of the people. But when King Louis heard of the laughter at Henry he was vexed. "Be still, be still," he said. "Do not mock him or try to make me hate him because you do."

And so King Henry returned home with as much triumph as if he had conquered all France.

CHAPTER 35

LOUIS THE SAINT—HOW THE KING TOOK THE 'CROSS OF THE VOYAGE' OVER THE SEA

SOME time after this war with England King Louis became very ill. It was thought that he would die. He lay so still and quiet that one of the ladies who watched by his side thought that he was dead. The other thought he still lived. As they whispered about it, the King suddenly sighed softly. Then he stretched out his arms and in a weak, low voice he murmured: "He who cometh from on high hath visited me and recalled me from among the dead."

As soon as he could speak well, he sent for two Bishops and bade them place upon his shoulder "the Cross of the voyage over the sea."

The two Bishops tried to make him give up the idea. His wife and his mother begged him on their knees to wait at least until he was well. But he would listen to none of them. At length the Bishops dared refuse no longer and with tears in their eyes they gave the Cross to the King. With great joy Louis took it, kissed it and laid it gently upon his breast. But when the Queen, his mother, saw it there, she wept as bitterly as if he had died.

The King got better. But three years passed, during which Louis found so much to do in ruling his kingdom that he was not able to keep his vow and go on a Crusade. No one wished him to go. His wise mother, his gentle, loving wife, all his friends and counsellors begged him to give it up.

"My lord King," said the Bishop of Paris, "remember when you took the Cross you were ill. To say truth you were not in your senses. God will forgive your words spoken unadvisedly. Stay with us. Look around and see the dangers you leave us to. England, Germany, Italy, are our enemies. Stay then and guard and rule your kingdom."

Queen Blanche too begged him to remain. "Dearest son," she said, "stay in your kingdom and the Holy Land will not suffer. God is just; He will forgive your oath by reason of your illness."

But Louis was deaf to all pleading. He looked from one to the other with unmoved face.

"You think I knew not what I did when I took the Cross?" he said. "You think I was out of my senses? Then I lay it aside. I give it up to you."

Then raising his hand to his shoulder he tore away the Cross. He held it out to the Bishop. "My lord Bishop," he said, "here is the Cross which I took. I give it back to you willingly."

When they heard this all around were filled with joy. Then again the King spoke.

"My friends," he said, "I am not now out of my senses. I am not ill. Therefore I ask you to give me back my Cross. For the Lord who knoweth everything knoweth that I shall neither eat nor drink until I wear it again."

Seeing how steadfast the King was in his desire, the Bishop returned the Cross and no one dared try to dissuade him more.

But times were changing. Knights and nobles were no longer so eager to forsake their own land to fight in a far-off country and Louis found it hard to gather an army. He fell upon many ways to gain his end. He even played pranks on his courtiers.

At Christmas time it was the custom of the King to give a new suit of clothes to the gentlemen of his court. The King asked all the gentlemen of his household and the barons who had gathered to spend Christmas with him to come to mass before dawn in the beautiful new chapel which he had built. So all the lords and gentlemen gathered, dressed in the new clothes which the King had given them

When the first rays of sunshine came through the painted windows each man saw with astonishment the sign of the Cross on his neighbor's shoulder. For the King had secretly caused a Cross to be sewn on each. The knights felt that it would not be respectful to the King nor honorable in them to tear off the Crosses. So they took it in good part and laughed at the King's jest until the tears came.

At length Louis set forth upon his long hoped for journey. He left his mother as Regent and she took leave of him sadly and tenderly. "Most sweet, fair son," she said, "fair, tender son, I shall never see you more. Full well my heart tells me so." She was right. Louis held his mother in his arms for the last time, for she died before he returned. His wife, Queen Margaret, went with him.

King Louis turned his Crusade, not toward Palestine, but toward Egypt, for he believed if he conquered the ruler of Egypt he could easily take possession of Palestine. After a long delay in the island of Cyprus the Crusaders at length landed at Damietta at the mouth the Nile.

Here a battle was fought in which the Saracens were defeated and Damietta was taken. But instead of marching on at once and fighting the Saracens again the Crusaders wasted five months at Damietta, giving the Saracens time to get over their first terror and prepare to fight again.

At length the Crusaders moved on, and a second battle was fought. This, too, the Crusaders won. But the victory was of little use to them. Food was growing scarce, sickness and death were thinning their ranks. King Louis saw they could do no more, and he tried to make peace with the Saracens. But they would listen to no terms unless the King was given up to them as a hostage. To this the Crusaders would not listen. "Rather let the Turks kill us all," cried a knight, "than that we should endure the reproach of having pawned our King."

There was nothing then to do but turn homeward as speedily as might be. The retreat began. Part of the army, chiefly the sick and wounded, went by boat on the Nile. They fell almost at once into the hands of the Saracens, who killed them nearly all. The rest, the King among them, although he too was very ill, went by land.

As they marched they were attacked again and again by small parties of Saracens, so that many a knight fell by the way, and was left to die on the burning sand beneath the pitiless blazing sun.

Soon the King became so ill that the army was forced to halt at the first village to which they came. Here the Saracens surrounded them and a fight began. But the French were weak and worn with hunger and sickness. They could scarcely defend themselves.

Then one of the French knights, with the King's leave, went to the Saracen leader to beg for a truce. The Saracens consented. But before the truce could be made known a French herald, either through fear or treachery, cried out, "My lords and knights, yield, yield! The King commands it so that you may not all be slain."

At once the French laid down their arms and yielded. When the Saracen leader saw this he turned to the knight, saying: "You see a truce is no longer needful. Your people are already our prisoners."

It was too true. Even the King was a captive.

A terrible slaughter then began. The Saracens had no pity or mercy. They killed all the sick and wounded and all the common soldiers. To the knights they offered the choice of becoming Mohammedan or having their heads cut off. Many chose rather to die than deny their faith. Only the King and a few of the greatest nobles who could afford to buy their lives were spared.

The King himself was threatened with torture and death. But nothing could shake his calm dignity. "I am your prisoner," he said; "do with me what you will," and his firm courage made even his cruel captors admire him.

At length the Sultan offered to set Louis free if he would give up Damietta and pay a large sum of money. To this Louis consented at once. It was such a huge sum that the Sultan had never expected it to be paid, and he was greatly astonished. "By the law of the prophet," he cried, "the Frank is truly frank and free. He does not bargain over so great a sum as if he were a pedlar or merchant. Tell him that I abate one fifth of the sum."

A truce of ten years was made and King Louis set sail, but not for home. He had done nothing for the Holy Land. He had not even seen it, and he felt it impossible thus to return home. So although, because of the truce he had made, he could not fight, he sailed for Palestine. There he remained for four years, rebuilding and strengthening the fortifications of some of the cities along the seashore which were still in the hands of the Christians. Yet, dearly as he longed for it, he never even saw Jerusalem.

CHAPTER 36

LOUIS THE SAINT—THE KING'S LAST VOYAGE

WHILE Louis stayed in Palestine, his mother, Queen Blanche, ruled France wisely and well. But at length she died. The news was brought to King Louis at Jaffa. Then, filled with great grief at the loss of so good and wise a mother, he set sail once more and landed in France amid the rejoicing of the people.

But Louis himself felt no joy at seeing his own land again. He brought back with him a heavy heart and a sad and smileless face. For he was unable to forget the failure of his Crusade. He could not forget that he had been made prisoner by the Saracens, and through it he felt that shame had been brought on the whole Christian world.

Yet for sixteen years he gave himself up to ruling his country, and no one guessed that he still kept in his heart a deep desire to free the holy places.

During these years Louis did much for his people, Private war was almost put an end to by the Quarantaine of the King. This word comes from quarante, meaning forty. By it barons were forbidden to go to war with one another until forty days after their quarrel. During that time their anger cooled, and very often they did not fight at all. It is said that Philip Augustus first made this law, but Louis forced the barons to keep it. Besides this, the barons learned that if they took their disputes to the King justice would be done. So often instead of fighting they settled their quarrels by law.

Many a time in summer Louis sat under a great oak tree in the forest of Vincennes. Here the people came to him without any hindrance. One after another they would tell their wrongs and Louis would listen patiently and give judgment. There are many stories told of his wisdom and kindness. Daily the love of the people toward their King grew greater. There was justice at home, there was peace abroad such as had never been before.

Soon, however, all the joy was darkened, for the King let it be known at length that he had made up his mind to go upon another Crusade.

But the world had grown weary of Crusades, and no one wished him to go. The people of France, the great lords and nobles, even the Pope, tried to persuade Louis to give it up. But he would listen to none, and with a small army he set out.

This time he did not go even so far as Egypt, but sailed across the Mediterranean to Tunis. From the beginning everything was mismanaged. Louis was a great and good man, but he had never been a great general. Now, even before he started, he was ill and quite unable to command. A month after he landed he lay dying of plague beneath the walls of Tunis. Feeling that death was near he called his eldest son Philip and charged him to rule his people wisely and well. Then having received the Sacrament he begged to be laid upon a bed of ashes. There he lay softly repeating now and again words of Scripture. Once he sighed "Jerusalem! Jerusalem!" At length he crossed his hands upon his breast and murmuring, "Father, into Thy hands I commit my spirit," he lay at rest.

Louis was not a great general. He was perhaps not even a brilliant statesman. But France never had a more truly good King. No King ever did more to make France great and happy. Yet his religion made him cruel to the Jews and to the "heretics." It made him leave his country, his duty, and the real good he was doing, and go to fight for an imaginary good far from his own land, thereby bringing on his people much sorrow and trouble. But that was the fault of the times in which he lived. We cannot judge him as we would judge a King to-day, and we must remember Louis as one of the great good men of the world. His people sorrowed for him so deeply and held his memory so dear that some years after his death he was made a saint, and he is known to all the world as St. Louis.

CHAPTER 37

PHILIP III THE BOLD—THE STORY OF PETER THE BARBER

LOUIS IX died in 1270 and was succeeded by his son Philip III, *Le Hardi* or the Bold. Philip had gone on the Crusade with his father, and after St. Louis's death he stayed about two months longer in Tunis. During that time two fierce battles were fought. Then at length a treaty was signed by which the Christians were allowed the freedom of their own religion, and the King of Tunis paid Philip a large sum of money.

By this time Prince Edward of England had come out to join the Crusade. He and his knights now set sail for Palestine, while Philip turned homeward.

It was a sad procession which reached France, for Philip brought with him no fewer than five biers. For besides his father, St. Louis, his brother John, his sister Isabella and her husband, and his own Queen, Isabella, had all died.

There was a great and splendid funeral for St. Louis, the King himself helping to carry his father's coffin to the Abbey of St. Denis. The great church was thronged with knights, nobles, and clergy, while the people crowded along the way mourning for their beloved King.

Philip III was twenty-five when he came to the throne, and how he came by his name of the Bold is hardly known. History does not tell us of any bold or brave deed he did.

Philip III was by no means a great King. He had been a good, obedient son. Now he showed himself a good man, but stupid and ignorant, and he allowed himself to be led by his favorites, by his wife, by his mother, by any and everybody.

It is during this reign that we find a French King for the first time making a favorite of a man of low degree. Philip's chief favorite was Peter de la Brosse, who had been barber to St. Louis. Philip loaded him with honors, gave him titles and lands and much money.

Peter ruled the King, and the great lords feared him because he made the King do everything he wished. They became humble before him and gave him rich presents. If they wished to speak to the King, it was Peter to whom they went.

Though the lords feared Peter they hated him too, for they could not forget that he was a man of low degree. But there was only one person whom Peter feared and hated. This was Marie of Brabant, Philip's young and beautiful Queen. He resolved to do her harm if possible.

Now Louis, Philip's eldest son, died suddenly. So Peter caused it to be whispered abroad that the Queen had poisoned him, for Louis was not her son, but the son of Philip's first wife, who had died during the Crusade. Peter sent a friend to Court who smiled meaningly, shook his head, and shrugged his shoulders as he spoke of the Prince's death as if he would say, "Oh! if I liked, I could tell you about that." So after a time the King really began to believe that the Queen had done this wicked thing.

The Queen was in great distress, but she had many friends. They persuaded Philip to consult a "wise woman" who knew both of things past and things to come. And this wise woman told the King not to believe the wicked things which were said about his wife, for that she was good and loyal both to himself and all dear to him.

When the King heard these words he thought to himself that he had in his Court and in his service men who were neither good nor loyal. The lords then hoped that Peter would be punished for the evil that he had tried to do. But for two years nothing happened.

Then one day a monk came to the King bringing with him a box full of letters. What was written in the letters no man knows. It is said, however, that they were written by Peter de la Brosse, and that he was therein proved a traitor to his King.

However that may be, Peter was seized and cast into prison, and the King sent for the barons to judge him. Right gladly they came, and when they had condemned him to death Peter was given over to the common hangman. And early one morning ere the sun was up he was hanged among the thieves and robbers. Many nobles followed him to the scaffold right glad to see the death of their enemy. But the common people of Paris were greatly troubled. Men and women crowded round to watch, scarcely believing it possible that one who had risen so high could fall so low.

Besides this barber who came to so unhappy an end, another commoner, the silversmith Ralph, rose to greatness. For Philip made him a noble. Never before had such a thing been known. Only through fighting had it been possible to win nobility. This showed that the idea that war was the only noble calling was passing away. It showed that the feudal system was coming to an end.

Philip reigned for fifteen years. He died in October, 1285, while returning from a disastrous war in Spain, by which he had tried and failed to win the throne of Aragon for his son Charles.

CHAPTER 38

PHILIP IV THE HANDSOME—THE WAR BETWEEN KNIGHTS AND WEAVERS

PHILIP IV, who succeeded his father, was only seventeen when he came to the throne. He was called Philip le Bel, or the Handsome. He was cold and selfish, very greedy of money, very greedy of power.

He took little interest in the Spanish war begun by his father. It dragged on for six years, and was at last ended by a treaty in which Charles gave up all his claim to the throne of Aragon.

For this Philip cared little. He was much more interested in increasing his own power and extending his own kingdom than in winning one for his brother. He tried to take from the King of England all that remained of his French possessions. But although Edward I was busy trying to conquer Wales and Scotland, the French King found it hard to get the better of him. So he made friends with the Scots and helped them against Edward, in order that the English King might be kept busy at home and have fewer soldiers to spare to fight in France.

Philip next turned his attention to Flanders. Flanders was at this time the richest country in Europe. The people were industrious and clever; Flemish cloths and woolen stuffs were known throughout the world; the country was full of wealthy towns; and as the land was not cut off from France by mountains or broad rivers it seemed natural to Philip to extend his kingdom in that direction.

Besides all this, although Philip was the over-lord of the count, the Flemish were friends with the English. For from England they got wool for their cloth, and found there a market for their wines. That the Flemish were friends with the English was enough to make them the enemies of the King of France. Besides, Philip was always in need of money, and he coveted the wealthy cities.

Now about this time Guy Count of Flanders secretly made arrangements with the King of England that his daughter should marry Edward Prince of Wales. When Philip heard of it he was very angry and made up his mind to stop the marriage. He asked the Count of Flanders to come to Paris, pretending that he wished to consult with him about affairs of state. Guy was afraid to go, but he was equally afraid to stay away. So in the end he went with his two sons. And thinking it wisest to be open, he told the King at once about the marriage between his daughter and the English Prince. "Nevertheless," he added, "I will still serve you loyally as it becomes a man to serve his over-lord."

Then Philip showed the Count traitorous letters which it was said he had sent to the King of England. "My lord King," said Guy when he saw them, "they are not mine. They are false letters sealed with a false seal."

But Philip would not listen, and the Count and his sons were thrown into prison in the tower of the Louvre, For six months they remained there and were only set free when the Count promised to send his daughter Phillipa to take his place. So the doors of his prison were opened only to close again on his young and lovely daughter. And in this gloomy prison she remained all her sad life, although her only crime was that her father had promised her hand in marriage to the heir of the English throne.

Although Edward was not yet twelve years old, this was the second time that he had been disappointed of his bride. The first, you will remember, was Margaret, the Maid of Norway, Queen of Scotland.

Angry and discontented, Guy returned to his own land and soon, aided by Edward, he declared war against Philip. But even with King Edward's help Count Guy was not strong enough to fight Philip. It was rather a war of money than of swords. Edward paid the great nobles to fight for him. Philip paid them to do nothing, and they did nothing. It was a question, not of which King had most soldiers, but of which had most money.

After a time Philip and Edward made peace. By this peace Edward left his friend Guy of Flanders in the lurch, for he was left out of the treaty altogether. Philip promised not to help the Scots any more. It was agreed also that King Edward should marry Philip's sister, and that Prince Edward should marry Philip's daughter Isabella. She was then only a little girl of six, so the marriage did not take place until nine years later.

Forsaken by the King of England, Flanders was now almost at Philip's mercy. Guy soon saw that it was hopeless to resist and yielded to him with his sons and chief nobles. Philip at once put them all in prison and declared Flanders henceforth a part of the kingdom of France.

The Flemish were not ill pleased to be rid of their Count, for they were ever a freedom-loving, unruly people and he had ground them down cruelly. So they had no love for him. They hoped that the King of

France would rule them more justly, and give them greater freedom. So when with his Queen he came to visit them, they gave him everywhere a splendid welcome. Every one dressed in their best and richest clothes and jewels, the houses were hung with colored cloths and flags. Everywhere there was show of wealth. At the sight of all this splendor the Queen was jealous. "What!" she cried, "I thought I was the only Queen in France, and now I behold around me six hundred queens."

But Philip, who was always in need of money, went back to France pleased with the thought that in Flanders he had an unending source of wealth. He had taxed his own people almost to the last farthing, now he taxed the Flemish. The governor he put over his new country was haughty and greedy and cared nothing for the rights or freedom of the Flemish cities. He oppressed the people without mercy until they rose in revolt.

Their leader was an old weaver called Peter Koning. He was a dried up, little old man, blind of one eye, and ugly. But he was wise, quick, and full of courage.

When the King heard of the revolt he sent an army to subdue it. They reached Bruges and were allowed to enter the town in peace. But that evening the French leader was heard to boast that next day many of the townsfolk would hang upon the gallows. Then they became desperate.

In the middle of the night they silently gathered. The great bell of the town was guarded the French; so it could not be rung, and the signal for battle was given by beating large iron pots. Awakened by this awful noise and by the sound of the Flemish war cry, "Our shields and our friends for the Lion of Flanders! Death to the Walloons!" the French sprang from their beds. Ere they were well awake they were slaughtered. Even women and children rushed upon them, slaying them almost in their beds. The butchery began before the sun was up, and all day the streets resounded with the cries of the dying. Almost the whole army perished, the leader and a few knights alone escaping.

When Philip heard of it he was bitterly angry. He sent another army to crush the rebels. But the weavers and merchants of Flanders gathered in force. "It is better," they cried, "to die sword in hand than with a rope about one's neck." And was it not well known that, in the French army, there were wagon loads of ropes wherewith to hang them?

Near the town of Courtrai the two armies met. Before the battle the Flemish knelt and confessed their sins. Then bending forward each man took a little of the earth and carried it to his mouth, thus silently vowing that he would free his country or die for it.

Then little one-eyed Peter Koning knelt before the lord of Namur, who struck him on the shoulder with his sword, and dubbed him knight. So with a sword by his side, and gilt spurs on his heels, the little weaver was ready to die for his country.

The Flemish stood waiting. In front of their position flowed a broad canal over which the French must pass to reach them. But the French knights were full of contempt for this rabble of weavers and tinkers. Over the plain they came dashing, with loosened rein, in careless disorder. On they thundered, clouds of dust flying from their horses' heels. Too late they saw the canal. Into it the first ranks plunged headlong. Unable to stop themselves others followed. Soon it was a struggling mass of men and horses. Unable to rise by the weight of their armor, crushed and beaten by their horses' hoofs, the French knights died in hundreds.

Seeing their helpless condition the Flemish advanced upon the broken and disordered ranks. They slew without mercy.

"I yield! I yield!" cried one of the French leaders.

"We understand not thy lingo," replied the Flemish, and slew him forthwith.

Never had there been such a slaughter of French nobles. When the fight was over all the best of the French lay dead on the field. So great was the number that gilt spurs were gathered by the basketful from the field.

But Philip was obstinate. In a year's time he had gathered another army and this time he led it himself. At Mons-en-Puelle the Flemish were defeated. Philip thought that at length he had conquered them. But he was mistaken. A few days after their defeat the Flemish gathered another and greater army. Every man who could hold a weapon hastened to the fight. Only women and children were left in the towns and villages.

Philip was dismayed. "I thought I had destroyed the Flemish," he cried; "now they seem to rain from heaven."

He did not care to fight any longer with sucn a determined people. So he made peace. The Flemings consented to receive the son of their old Count Guy as count. He did homage to Philip as over-lord and the first war of independence in Flanders came to an end.

CHAPTER 39

PHILIP IV THE HANDSOME—THE PRIDE OF ROME AND THE PRIDE OF FRANCE

WHILE Philip had been fighting with the Flemish, he had been fighting a different kind of war with the Pope. To get money for his wars, Philip had taxed his people very heavily. He wrung everything he could from the common people and from the nobles, and he tried to make the monks and priests pay still more, for they were the richest class in France.

Some of the Bishops refused to pay and asked the Pope for help. The Pope then wrote to Philip, forbidding him to lay any tax upon the clergy, without asking leave.

Philip replied by forbidding any one to send gold, or silver, or jewels out of France without his leave. This he knew would hurt the Pope, for the clergy of France paid him large sums every year.

Thus the quarrel began and went from bad to worse. Pope Boniface was a passionate, proud old man; Philip was just as proud, and he was cool and hard. The Pope was bent on showing that he was above all the kings in the world. Philip was bent on showing that he was not above the King of France.

"My power," said the Pope, "is over both things of the Church and things of the world."

"So be it," replied the French chancellor, "but your power is a thing of words. The King's is real."

The Pope at length sent to Philip a long letter, or Bull, as a letter from the Pope is called. It began: "Hearken, most dear son. God has placed me, though unworthy, over kings and kingdoms. Let no one then persuade you that you have no superior. For he who thinks so is a madman and a heretic."

The Bull went on among many other things to make a list of all the wicked deeds Philip had done. It made the King very angry. He caused part of it to be copied out and read to the people as well as his answer. It was very rude. It began "'Philip, by the grace of God King of the French, to Boniface, who calls himself Pope, little or no greeting. May your Supreme Foolishness know that we be subject to no man in things temporal: that the livings of churches belong to us by royal right; that we will support their possessions with all our power against your face and in your teeth."

The King also caused the Bull to be burned with solemn pomp in his presence. Then heralds were sent through all Paris to cry to every wind of heaven what he had done.

Immediately after this, Philip called a parliament together. He called people from the three estates; that is, from the nobles, the clergy, and from the common people. This was the first time that such a parliament had been called in France.

For many years meetings called parliaments had been held. But they were rather courts of justice. This meeting called by Philip was more like our Parliament, and because of the three estates that came to it is called the States-General.

All three estates wrote to the Pope telling him that they would no longer allow him to interfere. But the Pope did not care, and he ordered all the French Bishops to go to Rome to a council.

So the quarrel went on. At length Philip made up his mind to take the Pope prisoner. The Pope in fear fled to his native town, Anagni, where the people loved him. They greeted him with delight and, to show their love, they insulted the blue flag of France, dragging its golden lilies in the mud.

But one evening the quiet little town heard the tramp of armed feet, the clash of armor, and shouts of "Death to the Pope! Long live the King of France!" It was a band of Frenchmen led by William of Nogaret, the King's friend, and Sciarra Colonna, the Pope's deadly enemy.

The people of Anagni were so surprised and frightened that they could do nothing. But the Pope, old man though he was, was proud and brave. When he saw himself left alone and forsaken, his courage did not leave him.

"Betrayed like Christ," he said, "I shall die. But I shall die Pope."

So he dressed himself in his splendid robes, placed the triple crown upon his head, and, with the keys of St. Peter and the great pastoral cross in his hands, he awaited his enemies.

"Here is my neck," he said calmly. "Here is my head."

Colonna hated the Pope bitterly. With his steel-gloved hand he struck the old man in the face and would have killed him, but Nogaret prevented him. He took the Pope under his care. "See, caitiff Pope," he said, "the goodness of my lord of France who defendeth you by my hand."

The Pope was now a prisoner. He was not bound nor fettered with iron chains. But Nogaret kept him in his own room under his own eye.

It was one thing, however, to have taken the Pope prisoner in a little mountain town of Italy. It was another thing to carry him to France. When the Pope's friends saw how few the Frenchmen were they recovered from their first fear. Two days later new cries resounded through the streets. "Long live the Pope! Death to the strangers!"

The Pope was set free. Rejoicing, his friends brought him to the market-place to speak to the assembled people. With tears of joy running down his face and sobs choking his voice he tried to thank them. "Good people," he said, "ye have seen how my enemies have robbed me. Behold me standing here as poor as Job. I have neither food nor drink, and die of hunger."

Then the people carried him back to his palace, they crowded round him with offerings and words of comfort.

A few days later the Pope set out for Rome. But his spirit was crushed, his health shattered by all that he had gone through, and in a few days he died.

Almost at once a new Pope was chosen. He was the son of a simple shepherd and King Louis thought he could do with him as he would. But he found himself mistaken. In less than a year, however, this Pope died of poison. Some said that Nogaret had done this deed, some Colonna, some the King. It was never proved against any of them. But at least the King was not sorry when the Pope died. He plotted now so that a Pope should be chosen who would do his will, and a Frenchman named Bertrand de Goth was the man.

Philip sent for this man in secret. "Hearken," he said. "I can make you Pope if I please. I will do it if you promise me six things."

And to prove that he had the power he boasted of, Philip showed Bertrand letters from Rome. Having read these, Bertrand threw himself at the King's feet, promising to do all that was asked of him.

Philip then told five things he wished the Pope to do. "The sixth," he said, "I will keep to myself. But in due time you shall know it."

He then made Bertrand swear a solemn oath to fulfil this sixth thing as soon as it was asked of him. This Bertrand did, and six weeks later he was made Pope. But Philip, having chosen his Pope, wanted to rule him completely. So instead of letting him go to live in Rome, as all the Popes had done, he made him come to live in Avignon. For seventy years afterward all the Popes were Frenchmen, and they all lived at Avignon. This time has been called the Babylonish Captivity of the Popes, for so long as they lived in France they were little more than vassals of the French King.

The new Pope kept his promise. He did all the things Philip had asked of him, one being to make vile the memory of Pope Boniface. "Boniface was wrong," he said. All that Philip had done was right and good, and to the glory of the Church.

Philip soon let the Pope know the sixth thing. It was utterly to destroy the order of Knights Templar. This was an order of knights which had been founded after the first Crusade. At first they were very poor and called themselves "poor soldiers of Christ." They had a house near the Temple in Jerusalem and hence they received their name of Templars. They took vows like monks, but they lived the life of soldiers, fighting for the freedom of the Holy Sepulchre.

But although these soldier monks were at first poor, they soon grew rich and powerful. When the Crusade ceased they became idle and proud. And because of their pride and wealth they were hated and feared.

Philip was jealous of their wealth. He had already borrowed money from them. Now he made up his mind to destroy the order and take all its riches for himself.

Making believe that he wanted to plan a new Crusade, Philip asked the Grand Master of the Templars to come to visit him. Suspecting nothing, the Grand Master came.

At first he was treated with every honor. Then dark whispers began to be spread abroad of the terrible and unbelievable wickedness of the Templars. These whispers grew louder and louder until the King asked the Pope to look into the matter and find out the truth.

Then at once the Grand Master with all the Templars in France were seized and thrown into prison. They were then brought before the Inquisition for trial. There they suffered terrible things. Those who confessed to a wicked life were put to death as a punishment. Those who would not confess were tortured until they did confess. They confessed to anything rather than endure further tortures. But confession did not serve them. They were condemned to death, often in the end denying again those things to which they had confessed by reason of pain and fear.

For four years the cruel work went on. The knights were condemned to death and burned by tens and fifties at a time, and all the great wealth of which they were possessed was seized by Philip. Last of all the Grand Master was led to the stake. It was said that as he died he called upon the Pope and Philip to meet him before the judgement seat of God ere the year was gone. And when, within a month, the Pope died of a dreadful disease, and seven months later Philip died from a hunting accident, the people saw in it the judgement of God, and looked upon the Templars as martyrs, as they had long looked upon the King as a tyrant.

CHAPTER 40

LOUIS X, PHILIP V, AND CHARLES IV—THE SALIC LAW

PHILIP was the most cruel and vengeful King who had sat upon the throne of France and his people hated him. Yet it was he who first called the States-General together, it was he who broke the power of the Pope, who humbled the feudal lords. He may have been a hard man and a bad King, but his reign was a great one.

Very different were the reigns which followed.

Philip IV was succeeded by his son Louis X *le Hutin*, or the Quarrelsome. Louis X ruled only eighteen months and perhaps the thing best worth remembering about him is that he made a law forcing slaves to buy their freedom. He needed money, and he fell upon this new way of getting it. "According to the right of Nature," he said, "every one ought to be born free. But by old custom many of our people have fallen into bondage. This displeases us much. Seeing that our kingdom is named the Kingdom of the Franks (freemen) we wish that facts be in keeping with the name." Therefore the slaves were ordered to buy their freedom. But few had money enough; even those who had were too ignorant to know the value of what was offered them. So the King got little money; by this means. But from this time onward slaves, or serfs, became fewer and fewer.

Louis X died in 1316. He left no son and his little daughter was only six years old. A little child of six could not rule, so Louis's brother Philip *le Long*, or the Tall, seized the throne.

Philip was crowned at Reims, but hardly any of the nobles came to the ceremony. Indeed, knowing that many were against him, and fearing their anger, Philip ordered the gates of Reims to be closed and guarded until the crown was on his head.

Philip knew that he was only a usurper. So he determined to make his claim to the crown sure. He therefore made use of an old law of the Salian Franks which said that no woman might inherit land. Philip and his lawyers said that meant no woman might sit on the throne and rule over France. The old law did not really mean this at all. But that did not matter, many people believed it did, and it served Philip's purpose. Ever after, as long as Kings ruled in France, the Salic Law, as it is called, was held to.

But even after this law had been found many nobles were discontented, and it seemed as if there might be civil war. There was none. Philip married his daughter to the most powerful of his enemies, he promised to give his niece, whose throne he had taken, a good sum of money. In one way or another he persuaded the nobles to accept the new law and the new King in peace.

This institution of the Salic Law is the chief thing worth remembering in the reign of Philip V. It is very well worth remembering, for but for it the whole history of France, perhaps of England too, would have been different.

Philip V ruled for six years. He taxed the people heavily, he cruelly treated the lepers and the Jews, and robbed them of their money. He ground a great deal of money out of his people, yet he did nothing with it. He did not pay the debts which the kings before him had left, he did not go on a Crusade, he did not build fine churches and cathedrals. What then did the King do with all the money? the people asked. They were poor and miserable, and they hated and cursed their King. When he fell ill and died some said that his illness was brought on by these curses.

Yet Philip V tried to do some things for the good of his people. He tried to make all weights and measures alike throughout the country. He tried to make the money alike, so that people from distant parts of the kingdom could buy and sell with ease. But the people did not understand that these things were for their good. They only saw in them new ways of robbery, and they hated the King the more.

Philip V died in 1322, and like his brothers, he also left only daughters. According to the Salic Law they could not succeed, and so Philip's brother Charles IV the Handsome came to the throne.

Nothing very interesting happened in his reign, which lasted six years. He too, like his brothers, died leaving only daughters, and as he was the youngest son of Philip the Handsome there was no direct heir to the throne. It passed therefore to his cousin, Philip of Valois, who became Philip VI.

Thus after three hundred and forty years the direct line of the Capetians ceased. The Kings who came next were called the Valois, for Philip was Count of Valois before he became King of France.

CHAPTER 41

PHILIP VI OF VALOIS—WAR WITH THE FLEMISH MERCHANTS

ALTHOUGH the French people accepted Philip of Valois quietly for their King there was someone else who did not. This was King Edward III of England. You remember that Edward II had married Isabella, the daughter of Philip the Handsome. She was the sister of Louis X, Philip V, and Charles IV. Her son Edward III was their nephew, and he claimed the throne of France. Although his mother, Queen Isabella, because of the Salic Law, could not inherit the throne, there was no reason, said Edward, why her son should not. It is not easy to follow the claim, for of course, if Isabella never possessed the crown she could not give it to her son.

To begin with, however, Edward did not force his claim. Of all the French lands once possessed by the English he now held only Guienne. For that he consented to do homage to Philip, but, although only a boy of sixteen, he refused to kneel before the French King, and put his hands in his, and swear to be his man. He would give, he said, only homage of the mouth. And with this Philip had to be content. And for the time being, if there was not peace, there was at least no war between the two countries. Meanwhile Philip began his reign by fighting another foe.

The right to carry the royal sword at the coronation belonged to the Count of Flanders. Louis de Nevers, Count of Flanders, came to Philip's coronation with many knights. But when the herald stood forth and cried "Count of Flanders, if you are here come and do your duty," no one answered.

Again the herald called. Again no one answered.

A third time the herald called. Still no one answered.

Thereupon the King was greatly astonished. "Louis de Nevers," he cried, "what meaneth this?"

"May it please you, my lord King," answered the Count, "be not astonished. They have called the Count of Flanders and not Louis de Nevers."

"What then?" answered the King. "Are you not the Count of Flanders?' complains of

"Truly, my lord King," said Louis. "I have the name, but not the power. The Flemish have well-nigh driven me from the land, and there is scarce a town where I dare show my face."

"Fair Cousin," cried the King when he heard that, "we swear to you by the holy oil that this day hath anointed our head we will not enter into Paris until we see you once more at peace in your own land."

At this Louis de Nevers was greatly rejoiced. But many of the French knights were displeased, and desired to wait until the next year before beginning the war. The summer was too far advanced, they said. The winter would be upon them ere they were ready for battle.

At this the King was angry. "And what say you? he asked, turning to the Constable of France.

"Whoso hath good courage will find all times good for battle," he replied.

"Well said," cried the King as he clapped the Constable on the shoulder. "Who loves me follows me."

So the King and his men marched to battle. Nearly all the great lords of France followed. For they looked upon Count Louis's cause as the cause of chivalry. It was the cause of the nobles against merchants and tradesmen.

The rebels gathered to the hill of Cassel. It is a lonely hill from the slopes of which there stretch wide plains as far as the eye can reach. From their camp upon the slopes the Flemish looked down upon the great army of the King. They did not fear him or his brave show of knights, for in the heavy armor they wore it was impossible for these knights to charge uphill.

Over the rebel camp floated a banner on which was painted a cock and under it the words:

> "When this cock here shall crow
> The foundling King herein shall go."

They called him a foundling because they said he had no real right to the throne. He was only adopted like some orphan child by the people of France.

For three days the two armies lay watching each other. The Flemish would not leave their safe and strong position and come down, the French knights could not charge uphill.

At length the Flemish leader, who was a brave and reckless man, disguised himself as a seller of fish, and went down into the French camp to find out what they were about.

He discovered that they were very careless, and that they kept no watch. The knights he saw wandering about from tent to tent, amusing themselves by playing at dice and showing off their fine robes. Upon this the Flemish made up their minds to attack.

Down the hill they came very quietly without war cries or noise of any kind. They reached the camp. At first the French took them for new soldiers come to help. Soon they saw their mistake. In a moment all was confusion.

The King's standard bearer dashed into his tent shouting "To arms! to arms!" But the King had neither knight nor esquire near him. So his clerk and chaplain, who were there, did their best to arm him. In a few minutes he rode forth. And when his knights saw the oriflamme flickering in the afternoon sunshine like a tongue of flame, and heard the cry "Mont-Joie! Saint Denis!" they rallied to their King, though many of the common soldiers fled.

The knights and nobles rallied, and a fierce fight took place. The Flemish fought obstinately and bravely, but they were no match for the knighthood of France. Yet they would not give way, and almost to a man they fell. For French chivalry the disgrace of Courtrai was wiped out.

This battle ended the rebellion. Philip returned to Paris, where he was received with great rejoicing. "Count," he said before he went, "I give you back your land in peace. See to it that justice be done there. For if through your fault I am forced to return it will be for my profit and your hurt."

But far from remembering the King's words the Count began to establish order by terror. He punished and despoiled the people, and treated them so cruelly that soon the land was seething once more with wrath and discontent.

Before long the Flemish found a friend and supporter in the King of England. Robert of Artois, a Prince of the Royal family, was accused of trying to kill the French King, and he fled to England. There he did his best to persuade Edward into war with Philip. Edward was busy fighting the Scots, who were helped and encouraged by Philip.

"Sir," said Robert to him one day, "leave this poor country, and turn your thoughts to the noble crown of France."

DISGUISED AS A SELLER OF FISH, THE FLEMISH LEADER
WENT DOWN INTO THE FRENCH CAMP.

But Edward was slow to make up his mind. So Robert of Artois made cunning appeals to his pride. One day as the King sat at table two beautiful young girls came carrying a heron upon a dish. It was a present from the lord of Artois, and this was the message he sent.

"The heron is the most fearful of birds, for it fears its own shadow. It is for the heron to receive the vows of King Edward. For he, though lawful King of France, dares not claim that noble heritage."

As the King hears these words he was right wrathful. The dark blood flushed in his face. He rose to his feet.

"Sith coward hath been cast in my teeth," he cried; "I swear now and here on this heron, by the Lord on high, a year shall not pass ere I defy the King of Paris."

Then Count Robert smiled to himself, and whispered softly in his heart, "Now have I won. Now will my heron cause a great war."

Soon Edward had another call to fight. King Philip commanded the Count of Nevers to take prisoner all the English merchants in Flanders. The Flemish had long murmured under the cruel hand of their Count. This was now the signal for revolt. For the wool of English sheep was needed for the cloth of Flanders, and the whole wealth of Flanders was bound up with England. The Flemish rose in rebellion once more. Their leader was now Jacques van Artevelde. He was a brave and clever man, and loved freedom. He sent to King Edward begging him to help the Flemish, and proclaim himself King of France. "The Flemish would willingly follow," he said, "not the foundling King but the true King of France."

So in 1340 Edward proclaimed himself King of France, although he had conquered not an inch of French land. And from that day the fleur de lis of France was painted upon the English standard, and stamped upon English money, and the War of a Hundred Years was begun.

At first the war went badly for Edward. It is true he utterly destroyed the French fleet at Sluys, but by land he had little success. So after a time he was glad to make a truce with King Philip. This truce did not last long, for soon new causes of quarrel arose, and war burst forth once more.

Meanwhile Edward had lost a great supporter in Jacques van Artevelde. Jacques had promised that the Black Prince should be made Count of Flanders. But the turbulent Flemish had no mind to pass from the rule of a French prince to that of an English one. They wished to be altogether free. So they began to murmur against Artevelde. As he passed through the streets they whispered together. "Behold," they said, "yonder great master who will order all Flanders after his pleasure, the which is not to be suffered."

Also they began to whisper abroad that for nine years Artevelde had ruled them, and had gathered the taxes of Flanders, and given no account of the money. And many said that he had sent it to England secretly. These words set all Ghent on fire.

Then one day as Artevelde rode through the streets he felt that some evil was brewing against him. For those who used to greet him respectfully, and bow before him, now turned their backs upon him, and went into their houses. So he began to fear for his life, and as soon as he got to his house he closed fast his gates, and doors, and windows.

Scarcely was this done when all the street was filled with men who began to attack his house. When Jacques saw that he was hard put to it to defend himself, he came to the window bareheaded. "Good people," he cried, "what aileth you? Why be ye so sore troubled against me? Shew me in what manner I have displeased you and I will make amends."

Then the people cried out, "We would know what you have done with the great treasure of Flanders."

Humbly Jacques answered: "Certainly, sirs. Of the treasure of Flanders I have taken naught. Go now patiently to your houses, and come again to-morrow, and I will show you good account of all."

"Nay," they replied, "we will have account now. You shall not escape us so. We know of good truth that you have sent monies into England without our knowledge. Therefore shall you die."

Then Artevelde was sore distressed. "Sirs," he cried, "ye have sworn to defend me against all persons, and now ye would slay me without reason. Ye may do it an ye will, for I am but one man among you all. Ye know right well trade was well-nigh lost in this land, and I recovered it. Also I have governed you in great peace and rest. For in the time of my governing ye have had all things as ye would wish, corn, riches and all other goods."

Then they all answered as with one voice, "Come down to us, and preach not so high."

When Jacques saw that he could not appease them he drew in his head, and closed his window, and so thought to steal away by the back of his house. But already as he turned he found his house was full. About four hundred people had possession of it. And so he was taken and slain without mercy. Thus Jacques Artevelde, who had been so great a master in Flanders, ended his days. "Poor men first raised him up," it was said, "and evil men slew him at the last." And when the news was spread abroad some were sorry, and some were glad. Edward of England was right angry.

CHAPTER 42

PHILIP VI OF VALOIS—BATTLE AND PLAGUE

THE war with England continued. On the whole it now went ill with the French King, and in 1346 the English won a great victory at Crecy.

I think I need hardly tell you the story of that battle, you have read of it so often in English history. Never had France suffered such a terrible defeat. When night fell there gathered round the King and his oriflamme no more than five barons and sixty common soldiers. The rest of his great and splendid army lay dead upon the field, or were scattered in flight.

"Sire," said one of the five knights, "get you gone. It is time. Lose not yourself thus foolishly. If you have lost this time you will gain another time."

Then he took the King's bridle, and led him away by force. And being turned from the field the King rode until he reached a strong castle. There they found the gates closed, and the drawbridge up, for the night was dark and misty. Then the King called aloud for the governor.

He came quickly to the walls, crying, "Who is it that calleth there this time of night?"

"Open your gates," answered Philip. "It is the unfortunate King of France."

The governor knew the King's voice, so he let down the bridge, and opened wide his gates. Then the King entered and with him but five knights. But there he rested only a short time. Then taking guides with him who knew the country, he hastened forth again, and never drew rein until he was safe within the walls of Amiens.

Philip was now greatly disheartened, and he disbanded his troops, for he had no money to pay them. It seemed as if the way to the capital lay open for Edward. But instead of following up his victory by pursuing Philip and marching on Paris, he now turned northward to Calais. Calais was very strongly fortified. It could not be taken by assault. So Edward encamped with his army round it to starve it into surrender.

It was a sad winter for France. Besides the army before Calais another small English army, led by the Earl of Derby, marched through the land destroying and conquering. The people were in utter misery. They were ground down by taxes which if they paid they starved. Yet if they did not pay they were punished in many cruel ways. So miserable were they that it is said some even plotted with the King of England, and were ready to deliver their country into his hands.

At length spring came, and Philip began to think of gathering an army to aid the brave people of Calais who had held out all the long winter. But the nobles were so disheartened by their defeat at Crecy that they were slow to answer the King's call to battle. It was July before the army was ready to march.

To reach Calais was difficult. Philip tried to make friends with the Flemish, for he saw that if he could march through their land he could relieve Calais more easily. He promised them many favors. But although the Flemish had themselves killed their great leader Jacques van Artevelde, they were no more ready than before to yield to the King of France. They did not believe in his promises, and they refused to help him.

So Philip was obliged to march on Calais from the south. But when he came near he saw that the King of England was so strongly posted that to fight him would be impossible. He began then to propose peace.

Philip offered to give up Calais. Edward refused. Philip offered then all the French lands which Edward I had possessed.

"It is too little," said Edward III. At length, seeing nothing he offered would move Edward, Philip sent four knights to ask him to appoint a place where they could fight fairly.

"Sire," said the spokesman, "the King, my master, sendeth you word by us that he is come to do battle with you. But he can find no way to come at you. Therefore he would that you appoint certain of your counsel, and likewise of his, and that they between them advise a place for battle."

But Edward replied sternly: "Say to mine enemy who wrongfully keeps me from mine heritage that I am here, if so ye list. Say that here I have been nigh a whole year, and that he knew right well. He might have come sooner an he would. But he hath suffered me to abide here so long, greatly to my cost and charge. Having done so much to make myself master of Calais, I shall not depart from that which I am on the point of winning. If Philip and his men cannot pass this way, let them try another passage, if they think to come hither."

Then the knights departed sadly and told the French King all that Edward had said. And when the French King saw he could do nothing, he broke up his camp, and marched away in great wrath against Edward.

The brave people in Calais were starving, but their courage was unbroken. When they saw the King and his army come their hearts were glad, for in a few days, they thought, they would be free. When they saw him march away without striking one blow for them, their hearts sank. They could endure no more, and they yielded.

You have read in English history how six brave men gave themselves to save their fellows, and how Queen Phillipa begged on her knees for their lives, and saved them. So I will not tell it again here.

As soon as Edward had possession of Calais he sent all the Frenchmen out of it. From London he brought hundreds of men with their wives and families, so Calais became an English town. It remained so for two hundred years.

Both sides now were tired of this war, and so they made a peace for ten months, and Edward went home to England.

Philip was at peace with England for the rest of his life. But although France had relief from war for a little it suffered from another and terrible evil. This was the plague of the Black Death. This plague spread all over Europe, and when it ceased more than half the people were dead.

At Paris it was so terrible that five hundred people died every day. They died so quickly that it was impossible to bury them in proper graves, and they were laid hastily in great trenches. They were laid there, too, without prayer or chant or service of any kind. For many of the priests fled, leaving to poor orders of monks and nuns the task of caring for the dying and burying the dead. The plague spread like wildfire. Those who were well to-day were dead to-morrow. Those who visited the sick seldom escaped with their lives. Whole towns and villages were left empty and deserted. It was not only the common people who suffered. Great nobles and fine ladies too were attacked by the terrible disease, and even in the King's household many died.

It may interest those of you who have read about English literature to know that this Black Death was also called the Plague of Florence. It was from this plague that Boccaccio's ladies and gentlemen fled. And it was the stories they told each other which Chaucer later on told again in English in the famous Canterbury Tales.

For a year and a half the plague lasted, and when it ceased at last the people went mad with joy. There was nothing but feasting, and marriages, and merrymaking.

In 1350 Philip died. He had not been a good King, and he was a foolish general. He was proud and passionate and a spendthrift. He was careless of his people's happiness and he loved splendor and fine shows more than any King before him. His wars and his splendors cost a great deal of money, and he ground down the people mercilessly to get it.

He ordered a new tax called the *Gabelle*. This was a tax upon salt, which could only be bought from the King's warehouses. All the salt had to be brought to him, and he fixed the price. He fixed it so high that he earned the hatred of rich and poor. Besides this, he laid many other taxes on the people, so that the trade of France was well-nigh ruined.

Yet Philip added a great territory to the kingdom of France. Between the Alps and the Rhone there lies a great tract called the Dauphine. It was called so because the noble who ruled over it carried a dolphin painted on his shield. This ruler sold his land to King Philip, who made his eldest son Dauphin. Ever after the eldest son of the King of France was called the Dauphin, just as the eldest son of our King is called the Prince of Wales.

CHAPTER 43

JOHN II THE GOOD—HOW THE KING QUARRELLED WITH CHARLES THE BAD AND WAS TAKEN PRISONER TO ENGLAND

PHILIP'S son John was thirty-one when he came to the throne. He was just as proud and fond of show as his father, and he was even less a king and a general, although he was eager to win fame as a soldier. He was called John *le Bon*, or the Good. But that does not mean that he was good. It means that he was gay and good-natured with his favorites, and spent his people's money without stint upon them.

Almost at the very beginning of his reign John showed himself cruel and violent. The Constable of France, Ralph Count of Guines, had been taken prisoner by Edward of England. Now after six years he was allowed to return to France in order to find money for his own ransom. Joyfully he hurried to the King, by whom he believed himself much beloved.

John, however, looked darkly at him. "Count," he said, "come with me. I have that to say to you apart."

"Right willingly," answered the Count.

So the King led him into a room alone, and showed him a letter. "Have you before this day seen this letter?" he asked. The Count was troubled, and could not answer.

"Ah, wicked traitor, you well deserve death," cried the King. "And by my father's soul you shall not escape it."

So without more ado, or trial of any sort, the Count was led away, and his head was cut off.

No one knows what was in the letter, or why the Count was thus hastily killed. It was whispered abroad that there was treason in it, and that the Count had promised the town of Guines to King Edward as the price of his freedom. But the truth was never known, for King John did not deign to explain his cruel deed.

The King now possessed himself of all the Count's lands, and gave part of them to Charles de la Cerda, his favorite. Along with that he also gave him some land which belonged to Charles King of Navarre. This made Charles of Navarre furiously angry, and he became John's deadly enemy.

JOHN II THE GOOD—HOW THE KING QUARRELLED WITH CHARLES

Even before this Charles had hated John, although he had married his daughter and was his son-in-law. Besides this, they were nearly related. And had it not been for the Salic Law, Charles might have been King of France. He had indeed a better claim to the French crown than Edward of England. He hoped to make himself King, and cared not by what means. For he was a wild and turbulent Prince, and although he was at this time not more than eighteen his own people had already given him the name of the Bad.

Now that John had given part of the land which rightfully belonged to him to de la Cerda, Charles followed the King's favorite with undying hatred, and sought a means of avenging himself. At length he found a chance. One day de la Cerda was passing through a small town in Normandy. Charles heard of it, and sent a troop of soldiers to attack him.

In dead of night they rode into the town, while Charles awaited their return without the walls. They broke into the house where de la Cerda slept, and killed him in his bed. Then they rode back to where their master waited for them outside the city wall.

At daybreak Charles saw his soldiers come galloping toward him. "Tis done!" shouted the leader from afar, "'tis done!"

"What is done?" asked Charles.

"He is dead," was the reply.

Then, well pleased, Charles rode on his way. He made no secret of what he had done, but openly boasted that he had but executed judgment on de la Cerda because of his many misdeeds.

When, however, the King heard of the murder he vowed vengeance, and gathered his men to fight Charles.

Charles, too, gathered his men, and made friends with the King of England, who willingly offered him help.

Then John took fright. He was not prepared to fight so great an enemy, and he pretended to forgive Charles. Charles then came to the King and kneeling before him humbly begged for pardon. "What I did," he said, "I did not in scorn of the King or of his authority, but because I had good cause to do it."

But the King answered never a word.

Then as Charles rose from his knees two Queens, Jeanne the widow of Charles the Handsome, and Blanche, the widow of Philip VI, came and knelt at John's feet, begging him to forgive Charles.

Still never a word spoke the angry King.

Then the Cardinal of Boulogne stepped forward. In the King's name, and for love of the two Queens who begged for him, he pronounced the pardon of Charles. "But let him beware of such deeds in future," he cried, "for were the murderer the King's son himself, and the victim but the poorest in the land, justice should be done on him."

Once again Charles knelt at the King's feet to thank him for his mercy. Still without a word John rose and passed from the hall. In his heart there was no forgiveness, and he could not bring his lips to speak it.

Even after this make-believe peace Charles still went on stirring up strife against his father-in-law, for he was a scoundrel and a traitor, and he made strife for the love of it. He made friends with the Dauphin, and tried to make mischief between him and the King. He persuaded the Dauphin that his father hated him. So John's hatred of Charles grew ever greater and greater.

"I shall have no joy so long as he is alive," he said, and never ceased to seek for a way of getting rid of his enemy. At length he found it.

One day the Dauphin asked Charles of Navarre and some other friends to a feast. Hardly were they seated at table when the door was thrown open, and the King entered. Before him marched a noble, drawn sword in hand. "Let no man move," he cried, "if he desires not to die by this sword."

At these words all the guests sprang to their feet in fear and astonishment. King John advanced to the table. He seized the King of Navarre and drew him roughly toward him. "Know, traitor," he cried, "that you are not worthy to sit at table with my son. By the soul of my father I shall neither eat nor drink so long as you live."

As he spoke one of the King of Navarre's men threw himself on King John, dagger in hand. But ere he could do the King a hurt he was seized and bound. In a few minutes all the Dauphin's friends were made prisoners. With tears in his eyes the young prince threw himself at his father's feet.

"Ah, my lord," he cried, "you do me great dishonor. What will be said of me, if having prayed King Charles and his lords to feast with me, you do thus? It will be said that I betrayed them."

"Let be Charles," the King replied. "They are wicked traitors. You do not know all that I know."

Then with his prisoners the King rode forth to the field that is called the Field of Pardon. There he caused their heads to be struck off. Only with great difficulty was he persuaded to spare the life of Charles. He, instead of being killed, was put into prison. There at first he lived in constant dread and fear. For five or six times every day and every night he was told that his head was to be cut off, or that he was to be thrown into the river in a sack, at such and such a time.

But although Charles was wild and turbulent he had winning ways. He spoke so gently and kindly to his jailers that they began to be sorry for him, and ceased to torment him with threats of death.

Charles the Bad had made friends with Edward of England, and although at this time there was a truce between France and England it had never been kept very well. Now Edward made the imprisonment of Charles an excuse for breaking it altogether, and the Black Prince marched into France with an army, fighting and plundering near and far. John also gathered a fine army and marched after him. They met at length near Poitiers. And here the Black Prince, who had been marching through France fighting and destroying at will, found opposed to him a French army five or six times as large as his own.

To fight seemed folly. So the Black Prince sent to John offering to give back all that he had won during the war if he were allowed to depart in peace.

But King John was sure of victory, and by no means ready to listen to Prince Edward's terms. As the price of peace he demanded that the Prince and one hundred of his best knights should yield themselves prisoner. To this the English would not listen, and they prepared to fight. It was a fierce battle which now took place, and many a great stroke was given and received.

The English had the best of the position on the slopes of a hill well protected by high hedges. But the French were in far greater numbers, and had King John been anything of a general he could easily have won the victory. As it was, mistake after mistake was made, and the day went against him. Soon the French were in confusion, many were killed, and many fled, among them the three eldest sons of the King.

"Sire, ride forward," said a knight to the Black Prince when he saw the confusion of the French. "The day is yours. Let us seek out the King of France, for he is brave. He will not flee."

And he said truth. Where the fight still held out stood the King of France. For although he was no general he was a brave fighter. To right and to left he swung his battle-axe, dealing death at every blow. By his side his youngest son, Philip, a boy of thirteen, fought as for his life. He would not leave his father as his brothers had done. Now he watched over him lovingly. And above the clang and clash of battle rose his clear childish voice, shrill with excitement "Father, ware right! Father ware left!" he cried as now on one side, now on the other, he saw the enemy come.

Bravely fought the little group of knights about their King. The standard bearer was struck down. The oriflamme fell, and its flame-colored silk was trampled and stained with blood. Still the King fought on while all around him shouted: "Yield! yield! lest you die."

At length a knight forced his way to the King's side. "Yield Sire! I pray you!" he cried, in right good French.

"To whom do I yield?" asked the King. "Where is my cousin the Prince of Wales? If I might see him I would speak with him."

"He is not here," the knight replied. "But yield you to me, and I shall bring you to him."

"Who be you?" said the King.

"A Knight of France. But being banished from the realm of France, I serve the King of England," was the reply. Then the King gave the knight his right gauntlet saying, "I yield me to you."

But when the knight would have led King John to the Prince he could not. For the throng about them was great and every one was eager to claim the honor of having taken the King. He was snatched from one to another, each man crying, "I took him! I took him!" so that the King was like to be torn in pieces.

Then it seemed to John that having yielded he was in greater peril of his life than when he fought. "Sirs," he said, "strive not. Lead me courteously and my son to my cousin the Prince. Strive not for my taking, for I am so great a lord that I can make you all rich."

Then seeing the tumult that was made, two great English lords rode forward. "For what do your strive? " they asked.

"Sirs, "replied one, "it is for the French King, who is taken prisoner. And there be at the least ten knights and esquires who cry that he is theirs."

Then the great lords bade every man stand back. On pain of death they charged them to make no more noise, and taking the King and his son they led them right courteously to the Black Prince.

So ended this sad day for France. All the flower of French knighthood lay dead upon the field, and the King and his youngest son were prisoners.

CHAPTER 44

JOHN II THE GOOD—THE JACQUERIE

THE French King and his youngest son were taken prisoner to England, and the Dauphin Charles became Regent of France. He was only nineteen, and although he was clever he had as yet no knowledge of how to rule. Indeed the misery of the land was such that it would have needed a very wise man to bring it to peace and content. As it was, the country drifted toward civil war. It was a war between Prince and nobles on one side, and commons on the other.

The Dauphin had no money, and in order to get some he called the States-General together. Very many came, especially of the commons. They soon showed that they meant to have a real share in the ruling of the country. They formed themselves into a sort of league, choosing red and blue for their colors. This soon showed how powerful the commoners had become, for red and blue caps were to be seen all over Paris. Knowing their strength they refused to let the Prince have money until he had granted them certain privileges in return.

The Dauphin was helpless, and he granted all they asked. But secretly he sent to his father begging him to refuse his consent. This King John did. Although a captive he believed that he had nothing to do but send an order to his people to have it obeyed. He was mistaken. It was a signal for war.

The leader of the commons was a Paris merchant named Stephen Marcel. He was provost of the city, an office somewhat like that of the Lord Mayor of London.

Marcel and his followers decided that the Prince's counsellors gave him bad advice, and that these evil counsellors must be removed. So in a great company, all wearing hoods, half blue and half red, they set out for the palace.

On the way they met one of the Prince's advisers whom they believed to be one of their chief enemies. At the sight of the great crowd he was afraid, and took refuge in a baker's shop. But the angry citizens followed him there, and killed him without mercy. Leaving him dead they went on to the palace.

Right up to the Prince's chamber marched Marcel. Bitter words he spoke. As bitterly the Prince replied. Then suddenly Marcel put an end to the angry talk.

"My lord," he cried, "do not be alarmed at the thing that you shall see, for so it must be." Then turning to his followers, "Do quickly what you have come to do," he added.

Immediately those about him drew their swords, and seizing upon two of the Dauphin's friends killed them on the spot. So near were they to the Prince that his robes were bespattered with their blood.

At the sight all the gentlemen about the Dauphin fled. Thus left alone he was in much fear lest he too should be killed.

"Sire," said Marcel, seeing his fear, "you are in no danger." But he took off his red and blue hood and gave it to the Prince. For he knew that any one who wore the red and blue hood was safe from peril, for it was the badge of their party. Upon his own head he placed the Prince's cap of black velvet fringed with gold. The bodies of the two slain nobles were then dragged out into the courtyard, and there they lay all day as a warning to the nobles, no man daring to touch them till night fell. Marcel meanwhile went to the town hall, and there spoke to the people.

"What is done," he said, "is done for the good of the realm. For those who are slain were false and wicked traitors."

"We acknowledge the deed, and will support it," cried the merchants and work-people who had gathered to listen to him.

Marcel was now master of Paris. But he did not know how to use his power. He allowed the Dauphin to leave the city and go to Champagne. There many nobles gathered round him ready to fight the rebel merchants of Paris.

But while the merchants and the nobles were making ready to fight each other, war burst forth from another quarter. The peasants rose in rebellion. This rebellion was called the Jacquerie, from Jacques Bonhomme, or James Goodfellow, which is the name given to French peasants, just as John Bull is given to Englishmen.

All through the terrible wars which had made France a desert it was the peasant who had suffered most. And no one cared. They were there to be made use of, to bear burdens. "Jacques Bonhomrae," it was said, "has a broad back. He can stand anything."

But Jacques Bonhomme had been tried too far, and now he brok out into wild and terrible rebellion. Suddenly one day peasants armed with scythes, pruning hooks and heavy sticks rushed to the castle of Beauvais.

They killed the lord and lady and all their children in the most cruel manner. Then they plundered and wrecked the castle.

A second and a third castle were treated in the same way. The peasants were crazy with long suffering, mad with hopeless misery, and thirsting for revenge. Now in their madness they had no mercy. They killed their victims in the most cruel ways, sparing neither women nor children. Often enough had their wives and little ones suffered, now it was the turn of the fine ladies with their spoilt lordlings. Often enough had their cottages gone up in flames, now it was the turn of the castles.

Like wildfire the revolt spread. And wherever the maddened peasants passed they left a track of blood and ashes behind. Never was there insurrection more terrible and savage.

Even if he would Marcel could do nothing to stop the fearful slaughter, for he himself was hard pressed by the Dauphin and the nobles. So he helped and encouraged the peasants, for he thought they were working for him in slaying the nobles.

But at length the mad career of the Jacques was stopped. Before the town of Meaux they were utterly defeated by a small army of nobles. Seven thousand were slain, and when the soldiers grew tired of slaughter they drove the wretched peasants into the river, where thousands of them were drowned.

After this terrible defeat the rebellion fell to pieces at once. The peasants were cowed, and the nobles took an awful revenge. They hanged and burned and hunted the unfortunate rioters like wild beasts. "The nobles of France," says a writer of the time, "did in those days such evil that there was no need for the English to come to destroy the country. In truth those deadly enemies of the realm could not have done what was done by the nobles at home."

CHAPTER 45

JOHN II THE GOOD—HOW STEPHEN MARCEL WOULD HAVE BETRAYED PARIS

CHARLES of Navarre (the Bad), who you remember had been put in prison by John, had by his time escaped. He was as much a scoundrel and traitor as ever. And in those days of terrible confusion and distress he joined in turn whichever side seemed likely to serve his own ends. He made friends with the Jacques, and betrayed them, putting their leader to death with most frightful cruelty. He made friends with Marcel, he made friends with the Dauphin, and betrayed them both. All he wanted was to make himself King of France, and he cared not what means he used.

Marcel had trusted in the help of the peasants, and they were slaughtered and hunted like wild beasts. Now he put his faith in Charles the Bad. The Dauphin was at the gates of Paris. So Marcel begged Charles to go out and drive him away.

Charles went, but instead of fighting the Dauphin he made a league with him, promising to deliver up to him both Paris and Marcel. When Charles and his men returned to the City, having done nothing, the citizens suspected him of treachery and drove him out.

Marcel, too, suspected him, but he felt that without his aid his own cause was lost. For already the people of Paris had lost confidence in him, and many were willing again to submit to the Dauphin. Rather than do that Marcel plotted with Charles. He promised to open the gates of Paris to him, and to mark all the houses in which his enemies lived. And when Charles was once master of Paris, and his enemies had all been killed, he promised to proclaim him King of France.

Thus Stephen Marcel, who had loved his country and his town, ended by betraying both. He had begun with high desires. He had wished to free his people, and curb the too great power of the King. He failed, and became a traitor.

All was ready. But on the very day upon which Marcel had agreed to betray the town the plot was discovered by John Maillart, one of the chief citizens. Quickly arming himself, and gathering his friends about him, he hurried to the gate. For with many others of the citizens he felt that if yield he must he would rather yield to the Dauphin than to Charles the Bad. As the hour of midnight struck with slow deep tones on the great town clock Maillart and his men reached the gate. There already stood Marcel with the keys in his hand.

"Stephen, Stephen" cried Maillart, "what do you here at this hour?"

"John," replied Marcel, "what is that to you? I am here to guard the town of which I have the governing."

"By heaven," said John, "you do not so! You are not here at this hour for any good. That may well be seen by the keys in your hands. I think it is to betray the town that you are come."

"John, you lie falsely!"

"By heaven, traitor, it is you who lie!" returned Maillart, and as he said the words he struck Marcel in the face.

Then turning to his companions he pointed to Marcel and his men, crying, "Kill them, for they are traitors!"

Quickly Maillart's men set upon those of Marcel. Marcel tried to flee, but he could not, for he was surrounded on every side. With his own hand John Maillart struck him so that he fell dead to the ground. Yet once these two had been loving friends.

The fight thus begun went on until all Marcel's followers were killed or taken prisoner. The whole night long the city was in uproar and confusion, for the poor people hardly knew what was happening. But the next morning all the red and blue hoods had vanished, and the following evening the Dauphin rode once more into Paris.

The revolt of the people was over. Their attempt to put some check on the unlimited power of their kings had ended in utter failure. This was partly owing to Marcel having taken as a friend such a selfish traitor as Charles the Bad. Partly because neither Marcel nor the people really knew how to use the power they had fought for.

But although the civil war was at an end there was still Charles the Bad to fight. And for a year longer the war with him lasted. Then Charles the Dauphin and Charles of Navarre made peace.

King John was all this time a prisoner in England. And although he was treated as an honored guest rather than as a prisoner he had grown tired of his splendid exile. So he now made a treaty with Edward giving up to him the better half of France in return for his freedom. When, however, the Dauphin heard of this treaty he utterly refused to agree to it. Not even to free his father would he consent to the loss of half of his kingdom.

But Edward meant to force the Dauphin to yield, and he once more invaded France. The Dauphin had hardly any soldiers, so he avoided a battle. He fortified the towns, and left Edward free to march through the barren, deserted land, already wasted to the utmost by fire and sword. The nobles shut themselves into their strong castles, the townsfolk into their walled cities, and it was upon the peasants again that the misery fell.

But at length Edward grew tired of this sort of warfare which brought him little glory and much loss. He made peace with the Dauphin. This peace was called the Treaty of Bretigny. By it Edward's right to a large part of France was acknowledged. For himself and his son he gave up his claim to the French crown, and in return for a huge sum of money consented to set King John free.

So after four years' imprisonment King John once more returned to France, where he was received with great joy. But three years later one of his sons, who had promised to remain with the King of England until the whole of his father's ransom had been paid, grew tired of living in exile and ran away.

John, who was a true knight if not a great King, was deeply grieved at this. He felt that it was a slur upon his honor and he returned to England. Edward received him as a friend, and made great feasting and rejoicing at his return. In the midst of this display and splendor King John fell ill and died.

He was buried very splendidly in St. Paul's, but a few years later his body was taken to France and buried in the abbey of St. Denis.

CHAPTER 46

CHARLES V THE WISE—HOW AN UGLY BOY BECAME A GREAT KNIGHT

CHARLES V was twenty-seven when in 1364 he came to the throne. It could hardly be called a new reign, for already he had ruled for several years. He was a weak and sickly man, and to begin with had not shown himself a wise ruler. He was nothing of a soldier. He had been among the first to flee at Poitiers. He seemed nothing of a statesman, for during the revolt in Paris he had been unable to hold his own.

But Charles had learned many things since first he tried to rule. Now he earned for himself the name of Charles *le Sage*, or the Wise. He had need of all his wisdom, for he had three great enemies to fight, the King of England, the King of Navarre, and the Free Companies.

These Free Companies were the result of the many wars which had wasted France. When Kings and Princes went to war they no longer trusted only to their own vassals. They hired soldiers who were willing to fight for any king or country so long as they were paid. When the war was over these men were paid off. Their trade was war, and in peace there was nothing left for them to do. So they banded together under their chosen captains, and calling themselves Free Companies roved the country, a terror to all.

In these companies was to be found the very dregs of the armies. There were among them Englishmen, Dutchmen, Germans, Italians, Bretons, Spaniards, indeed people of almost every nation of Europe. They were of every class too. There were nobles among the leaders. Even in the ranks, outcast nobles fought side by side with thieves and cut-throats, runaway priests, peasants, laborers, and all the riff-raff of the towns.

They were absolutely lawless and pitilessly cruel. And as they grew rich in their spoils they lived lives of savage luxury, liking best the richest parts of France, where there was fine pasture for their horses, and good wine for themselves.

Charles fought his three great enemies with his brain. He it was who first taught the knights of France that reckless valor is not enough if one would win. He taught them that it was not enough to dash madly onward with spur in side and lance in rest. He taught them that cunning must be met with cunning, stratagem with stratagem.

Yet Charles never led his army himself. He was the first King who sat at home and from there directed his men. It was his good fortune to know how to choose his generals, and choose them well.

Chief among them was a Breton gentleman, Bertrand du Guesclin, whom Charles made Constable or Commander-in-Chief. du Guesclin was a true knight. Yet no one could be more unlike our ideas of the splendid knights of old. He was not tall and handsome, he was an ugly, broad, thick-set man with a dark-brown face, a flat nose, and green eyes. When he was a little boy he was so ugly that even his mother would not look at him. Although he was the eldest, she would not let him sit at table with his brothers, but made him eat at a small table in a corner of the great hall.

As you may imagine, to be treated like this made Bertrand feel very sore and angry in his little heart. He could not help his ugly face, and it seemed hard to him to be punished for it. And as he was always treated rudely he too became rude and rough.

One day there was a great feast, and as usual Bertrand was seated by himself in the corner eating his heart out with rage at seeing his younger brothers seated at the high table beside their mother. But when he saw her help them first he could no longer contain his fury. Rising from his seat he darted at his brothers. "You eat first while I have to wait like a servant!" he cried. "Get up! This is my place, for I am the eldest."

Quite frightened at the angry tones and fierce flashing eyes of their big brother, the younger ones moved, and Bertrand took his proper place.

As soon as he was seated he began to eat so greedily that the lady Jeanne, his mother, was shocked.

"Bertrand," she cried, "if you do not leave the table at once I shall beat you."

That was more than Bertrand, proud and hurt as he was already, could stand. He rose quickly, and with a great push overturned the table so that bread, and meat, and wine, plates and dishes went rolling on the floor.

Amidst all the confusion an old wise woman came into the hall. "What is it all about?" she asked.

"Ah," replied the lady, "it is my ugly, wicked boy, and I wish he had never been born."

The old wise woman looked kindly at Bertrand, and spoke to him gently. But Bertrand was not used to kindly looks and speech. He thought she was making fun of him. He glared at her darkly from underneath his rough hair. "Let me alone," he said. "If you make fun of me I have a stick, so you had better look out." When his mother heard Bertrand speak so rudely she was more distressed than ever, and began to scold him afresh. But the wise woman stopped her.

"Lady," she said, "you are wrong. This child here whom you treat so badly will be greater than any of his forefathers. There shall not be his equal under heaven, and he shall be loaded with honors by the King of France. They may burn me alive if I speak not the truth."

Bertrand was so pleased to hear any one speak well of him that he was at once sorry for his rudeness. The table being again spread, he seized the dishes from the servants, and himself waited upon the old wise woman. He poured out wine for her to drink, but so clumsily that it ran all over the table. Yet for once Bertrand was not scolded, and from that day he began to take his proper place among the family.

As he grew older his greatest joy was to collect forty or fifty of the village children and make them fight tournaments. Sometimes these mock battles were so fierce that Bertrand returned home with his clothes all torn and blood-stained. And from playing soldier as a boy he grew up to be a soldier and leader of men. One could fill a whole book with stories about du Guesclin, for this ugly Breton knight was full of courage and wisdom. He too, like Charles the Wise, saw that war was not a game, that blind bravery was not enough, and that to succeed one must fight with the brain as well as with the sword. He was as brave as a lion and as true as steel. The Bretons had always been the most rebellious people of France, but in du Guesclin, Breton though he was, Charles found a most faithful friend.

And it was really by his help that Charles got the better of all his three great enemies. The very day that Charles was crowned du Guesclin fought and defeated the King of Navarre. After this he was no longer to be dreaded as he had been. Thus at the very beginning of his reign Charles was well-nigh rid of one enemy.

CHAPTER 47

CHARLES V THE WISE—HOW DU GUESCLIN FOUGHT THE KING'S ENEMIES

AT this time there was civil war in Spain. Pedro the Cruel ruled so badly that his brother Henry rebelled against him and tried to take the throne from him. Henry asked the French King to help him and Charles very gladly sent to him the Free Companies under du Guesclin. Very soon du Guesclin routed Pedro's troops and placed Henry on the throne. Then Pedro appealed to the King of England for help, and the Black Prince came with a great army.

At Navarette there was a great battle fought in which once more the Black Prince was the victor. Du Guesclin was taken prisoner, the soldiers of the Free Companies were killed in thousands, and Pedro the Cruel was once more set on the throne.

The Black Prince was glad to have taken prisoner so powerful an enemy as du Guesclin. All the other great nobles were allowed to ransom themselves. For du Guesclin only Edward would take no ransom. But one day it was told the Prince that every one said he dare not let du Guesclin free because he was afraid of him.

The Prince was angry that any one should think this. So he sent for du Guesclin. "Bertrand," he said, "you shall yourself fix your ransom, be the price as small as you will."

But du Guesclin was proud and as generous as the Prince. "My ransom is a hundred thousand pounds,'* he said.

Even to the Prince this seemed a huge sum. "A hundred thousand pounds?" he cried. "And where do you suppose you will get it?"

"Sire," replied du Guesclin, "Henry of Spain will gladly pay half, Charles of France will gladly pay the second half. And if anything lacks there is not a young girl in all France who will not spin to free me out of your clutches."

So du Guesclin was ransomed. He soon returned to Spain with another army, and once more there was fighting. In the end Pedro was killed, and Henry set upon the throne.

In this way Charles freed Spain from a tyrant and himself from a second of his enemies. For by the time the fighting in Spain was over most of the soldiers of the Free Companies had been killed, and the rest so scattered that they were no longer a danger to France.

But the Black Prince meanwhile got little good out of setting a tyrant on the throne who was so soon driven from it again. For Pedro died without paying the money he had promised to the Black Prince, so that he had not enough to buy food for his soldiers. Want of proper food and the heat of Spain made them all ill, and many of them died. To get money the Black Prince was obliged to tax his own French provinces, so that the people there grew angry and discontented and ready to revolt.

Charles then seeing Edward with a shattered, worn out army, with his vassals in Gascony and Aquitaine in a state of revolt, thought that it was a good time to rid himself of the English King.

So as overlord he sent a letter to Prince Edward commanding him to appear before the peers of France to answer the complaints made against him by his French vassals.

When the Black Prince read the letter he looked fiercely at the messengers. Then he proudly answered: "Sirs, we will right willingly go to Paris to our uncle, but it will be with a helmet on our head, and sixty thousand men at our back."

So there was war once more between France and England. But Charles warned his soldiers not to fight a battle, but rather to protect the strong castles and walled towns.

Things went badly for the English. "Never was there King of France who less took sword in hand," said King Edward. "Never was there King who gave me more to do."

At length the Black Prince became so ill that he was obliged to return home. After that things went from bad to worse, until at length only three towns were left in the hands of the English. Then the Pope persuaded the two Kings to sign a truce for two years. Before the two years were over both the Black Prince and Edward III had died. So Charles was freed from the third of his enemies.

At this time Brittany was without a duke, and Charles thought it would be a good time to add it to the Crown of France. But the Bretons still held proudly to their independence. Charles then told du Guesclin to march against them, and compel them to own the French King as their only lord.

But du Guesclin would not fight against his own countrymen. Rather than that he sent his sword to Charles, giving up the post of Constable of France. But Charles could not thus lose his greatest soldier, and he sent his two brothers to beg him to take again his sword. This du Guesclin did, but he would not fight against Brittany. Instead he turned his sword against some English and Gascons who had formed themselves into a Free Company once more. Du Guesclin set out to besiege them in a castle of which they had taken possession. Thinking it hopeless to fight against so great a soldier the English leader promised to yield if no help came within fifteen days. To this du Guesclin agreed. But before the fifteen days were over he fell ill and died.

Not knowing what had happened the Governor came on the appointed day to give up the keys. He was received, to his indignation, by another leader. This, it seemed to him, was an insult. "Nay," he said, "it was to du Guesclin I yielded. To him only will I give up the keys."

"Du Guesclin is dead," was the mournful reply.

For a moment the haughty Englishman was taken aback, then he said proudly, "I shall still yield to him, I shall lay the keys upon his bier." And so it was done. The English leader knelt beside the coffin of the great soldier and laid upon it the keys of the castle he had held against him. He felt that it was less disgrace to yield to du Guesclin dead than to any man alive.

When the news of du Guesclin's death was known there was great sorrow throughout all France. Both peasants and soldiers wept for his loss. To the soldiers he was a great and glorious captain who had ever led them to victory and who had loved them like a brother. To the people he was a father, for he had cared for the poor and helpless, and given them rest from the terrible Free Companies, and from the yet more terrible English.

The King too grieved. He gave du Guesclin a splendid funeral, and caused his body to be laid among the kings of France in the great Abbey of St. Denis. Before the tomb he placed a lamp which night or day was never allowed to go out.

Two months later the King himself lay dead. His death was a great misfortune for France, for he had done much for his country. He was thoughtful and kindly and always ready to listen to those in trouble. Although he hated war he spent much in fortifying towns and castles to make them strong against the enemy. But he spent little on splendor and fine shows. So in spite of the wars the people's lives grew happier, the country more prosperous.

Charles had found France beggared, he left it rich. He had found France in misery, he left it prosperous. But, alas! he left a child of twelve to succeed him.

CHAPTER 48

CHARLES VI THE WELL-BELOVED— THE MADNESS OF THE KING

CHARLES VI was only a child when in 1380 he came to the throne. His father was hardly dead before his uncles, the Dukes of Anjou, Bourbon, and Burgundy, began to quarrel as to which of them should be Regent. Hardly were these quarrels settled when revolts broke out both in Paris and in Flanders.

The Flemish leader was Philip van Artevelde, son of that Jacques van Artevelde under whom they had risen once before.

The King's uncles were eager to go to fight the Flemish. One day while they were talking about it the young King came in with a hawk on his wrist.

"Ah, my fair uncles," he said, "of what matter is it that ye speak in so great counsel. I would gladly know if I might."

"Sir," replied one of his uncles, "you know it right well. Sir, behold here your uncle, the Duke of Burgundy, who complaineth greatly of them of Flanders. For these false villains of Flanders have driven out the Earl and all his noblemen. And now they lie besieging the town of Oudenarde, where be many gentlemen. Therefore, sir, how say you. Shall ye aid your cousin of Flanders, and conquer again his heritage, the which these proud villains have taken from him?"

"By my faith," said the King, "fair uncles I have great will thereto. I desire none other thing but to be armed, for as yet I never bare armor."

So the King with a great army set out. At Roosebeke a battle was fought in which the Flemish were utterly defeated and their leader slain. Then the King returned to Paris greatly pleased with the result of his first battle.

But the boy King had not only conquered the Flemish, he had cowed the people of Paris. No sooner had he returned than he began to punish them for their late revolt.

Three hundred of the richest citizens were put to death, the others were gathered together and told of all their misdeeds and the punishments they deserved. Then when they were feeling utterly downcast and afraid, the King's two uncles threw themselves at his feet and begged for mercy for the people of Paris. So the King said he would change the punishments to a fine.

This the King's uncles did for their own profit, for they were greedy of money, and the young King only did as he was told.

Two years after this, still delighted with their success in Flanders, Charles VI, or his uncles, decided to strike a great blow at England. So at Sluys an immense fleet was gathered, fourteen hundred ships, great and small, "enough to make a bridge from Calais to Dover."

The nobles came in crowds. They had no fear of ruining themselves in this expedition, for they knew that they would find ten times as much wealth when they had crossed the narrow seas.

They made no doubt of conquering England, and all their talk was how the realm of England should be utterly vanquished, and all the men, women, and children either killed or led prisoners to France. It was to be a second conquest of England, and the nobles meant to do it splendidly. So they painted the masts of their ships with silver, the prows with gold. Silken tents and awnings were spread on the decks, while pennons and flags, decorated with lions and leopards, dragons and unicorns, and all the strange beasts of heraldry fluttered in every breeze. Gold and silver, it was said, were no more spared than if they had rained out of the clouds, or been thrown up by the sea. Not the oldest man living could remember such great splendor and display.

But day by day passed and the splendid fleet did not set out. For one of the King's uncles was not willing to attack England and so delayed coming day after day and week after week. When at length he set out he travelled as slowly as possible. So when he did arrive it was nearly winter. It was too late to think of crossing the stormy sea that year. The great invasion was therefore given up, and all the soldiers sent home until April of next year. But as soon as there was a calm the English sailed across to Sluys, attacked the French fleet, and captured and destroyed a large part of it. So the great invasion never took place at all, and the immense sums of money spent on getting the fleet ready were wasted.

The King's uncles were blamed for the failure of this expedition. It is even said that one of them had been bribed by English money to break it up. In any case the people were very tired of their misrule and now that the King was twenty he made up his mind to rule himself.

So calling together a great assembly of nobles and bishops he thanked his uncles for the care they had taken of his kingdom and told them that he could now govern for himself. The two dukes were quite taken by surprise. They were also very angry. But seeing no help for it for the time being they went away quietly to their own estates.

Charles then called back many of his father's old advisers, he did away with some of the heaviest taxes, and opened Parliament again. This caused great joy among the people. They blamed the dukes for all their past troubles, and believed now that they were at an end.

But Charles was not really a good ruler. He was fond of show and magnificence, of balls and parties, and he spent enormous sums of money. Soon his treasury was empty, and once more the people had to be taxed to fill it.

Meanwhile his two uncles were becoming more and more angry at the rule of the Monkeys, as they called the King's new advisers. So they leagued with the Duke of Brittany to get one of them killed. This was De Clisson the Constable, whom they had long hated.

So one dark night as De Clisson rode homeward he was set upon by a company of armed men. "Death! death!" they cried. "Here you must die!"

"Who speaks such words?" cried he.

"I am Peter de Craon, your enemy, to whom you have so many times done evil. You shall now pay for it all."

De Clisson defended himself as best he could. But presently, severely wounded, he stumbled against the door of a baker's shop. The door gave way and he fell into the dark shop. Thinking he was dead, the murderers rode off as fast as they could.

But De Clisson was not dead. And when the King heard of this attack on his friend he was very angry. "Constable," he cried, "take care of yourself and think of nothing else but to get well. For never was misdeed so punished or dearly paid for as this shall be. It is my affair."

Then, finding that Peter de Craon had taken refuge with the Duke of Brittany, the King set out to fight the duke. His two uncles dared not oppose him, but they did everything they could to prevent the war.

It was the beginning of August when the King set out and the weather was very hot. He had been ill and his doctors warned him that he was not yet fit to go to battle. But Charles would not listen to their advice.

The day was sultry, the roads were dusty. The King rode alone so that he might not be troubled by the dust of the horses' feet.

Suddenly as he rode through the forest a man with bare head and feet, and clad in a poor rough coat sprang out from among the trees. His hair was long and shaggy, his eyes gleamed with excitement, and dashing at the King's horse he seized the bridle.

"King," he cried, "ride no farther! Turn! Turn! you are betrayed."

These words startled the King. He trembled and knew not what to do. But at once his attendants rode up and forced the man to let the bridle loose. They saw that the man was but a poor mad creature. So they let him go. But for a long time he continued to follow the King at a distance, calling out, "You are betrayed! You are betrayed!"

The King and his followers rode onward. By midday the wood was cleared and they rode through a sandy plain. The sun beat down upon their heads mercilessly.

There was no shelter and the air seemed to quiver with heat. The country round was still and silent save for the hot hum of insects.

Behind the King rode two pages, one carrying his lance, the other his helmet. The heat was so great that the one who held the lance fell asleep as he rode. The lance slipped from his hand and fell clattering against the helmet held by his companion. In the sultry quiet the clash sounded loud and clear.

The King started. Drawing his sword he cried out wildly: "Forward, forward! At the traitors!"

Turning, he rushed madly upon his pages. His eyes were wild and wide and unseeing. He struck about him furiously, killing and wounding several of his followers before he could be disarmed. At length one of them caught him from behind and laid him gently on the grass by the roadside.

The poor King was mad. And so for the rest of his life he remained, now and again coming to his right senses for a short time, only to be plunged once more into deeper darkness.

CHAPTER 49

CHARLES VI THE WELL-BELOVED—THE BATTLE OF AGINCOURT AND AFTER

THE power was once more in the hands of the King's uncles. And for the rest of the reign the country was torn asunder by quarrels between them and their sons and the King's brother, the Duke of Orleans.

These quarrels became so bitter that at length the Duke of Burgundy, who was the youngest and most powerful of the three, caused the Duke of Orleans to be slain in the streets of Paris. So evil were the times that the Duke of Burgundy was not punished. He fled away for a time and when he returned he was received with joy by the people. But the young Duke of Orleans was eager to avenge his father's murder. So there was war between the Orleanists and the Burgundians.

The Orleanists took the name of Armagnacs from the Count of Armagnac, whose daughter the Duke had married. They wore for a badge a white scarf with a St. George's Cross, while the Burgundians wore a red scarf with a St. Andrew's Cross.

Each side tried to get possession of the King, and of his son the Dauphin, who was now supposed to govern. Now the Armagnacs were in power, now the Burgundians, but whichever was uppermost there was misery for the people. For they did little but suppress the people and kill and put to death those whom they hated. Those were sad days for France.

All this time the war with England had been carried on in a halfhearted way. But now Henry V had come to the throne. He was young and ambitious and, like Edward III, he laid claim to the crown of France, and while the French were thus quarrelling among themselves seemed to him a good time to press his claim. So he asked for the hand of the French King's daughter Catherine in marriage, a large sum of money as her dowry, and all Normandy and much of France besides.

His demands were refused; so gathering a great army he sailed over to France. He landed near Harfleur and after a month's siege took the town.

But this success was of little use to Henry. For already he had lost half of his army from wounds and sickness. He saw that it was impossible to push his conquest farther that year. So he resolved boldly to march across French land from Harfleur to Calais and there spend the winter.

It was a miserable march, for many of the men were sick, and the autumn was wet. Hungry and worn they tramped day by day through the mud and rain.

Had the French fallen on them they must surely have been cut to pieces. But day after day went past and they saw no French army. For the French nobles had been so busy with their own quarrels that they were slow in arming against the English.

But at length the two armies met near the castle of Agincourt. All that night it rained; most of the French, both men and horses, had no protection from it, and passed the night in the middle of muddy, ploughed fields. Their feet sank in the mud, while the rain beat upon them and the wind chilled them to the bone.

When morning dawned they were already exhausted. The English, on the other hand, although they were a worn and ragged, hungry company, had at least been under cover. They were dry and rested.

In those days both men and horses were covered with heavy plate armor, and now, finding it impossible to ride thus heavily weighted over the soaked fields, most of the French knights sent away their horses and resolved to fight on foot. So ankle deep in mud they stood awaiting the attack. Among them were the greatest nobles of France. In glittering array of steel, they stood, their embroidered surcoats and gay pennons making a brave show.

Against them was a mere handful of ragged, hungry men. King Henry hesitated to fight. At the last minute he sent to the French offering to make peace. The French leader said he would grant it if Henry would give up all claim to the crown. This Henry refused to do, and the battle began.

Uttering a loud cry, the English archers advanced a few steps. The French remained still.

Again the English shouted, and again advancing a few steps let fly their arrows.

Then the French horsemen advanced. But as they rode over the sticky, heavy mud, the first stumbled and fell, those who followed fell upon them, and soon the whole field was a scene of utter confusion. The English archers then threw away their bows and, seizing swords and battle-axes, rushed upon the French, slaying them at will.

The French were utterly defeated, and among the ten thousand who lay dead, eight thousand at least were of noble blood. Not even at Crecy or Poitiers had the French suffered as at Agincourt.

But even after this great victory Henry did not feel himself strong enough to enforce his claim to the French throne. So he marched on to Calais and set sail for England.

Thus once more France was left to the fight for power which raged between Burgundians and Armagnacs round its poor mad King. But Henry of England had no mind to give up his claim to the French throne, and he soon returned.

He overran Normandy, took Rouen, and was marching on Paris. Then the rival princes agreed to make friends and join against this common foe.

The Duke of Normandy, John the Fearless, was asked to meet the Dauphin, who was now of the Armagnac party. They met on a bridge across the Seine. In the middle of the bridge a pavilion had been built. Into this each of the princes entered with only a few followers.

As he came into the presence of the Dauphin John the Fearless took off his velvet cap and bent his knee. "Sire," he said, "I am come at your command. You know the desolation of the kingdom which will one day be yours. As for me, I am ready to give for it myself, and my goods, my vassals, my subjects, and my friends. Do I say well?"

"Fair Cousin," replied the Dauphin, "you say so well that no one could say better. Rise and be covered."

But soon the talk which had begun in friendly wise grew bitter. "It is time!" suddenly cried one of the Dauphin's men, and struck the Duke with his battle-axe.

The Duke fell to the ground, and soon lay dead, pierced by many wounds. All his attendants were also slain, only one escaping. Thus was the Duke of Orleans avenged.

It is not known whether or no the Dauphin knew that this murder was intended. But whether he knew or not it did his cause much harm. What neither Crecy nor Poitiers nor Agincourt had done, the murder of the Duke of Burgundy did. It gave the crown of France to the King of England. For John the Fearless left a son, afterward called Philip the Good. He was eager to avenge his father's death, so he turned to the King of England and offered to help him. The Queen, too, who was not a good woman, and hated her son, the Dauphin, offered to help Henry

The young Duke and the Queen were so powerful for the time that on May 21, 1420, the treaty of Troyes was signed. By this treaty Henry V of England married the French Princess Catherine and became Regent of France. It was arranged that as soon as Charles died Henry should become King, and that France and England should be one kingdom forever after.

So weary were the people of constant war and struggle that many of them were really glad when this wicked and foolish treaty put an end to them.

But Henry of England was never to be Henry of France; for two years later, in 1422, he died, still young and in the very height of his splendor. He left a baby boy of only nine months to succeed him.

Two months later Charles VI also died. He was but a poor mad old man, yet the people wept for him. In spite of all the miseries they had suffered during the forty-two years he had borne the empty title of King, to them he was still the Well-beloved.

CHAPTER 50

CHARLES VII THE VICTORIOUS—THE STORY OF THE MAID OF ORLEANS

THE unhappy, mad old King lay dead. The new King was proclaimed. To all the winds of heaven the French heralds cried, "May God have mercy and pity on the soul of King Charles VI, and grant long life to Henry our sovereign lord, King by the grace of God of France and England."

John Duke of Bedford came to France to rule for the baby King. But there were two Kings in France. For though the Burgundians and the English had proclaimed Henry, the Orleanists had proclaimed the Dauphin. "Long life to Charles VII," they cried, "by the grace of God King of France." He made Bourges his capital, and so the English called him scornfully "King of Bourges."

It was little wonder that many of the French should prefer for a King one of their own nation. Yet Charles VII was no hero. He was now nineteen, but he was idle and frivolous, caring more for pleasure than for the troubles and dangers of a throne.

Careless and indolent though he was, the people fought for him. But at first they had no success, and it seemed as if France was fated to have an English King.

The English were besieging Orleans and the people were so hard pressed that they were ready to yield. Charles was thinking of running away to Scotland or to Spain, when a great change came over his fortunes.

Far away from the sounds of war in a little village called Domremy there lived a young girl called Joan d'Arc. The wars which had made France a desert had never reached this village, but soldiers came from time to time who told the sad story of loss and ruin. Men and boys left the village to go to fight. Some never returned. Others returned wounded and disheartened. They all told the same tale of towns in ruins, of desolate country, of lost battlefields red with the blood of Frenchmen.

As Joan listened her heart beat fast, tears rose to her eyes. She longed to do something to save her country and her King. But she was only a weak girl of seventeen. She could neither read nor write. What could she do but pray? So she prayed very earnestly to God and His saints that they would help her beloved country.

Joan thought and prayed so much that at length it seemed to her that she heard voices whisper to her. "Joan," they said, "go and deliver the King of France and give him back his kingdom. Put on the courage and armor of a man and lead the armies to victory."

So Joan cut off her long hair, dressed herself in armor, and mounting upon a war horse she set out upon the long and dangerous journey half across France to Chinon, where the Dauphin was. It was a terrible journey for a young girl to venture upon; for the whole country was full of rough soldiers and robbers, but Joan was not afraid.

She reached Chinon in safety and after much trouble was allowed to see the Dauphin. Among all his courtiers she knew him at once, although to prove her he tried to hide himself among them.

Joan went straight to him and knelt. "I am not the King," he said; "there he is," he added, pointing to one of his attendants.

"Nay," replied Joan, "it is you and no other. Gentle Dauphin, why will you not believe me? I tell you God has pity on you and your kingdom and your people. Give me soldiers and I will raise the siege of Orleans and lead you to Reims to be crowned. For it is God's good pleasure that the English be chased from the land and the kingdom be yours."

Neither the Dauphin nor his court would at first believe Joan. But she was so earnest and so gentle, and yet so ready with an answer for every doubter, that at length she won the faith of all who listened to her. So Joan was given a company of soldiers. She chose for her standard a flag of white silk sewn with golden fleur de lis. Upon one side was Jesus blessing the fleur de lis, upon the other the Virgin Mother and the words "Jesus Maria."

Thus clad in shining armor, with her white flag carried before her, Joan set out for Orleans.

As soon as she arrived she put fresh courage into the hearts of the defenders. She was a simple peasant girl who knew nothing of war, yet the rough soldiers gladly followed her. They ceased to drink and swear in her presence. They looked up to her as to one divine and were ready to die for her. They knew she would win. And she did.

Ten day s after Joan reached Orleans the English broke up their camp and marched away. They said she was a witch. They could not fight against witches.

BESIDE THE ALTAR STOOD JOAN, HER WHITE STANDARD IN HER HAND.

But Joan was no witch. She was a simple, earnest woman filled with splendid purpose and splendid faith.

When it became known that Orleans was relieved there was rejoicing from one end of France to the other. Wherever men were true to their King, solemn services were held in the churches, the people lit bonfires, and poets sang mocking songs about the English.

Ever since Joan has been known as the Maid of Orleans. Yet in the midst of all this excitement Charles remained idle and hopeless. Joan went to him and he received her with great honor. But it was in vain that she tried to pour into him something of her own grand purpose. She begged him to come to Reims to be crowded. He remained cold and indifferent. The way was long, he said, and beset by enemies; he had no money either for the journey or for the grand ceremony.

"'Gentle Dauphin," she said, kneeling before him, "do not hold such long counsel. Come to Reims with all speed and take your crown."

Meanwhile Joan returned to fight. She took several towns and won a battle. Everywhere the people rejoiced. They ran to kiss her hands or touch her armor as she passed. They knelt to kiss the footprints of her horse's hoofs.

At length Charles set out for Reims. It was a triumphal progress. Town after town opened their gates to him as he passed. For the love of the Maid they laid down their arms and greeted him as King. As he rode through the streets of Reims the people thronged around him, cheering and sobbing aloud for joy.

In the great Cathedral the crown was placed upon his head, he was anointed with the holy oil, and once more proclaimed King of France. Beside the altar stood Joan, her great eyes shining with holy joy, her white standard in her hand. "It has been through the strife," she said looking at it lovingly, "it is right that it should have the honor."

CHAPTER 51

CHARLES VII THE WELL-SERVED—THE END OF THE HUNDRED YEARS' WAR

THE King was crowned, but all was not yet done, for there still remained many English in the land. Paris was in their hands. Paris the capital must be freed, and with the same splendid courage and purpose which had led her until now, Joan marched to Paris. On the way town after town yielded to her, but Paris itself she could not take. For she was ill aided, indeed wellnigh betrayed by the languid, idle King. With a heavy heart Joan turned back from Paris.

Next spring she again led her soldiers into the field. But at the siege of Compiegne she was wounded and taken prisoner. Then for a year Joan suffered cruel imprisonments. Both the Burgundians and the English hated her. They feared her, too. She was a witch, they said, and it was from the Evil One she drew her power. So they resolved that she should die. After a long cruel and unfair trial they condemned her to death. On May 30, 1431, she was burned to death in the marketplace of Rouen.

Alas for the glorious Maid of Orleans!

Yet the King for whom Joan had worked and suffered did nothing. He raised not a finger to save her from a horrible prison and a ghastly death.

Now that the witch was dead the English and Burgundians hoped that all would go well for them. But they were mistaken. Joan they had killed, but they could not kill her work.

For in one year this simple girl changed the fate of France. She awoke in hearts of Frenchmen something unknown before—love of country—patriotism. In one year she carved for herself such a name that wherever brave deeds are told the name of Joan of Arc is known. In the heart of every true Frenchman who reads the story of Joan, must rise the cry " France forever!" And surely it may find an echo in the heart of every generous Briton. She takes so high a place among the great men and women of the world that wherever noble deeds and noble lives are held in honor the name of Joan of Arc is reverenced.

Everywhere now the English began to lose. The Burgundians, tired of the strife, made peace with King Charles, and thus the quarrels between

Burgundians and Armagnacs, which for twenty-five years had torn France asunder, were at an end. The English were driven out of Paris and the King entered in triumph. And now Charles showed himself in a new light. He was no longer idle and listless, but became a wise and skillful ruler, and did much for the good of his people and country. At length in 1445 a truce with England was signed.

A few years later this truce was suddenly broken and the last campaign of the Hundred Years' War began. When it ended there remained to the English nothing of their once great French possessions save Calais.

Charles VII was the first king to have a standing army—that is, an army which was always at command. Instead of hiring a lot of soldiers when he went to war and paying them off when it was over he kept his soldiers and paid them all the year round. This was of great benefit to the country, for bands of idle soldiers no longer strayed about, a terror to peaceful folk.

Charles made many other good changes in the realm, and he found so many people willing to do his bidding and help him that he came to be called Charles the Well-served. Among those who served him best was Jacques Coeur, a wealthy merchant of Bourges. When the King was penniless, with no money to pay his soldiers to fight the English, Jacques Coeur came to him.

"Sire," he said, "all that I have is yours." So the King took Jacques's money and used it. Jacques soon rose to great power. He took charge of the money of the kingdom and made those under him give account of how it was spent. Soon the money affairs of the kingdom were in a better state than they had ever been.

But Jacques made many enemies, for the nobles hated this rich merchant who had such power with the King. They hated him because of his wealth. He had so much money that "As rich as Jacques Coeur" became a proverb. So they began to whisper all sorts of evil about him. Charles had no spark of gratitude in his being. He forsook Jacques Coeur as he had forsaken Joan of Arc. Charles believed, or pretended to believe, the evil things which were said of Jacques, and, forgetting all he owed to him, cast him into prison. For three years Jacques remained a prisoner. Then with the help of some faithful friends he escaped. He fled from the country, and two years later died in exile.

But Charles, who had shown himself so ungrateful to others, had himself to suffer from ingratitude. His last years were troubled and made bitter by the plots and revolts of his son Louis the Dauphin. Louis went against his father in every way he could, till at length Charles hated him. At length, Louis fled from his father's anger and took refuge with the Duke of Burgundy. "Ah," said Charles when he heard of it, "he has taken into his house a fox who will soon steal his chickens." By this he meant that Louis would repay the Duke's kindness with treachery.

Year by year the King's unhappiness increased. By degrees he lost faith in all his friends, and at length believed himself to be surrounded by rebels who sought to poison him. He feared poison in everything. At last he refused to eat or drink. In vain his friends told him it was madness to cause his own death by fear of dying. In vain his favorite son, Charles, tasted the food before him to prove that it held no poison. The King would listen to no one. For eight days he touched no food and at length died of starvation. He was fifty-eight and had reigned thirty-nine years. The black blot of ingratitude can never be wiped from the name of Charles VII. But apart from that he did much for this country, and left the kingdom prosperous and at peace.

CHAPTER 52

LOUIS XI THE SPIDER—HOW THE KING FOUGHT WITH CHARLES THE BOLD

CHARLES VII was succeeded by his son Louis XI, who was thirty-eight years old when he came to the throne. He was an ugly little man, with a wizened face, a nose much too big, and wonderful shining eyes.

His legs were thin and bent so that he shambled in his walk. Added to this, he dressed very badly. While the nobles around him were gorgeous in cloth of gold and sparkling with gems, Louis, as a writer of the time says, "wore apparel marvelous uncomely, and was clad in very coarse cloth."

He was so poorly dressed that the country people when they saw him were greatly disappointed. "Is that the King of France!" they would say; "the greatest King in all the world? Why, everything he has on, horse and all, isn't worth twenty francs!"

Yet for all his shabby clothes and mean little body no one could despise Louis. His piercing eyes and strange smile, of which no one could tell the meaning, yet which made every one uncomfortable, saved him from that. Few, if any, loved him. All feared him. "He was the most terrible of all the Kings of France," said one who knew him.

He was the most terrible and one of the greatest. He greatly enlarged the boundaries of France, he greatly increased the power of the King, lessened the power of the nobles, and left the kingdom at peace. Louis was a great statesman. He knew very well what he wanted and he liked better to gain his ends by wile than by open war. He never fought if he could avoid it, which was a good thing. But he never took the straight path if there was a crooked one, which was a bad thing. He was sly and subtle and false. He would promise anything to get his way, and then without a qualm break his promises when it suited him. He had spies everywhere. No one knew better than he how to make friends quarrel, and when to profit by these quarrels.

Louis had no pity. He loved revenge and he knew how to wait for it. He never hesitated to send to death or to some yet more fearful imprisonment those he hated. On the other hand, he loaded with money and honors those who served him well. He had no belief in faith or honor, but thought that every man could be bought. And if the price was high he was quite willing to pay it.

With all his cruelty and his treachery Louis was pious. But he treated God and heaven as he treated men. He believed of them as he believed of men, that they could be bought. He wanted to have heaven and all the powerful saints and angels on his side. So he loaded them with presents. He built new churches, he restored others. He presented splendid altars, golden vessels, jeweled vestments to many of the saints. He went upon pilgrimages, and he always wore a shabby old pilgrim's hat, which was stuck round with leaden images of saints, to which he would pray at any moment when he thought his schemes were going wrong.

But in spite of his cleverness when he first became King, Louis tried to get his way too quickly. And he had not been long upon the throne before he found that he had made enemies of every one. The nobles and the clergy and the townspeople were all angry with him. With some of the greatest nobles in the land at their head they joined together in what they called the League of the Public Good and declared war against the King.

Chief among Louis's enemies was Charles the Bold, the son of that Duke of Burgundy who had befriended Louis when he was Dauphin. Louis had made an enemy of Charles through persuading the Duke to give up a number of towns which Charles looked upon as his inheritance. Thus the words of King Charles VII came true and the Duke of Burgundy found that the fox had stolen his chickens.

Near Paris a battle took place between the League and the King. The victory was uncertain, but the King was able to get possession of Paris. And having possession of Paris he began to make terms with the leaders of the revolt. To each one Louis granted what he asked. Some got money, some got lands, some posts of honor. No one was refused. Thus Louis broke up the League of the Public Good. He did not mean to keep his promises. He only meant to bide his time and take back from each one in turn all that had been granted to him. It would be much easier to fight them one by one, he thought, than all at once.

The King's own brother had been among the rebels and he had received Normandy as his share of the spoil. Louis had no right to give away Normandy, as by a law of Charles V it could not be separated from the French crown. But Louis never meant his brother to keep it. Very soon he found a cause of quarrel with the Duke, marched into Normandy, and in a few weeks was master of the province.

When Charles the Bold heard of this he was furiously angry. He made the Duke's quarrel his own and demanded that Normandy should be restored to him.

Charles was a blustering soldier. Louis was a subtle, cunning statesman. He had no wish to fight, so he proposed instead that they should meet and talk matters over.

To this Charles the Bold consented and the King and Duke met at Peronne. The Duke received the King with every honor, and for a few days all went well. But meanwhile the King had forgotten that he had sent messengers to the people of Liege encouraging them to revolt against Charles their Duke.

Then one morning news was brought to Charles that the people of Liege had revolted against him. When Charles heard that he was very angry.

"Ah, this traitor King," he cried, "he has come then under a false pretense of peace merely to deceive me. By St. George! he and these wicked folk of Liege shall pay dearly for it."

He commanded that the gates of the town should be shut. The King found himself a prisoner. For three days Charles raged up and down. He was in such fury that at first he thought of nothing less than killing the King or shutting him up in prison for the rest of his life. But by degrees his anger cooled.

Meanwhile Louis was very much afraid. But he lost no chance of making friends among the servants of the Duke, and he scattered money and promises all around. The third night after the news came the Duke never undressed at all. He lay down on his bed in his clothes, and every now and again he got up and paced his room in angry thought. When morning came he seemed more angry than ever. But at length he allowed himself to be persuaded to more peaceful thoughts. He decided that the King should be set free on certain conditions. One was that he should give up a large part of France to his brother the Duke of Berry, another that he should go with Charles to quell the revolt of Liege which he had himself encouraged.

When the Duke came into the King's presence he bowed low and humbly. But his look was furious, and when he spoke his words were bitter, and his voice trembled so with rage that it seemed as if he would burst out again in fury.

Sharply he asked the King if he would swear to the treaty and keep it.

"Yes," replied Louis, "and I thank you for your good will."

"And you will come to Liege and help me to punish these traitors?'

"Yes, truly," said the King, "for I am astonished at their wickedness."

Then a holy relic which Louis always carried about with him and which he reverenced above all things was brought out. And upon this the treaty was sworn. Whereupon all the bells in the town rang for joy and all the people were right glad.

The next day the King and Duke set out for Liege. In a short time the revolt was put down and the Duke avenged himself with dreadful cruelty. Then the King took his leave with a great show of friendship and much flattery. "Next summer we must meet again," he said. "I will come to visit you in your duchy, and we will pass a week joyously together making good cheer."

But the King's words were a mockery. Nothing was farther from his thoughts than to place himself again in the power of the terrible Charles. There could be no real peace or friendship between the two. If there was peace to-day there was war to-morrow. Louis had many enemies and Charles sided against the King with each one of his enemies in turn. The League of the Public Good, the Duke of Berry, the Duke of Brittany, the King of England, all were the friends of Charles so long as they were the enemies of Louis.

But although the King was constantly at strife with Charles he had leisure enough to get rid of others of his enemies by craft and wile. These were means which he liked better to use than the sword. He was like a great spider, it was said, who spread his nets in the hope of catching flies. So in one way or another he got the better of all his enemies.

CHAPTER 53

LOUIS XI—THE TROUBLES OF THE DUCHESS MARY

KING Edward IV was now on the English throne. He made up his mind once more to claim the crown of France. Both Charles of Burgundy and the Duke of Brittany promised to help him, and in 1475 Edward landed at Calais with a great army. But to his surprise and disgust, instead of finding a large army of Burgundians ready to join him he found only a very few. For Charles had been away fighting a useless war in Germany and had thus lost many of his men.

The King of England had already sent a letter of defiance to Louis in which he claimed his realm of France. But Louis did not greatly care for Edward's threats. He thought that the friendship between the Duke and the King would not last long. And he was right. Misunderstandings soon arose, the English murmured of treachery, and Charles marched away to his own land and was seen no more.

Almost as soon as Charles had gone a herald arrived from Louis. He offered to make peace and pay Edward a large sum of money to go away.

The English being already weary of the expedition were glad to accept Louis's offer.

Upon a bridge over the Somme the two kings met; right across the bridge there was placed a wooden grating such as one might put to separate wild beasts, This was done because Louis remembered how in his father's lifetime the Duke of Burgundy had been slain at the Bridge of Montereau.

To the one side of the grating came the little, clever, shabbily dressed King of France. To the other came the tall, handsome, splendidly dressed King of England.

When Edward came near the grate he took off his black velvet cap, wherein was set a splendid jewel made like the French fleur de lis, and bowed low. Louis too bowed low. "Cousin," he said, "you are heartily welcome. Praised be God that we be met here to such good purpose,"

The King of England answered in right good French. Then the two kings came close to the grating and kissed each other. The talk went pleasantly enough, although Edward called himself King of France and England and gave Louis merely the title of Prince. For Louis cared little for such empty forms. To get rid of the King of England was all he desired. "There is nothing in the world I would not do," he said, "to cast the King of England out of my realm except give him an inch of land."

So Louis promised to pay Edward a yearly sum of money, a seven years' peace was signed, and a marriage between the little Dauphin and Edward's eldest daughter was arranged to take place as soon as the children were old enough. Then after being feasted and flattered for a few days more Edward sailed home to England. "I love the King of England very much," said Louis, "when he is on the other side of the sea."

Seeing himself thus forsaken by his friend the King of England, Charles the Bold hastened also to make peace with Louis. This Louis was willing to do. But Charles must always be fighting. He wanted to conquer Switzerland and add it to his own lands. So he marched away to fight the Swiss.

After this the fortunes of Charles became always worse and worse, and less than two years later he was killed in battle.

When Louis heard the news he was delighted to be thus rid forever of his greatest enemy, and he at once began to scheme to add the whole of Burgundy to France. For Charles had left no son, but only a daughter named Mary.

An easy way would have been to marry the young duchess to the Dauphin. The Dauphin, you remember, was already engaged to the little English princess. Louis would have cared little for that. But unfortunately for his schemes, the Dauphin was only seven and Duchess Mary a grown-up lady of twenty.

Still Louis let it be known that he intended they should marry. Then he announced that as a woman could not inherit the duchy, Burgundy henceforth belonged to the Crown of France.

It was quite in vain for Duchess Mary to say that Burgundy did not belong to the Crown of France and that a woman could inherit it. The King took possession of it.

Mary had still all Flanders left to her. Then, while swearing that he would guard her rights as if they were his own, Louis deceived Mary and robbed her, stirred up strife among her people and plotted so that two of her wisest counsellors were put to death.

At length driven to distraction, wearied with struggling against so powerful and wily a foe, Mary married her marriage; Maximilian of Austria, son of the Emperor Frederick III.

Maximilian at once began to fight with Louis. But the sword was not the weapon with which the wily King liked to fight. He liked much better to fight with craft and wile. So after being defeated at Guinegate he made peace. And so clever was he that he managed to keep all the land he had seized.

Three years later Mary of Burgundy died, leaving two little children. As long as Mary lived the Flemish had looked upon Maximilian as their ruler. Now that she was dead they thought that he had no longer any right over them. So they appointed Regents to take care of the children and rule for them until they were old enough to rule themselves.

This made Maximilian very angry. He had no money and few soldiers, but he tried to force the Flemish to give him the power. The Flemish then turned to their old enemy, the King of France, for help. This Louis very gladly gave them, proposing that the little daughter of Mary and Maximilian should marry the Dauphin.

Little Margaret was not yet three, but the Flemish agreed that she should go to live in France until she was old enough to be married. And as a wedding gift Louis managed to get still more counties and towns which had belonged to the Duke of Burgundy. In return Louis gave up all claim to the rest of Flanders, and so there was peace once more.

But this peace nearly made another war. For the Dauphin was already promised in marriage to the Princess Elizabeth of England. But Louis did not care for that. He was less afraid of the English over the sea than of the Flemish on his borders. Besides, he wanted to make France larger. When, however, Edward IV heard that Louis had broken his word and insulted him he was very angry. He began to make ready to invade France, and only his sudden death prevented the war.

By this time Louis too was near death. He lived in daily terror of being killed by one or other of the many he had cruelly wronged and oppressed. So he shut himself up in a gloomy palace called Plessis-les-Tours. This was more a fortress and prison than a palace, and was surrounded by a deep ditch and thick strong walls. The entrance was guarded by bolts and bars and gates of iron. Night and day soldiers were ever on the lookout, and they had orders to shoot any one who, without express leave from the King, might come near after the gates were shut. The trees round the castle hung thick with the dead bodies of people who had been hanged because they were found near. The prisons were full of innocent prisoners.

No nobleman or any great person was allowed to live in the castle. Even the Queen and her children were sent away. The King often changed his servants, for he suspected every one, and his chief companions were two men of mean birth, scoundrels both, who had helped him often in his craft and wiles.

Thus in gloomy solitude the King dragged out his last days. His little form, wrapped in a rich robe of crimson silk edged with fur, he crouched in his chair, "seeming rather a dead body than a living creature, for he was leaner than a man would believe." There he sat thinking out schemes for making the world believe that he was still vigorous and dangerous. He caused himself to be more spoken of than ever king was, and all for fear lest men should think him dead. Few saw him, but when men heard of his doings they feared him and little thought that he was sick unto death.

He longed passionately to live. At times in weak and trembling tones he would pour out passionate prayers to the leaden saints upon his cap for longer life. Again he would drag his faltering steps along the dimlit gallery to the chapel beyond, there to implore the help of the holy Virgin. But all his prayers and tears were of no avail, and on the August 25, 1483, he died.

Louis was a terrible king, but he was a great king. He broke the power of the nobles, enlarged the borders of his work France, and left the country at peace and great among the countries of Europe.

CHAPTER 54

CHARLES VIII THE AFFABLE—THE DREAMS OF GLORY AND DOMINION

LOUIS XI was succeeded by his son Charles who was a boy, barely fourteen years old. Besides being naturally stupid he was also very ignorant for his years, for Louis did not like him, and had taken no trouble to have him taught. When he came to the throne he could not read, and all the Latin Louis had allowed him to learn was one sentence meaning "who does not know how to dissemble does not know how to reign." It was Louis's own guide in ruling.

Fourteen was by law the age at which the Kings of France came of age. Thus by law Charles had the right to rule in his own name. But of course he was really too young to rule. So, as might be expected, a struggle for the real power began at once. The struggle was between Princess Anne, Charles VIII's elder sister, and Louis Duke of Orleans, the husband of his younger sister.

This Duke of Orleans was the grandson of the Duke of Orleans who made so much trouble during the reign of Charles VI. He was therefore the King's cousin.

Anne was a clever woman. Even her father, Louis XI, acknowledged that. She was the least foolish woman in the kingdom he said, since clever women there were none. She succeeded in getting all the power, and she used it well. She set free many of the wretched prisoners shut up in iron cages by her father. She restored lands to many from whom they had been unjustly taken. She brought back others who were banished, and she caused to be hanged Louis's two evil advisers. She ruled so well that the people called her Madame la Grande, or The Great Lady. Thus once again a woman ruled in France. For it is strange that the French, who made such a point of the Salic Law should have been again and again ruled by women as regents.

Finding that Anne had all the power, the Duke of Orleans rose in revolt. He was helped by the Duke of Brittany and several lesser nobles. They were, however, defeated, and the Duke of Orleans was taken prisoner. Anne kept him prisoner for three years. She shut him up in a strong castle where at night he was made to sleep in an iron cage like a wild beast.

Soon after the Duke of Orleans was taken prisoner the Duke of Brittany died. Brittany was the last of all the great feudal lands to remain free. Ever since the days of Clovis the Dukes of Brittany had given trouble to the Kings of France. Now Anne of France saw a chance of making an end of that, and of joining Brittany to the crown of France. For the Duke had left only a daughter named Anne to succeed him.

Anne of Anne of Brittany was a young girl just the right age to marry the young King, so Anne of France made Charles claim the right of guardianship over her, and then demand her hand in marriage. You will remember that Charles was already betrothed to Marguerite of Flanders. But that did not seem to matter to Anne of France.

Anne of Brittany, however, did not want to be Queen of France. She was only a girl of fifteen, but she had a will of her own, and she refused to marry Charles. She was a great heiress, and many princes wished to marry her. Now she betrothed herself to Maximilian of Austria, who once before, you remember, had married an orphan Duchess and who, to make confusion still worse, was the father of the lady Charles ought to have married. Anne of France did all she could to stop this marriage, but Anne of Brittany would have her way.

She was married to Maximilian by proxy—that is, he did not come himself, but sent an ambassador, who took his place at the marriage ceremony.

This after all was not a real marriage, and it did not stop Anne of France or the young King Charles. He, seeing that he could not win Anne for his bride peacefully, made up his mind to win her by force, and he marched into Brittany with an army.

Brittany was in a state of utter misery, worn out by wars. Maximilian sent no help to his girl bride, and her ladies and advisers pressed her daily to yield to the King of France. So at length, wearied of the struggle, feeling herself friendless and forsaken, Anne of Brittany gave way. She promised to marry this lover who wooed her with cannon and with sword, by wasting her land and laying her castles in ruins.

Almost at once the marriage took place and little Marguerite of Flanders, who had been brought up in France with the idea of one day being Queen, was sent back to her father. Maximilian was furious. He had been robbed of his bride, and his daughter had been insulted. He "openly railed upon the King and vowed to destroy France with fire and sword." But soon after this Maximilian's father died and he became Emperor. Then, so that he might rule his empire quietly, Maximilian made peace with Charles.

Soon after the King was married, Anne of France gave up all the power and went away to live quietly on her own lands. She had ruled for eight years. Now she left the land at peace, the King and people better off than they had been for many a long day.

Charles, however, did not long remain at peace. He was a sickly little man, but his head was full of ideas of glory and battles. He loved to read and hear stories of knightly adventure. Above all he loved the stories of Charlemagne and his Paladins. He longed to be a great conqueror like Charlemagne, so he set out to conquer the Kingdom of Naples.

Long before this time a prince of Anjou had become King of Naples, and Charles now claimed to be the heir to the throne. Besides this, in all the states into which Italy was at this time divided there was misrule and disorder. They seemed an easy prey for any one who would take them. Charles resolved to be that one. So gathering a great army he marched into Italy.

Through all the north of Italy his march was a triumphal progress. Peoples and rulers welcomed him; towns threw open their gates to him. For at first the Italians looked upon him as a deliverer.

Now and again there was a little battle, now and again a town was taken. But for the most part the march was like a glittering pageant, the knights scarcely troubling to wear armor. To the sound of trumpet and drum the army moved along, men and horses clad in richly colored velvets and stuffs, gold and jewels gleaming in the sunlight, silken banners floating in the breeze. Under a canopy of cloth of gold, carried by pages clad in cloth of gold and velvet, rode the King upon a coal black horse. Over his glittering armor he wore a cloak of blue velvet richly embroidered with gold and pearls and precious stones. Upon his head he wore a white hat decked with long black feathers, and surrounded by a golden crown. So through the land he marched, proclaiming himself the "Friend of Freedom, the Enemy of Tyrants."

When he reached Naples the King fled, and the people greeted Charles with mad joy. They bowed to the ground before him, reverently touching his clothes and hands with their lips. As he passed through the streets the people showered flowers upon him and acclaimed him king.

CHARLES VIII THE AFFABLE—THE DREAMS OF GLORY AND DOMINION

Never had there been so easy a conquest. But Charles did nothing to make his conquest sure. He and his companions gave themselves up to riotous pleasures. All the chief posts were given to Frenchmen. Frenchmen were married to rich Italian ladies. The Italians were neglected and insulted. At first they had looked on Charles as a deliverer. Now that they saw Frenchmen robbing and plundering on every side they changed their minds.

So in feasting and rioting two months passed. Then one day the King received news that the states of Northern Italy were leaguing against him, helped by all the Kings of Europe. It was time, he felt, to turn homeward.

Before he went he caused himself to be crowned with gorgeous pomp King of Naples, King of Jerusalem, and Emperor of a make-believe empire of the East.

This done, and having received the homage of the people, he returned homeward, leaving about half his army to guard his new Kingdom of Naples.

With great difficulty he crossed the Apennines, and on reaching the farther side found his way barred by an army of the League, more than three times as large as his own. But he determined to cut his way through and thus reach France. So at Fornova a great battle was fought.

The Italians were not used to desperate fighting. Their battles were more like tournaments where men fought not to kill but to overthrow and take their enemies prisoner. They were unused to cannon also, and were quite unable to stand against the furious onslaught of the French. In an hour the great fight was over and the army of the League in flight, and for many a long day the "French Fury" was a proverb in Italy.

Charles then went on his way, feeling himself more than ever a great warrior and conqueror. But as soon as he had reached France he seemed to forget all about Italy and to care no more for his conquests. Meanwhile, the soldiers he had left in Naples had been driven out, and the people had welcomed their old King once more. Charles did nothing to help his soldiers, and after much wandering and suffering, a shattered remnant of the once fine army reached the shores of France. Of all the French King's famed conquests not a foot remained to him. His Empire was but an empire of dreams, his titles empty as bubbles.

Charles VIII reigned for about three years longer, doing little but amuse himself. Then one day, as he was going to watch a game of tennis, he passed through a low dark gallery and forgetting to stoop down enough he struck his head against the doorway. He paid no heed to the blow at the time, and watched the game, talking and laughing with those around. Then suddenly in the middle of a sentence he fell backward in a fit. A few hours later he died. He was only twenty-eight.

Charles VIII was an ugly little man, and his speech was slow and stuttering. But his ways were so pleasant, and his manners so kindly, that he earned for himself the name of the Affable. His reign was not a great one. He was too vain and pleasure-loving, his head was too full of dreams of empty glory to be a truly good King. But after the tyranny of Louis the rule of Charles was grateful to the people. They called him their "good little King," and wept for him when he died.

CHAPTER 55

LOUIS XII THE FATHER OF THE PEOPLE—THE KNIGHT WITHOUT FEAR AND WITHOUT REPROACH

CHARLES VIII had four children, but they all died as mere babies. The Dauphin alone, whom he named Roland after his favorite hero, lived to be three, but died before his father. So the next heir to the throne was Louis, Duke of Orleans, who had been taken and held prisoner for three years by Anne of France.

Now many who had been his enemies in those days feared him. But Louis bore no malice. "It would not become the honor of the King of France to avenge the wrongs of a Duke of Orleans," he said. From being a gay and frivolous prince, Louis became a just and merciful King. His old enemy Anne was loaded with gifts. La Tremouille, the famous general who had taken him prisoner, far from being punished, was honored. He had been one of Charles VIII's greatest generals, and had earned for himself the name of the Knight Without Reproach. He now became Louis's greatest general, and made himself so famous in the Italian wars that an Italian writer called him "the greatest captain in the world."

Anne of Brittany, now that her husband was dead, went back to her duchy. She was far more proud of being Duchess of Brittany than of being Queen of France, and it seemed as if France and Brittany would once more be separated. True, when Anne had married Charles she had promised that when he died she would marry his successor. But Louis was already married to Jeanne, the good, little, deformed daughter of Louis XI. She was good and gentle, but Louis had never loved her, and now he asked leave of the Pope to put her away and marry Anne of Brittany.

The Pope of the time was the wicked Alexander VI. He wanted Louis to help his son Caesar Borgia, and so he consented. Louis made Caesar Borgia a duke, and gave him a large sum of money, and in return the Pope allowed Louis to put away his wife.

So poor little Jeanne went away to end her days in a convent. Once more Anne of Brittany became Queen of France, once more Brittany was joined to France, this time forever.

Louis XII was a good and kindly King. He spent little money on himself, he lightened the taxes, and did what he could to make his people happy, so that he was called the Father of the People. But unfortunately, like Charles VIII, he loved adventures and war. Like Charles VIII, Louis XII wanted to be King of Naples. He also claimed to inherit the Duchy of Milan from his grandmother. So he resolved to conquer Milan first, and thus gain a foothold in Italy before venturing upon the long march right down the peninsula to Naples.

Louis had some splendid generals and knights in his army. La Tremouille, called the 'Knight Without Reproach', was one of them. Bayard, called the 'Knight Without Fear and Without Reproach', was another.

So Louis conquered Milan. The Duke, an unruly scoundrel, was taken prisoner to France. There he remained for fourteen years in miserable exile, eating his heart out in desire for freedom. But he never gained it, for when at length he was told he might go free the shock was too great and he died.

Having conquered Milan, Louis next desired to conquer Naples. But Ferdinand of Spain also desired Naples. He was powerful, and he was crafty. Louis dared not fight him, so he made a bargain with him, and they agreed to seize Naples and divide it.

Ferdinand had pretended to be the King of Naples's friend, and the King had opened his gates to the Spanish troops. But when he asked for help against the French he found himself betrayed. Unable to fight two such powerful kings he yielded. Feeling that he would rather yield to an open enemy than to a false friend he set sail for France and gave himself up to Louis. Louis received him kindly, gave him some land and money, on condition that he should not try to leave France. And there he lived quietly until his death, nearly four years later.

But now Louis was to learn with what a wily rascal he had to do. For no sooner had Naples been conquered than the two allies began to quarrel over the division of it, and war broke out between France and Spain. During this war the knight Bayard gained for himself great fame. Upon the banks of the river Garigliano a battle was fought in which the French were utterly defeated and all their baggage fell into the hands of the enemy, together with many prisoners. The splendid courage alone of Bayard saved the defeat from being utter disgrace.

The Spaniards were making for a bridge over the river. Had they gained it it would have meant total destruction to the French army.

Seeing the movements of the enemy, Bayard said to a friend who was near, "Go quickly and get help to guard the bridge; otherwise we are lost. Meanwhile I will amuse these folk until you return. But be quick."

The friend went, and Bayard, lance in hand, took possession of the end of the bridge, upon which the Spaniards already were. Seeing only one man to oppose them they continued to advance. Four men at once attacked Bayard. But he overcame them. Two he slew, and two fell into the river and were drowned. Another and another followed, but all fell beneath the blows of Bayard's sword. Like a hungry tiger he crouched at the end of the bridge, and so mighty were the blows of his sword that the Spaniards doubted whether it was a man or a demon with which they had to do.

Well and long Bayard kept the bridge, until at length his friend came galloping back with a hundred men behind him. They put the Spaniards to flight and chased them for a good mile. Then said Bayard, "Sirs, we have done enough to save the bridge; let us return in as good order as we can."

But in spite of Bayard's bravery, and the bravery of many another famous knight, the war ended in disaster, and Louis lost again all the kingdom of Naples.

Louis's grief and wrath were great.

"Twice has Ferdinand deceived me!" he cried.

"What?" said Ferdinand when he heard it. "The King of France complains that I have deceived him twice? He lies, the fool; I have deceived him ten times and more."

CHAPTER 56

LOUIS XII THE FATHER OF THE PEOPLE—THE BATTLE OF THE SPURS

HAVING lost Naples, Louis desired more than ever to make safe and to enlarge his Duchy of Milan. So he entered into a league called the League of Cambrai with the Pope (now Julius II), with the Emperor, and with his late enemy Ferdinand against Venice. This was a very foolish thing to do. For the Venetians were friendly with Louis, and had more than once helped him in his wars. But Louis was so anxious to increase his territory that he forgot all else, and gathering his army marched across the Alps.

The Venetians, too, made ready, and at Agnadel a great battle took place in which the French were victorious. This battle decided the fate of the Venetians. After it town after town yielded to Louis. And he who was so good to his own people that he gained for himself the name of the Father of the People, proved himself pitilessly cruel to the Venetians, and those who fell into his hands were slaughtered without mercy.

The spoils were divided among the conquerors, the Pope receiving the towns of Romagna as his share of Venetian territory. That was all he wanted of the League. He had used Louis as a cat's-paw to win these towns. Now having got what he wanted he made up his mind to drive the French and all "Barbarians," as he called them, out of Italy. So he made a new League which he called the Holy League.

This was much the same as the League of Cambrai with Louis left out, and instead of being formed against the Venetians it was formed against the French.

At first the French were victorious. They won a great victory at Ravenna on Easter Sunday, 1512. But in the very moment of victory their gallant leader, Gaston de Foix, was killed. He was only twenty-two, but he was, said an Italian writer, "A great captain before he was a soldier. With him vanished all the strength of the French army."

"I would fain," said Louis, when he heard of Gaston's death, "have no longer an inch of land in Italy, if I could by that price bring back to life my nephew Gaston and all the gallants who died with him. God keep us from often winning such victories."

After this young leader's death things went badly for the French.

And before Julius II died he saw his desire fulfilled and Italy delivered from them. But it was only freed from the French to be given over to the Spaniards. It was not true freedom, but only a change of masters.

But in spite of all defeat and disaster Louis could not yet give up his wish to conquer Italy. So when Julius II died he made peace with the Venetians and once more sent an army to conquer Milan. La Tremouille, the aged general, was the leader of this expedition, and as soon as he appeared many of the Italians flocked to join him. Almost without striking a blow the whole of the Duchy was reconquered. La Tremouille was triumphant. But his triumph was short lived. Fortune changed once more. The French were defeated and at last driven out of Italy. After thirteen years of war Louis had gained nothing. He had lost many splendid soldiers, and brought sorrow and suffering to many of his people.

Now that the French were utterly defeated in Italy, other enemies attacked them. Louis's old and wily enemy, Ferdinand of Spain, aided by Henry VIII of England, invaded France.

Henry landed and began to lay siege to the town of Terouenne, and there the Emperor of Germany joined him, for he too wished to crush Louis. The French marched to relieve the town, and the two armies met near Guinegate. But hardly had the battle begun when the French were seized with panic and fled madly in a Indirect ions.

The knight Bayard and several other brave generals tried to rally the men. "Turn, men at arms!" they cried. "Turn; it is nothing!" But it was all in vain. Nothing could stop the mad flight.

This battle, if so it might be called, was named the Battle of the Spurs. For that day spurs were of more use than swords.

Bayard, however, disdained to flee. With forty or fifty brave men about him he fought gallantly. But they could do nothing against a whole army, and he and many other brave knights were taken prisoners. When the Emperor heard that Bayard had been taken prisoner he sent for him. "Sir Bayard, my friend," he said, "I have great joy in seeing you. Would to heaven I had men like you. If I had I should in very short time avenge all the bad turns your master the King of France has played me. But it seems to me," he continued, smiling, "I had heard that Bayard never flees."

"Sire," replied Bayard proudly, "had I fled I should not be here."

As they two thus spoke together King Henry entered. "Do you know this French gentleman?" said the Emperor.

"I' faith no," said Henry.

"You have often heard him spoken of," replied Maximilian. "He is the most famous of Frenchmen, more hated and feared by the Spaniards than any other."

Then said King Henry, "Sir, I believe it is Bayard."

"Right, brother," said the Emperor, "you have guessed well this time."

The King then embraced Bayard as if he had been a prince. "Sir," he cried, "I am right glad to see you. But I would for your honor and profit it had not been as prisoner."

Thus Bayard was received and treated with great honor. The Emperor, it is said, would himself have paid his ransom, but as soon as Louis heard that his knight was a prisoner he sent money in haste to free him.

Louis was at length tired of wars by which he gained nothing, and he made peace with all his enemies. Henry VIII at first was unwilling to make peace, but at length he too yielded. And as Anne of Brittany had died, Louis married Princess Mary, King Henry's sister.

She was a girl of sixteen, Louis a gray man of fifty-three. He had for some years been in bad health, and therefore had to live very carefully. In the simple ways of the time he used to dine at eight in the morning, and go to bed at six. Now to please his gay young wife Louis gave up his simple ways of life. He went to tournaments, balls and parties, dined at the fashionable hour of twelve, and often sat up till midnight. His feeble health could not stand it, and in a few months he died.

When one morning the bell ringers went through the streets of Paris ringing their bells and crying out, "The good King Louis, the father of his people, is dead!" the whole city was filled with mourning and tears. Never for the death of any King had there been such grief.

For apart from his foolish wars Louis had been a good King. Within his kingdom he had done all he could to make his people happy. He had made good laws, and seen that they were kept. In spite of his wars, which cost him a lot of money, he had taken away many of the taxes, for he spent little on empty show and pomp.

"I would rather have you laugh at me for my stinginess," he said to his courtiers, "than have my people weep because of my extravagance."

So, free from grinding taxes, and free from civil war France grew wealthy. Trade and agriculture flourished. Never at any time had France been so prosperous. And the poor people, who had been used to princes who looked upon them as mere beasts of burden, loved the King who brought them wealth and ease.

In all his wise ruling, Louis was helped very much by his minister, Cardinal Georges, and the people were grateful to him too. They trusted him. "Let Georges alone," they said, for they knew he would advise the King well.

CHAPTER 57

FRANCIS I THE KING OF GENTLEMEN— HOW BAYARD KNIGHTED THE KING

LOUIS XII left no sons, so he was succeeded by his cousin Francis, Duke of Angouleme. He was the next heir to the throne, and he had strengthened his claim by marrying the Princess Claude, Louis's eldest daughter. Francis was young and gay, he loved splendor and show, fine clothes and magnificent pageants. He cared little for the tears of his people. Louis XII had watched him grow up with grief. When he was trying hard to make good laws he would sigh and say, "We labor in vain; this great boy will spoil it all."

But Francis was the most knightly knight in all France at a time when France rejoiced in many knights of fair fame. He was gracious and winning; the people believed that he would be a good king and greeted him with joy.

Francis loved tournaments and he loved war. For war to him was little more than a tournament with an added spice of danger. Almost at once, eager to win back Milan, he renewed the war with Italy. With a great army led by the greatest soldiers of the day, among them the aged La Tremouille and the young and famous Bayard, he set out across the Alps.

This time the war went well for the French. Near the village of Marignano a great battle was fought. It began at four o'clock in the afternoon and lasted till midnight, for the bright September moon shed its light upon the deadly strife. The French soldiers fought with desperate rage, anxious to prove their courage. For ever since they had fled almost without striking a blow at Guinegate their enemies had laughed at them, nicknaming them the "armed hares," and they longed to wipe out that reproach.

But when the moon set and darkness covered the ghastly field the victory was not sure. The foot-soldiers lay down to rest upon the field where they were, with their helmets on their heads, and their lances in their hands. The horse-soldiers sat upon their horses fully armed awaiting the dawn, the King himself among them.

With the first streak of dawn the battle again began. For hours the strife lasted, but at length the Swiss, who were fighting on the Italian side, gave way, and the victory belonged to France. It was such a terrible battle that one of the oldest and most tried leaders there said that all his other battles had been as child's play to it. This, he said, was a true battle of giants.

In the French camp there was great rejoicing. The King had won his spurs nobly, and wished to be made a knight. So he commanded Bayard, the Knight Without Fear and Without Reproach, to come to him.

"Bayard, my friend," said Francis, "I wish to-day to be made a knight at your hands. For you have fought valiantly and proved yourself a true knight in many lands and many battles."

But Bayard, the valiant knight, was humble. "Sire," he said, "he who is crowned and anointed with the holy oil, and King of so noble a realm, is knight above all other knights."

"Nay, Bayard, haste you," said the King. "Do rny will and commandment if you would be counted among my faithful nobles and servants."

"I' faith, Sire," said Bayard, "if it pleases you I, all unworthy as I am, will even do your will and commandment."

So the King knelt before his knight. Then drawing his sword Bayard struck the King on the shoulder, saying, "Sire as valiant as Roland, or Oliver, or Godfrey, or his brother Baldwin, you are certainly the first prince to be made knight in this manner. God grant that you may never flee before an enemy."

Then raising his sword high in his right hand Bayard cried aloud, "Thou art most happy, O my sword, in having this day given to so splendid and powerful a King the order of knighthood. I' faith, my good sword, thou shalt be carefully guarded as a relic, and honored above all others. And I will never draw thee again unless against Turks, Saracens, or Moors." Then leaping twice for joy he thrust his sword into its scabbard.

Having thus been knighted, Francis in his turn knighted several of the young nobles who had fought bravely around him.

Soon after this battle the city of Milan was taken, and the Duke Maximilian, the son of the Duke Lodovico who had died a prisoner in France, gave himself up. He too, like his father, went to live in France. Like him, he lived neglected and forgotten, and died in Paris fifteen years later.

The Swiss at this time were considered the best foot-soldiers in Europe. They took part in all the wars, and were often to be found on both sides, for they fought not for any one country or for any particular cause, but for money. When Francis saw how gallantly they fought, and remembered that Switzerland lay upon the borders of France, he resolved to make friends with them. So he made a treaty with them called the Perpetual Peace, and, if they would allow him to raise as many troops in their country as he liked, promised to give them a large sum of money. By this means he gained a very useful friend. And although not quite perpetual the treaty between the two countries lasted for two hundred and fifty years; that is as long as the French monarchy lasted.

Soon after Francis had conquered Milan, Ferdinand of Spain died. He was succeeded by his grandson, Charles of Austria. This made Charles very powerful. For besides being ruler of the Netherlands he was now King of Spain and Naples. Added to this, America had been by this time discovered, and Spain owned a great part of the wonderful new western lands. Spain, it has been said, was like a great vessel, the prow of which was in the Atlantic, the poop in the Indian Seas. But all these possessions were not enough to satisfy Charles. He had for a motto the words, *"Toujours plus oultre"* that is, "always farther."

Two years after Charles became King of Spain the Emperor Maximilian died. The title of Emperor did not pass from father to son, but each new Emperor was chosen by the princes of the Empire. Charles and Francis were the two most powerful rulers in Europe. Each hoped to be chosen. Each did everything he could to make the princes of the Empire choose him. "We are lovers striving for the hand of a fair lady," said Francis. "As only one can win, the loser must by no means bear malice against his more fortunate rival." He said this hoping that he would be the fortunate one.

It was Charles, however, who was chosen. Soon it was plain that the pride of Francis could not bear the slight. Besides, he could not but know that the great power which Charles now had was a danger to France. For the lands of Charles enclosed France on north, south, and east. Francis therefore became very eager to swear friendship with King Henry of England. For he was the only other great King in Western Europe at the time. So a meeting between the two Kings was arranged.

But the Emperor, too, was anxious to have Henry's friendship. He determined to be beforehand with him and he set sail in haste, and paid Henry an unexpected visit in England. He flattered and made much of Henry's favorite, Cardinal Wolsey, loaded him with presents and promises, and then set sail again, pretty sure that he had a friend in Henry.

But all the same, as soon as the Emperor had gone, Henry set out for France to meet the French King. The place of their meeting was near the town of Guines, and everything about it was so gorgeous and rich that it is known as the Field of the Cloth of Gold. The knights and nobles who followed the two kings tried to outdo each other in magnificence. Many ruined themselves to make a brave show, so that it was said they carried on their backs their mills, their forests, and their meadows.

The two Kings, clad in the utmost splendor, met and embraced each other before getting off their horses, and exchanged words of courteous greeting. Then alighting they went arm in arm, like loving brothers, into a great tent in which they were to sign a treaty.

But in spite of all this show of affection, cause of quarrel was not far to seek. The King of England being seated took up the treaty and began to read it aloud. The first part was all about the King of France, the second part was about the King of England. When he came to that part Henry read, "I, Henry King" then he hesitated. He wanted to say "of France and of England." But instead he turned to Francis with a jest, "I will not put it in, seeing you are here," he said, "for I should lie." So he left out the title so far as France was concerned, and said only, "I, Henry King of England." Yet he did not strike it out of the treaty. And from this we may see, that in spite of all the show of it, there was little real friendship between the two Kings. How could there be, when one was only awaiting a chance to wrest his crown from the other?

Yet for more than a fortnight the days went pleasantly past in tournaments and wrestling, shows and pageants. Then the Kings parted, to all seeming the best of friends. But Francis had made the mistake of making too much display of wealth and grandeur. He had outdone the splendor-loving King of England, and before even he left France, Henry once more had a meeting with the Emperor Charles V.

In the following January King Francis was nearly killed by accident. On Twelfth Night the court had games and revels, during which one of the nobles was crowned as King of the Fete. Francis came to besiege this King of the Fete in his castle.

Both sides used snowballs for ammunition. But after a keen fight the store of snow within the castle gave out, and the besiegers rushed in in triumph. Just as the gateway was stormed some thoughtless person threw a live coal from one of the windows. It fell upon the head of the King, and wounded him sorely. Thus a sudden and sad end was put to the fun.

For some days it was not known if the King would recover. Wild rumors were spread abroad. Some said the King was dead, some that he was blinded. But Francis got well quickly, and as soon as he was able he showed himself everywhere, to prove to his people that he was still alive.

Up to this time the Kings of France had worn long hair, like the Frankish Kings of old, and shaved their faces. But after his accident Francis was obliged to cut his hair short. He let his beard grow too and so set a new fashion, for the Court soon followed the King, and the people the Court, and for a century and more Frenchmen wore short hair and beards.

CHAPTER 58

FRANCIS I THE KING OF GENTLEMEN— HOW THE KING WAS TAKEN PRISONER

A year after the peaceful Field of the Cloth of Gold Francis was once more at war with Spain and with Italy. The Pope and Emperor (who was also the King of Spain) joined against him. The French were beaten, and for the third time Milan was lost to France. Henry VIII also joined with the Emperor, and Francis saw himself surrounded by enemies on all sides. To these enemies there was soon added the greatest noble in France, Charles Duke of Bourbon.

All the mighty feudal princes who had caused France so much trouble had disappeared. There was no longer a Duke of Normandy, there was no longer a Duke of Brittany; their lands and their titles now belonged to the King of France. The Duke of Bourbon alone possessed lands over which he held sway as a King.

Charles of Bourbon was handsome and fiery tempered, a splendid knight and soldier, and he kept state as brilliant as the King himself. "If I had a subject like that in my kingdom," said Henry of England, "I would not leave his head very long on his shoulders."

Francis indeed may well have been jealous of his great vassal, and his mother, who was a headstrong, proud woman, greedy of power, hated him. She claimed all the Duke's possessions and succeeded in robbing him of them.

Burning with wrath at this unjust and wrongful treatment, Charles revolted against his King, and joined his enemies.

When it was too late Francis tried to bring back Charles of Bourbon to his faith. He tried in vain, and soon the Duke was leading a hostile army against the French in Italy.

It was in this war that Bayard, the Knight Without Fear and Without Reproach, met his death. The French were retreating before the enemy; Bayard, fighting bravely, covered the retreat, giving more trouble to the foe than a hundred other men.

But at length he was struck by a bullet. When he felt the blow he cried out, "Alas! I am killed." Feeling that indeed his last hour had come he drew his sword, and taking it by the hilt he kissed the cross upon it, murmuring, "Have pity on me, O God, according to Thy great mercy."

Then he begged his comrades to lay him at the foot of a tree, with his face to the enemy; for all his life he had never turned his back to the foe, and would not do so now in death. This being done, he bade his comrades save themselves, for, he said, "There is no more to do for me in this world." But they would not leave him. A few moments later Charles of Bourbon, who was in hot pursuit of the French, passed near the tree under which Bayard lay dying.

"Ah, sir," he cried, "it is great pity to see you thus. For you are a good and valiant knight."

"My lord," answered Bayard, "there is no need to pity me. I die as a soldier should. But I have pity for you to see you thus in arms against your King, your country, and your oath."

Charles made no answer. In silence he turned away.

In vain Bayard begged his comrades to flee. "I pray you get you gone," he said, "else you will fall into the hands of the enemy. That would profit me nothing, for there is nought more to do for me in this world." Yet they stayed, until after a few hours the gentle knight closed his eyes and died. He was mourned for alike by friend and foe.

The war still went on. Before the town of Pa via a great battle was fought. It was a desperate fight, and went ill for the French. Knight after knight went down, the foot soldiers were broken and scattered, the artillery useless. But the King, wounded and exhausted, still fought on amid the dead and dying. His horse was killed beneath him. Then some Spanish soldiers, seeing him unhorsed and at their mercy, knowing not who he was, but sure that he was some great noble, began to quarrel for the prize. But at the moment a French gentleman came up who knew the King. He beat off the Spanish soldiers, and begged Francis to surrender to Bourbon.

"Nay," said the King in wrath, "I would rather die than pledge my faith to a traitor. Where is the Viceroy of Naples?'

The Viceroy was found. He came to Francis, and kneeling on one knee before him, received the King's sword, and gave his own in exchange.

The battle was over, and the King of France a prisoner. "Madame," he wrote to his mother the same evening, "all is lost but honor."

During more than a year Francis remained a prisoner, for the terms upon which alone Charles would set him free were so hard that at first

Francis swore he would rather die in captivity than sign them. But at length, weary of his prison, he yielded, and signed what is known as the Treaty of Madrid. By this treaty he gave back to Charles of Bourbon all the land which had been unjustly taken from him, yielded to the Emperor Burgundy and Flanders, and agreed to send his two little sons to live in Spain as hostages, and to return himself if within four months he had not kept all his promises.

Francis was then led to the borders of the two kingdoms. There on the river Bidassoa a large barge was anchored. From the Spanish side came the King, from the French side came the two little princes. As they met the King took them in his arms. With tears in his eyes he kissed and blessed them. Then they passed on to Spain and captivity, he to France and freedom.

When he reached the French shore Francis sprang upon his horse, which was ready waiting him. "Once more I am King!" he cried exultantly, and setting spurs to his fiery steed he dashed away toward Bayonne.

But Francis had never meant to keep his promises, and he did not keep them. The nobles of Burgundy gathered together, and swore that the King had no right to give away their land, and that nothing would ever persuade them to live under Spanish rule.

So there was more fighting again in Italy. The Duke of Bourbon was killed, but for the most part things went so badly for France that Francis at length was willing to make peace. The Emperor Charles, too, was anxious to make peace, for he saw himself surrounded by other enemies.

So at Cambrai there was a meeting between the aunt of the Emperor and the mother of the King, and these two ladies arranged a peace known as "The Ladies' Peace." It was much the same as the Peace of Madrid. except that the Emperor Charles consented to take a large sum of money instead of Burgundy.

For six years now France had peace, and Francis strengthened the position of his kingdom by making treaties with other countries of Europe, and by improving the condition of his army. But the great passion of the French King's life was hatred of Charles. So it was not wonderful that war broke out between the two rivals again and yet again.

And it is to the credit of Francis that he held his own against his powerful rival, and left his kingdom when he died as great as when he inherited it from his cousin.

Even although Francis at times made peace with Charles he was constant in his hatred of him. In all else he was fickle. At times he made friends with the English King, at times he fought with him. The Reformation had begun. In Germany, Martin Luther had defied the Pope. In France, John Calvin had followed his example. At times Francis tried to make friends with the Protestants, at times he treated those in his own lands with frightful cruelty. But all this changeableness was the outcome of his hatred of the Emperor. Many of the princes of Germany had become Protestant, and Francis tried to make friends with them in order to win them to his side. His one desire was to get the better of the Emperor.

The worst and cruelest persecutions in the reign of Francis were against the Vaudois. They were quiet, peaceful folk who lived in little towns and villages in the south of France. It is said by some that they had followed their own simple ways of religion ever since the days of Philip Augustus, and that they needed no Calvin, no Reformation, to teach them to worship God in simple fashion.

For long years they had lived untroubled in their lonely villages. Now the order went forth that they must die. Armed men poured into the peaceful valleys, the defenseless villagers were slaughtered without mercy. Some fled to the mountains and died there of hunger and cold. Many children were sold into slavery, and over three thousand were slain in less than a week.

Yet Francis himself was not actually cruel, though he was selfish and pleasure-loving. By this time he had grown worn and ill, and he allowed the Constable, Anne of Montmorency, a hard and cruel man who had grown to great power, to do as he liked among the wretched Protestants.

CHAPTER 59

HENRY II—HOW THE DUKE OF GUISE DEFENDED METZ

WHEN Francis I died, in 1547, he was succeeded by his son Henry, a weak and stupid man of twenty-eight. He left the government very much in the hands of powerful and self-seeking counsellors, among whom were the Guises, the Duke of Guise and his brother the Cardinal. They claimed to be descended from the House of Anjou and even from Charlemagne. They now rose to power and for many years played a great part in the history of France. They were courteous, and brilliant, while their great rival, Anne of Montmorency, the Constable of France, was a big, rough bully, carrying everything with a high hand, shouting down those who did not agree with him.

Meanwhile, although a new King was on the throne, the hatred between the Emperor and the King of France still continued, and about four years after Henry succeeded to the crown there was war once more.

The Emperor by this time had grown into a tyrant. Many of the princes of the Empire had become Protestant, but he fought and imprisoned them tor it. He settled matters of religion without asking advice of the Pope, he settled matters of the Empire without asking the advice of the princes. He did as he liked.

At length his tyranny was not to be borne, and many of the Protestant princes entered into a league against him. By this league they bound themselves to resist in every way in their power the schemes by which, they said, "Charles of Austria tried to bring Germany into a bestial, unbearable and eternal slavery, such as he had done in Spain and elsewhere."

In secret Henry joined the league, and with a great army marched into Lorraine, and took possession of Metz, Toul, and Verdun. Delighted with his success, Henry marched farther into the country. But he was driven back from the walls of Strasburg, and boasting that he had watered his horses in the Rhine he returned to Verdun. The Emperor had been completely taken by surprise, and he now hastened to make peace with his Protestant princes. He set free those he had imprisoned, and agreed to allow them to follow their own religion. But Henry refused to be a party to this treaty, for he had no wish to give up the towns he had taken. So the war between him and the Emperor went on.

The Emperor was determined to recover Metz, Henry was just as determined to keep it. Francis Duke of Guise was chosen to command the French within the walls. The defenses were poor, but by his orders houses, churches, abbeys were pulled down, and with the stones new walls were built. The work went on apace. Great nobles, even the Duke of Guise himself, might be seen wheeling stones and carrying mortar like any common laborer, such was their eagerness.

All who could not fight were sent out of the town, while hundreds of French gentlemen, among them the greatest lords in the land, crowded into Metz eager to take part in defending it. Food was gathered in great quantities and brought within the walls, and the country for miles round left a desert. The Emperor was slow to move, and Guise had time to make all his preparations before the enemy appeared. But at length they came with great guns and cannons. "I mean to knock the town about the ears of Monsieur de Guise," said the Emperor.

The bombardment was so tremendous that the sound of it was heard on the banks of the Rhine. The walls were broken down. But as quickly as they fell they were built up again. Sometimes even when the old wall had been battered down, the besiegers found that there was already a new wall within the old, so that the town was as safe as before.

"If they give us peas we will give them beans," said the Duke of Guise. So when the Germans dug mines the French dug counter mines. The German cannon thundered against the walls, the French poured shot into the German camp.

Week by week the siege lasted. Cannon roared and thundered all day long, and the air was bitter with the smell of gunpowder, heavy with smoke. The weather too was awful. Rain and snow poured down in torrents, until the camp of the German soldiers was a reeking marsh. Their sufferings were terrible, disease carried them off in hundreds. Still the Emperor set his teeth, and swore that he would have Metz, if it cost him three armies, one after the other.

But sufferings sapped the courage of the soldiers. Many deserted, the rest fought on sullenly. At length Charles gave way. On the first of January, 1553, he marched away. "Fortune," he said sadly, "I well see is but a fickle jade. She prefers a young King to an old Emperor."

The retreat was disastrous. In the silence and darkness of the night the troops marched away. Tents, baggage, and a great part of the guns and ammunition were left behind. For the wheels of wagons and gun carriages stuck axle deep in mud, and neither horses nor men could dislodge them.

When the French reached the deserted camp they found it in a fearful state. On every side, amid dead and dying horses, abandoned arms, knapsacks, cooking utensils, were dead and dying soldiers. Some lay half-buried in the mud, others sat on stones with their legs sunk in half-frozen mud to the knees, unable to move. When they saw their enemies some cried aloud for mercy, others prayed for a speedy death, so that their sufferings might be ended. The French soldiers were filled with horror and pity at the sight. They had mercy on these poor forsaken wretches, carried them into the town, and took care of them so generously that for many a long day the "Courtesy of Metz" was a proverb.

Soon after this Charles V, weary of all the glories and troubles of an empire, gave up his throne and went into a monastery, there to end his days. He divided his lands and power. Austria and the title of Emperor he gave to his brother Ferdinand; the Netherlands and Spain to his son Philip.

In the great hall of his palace at Brussels the Emperor called his nobles together. Clad in black velvet with a golden chain about his neck, the bent old man limped painfully to his throne, leaning heavily with one hand upon a stick, with the other upon the arm of William the Silent.

Turning to the waiting nobles he told them of all that he had done since, when a boy of seventeen, he had become King of Spain. His had been a stormy life. Nine times he had journeyed to Germany, seven to Italy, six to Spain, ten to Flanders, four to France, and twice to England and to Africa. Three times had he crossed the ocean, eight times the Mediterranean. But now he was old, he was already half dead. He could no longer bear the burden of the Crown. He begged his people to forgive him all the wrongs he had unwillingly done them, and to accept his son Philip as their ruler.

Then while Philip knelt before him he kissed him, and laying his hand upon his head proclaimed him to be the ruler of the Netherlands in the Name of the Holy Trinity. As the Emperor spoke tears ran down his cheeks. And as he fell back exhausted upon his throne the silence was broken by the sobs of those who listened to him.

CHAPTER 60

HENRY II— HOW CALAIS ONCE MORE BECAME A FRENCH TOWN

THUS Philip II became ruler of the Netherlands and of Spain. Already two years before he had married Mary of England. So the King of France was more than ever in danger; for Spanish possessions enclosed his kingdom on north, east, and south; on the west England threatened him across the narrow sea, for so long as Philip and Mary were husband and wife France could never hope for peace with England.

Yet with such danger surrounding him on every side, Henry, like the kings who had gone before him, kept the foolish desire for power in Italy. And while his soldiers had been defending Metz there had been fighting in Italy also. But there the French had little success, even after the great Duke of Guise took command. He was still fighting there when Henry hastily recalled him to France. For once more there was war, and Philip of Spain had marched into France, and had defeated the French in the Battle of St. Laurent. The French army was utterly shattered, the Constable taken prisoner.

When the Emperor Charles V in his quiet monastery heard of this Spanish victory he was delighted. It seemed to him that now the conquest of France was sure. "Is my son the King at Paris?" he asked impatiently. And indeed the way to Paris lay open, the fair city was at the mercy of the Spaniard. But happily for France Philip had none of the daring of his father. He did not march on Paris, but stayed to besiege the town of St. Quentin. The walls were crumbling, the garrison small, but the town held out gallantly. For well the people knew that there was not a town between St. Quentin and Paris which was strong enough to stop the triumphant march of the enemy. It was the last outpost and must be held. So bravely they held out, townsfolk and monks fighting side by side with soldiers. And even when at last the town was taken by storm, and the enemy poured in at eleven breaches at one time, they fought on and fell where they stood almost to a man.

Meanwhile the Duke of Guise was returning with all haste. He was a great soldier, and when he arrived he saw that to save France he must do something striking. The mere retaking of St. Quentin would not be enough. So instead of marching to St. Quentin he marched to Calais.

The fortress of Calais was in a bad state, the garrison was small, for the English thought that the fame of the town was enough to keep it safe. Over one of the gates indeed was written:

> "The French may think this town to win,
> When iron and lead like cork do swim."

But with such speed and skill did Guise strike that before a week had passed Calais was taken. The governor and about fifty other Englishmen were made prisoners, and the rest of the inhabitants were sent back to England, leaving all their money and possessions behind them.

Thus the gallant town which for more than a year had withstood Edward III, and which for more than two hundred years had belonged to England, became French once more.

To Mary of England the loss was bitter. "If you open my heart," she sighed, "you will find Calais graven upon it." She never ceased to grieve for the loss of it.

But in France the news was greeted with an outburst of joy. Nothing could have served so well to raise the drooping courage of the soldiers. Nothing could have made the Duke more dear to the hearts of the people. He was their idol, their darling, and the conqueror of Calais was greeted with cheers and applause wherever he went. His fame was at the highest, it seemed, when he and his family were raised still higher; for his niece, the Queen Mary of Scotland, married Francis, the Dauphin of France.

Francis was but a weak boy, and the Duke of Guise hoped when he became King that he, as his uncle, would have great power both in France and in Scotland.

After the taking of Calais the war lingered on for more than a year, but at length both sides were weary of it, and a peace called the peace of Cateau-Cambresis was signed in April, 1559. At this peace there was great rejoicing, and feasting, and marriage giving. For to make the peace sure Henry's little thirteen-year-old daughter was married to her father's old enemy Philip (for Mary of England had died). Henry's sister too was married to a Spanish noble. Before these princesses went away to their new homes there were great shows, and among other things a magnificent tournament. The King himself took part in this tournament, and showed himself a skillful knight.

Henry was so proud of his skill that when the jousting was at an end he wanted to run one more course, and break one more lance. So he challenged a young knight. The knight tried to excuse himself, but the King ordered him to lay his lance in rest, so he obeyed.

From either end of the lists the two horsemen galloped furiously toward each other. They met with tremendous shock, and their lances were shivered in their hands. But the young knight did not lower the broken shaft of his lance quickly enough. It struck the King's helmet, forced open his visor, and a splinter of wood entered his eye. King Henry fell forward sorely wounded on his horse's neck, and the horse feeling the reins loosened galloped madly down the lists, until it was stopped by the King's esquire.

Gently Henry was lifted from his horse and carried to his room. Doctors and surgeons were sent for in haste; but there was nothing to be done, the wood had entered his brain. For eleven days the King lingered painfully on, then he died.

CHAPTER 61

FRANCIS II—THE RIOT OF AMBOISE

HENRY II was succeeded by his son Francis II, a sickly boy of fifteen. He was the husband of beautiful Queen Mary of Scotland, and they were both children in the hands of the powerful Duke of Guise and of his brother the Cardinal of Lorraine.

During the last reign the Protestants, or Huguenots, as they were now called, had been growing stronger and stronger; this, too, in spite of bitter persecutions. Some of the greatest nobles had become Protestants, the greatest of all being the Bourbons.

These Bourbons were of the same family as that Charles of Bourbon who, you remember, rebelled against Francis I. They were thus cousins of the King, and the head of the house was Anthony King of Navarre. He received this title through Jeanne, his wife, who was Queen of Navarre of Navarre in her own right. Navarre was a small kingdom carved out of the north of Spain, the boundaries stretching over the Pyrenees a little way into France. It was really from this French Navarre that Jeanne took her title, for the Spanish province was in the hands of Philip of Spain. It was a tiny mountainous kingdom. The people were simple shepherds and peasants, and the King and Queen lived almost as simply as their subjects.

King Anthony was not really a sincere Protestant, like his wife Queen Jeanne, but he was an enemy of the Guises. He thought, too, that as the King's nearest relative he ought to be his chief adviser. The Duke of Guise, however, had no idea of giving up his office, and he insulted and neglected Anthony of Navarre and his brother, the Prince of Conde, in every way possible. So there began a struggle for power. On the one hand were the Guises at the head of the Catholics, on the other the Prince of Conde (for he was the real leader) at the head of the Protestants.

The Protestants now formed a plot to rescue the young King from the power of the Guises. Through all the land messengers were sent secretly to persuade all people who hated the rule of the Guises to take up arms for the "Dumb Leader." This was the name given to Conde, who dared not yet openly appear as the champion of the Protestants.

All went well. Hundreds and thousands joined the conspiracy. In the very castle itself where the King was there were conspirators. Plans were made, everything was ready. It was arranged that upon the day fixed the castle should be surrounded. Then, at a signal given by friends within the castle, it should be attacked on all sides, and the doors forced. The Guises were to be taken prisoner, but no harm was to be done to the King.

There was, however, a traitor within the camp. Before the day arrived Guise knew all the plans of the Protestants. He acted quietly and swiftly. He sent soldiers to every meeting place to scatter the conspirators. He changed the guards around the castle, replacing them with men he could trust; he walled up the gate of the town by which the conspirators hoped to enter. Thus when they arrived they were easily taken prisoner or scattered in flight, and the rebellion was at an end. It was called the riot of Amboise from the name of the castle in which the King then was.

But if the riot was over, not so the anger of Guise. He now caused himself to be made lieutenant-general of the kingdom, with power to do as he liked. And for a month the wretched conspirators were hunted from place to place. They were taken prisoner by dozens, and tortured and killed in many cruel ways.

For one long month there was nothing but hanging, and drowning, and beheading of people. They were led to death without any trial. "My business is not to talk, but to cut off heads," said Guise.

It was for him a horrible orgy of triumph. He delighted in the sight, and kept the chief executions as an after-dinner amusement, when even the ladies of the court sat at the windows of the palace to watch the terrible show.

The Duchess of Guise, it is said, turned from the sight in horror. "What is the matter?" asked the Queen, as she saw her turn away pale and stricken.

"What is the matter?" she answered. "Ah, Madame, I have just seen a most piteous sight, the blood of the innocent shed, the good subjects of the King done to death. Alas! some awful misfortune will fall upon our house."

The King too was uneasy. "I don't know how it is," he said to Guise, "but I hear it said that it is only you the people hate. I wish you would go away for a time, so that I might see whether it is you or I that they are against.'

But the Guises had no thought of going away. "If we left you," they said, "neither you nor your brothers would have an hour longer to live. The Bourbons want to kill you all."

Although so many of his followers were killed or imprisoned the Prince of Conde was at first allowed to go free. For even Guise did not dare to put a prince of the royal house to death. But after a time both Conde and his brother, King Anthony, were ordered to come to the court. They came, and Conde was imprisoned, tried, and condemned to death, and although the sentence was not carried out he was kept in prison. Thus one enemy was got rid of. The Guises wanted to get King Anthony, too, out of the way, but nothing could be proved against him. So, it is said, the Duke persuaded the King to kill him. It was arranged that Anthony should be sent for to speak with the King, and that the King should accuse him of being in league with his brother. If Anthony denied it the King should then draw his dagger, and at that signal men hidden there for the purpose should rush in and put King Anthony to death.

Thus it was arranged. Anthony was summoned to speak with King Francis. But before he went he was warned of the plot. Still he went. "If I die yonder," he said, "carry my bloodstained shirt to my wife, so that she may send it to every prince in Christendom, that they may avenge my death. For my son is not yet old enough to do it."

The first part of the plot had succeeded perfectly. But the young King's heart failed him. He could not strike a man in cold blood and Anthony left the King's presence in safety. "Was there ever a greater coward known?" muttered Guise, disgusted at the soft-heartedness of his royal slave, and at the failure of his plans.

Francis could not bring himself to kill a fellow creature. But he himself was soon to die. He had always been a sickly boy; now one day as he was mounting his horse he fell back fainting. It was quickly seen that he was dangerously ill, and that he could not live long. The Guises were in an agony of fear and rage. The Duke cursed and blasphemed, and threatened to hang the doctors. The Cardinal ordered prayers and masses to be said for the King's recovery.

Neither threats nor prayers were of any avail, and Francis died on December 5, 1560, having reigned less than a year.

CHAPTER 62

CHARLES IX—HUGUENOT AND CATHOLIC

AT the deathbed of Francis II there knelt two Queens, the one, his fair and beautiful wife, Mary of Scotland; Medici the other his mother, Catherine of Medici.

Mary had done all that womanly tenderness could do to make her young husband's last hours peaceful. Now that he was gone, she wept bitter tears of loneliness. He had been but a weak and sickly boy, but he was King, and Mary, who all her life had been loved and tenderly treated, had been the greatest lady in the land. Now she had no longer a place in France, she was no longer of importance. Her day in France was over. As the France months went on she felt it so more and more. France was no longer her home, and with tear-dimmed eyes she set sail for Scotland.

But for Catherine, her days of power were only beginning. She had been the neglected wife of Henry II. During the reign of Francis II, the Guises and their beautiful niece had overshadowed her. But now, Francis having no children, her second son, Charles, came to the throne. He was a weak and passionate boy of ten, and his mother became Regent.

Queen Catherine cared little about religion one way or another. She was neither on the side of the Catholics nor of the Protestants. She wanted neither side to be very powerful, for she wanted to be powerful herself.

But the country was now on edge for civil war and Catherine at first did her best to avoid it. Conde, who was still in prison awaiting death, she set free, and both he and his brother were made members of the Council, in which the Duke of Guise and the Cardinal were also allowed to keep their places. The persecution of Protestants was stopped, and those who were imprisoned were set free, being warned, however, to live like good Catholics henceforth. In these matters she took as her chief friend and adviser the Chancellor Michel de l'Hospital.

Michel de l'Hospital was a wise and kindly old man. He hated the cruel war of religion, and longed for it to cease. "Do away with these dreadful words Huguenot and Papist," he said; "let us not change the beautiful name of Christian."

So, to try if possible to come to a peaceful understanding, a meeting between Catholic priests and Huguenot ministers was held at Poissy, about twenty miles from Paris. The little King sat at one end of the great hall with the Queen beside him, his court surrounding him in glittering array. At the sides sat the priests in their splendid robes.

There seemed no place for the Protestants. There were no chairs set apart for them. But after the meeting was begun they were brought in guarded by soldiers, and made to stand at a barrier which separated them from the priests. It was as if they were prisoners brought before their judges, and their quiet and simple clothes were in strange contrast to the gorgeous robes and jewels of the courtiers and priests.

As might have been expected, no good came of this meeting. The two parties could not agree. Neither side would give way an inch. But a few months later the Regent passed a law by which the Protestants were allowed to hold meetings in private houses and outside the walls of towns.

This made the Catholics very angry. They began more than ever to fear the growing power of the Huguenots.

Meanwhile the Duke of Guise found much of his power gone. In order to regain it, and in order to defend the Catholic faith, he made friends with his old enemy, the Constable Montmorency. The Marshal, Saint Andre, also joined them, and these three were called the Triumvirate. Triumvirate comes from two Latin words, *trium*, of three; *vir*, a man. The Huguenots greatly feared this Triumvirate.

Thus on both the Protestant and Catholic sides there was anger added to fear. It needed but a touch to make the flame of war burst forth. It was not long before the touch was given.

It happened that the Duke of Guise was on his way to Paris with his family. On Sunday he passed by the town of Vassy and stopped to hear mass. The church was quite near the barn in which the Huguenots held their service. Just as the Duke was going into the church he was told that the Huguenots to the number of five hundred were gathered to hear their preacher.

This seemed to the Duke nothing less than insolence, and turning from the door of the church he rode to the barn. A few of his men rode on in front and dashed rudely into the meeting with shouts and gunshots. In a moment everything was in an uproar. The Duke's men poured into the barn. The Huguenots, among whom were many women and children, were seized with terror. They defended themselves with sticks and stones as best they could, against the swords and guns of the Duke's men.

Between twenty and thirty men were killed and many more were wounded; the rest were scattered in flight. The preacher was taken sorely wounded and led before the Duke.

"Why do you lead the people into rebellion?" asked Guise.

"Sir," replied the preacher, "I am no rebel; I but preach the Gospel to them."

Ordering him to be hanged, the Duke turned his back upon him in silent wrath. But the order was not carried out, and some months later the preacher was set free.

The massacre of Vassy, as it was called, was the signal for civil war. All over the country the Huguenots rose in arms, with the Prince of Conde as their leader. There were combats, and massacres, and riots. Towns were taken and retaken, castles were burned, churches were ruined and pillaged, and all the land was filled with violence and war. At length, near the town of Dreux, a great battle was fought, in which Conde was taken prisoner, and which ended in a victory for the Catholics. But it was for them a hard won fight. For St. Andre was slain and Montmorency made prisoner, and some who fled from the field took to Paris the news that the Huguenots had won.

"Well," said the Queen Regent, quite unmoved, "we must now say our prayers in French."

Guise was now alone at the head of the Catholics, for of the other two of the Triumvirate one was dead and one a prisoner.

The war went on. Once again, as in the days of Joan of Arc, Orleans was besieged. It was the great stronghold of the Huguenots, and the people within trembled in fear, for it was said that Guise had sworn to kill every living thing within the walls, both man and beast, and to sow the ruins with salt.

But one dark February afternoon a horseman sat silently waiting in the gloom ot a little wood. In his hand he held a pistol, his eyes shone with the light of mad zeal. He believed that what he was going to do was God's will.

The minutes slipped by. Then through the stillness of the evening hour came the clatter of horses' hoofs, the sound of voices. It was the Duke of Guise who came. The silent horseman raised his pistol and waited. Nearer and nearer rode the Duke. Then suddenly three shots, one after the other, rang out. The Duke fell forward on the neck of his horse. "Those shots have been in keeping for me a long time," he groaned.

The murderer did not wait to see the result of his work, but galloped furiously off into the darkness. But his work was done, for although the Duke was not killed, he was mortally wounded, and he died a few days later. It was a pitiful end for the defender of Metz, the conqueror of Calais.

For four years now there was peace. But both sides were ever ready to take up arms again. And a second and third civil war were fought.

At the battle of Jarnac the Huguenots were defeated and the Prince of Conde was killed. In spite of a broken leg, he had charged the enemy with great fury and broken through their ranks. But soon his little company was surrounded. The Prince's horse was killed under him, but he still fought on, his back against a tree. His men fought round him till one by one they fell. Then seeing among the enemy two Catholic gentlemen to whom he had once been kind, Conde called to them. Drawing off one of his gauntlets he yielded to them. Courteously the two gentlemen with their followers stood by their prisoner protecting him.

Presently the soldiers of the Duke of Anjou, Conde's deadly enemy, rode by. "Hide your face," said one of the gentlemen to the Prince.

Conde hid his face, and the soldiers rode on. But hardly had they passed when their captain found out the name of the prisoner.

Crying, "Slay! slay!" he wheeled his horse. He reached the spot, and bending down he held his pistol close to Conde's head and blew out his brains.

The Admiral Coligny, another of the great Protestant leaders, now became their head. Although he was also defeated the Catholics saw that he was an enemy to be feared; and at length peace was signed once more. In spite of all their losses and defeats the Huguenots gained great privileges by this peace. Indeed, they were given almost entire freedom.

This made the Catholics angry and jealous. Other things made them still more angry. Admiral Coligny came to court, and was received with great honor. Soon the young King came to like him so much that he did everything Coligny wished.

It was also arranged that the young King's sister Margaret of Valois, should be married to Henry of Navarre, King Anthony of Navarre had been killed in the wars, fighting on the Catholic side. For he was unstable and easily led, and had been readily persuaded to change sides. But his wife remained a staunch Protestant, and in her little mountain kingdom she brought up her young son Henry to be the champion of the cause.

That a Princess of France should marry a heretic made the Catholics very angry. Still the wedding took place.

But now tne Queen Mother had no wish that the Protestants should become too powerful. She wanted neither side to be strong, but wanted to have all the power herself. So she was angry when she saw Coligny's growing sway over the King. Henry, the young Duke of Guise also hated Coligny, and wished to avenge his father's death. The Admiral had many other enemies, and Catherine was easily persuaded to join in a plot to kill him.

So one day as he was walking slowly through the streets of Paris a shot was fired from a window. The shot, however, went wide of its mark, and Coligny was only wounded. Calmly he pointed to the window from whence the shot came. But although the house was entered at once, and the still smoking gun was found, the murderer had gone. He had had a horse ready waiting, and was already speeding far away into the country.

A messenger was sent in haste to the King to tell him of the Admiral's danger. Charles was playing tennis when the messenger came.

"Am I never to have peace?" he cried, as he threw away his racket in anger.

He went at once, however, to visit Coligny, swearing to avenge him. But this was not what Catherine intended. She talked to Charles until she made him believe that the Huguenots were ready to rise in rebellion, that Coligny was a traitor, and that unless he was killed the whole country would soon be ablaze with war. Long she struggled with her son, and at length driven to desperation the King started up in wild wrath, "Since you think it good to kill the Admiral," he cried passionately, "I will it. But kill also every Huguenot in Paris, so that there be none left to reproach me. Give the order at once." Then the King flung himself out of the room like a madman.

CHAPTER 63

CHARLES IX—THE MASSACRE OF ST. BARTHOLOMEW

THE hot August night was drawing to a close when through the deserted streets of Paris companies of soldiers crept noiselessly. They seemed but dark shadows as they slid along the walls in the blackness of the night. But soon the first faint gray of dawn shivered up the sky, paling its blue and dimming the stars. And in the dusky light it was seen that every man wore a white badge on his arm, a white cross in his hat. With faces strangely pale in the dawn they looked at each other and waited.

Paris slept peacefully. Save for a furtive footfall not a sound was heard far or near. Then suddenly on the stillness of the morning a harsh sound fell. A bell rang out. There seemed something awful in its tone as it clanged and clanged over the sleeping city. It carried with it some terrible foreboding of evil. Men leaped from their beds affrighted.

With the clanging of the bell all Paris was awake. The streets were suddenly full of armed men. Lights appeared in every window, blows, and shots, and cries resounded, and from far and near bell after bell took up the note of terror, till the whole city from end to end was full of the horror of noise.

The Catholics had taken the King at his word. They had sworn that not a Huguenot should be left alive to reproach him or them. And in the gray morning they began their deadly work. They had chosen a time when many Protestants were gathered in Paris. The houses in which they lived were marked, while the Catholics were known to each other by a white cross in their hats and a white bandage on their arms.

The Admiral Coligny was among the first to die. His house had been surrounded, and soon he was awakened by gunshots fired in the courtyard. Weak and wounded as he was he sprang from his bed and stood leaning against the wall. Well he knew that his last hour had come.

"Say a prayer for me," he said to his minister, who was with him. "Into my Savior's keeping I give my soul," he added.

"What means this riot?" cried a gentleman, running into the room.

"My lord, it is God calling us," answered another.

THEY SEEMED BUT DARK SHADOWS AS THEY SLID ALONG THE WALLS.

All knew the end was near. There was no time to waste.

"Sirs," said Coligny, "for a long time I have been ready to die, but you others save yourselves if it is possible." So they fled to the housetop; it was the only hope of escape. Even there some were taken and killed. Only one man remained by Coligny. He would not forsake his master.

The noise in the house grew louder and louder, the tramp of armed men nearer and nearer. In a few minutes the door was burst open, and the Duke of Guise's men rushed in.

"Are you the Admiral?" asked one.

"I am," replied Coligny proudly. "Young man, you ought to have respect for my old age and weakness. But do your will; you cannot shorten my life by much."

336 Uttering a dreadful oath the soldier lunged at Coligny with his spear. As the old man fell all the pride of name and fame rose in him. "Ah!" he cried, "had it but been a man and not this stable boy." Then one after another the soldiers crowded round him, plunging their daggers into his heart.

Suddenly from the courtyard came the voice of the young Duke. "Is it done?" he cried.

"It is done," was the reply. And raising the body the murderers threw it into the court below.

The day had hardly dawned, and the light was still dim. Guise bent down and wiped the blood from the face. "Yes it is he," he said, and giving the poor dead body a kick he turned on his heel. "We have begun well," he laughed.

So the work began, and so it continued all through the long summer Sunday till night ended the fearful carnage. None was spared; men, women and children alike were slain. The streets ran red with blood, the houses were piled with dead. All over the country the rage of killing spread, and before it was sated thirty thousand were slain.

This terrible slaughter is called the Massacre of St. Bartholomew, for it happened on St. Bartholomew's Day, Sunday, August 24, 1572.

It was meant utterly to root out Protestantism from France, but it failed. The Protestants were at first stunned with horror. Soon, however, they recovered, and a fourth civil war began. It was brought to an end by the Peace of Rochelle, which gave the Protestants all the privileges they had been given at the last peace. So the Massacre of St.

Bartholomew was an act of utterly useless, mad cruelty.

Charles never recovered from the horror of that awful Sunday. Before it he had been good-natured and easy-going. Afterward he became stern and melancholy, never smiling, never looking any one in the face. He was haunted by awful dreams in which he saw hideous faces covered with blood looking at him out of the darkness; he seemed to hear heartrending cries. Day and night were terrible to him.

His old nurse, who was a Huguenot, had been saved from the massacre and she, at the end, tried in vain to comfort him. "Ah, nurse, nurse," he cried, "what blood, what murders! Ah! I have followed evil counsel. Oh, may God forgive me and grant me grace."

"Sire," replied she, "the murders and the blood be upon the heads of those who counselled you."

And the world has followed his old nurse and blamed the powerful, scheming mother, more than the weak, easily led son.

CHAPTER 64

HENRY III—THE WAR OF THE THREE HENRIES

IN May 1574, Charles IX died. He was only twenty-three, and had reigned fourteen years. He left no son, and his brother, Henry Duke of Anjou, succeeded to the throne. When Charles died Henry was in Poland, for the Poles had chosen him as their King. But as soon as he heard that he was King of France, he gave up the crown of Poland and returned home.

The confusion in France was now worse than ever. The great leaders of the two parties were dead, but their sons took their places. On the Catholic side there was the young Duke Henry of Guise. On the Protestant side there were Henry of Navarre and his cousin, Henry of Conde, the sons of King Anthony of Navarre and of his brother, the Prince of Conde. Besides the Catholics and the Huguenots there was also a third party called the "Politics." Many of these were Catholics who wanted to see the rebellion put to an end, and who yet wanted to allow the Huguenots to worship God in their own way. At the head of this party stood the King's youngest brother, Francis Duke of Alencon.

Henry III was twenty-two when he came to the throne. He was a bad and silly king. Very proud of his looks, he spent nearly all the morning dressing himself. He painted his face, dyed his hair, wore ear-rings, thought more of his clothes than any vain woman, and gave a great deal of time to inventing new fashions. He thought so much of these things that it became the fashion for the favored people in the court to come to watch the King get up and dress, and a great ceremony was made of it.

Henry surrounded himself with courtiers as silly and empty-headed as himself. They were called his Mignons or Darlings. Both he and they made great pets of tiny dogs, monkeys, and parrots. Henry would often walk about with a sword by his side, a turban on his head, and a basket full of tiny dogs hung around his neck.

But besides being silly, Henry was bad. He would spend days and nights in shocking wickedness. Then afraid of being punished for what he had done he would walk barefoot through the streets clad in sackcloth, beating himself with knotted cords in penance. But this was not religion, only fear of punishment. He was afraid of death, afraid of hell, and when there was a thunderstorm he would run to hide himself in the lowest cellar of his castle, weeping and trembling with fear.

Such a King could do little to quiet the angry passions which had been raised, and the dreadful wars of religion went on. Between 1574 and 1580 the fifth, sixth, and seventh civil wars are counted. Each peace granted the Protestants some rights. Each peace made the Catholics angry, and afraid lest their power should wane. In 1584, too, the Duke of Alencon died. He was the King's only remaining brother. Henry had no children. So the next heir was Henry of Navarre, a Protestant. This made the Catholics still more fearful. So all over France they began to form a league for the defense of their religion. It was given the name of the Holy League. Henry of Guise was the head of it, and he soon became so powerful that the King was afraid of him and did everything he asked. All the chief posts in the kingdom were given to Guise and his friends, and Henry promised to undo all the laws giving freedom to the Huguenots.

When the Protestants heard of it they were filled with dread and once more they took up arms. This eighth civil war is called the War of the Henries because the leaders on all sides were named Henry— King Henry III, Henry of Guise, and Henry of Navarre.

Henry III had been forced to throw in his lot with Henry of Guise, but he did not love him. His real hope was that both Protestants and Catholics would be killed in such numbers that he would be left free to do as he liked.

But although, at Coutras, the Protestants won the greatest victory they had ever won, the war ended in a triumph for Henry of Guise.

The people of Paris, who were nearly all Catholics, were delighted with the Duke's success. They praised him as a hero almost as they had praised his father after the taking of Calais. But the King, jealous of the love the people gave him, fearful of his growing power, forbade Guise to come to Paris.

When King Henry himself returned to his capital the people looked coldly on him. As he rode through the streets hardly a voice was raised to cheer him. The people wanted their hero, and Henry had forbidden him to come.

But in spite of the King's command Guise came. As he rode through the streets the people recognized him, and cheer after cheer burst forth from them till from street to street the sound rolled in a thunder of applause.

"Long live Guise! Long life to the Pillar of the Church."

The people crowded round him to kiss his hand, to touch his coat, weeping, laughing, blessing him, scattering flowers in his path. It was a splendid triumph; all Paris went mad. Gallant, young, smiling and gracious, the Duke rode through it.

But there was one man in Paris who was ill pleased. That was Henry III. "He has come!" cried the King when he heard of it. "By heaven he shall die for it!"

"Sire, if it please you to honor me with the command," said a courtier, "to-day I will lay his head at your feet."

But the King was not yet ready for that.

Guise came to the King and bowed low before him. White and trembling with passion, Henry bit his lip.

"Sir Duke," he said, "I find it passing strange that you have the hardihood to come to me against my will and my command."

"Sire," replied the Duke, "I come to defend myself from the falsehoods of my enemies."

Shaken with anger, the King turned away in silence, and the Duke quickly left the court, glad to escape with his life.

The King now filled Paris with troops, who took possession of all the chief places. But the people rose in revolt. They overpowered the soldiers. They threw up barricades and stretched chains across all the streets leading to the palace, so that the King was really in a state of siege. Shops were shut, alarm bells were rung, and Paris from end to end was in uproar.

For hours the Duke looked on, doing nothing. Then later in the afternoon he left his house, and rode unarmed through the seething streets, carrying only a stick in his hand.

He was greeted with shouts of joy, "Long live Guise! Long live Guise!" And he, taking off his large hat, bowed and smiled to the yelling crowd, saying, "My friends, it is enough. Sirs, it is too much. Cry, "God save the King!'"

At the sound of his voice the fury of the people was quieted. But the barricades were not taken down, the people were still in revolt and ready to besiege Henry and take him prisoner. He knew it, and fled away in haste, swearing never to re-enter the town but through a breach made by his cannon.

Guise was now master, and the King was obliged to do everything he wished. Guise found many ways of showing his power, and of insulting and humiliating the King. Henry's anger against his rival grew hotter and hotter, until he resolved to be rid of him.

Very early on the morning of Christmas Eve, 1589, in his castle at Blois, Henry called together his council and his special bodyguard called the "Forty-five" because of their number. First he met his council. "The Duke," he said, "is so blinded by ambition that he is ready to take both my crown and my life. It has come to this, either he or I must die. And it must be this day. Will you aid me?"

"You may count upon our aid and our lives," they cried.

Then Henry went to the Forty-five. "You know all the insolence and the wrongs I have had to suffer these many years from the Duke of Guise," he said. "At last it has come to this that this morning either he or I must die. Will you promise to serve me and to avenge me by taking his life?':

With one voice they cried. "He shall die!"

"Let us see," said the King, then, "which of you have daggers?"

There were eight who had them. These men the King hid in the gallery through which the Duke must pass, and bid them kill him. Then as he waited, Henry walked back and forth in great excitement, unable to sit still. He already rejoiced in the thought of the Duke's death. "He is great and powerful," he said, "and I shall be right merry."

At length the Duke came. He had been warned not to go to see the King that morning, for already it was whispered abroad that the King meant to kill the Duke. But Guise paid no heed to the warning. "He will not dare," he said proudly.

Dressed in gray satin, a cloak about his shoulders and his sword by his side, his head held high, for was he not the greatest man in all France? he stepped toward the King's room.

Suddenly, as he walked jauntily along, a man darted upon him and struck him in the breast, crying, "Ha, traitor, you shall die!" another threw himself at his knees, a third struck him in the back.

"Help! my friends, help!" cried the Duke. But no help came. He tried in vain to draw his sword; it was entangled in his cloak. But with his bare hands he fought, and so strong was he that he dragged his murderers with him from one end of the room to the other and fell dying at the feet of the King.

"My God," said Henry, suddenly awed at the sight, "how tall he is!

He looks even taller than when he was alive!" Then he brutally kicked the poor, dead body as once Guise had kicked that of Coligny, and turned away.

"I am King of France at last," he said to his mother; "the King of Paris is dead."

"You have killed the Duke of Guise!" she cried, struck with horror. "God grant that by this death you become not King of nothing at all. You have cut your coat, but can you sew it?"

Queen Catherine did not live to learn the answer to her question. For a few days later this scheming woman who had used and betrayed Huguenot and Catholic alike in her desire for power, died hated, and despised by all.

When the news of the Duke's murder reached Paris becomes the people rose in fury. They took as their leader the Duke of Mayenne, a brother of the murdered Guise.

To meet this outburst Henry knew not what to do, for he had few soldiers and no money. So, strange to say, he made friends with Henry of Navarre. At once the Huguenots gathered to him in great numbers, and together the two Kings marched to besiege Paris.

The siege had scarcely begun when one day a friar came seeking the King, saying he had business with him. It was already late, so the friar was told he must wait till morning, and then he should surely see the King.

So early next morning the friar was brought to Henry. The King had not yet put on his buff coat, being only half dressed, and was sitting in his bedroom in a loose silk undercoat.

The friar bowed low before him, and gave him a letter, saying he had also a secret to tell. Henry took the letter and began to read it.

As soon as the friar saw that his thoughts were upon the letter he quickly drew a knife from his sleeve. One moment it flashed, the next it was buried in the King's body.

"Ah, the wicked monk!" cried Henry; "he has killed me! he has killed me!" With all his strength he drew the knife from the wound and struck at the friar's forehead. Hearing the cry and the noise, the King's guards rushed in, and in a moment the friar lay dead at Henry's feet, pierced by many wounds.

At first it was thought that the King's wound was not dangerous. But during the night he became very ill, and in a few hours he died. He was thirty-six and had reigned for fifteen years.

CHAPTER 65

HENRY IV THE GREAT—THE PROTESTANT KING

HENRY III was the last of the Valois, for his youngest brother had died before him, and he left no son. The heir to the throne then was the Bourbon Prince, Henry of Navarre. Before Henry III died he had acknowledged him as his heir, and kissed him. But in his dying voice he murmured, "Brother, I assure you, you will never be King of France if you turn not Catholic, and if you humble not yourself to the Church."

So true was this that when with tears in his eyes Henry of Navarre entered the room where his cousin lay dead, he was greeted with sullen looks. With clenched fists and dark frowns the Catholic nobles muttered, "Death, rather than a Huguenot King."

Yet many rejoiced at the death of the King. The friends of the Duke of Guise who had worn mourning now dressed themselves in green to show their joy. His sister drove through Paris shouting with delight, crying out to all the passers-by, " Good news, my friends! Good new r s! The tyrant is dead. There is no more a Henry of Valois in France!"

The Huguenots and some of the less zealous Catholics now acknowledged Henry of Navarre to be their rightful King. But the Leaguers would have none of him, and they proclaimed the Cardinal of Bourbon King, under the title of Charles X. King Philip of Spain, too, setting Salic Law at naught, claimed the throne for his daughter Isabella. For, you remember, Philip had married a French princess for his third wife, and he now claimed the throne in exactly the same way as King Edward had claimed it so long before.

Seldom has a King in coming into his kingdom found it in greater confusion. Henry of Navarre had to fight for his throne, and he had to fight in poverty, for his tiny kingdom of Navarre supplied him with little money. He had not even money enough with which to buy clothes. He could not have worn mourning for the dead King had he not taken Henry III's own clothes and had them made to fit himself. How then could he pay for an army to fight his cause?

He had not enough soldiers to go on with the siege of Paris, so he moved away to Normandy and took possession of Dieppe. This was of great use to him. For Queen Elizabeth had promised him help. And in Dieppe he found a port by which he could receive the soldiers which she sent to him.

It was the ninth war of religion which had now begun. And very soon the skill and bravery which Henry showed won many hearts for him. Province after province yielded to the new King.

At length Henry won a great victory at Ivry. The army of the League was much larger than Henry's. But in the hour of danger the King was ever gay and courageous. It was a cold and windy March morning, the ground was heavy with rain, and dark rain clouds drove overhead. But gloomy though the day was, it did not damp Henry's spirits.

Gallant and gay and every inch a King he looked as he rode up and down in front of his troops. On his helmet he wore a great white plume which the March wind tossed this way and that. Upon his horse's head there was another.

"Comrades," cried Henry, "God is with us! There are your foes! Here is your King! Up and at them! If lose your standards follow my white plume. You will find it ever on the road to honor, and please God to victory."

Then throwing his reins over one arm Henry clasped his hands, and raised them to heaven. "O Lord," he cried, "Thou knowest my heart, and with Thine eye dost pierce my secret thoughts. If it be best for this people that I win the crown, aid us. But if it be Thy will to take away my kingdom take my life also; let me die fighting at the head of these brave soldiers who give their lives for me."

When he had finished these words there arose from the army a great shout, "God save the King!" From rank to rank it echoed and thundered, in mighty waves of sound.

Who would not follow such a leader? Who would not gladly die for him? Behind their King the knights and nobles charged amain, they carried all before them, and the Leaguers were scattered in flight.

But even after the great victory of Ivry the war went on for nearly three years. Paris still held out against a Protestant King. At length, however, both sides grew weary of the strife. The Cardinal King, the so-called Charles X, had long been dead, and the Leaguers knew not whom to choose in his place. The young Duke of Guise, the Duke of Mayenne, and the Spanish Princess Isabella all claimed the right. So there was strife within the Catholic party.

And now Henry chose this time to take a great and hazardous step.

"FOLLOW MY WHITE PLUME," CRIED HENRY.

He had never been a bigot that is, he had not clung blindly and without reason to the Protestant religion. The peace of France was more to him than any form of religion. So now, seeing no other way, he determined to take the perilous leap and become a Catholic. "Paris is worth a mass," he said a little lightly.

But he was grave enough at heart. He sent for the bishops and argued long with them.

"See," he said at length, while the tears stood in his eyes, "to-day I put my soul into your hands. I pray you guard it well. For where you make me to enter, there I shall abide. I shall not go thence until I die. That I protest and swear to you."

Two days later, clad all in white satin, with a black cloak hanging from his shoulders, he went to the great church of St. Denis. With him were the princes and lords of the kingdom, and the whole court. Before him marched a bodyguard of soldiers in full armor.

With trumpets blowing, and drums beating, Henry passed through gaily decorated streets. Flags and silken hangings fluttered in the breeze, flowers carpeted his path. And all along the way the people cheered and cried, "God save the King!"

When the procession reached St. Denis they found the great gates fast shut. The Lord High Chancellor advanced, and knocked loudly upon them. Slowly they were swung open. And there at the great west door Henry saw a crowd of priests and bishops, clad in splendid robes and carrying the cross, the gospels, and the holy water. In front of them the Archbishop of Bourges was seated in a chair covered with white silk, and decorated with the arms of France and of Navarre. As the King mounted the steps, the Archbishop rose. "Who are you?" he asked.

"I am Henry, the King of France and of Navarre," was the reply.

"What do you want?"

"I want to be received into the Catholic Church," replied Henry.

"Do you desire it sincerely?"

"I wish it and I desire it," said Henry, kneeling at the Archbishop's feet. Kneeling there he repeated the Creed in a loud, clear voice. Then amid the shouts of the people and the firing of cannon he was led into the church. There before the altar he once more knelt.

When at last the long ceremony was over, the King, followed by a wonderful throng of people, returned to his palace through the same flower-strewn streets, resounding with cries of "God save the King!"

Whether we think that Henry was right, or whether we think that he was wrong, in thus denying the faith in which he had been brought up, he was certainly wise. It was the only way in which to bring peace to France. Many even among the Huguenots saw that, and Henry's chief adviser, Sully, himself a staunch Huguenot, advised at which him to take the step. But some too of his best friends were hurt to the heart at what seemed to them treachery. They sadly went to their own homes, and took no more part in the ruling of the land.

CHAPTER 66

HENRY IV—THE EDICT OF NANTES—FRANCE AT PEACE

BUT although by becoming a Catholic Henry had reconciled many of his people to him, much remained for him to do. For the Leaguers still held out, and they had possession not only of Paris, the capital, but of Reims, the city in which the Kings of France were crowned.

Henry felt that he must be crowned, that never until he was, would the common people really look upon him as their true King. So with great and solemn ceremony he was crowned at Chartres.

Then he marched to Paris, and Paris opened her gates to the King. While all the bells in the city clashed and clanged with joy the people shouted, "God bless the King and the Peace! God save the King!"

And as he rode along Henry with kindly eyes looked upon the eager crowd which surged around him. "Poor people," he said, "they are hungry for the sight of their King."

As he crossed the threshold of the splendid palace of the Louvre and heard the shouts in his ears it seemed to Henry he must be dreaming. "My lord," he said, turning to the Chancellor, "dare I believe that I am where I am?"

"Sire," replied he, smiling, "I think there is no doubt about it."

"I do not know," said the King, "the more I think about it the more I am astonished."

But Henry was in deed and in truth at last King of France. Even the young Duke of Guise and the leaders of the League yielded to him. He still had, however, a great enemy in Philip of Spain.

The Leaguers had been helped by King Philip of Spain, and there were many Spanish soldiers in Paris when the King entered in triumph. Henry sent them all away. "Give my compliments to your master," he said, "and don't come here again." But Philip still continued plotting against him, and Henry once more declared war. This war lasted for three years and was ended by the Peace of Vervins. This peace left things in almost the same position as at the Peace of Cateau-Cambresis, signed forty years before in the reign of Henry II.

Thus France had endured forty years of war and bloodshed for nothing. But at least peace had at last been won. And Henry now began this time of quiet by signing the Edict of Nantes. It is the act for which perhaps his reign is most remembered. By this Edict the Protestants were allowed the freedom of their religion throughout the kingdom, they were made equal with the Catholics in every way, and were allowed to serve their country in the state and in the army. They were also given certain towns as places of safety.

These favors to the Huguenots made many of the Catholics angry, and the Parliament at first would not pass the Edict. Some of its members even went to see the King to try to persuade him against this act. He listened to them patiently, and then he spoke.

"I come to speak with you," he said, "not in my royal robes, not with my sword by my side and my helmet on my head, nor yet as a prince who receives foreign ambassadors. But dressed as the simple father of a family I come to speak to my children."

But although his words were gentle he was firm. "Those who do not want my Edict to pass want war," he said. Then he grew more stern. "And I will declare it to-morrow, but I will not make it. You will make it. I have made the Edict, and I command you to serve it, I am King now, and I speak as King. I will be obeyed."

Again he grew more gentle. "Do what I command you," he pleaded, "or rather what I beg of you. You will do it not only for me, but also for yourselves, and for the good of peace."

So at length the Edict was passed. And in the calm which followed Henry did much for the happiness of his people. In this his chief friend and helper was the great Duke of Sully. He had been Henry's friend in the old fighting days. He had shared all his hardships, had marched beside him in rags and hunger, in weariness and want. Now he shared his good fortune and his splendor, and to the last day of his life he remained the King's greatest friend.

Sully looked after the money of the nation, and he looked after it so well that although the taxes were made less the King had far more money to spend. When Henry came to the throne he found nothing but debts. When he died he had paid off a great many of these debts and left his treasury full.

Yet he spent much money for the good of the country, Roads and canals were made, bridges were built, marshes were drained, much was done in every way for the farmers. For in farming Sully saw the great wealth of France.

Much was done too for manufactures. For in manufactures Henry saw the great wealth of France. Here he and his adviser Sully differed. Henry was specially interested in silk manufactures. He had mulberry trees planted, and encouraged the people to raise silkworms, from which to get the raw silk.

Sully did not like to see so much money being spent on mere fashion and finery, and he tried to stop the King. What need was there for people to wear silk and velvet, he asked. He declared that he would make a law forbidding people to wear such splendid clothes. But the King laughed.

"I would rather fight the King of Spain in three pitched battles," he said, "than face the judges and great people, and above all their wives and daughters, if I made such stupid rules."

So he had his way. He encouraged the silk manufactures as much as he could, and the first time he wore a pair of silk stockings made in France he showed them off to all his courtiers with great pride. The beginnings were small. But to-day the French silk industry is worth millions to the country.

It was now too that Frenchmen first settled in Canada, and that Quebec was founded by Champlain, and France, at Peace at home, began to build up a great colonial empire.

But at length Henry turned his thoughts from all these peaceful things to war once more. At the treaty of Vervins he had forced Philip of Spain to make peace, but he had meant to begin the struggle again, and break the power of the King of Spain and Emperor of Germany as soon as France was strong enough. For as long as Spain remained as powerful as in the days of Philip II the peace of all Europe was threatened.

Henry now thought that the time had come, and he began to make great preparations tor war with Spain, It was not to be a French war only. It was to be a war of all Europe. A Catholic, Henry placed himself at the head of the Protestant armies. The Dutch and the reformed princes of Germany joined him, as well as the Italian princes who wished to be free of Spanish interference. Henry hoped for an easy victory. Then he meant to rearrange the states of Europe so that war would no more be possible.

Henry was already fifty-seven, a great age at which to begin so tremendous an undertaking. Still he hardly hesitated, although he was sometimes haunted by dark forebodings of evil.

A few days before the date fixed for his setting out for battle he was talking with some of the nobles. "Ah," he said suddenly, "you do not know me now, you others. But I shall die one of these days, and when you have lost me then you will know what I was worth, and the difference between me and other men."

"By heaven, Sire," cried one of them, "will you never cease vexing us by telling us that you will die soon? Why, you are only in the flower of your age. You will live, please God, some good long years to come."

Still all morning Henry was restless and uneasy. But when a young gentleman of the court came to tell him that an astrologer had foretold that the day would be one of danger, Henry laughed.

"The astrologer is an old rascal," he said, "who wants your money, and you are a young fool to believe him. Our days are in the keeping of God."

Yet Henry could not get rid of his sadness and gloom.

"Sire," said one of his household, "you are sad and thoughtful. Will you not go out a little, and take the air? That will refresh you."

"A good idea," said the King. "Order my carriage. I will go to the Arsenal and see Sully, who is not well."

So the carriage was made ready, and Henry set out with several gentlemen. As they drove through a narrow street the carriage met two carts which blocked the way. The horses drew up for a few minutes until the road could be cleared to allow the King to pass. While the carriage waited a man suddenly leaped on to the wheel at the side next the King. He was a wild, half-mad bigot, who hated the King because of the Edict of Nantes, and had vowed his death. He raised a knife and struck.

"I am wounded!" cried Henry. Again the knife flashed. The King gave a deep sigh and lay still.

At once the street was in an uproar, the people crying aloud in rage and sorrow. But one of the gentlemen who was with the King shouted to the people that he was only wounded. The horses' heads were turned, and quickly they drove back to the palace. Gently the King was lifted from his carriage, and carried to his room. He neither spoke nor moved. He was quite dead.

No greater King has ever ruled in France. No King who cared so much for the happiness of his people ever sat upon the throne. He was a great soldier, and a great statesman, and above all he loved justice and toleration. And when it was known throughout Paris that Henry the Great was dead the people wept as they had never wept for any King before.

CHAPTER 67

LOUIS XIII—THE REIGN OF FAVORITES

HENRY IV, you remember, had been married to a Princess of France. He never loved her, they had no children, and some time after he became King of France the Pope allowed him to put away his wife. Soon after he married an Italian lady, Mary of Medici. Her son Louis, a little boy of nine, now came to the throne as Louis XIII.

Louis was of course too young to rule, so Mary of Medici was made Regent. Unfortunately, Mary was a weak and foolish woman, and allowed herself to be ruled by favorites. The chief of these were an Italian named Concini and his wife. Mary heaped honors of all kinds upon this man, making him Marshal of France, although he had never so much as seen a battle.

When Henry IV died all his projects for a great war died with him. Instead of fighting with Spain Mary arranged that Louis XIII should marry the Infanta Anne, and that his sister Elizabeth should also marry a Spanish Prince.

Sully could not consent to this, and as Mary would not give up her plans he gave up his posts and went away to live quietly in the country, taking no more part in ruling the land.

Daily Concini grew more insolent, for his pride knew no bounds, and daily hatred against him increased. As Louis grew up he, too, hated his mother's favorite, for he had one of his own. This was a gentleman named Luynes, the keeper of his falcons. For Mary of Medici took little trouble to teach her son the duties of a king. Instead, she did all she could to shut him out from any part in the government, and even allowed people to think that he was lacking in sense and unable to rule. He was allowed to grow up among his servants, and his favorite amusements were cock fights and bull fights, and setting falcons to catch sparrows in the gardens of the Tuileries. He made a very good stable boy, and he helped the gardeners cutting turfs and driving cartloads of earth, and was very clever with his hands.

Luynes hated Concini, and he did everything he could to increase Louis's hatred of him. He made Louis believe at length that his throne and his very life were in danger. Then the King plotted with his falconer, a gardener, a clerk, and some soldiers to kill Concini. They also persuaded a Captain of the Guard to help them.

One morning Concini went as usual to the Louvre to visit the Queen. Just as he was crossing the drawbridge before the great door, the Captain of the Guard ran out upon him, followed by several soldiers.

"I arrest you in the name of the king," he said, laying his hand on Concini's arm.

"What, I?" cried he in astonishment.

He had not time to say more, for several shots rang out and he fell dead.

Louis and his favorite, Luynes, were waiting anxiously for news, ready to fly if the plot failed. In a few minutes shouts of, "Long live the King!" rang out.

"Sire," cried an officer, rushing in, "from this hour you are King. Concini is dead." Then lifting Louis in his arms he held him up to the high window, so that he might be seen by the people who were rapidly gathering in the court below. Louder and louder rang out the cheers and cries of "God save the King!"

The news soon reached the Queen. She knew her day was over. "Poor me!" she cried; "I have reigned seven years. Now the only crown I can hope for is a heavenly one."

She asked to see her son. He refused, and held her prisoner in her own rooms. Later on she was banished to the Castle of Blois.

One of Louis's first deeds was to send for his father's old advisers. When they came he received them with tears of joy. "I am now your King," he said. "I have been your King, but now I am and shall be your King more than ever."

It was not however the advisers of Henry IV who were to have the power, but Louis's favorite, Luynes. He soon rose to be of great importance. He was made a duke, married a great lady, while Louis heaped upon him all manner of honors. But he was no more fitted to rule than Concini had been. His one idea was to make himself and his family great and powerful. So in a very short time he was hated by every one. Then many of the nobles, angry at the power of this upstart, remembered the exiled Queen. So they began to plot with her, and at length helped her to escape.

Mary was kept a prisoner, the doors of the castle were locked and closely watched. But having made up her mind to escape she cared little for bolts and bars. Was not the window open?

So one dark February night when every one in the castle had gone to sleep Mary alone waked. She made bundles of all her jewels and treasures, and then awaited the signal. At length it came.

A knight climbed the ladder which had been placed against the high terrace that surrounded the castle. Then he climbed the second ladder from the terrace to the high window of the Queen's room. When he reached the window he tapped upon it, and it being opened he leaped into the room.

The Queen wasted no time in talk, but gathering her wide skirts about her she gave her hand to the knight and stepped out of the window. The knight went first, the Queen next, and then a few faithful servants followed. Silently and anxiously they climbed down. To a lady utterly unused to danger it was a terrible descent.

The window was at a great height, and in spite of all her courage Queen Mary was breathless and shaken when she reached the terrace beneath. Still she was not free; the terrace was a long way from the ground. But she could not face the perilous climb down the second ladder. So sitting on a cloak she slid down the steep slope and safely reached the bottom.

The ladders were at once thrown into the Loire so that no one might know how the Queen escaped. Then through the darkness she sped, until at the end of the bridge she reached her carriage. Getting in, she was quickly driven away, and reached the spot where soldiers and friends awaited her without any adventures.

So quietly had the Queen slipped away that in the castle no one had the slightest idea of it. Next morning as it grew later and later her servants began to wonder why she slept so long. They listened at her door and could hear no noise. At length they burst into her room and found it empty. They were greatly troubled and knew not what to think. In a few days they heard that she had escaped and was far away.

When Louis and Luynes heard of the Queen mother's escape they were both much afraid. But Louis decided it would be best to make friends with her, before her followers had time to rise in revolt. So mother and son met and forgave each other. With tears running down her cheeks the Queen kissed her son, crying, "God bless us, how the boy has grown!"

But although war between the King's party and the Queen's party was avoided, war broke out in another quarter. The Protestants had become very uneasy, for they were no longer treated as they had been in the time of Henry IV. Now Louis let it be known that the Kingdom of Navarre should henceforth not only be a part of France but that it should be Catholic. As Navarre, and especially Beam, the birthplace of Henry IV, was the most Protestant part of France, the Protestants began to fear for their religion. They would not give way to Louis, and once more a war of religion began.

Louis marched against the Huguenots, resolved to crush them utterly. But for leader he had Luynes, who knew as little about war as Concini had done. So although he had a fine army he won no victory, but made mistake after mistake.

This made the nobles very angry, and Louis himself was at length growing tired of his favorite, when he suddenly died of fever.

CHAPTER 68

LOUIS XIII—THE TAKING OF LA ROCHELLE

AND now there rose to power the greatest man of Louis's reign. This was Cardinal Richelieu. Richelieu had been Queen Mary's friend. Now she no longer liked him, and indeed plotted against him time after time. Neither did Louis really like Richelieu. But he had no strength of character of his own. He had to have some one on whom to lean. He saw at least that Richelieu was wise, and so although he disliked him he kept him in power. For the last eighteen years of Louis's reign it was really Richelieu who reigned.

Richelieu was one of the greatest of French statesmen. He loved France well, and he understood France and Frenchmen perhaps better than any man has done. He was a man with a terrible strength of will, and he bent all things and all men to his own ends and aims. He would be obeyed, and he made even the King his slave. He had three great aims. One was to lessen the power of the great nobles, another to lessen the power of the Huguenots, the third to lessen the power of the German Emperor and King of Spain. By the first two he strove to unite France into one great whole. By the last he strove to make France great among the countries of Europe.

In order to lessen the power of the nobles Richelieu ordered that the fortifications of all towns and castles should be destroyed except those which were needed to defend the borders of the kingdom. He also did away with the posts of admiral and constable, as these posts put too much power into the hands of one noble.

The nobles were wild and lawless, but Richelieu showed them that they must bow to the laws of the land. They had a perfect passion for dueling. They fought duels for the slightest cause, because a man looked at another, or because he did not look, because a man trod on another's toe, because he wore a coat of a colour another did not like. Anything served as a reason. They fought at all times and in all places, in crowded streets, on lonely moors, by day, by moonlight, by torchlight. The two who began the quarrel each had a friend called a second who came to watch the fight. These seconds fought too, often without knowing in the least what the quarrel was about. And so many nobles and gentlemen were killed in those duels that it was said more died in that way than in all the wars of religion.

Richelieu made up his mind to stop all this, and he made the laws against dueling very strict. Death was the punishment for any man who killed another in a duel, and those who took part in it were banished or imprisoned. One of the greatest nobles in the land was banished for fighting twenty-two duels. In spite of that he returned and fought a twenty-third in the streets of Paris in broad daylight, just out of bravado.

Richelieu would not allow any one thus openly to flout his laws. As an example to others he caused both this noble and his second to be seized, and in spite of the prayers of their friends they were both condemned to death.

With deeds like these Richelieu showed himself powerful in the state. But Richelieu was not only leader of the state, he was leader of the army. When he went to battle he laid aside his red Cardinal's robes and wore a sword and breastplate, a coat embroidered with gold, and a plumed hat.

Richelieu continued the war against the Protestants which Louis had begun. For although he did not wish to take away their religious liberty he wished to make them of no account in the state. The struggle was nearly brought to an end with the taking of La Rochelle.

La Rochelle was the chief port of the Protestants and it was very strongly fortified. The King's army entirely shut it in upon the land side. But the British had offered the French Protestants help, and Richelieu soon saw that La Rochelle could never be taken so long as the British ships could enter the harbor freely, bringing food and men. So he began to build a huge dyke more than half a mile long right across the entrance of the harbor.

It was a tremendous undertaking, and more than once the wind and waves swept away in one night what had taken weeks to build. But nothing daunted the great Cardinal. The ruined work was begun again and again. Old ships were filled with stones and sunk along the line, piles were driven in, and thousands of loads of stone were brought to the great wall. At length the dyke rose above the waves, forts were built, cannon were mounted.

Helplessly the people of La Rochelle watched the work go on. They could do nothing to stop it. For the dyke was built just beyond reach of their cannons. Anxiously they awaited the promised help from Britain.

At length one May morning the British ships appeared in sight. The people of La Rochelle were filled with joy. They greeted the approaching fleet with loud thunder of guns, and flags were run up upon every flagstaff in the town.

But the British Admiral had expected to have nothing more to do than sail into the harbor and unload his vessels full of food. Now when he saw his way barred by the huge dyke, with forts and batteries, and French battleships to right of him and to left of him, bristling with cannon, his heart misgave him. For a week he hesitated, for a week he lingered, skirmishing with the enemy. Then one morning in the horrified gaze of the people of La Rochelle he turned about and steered for home.

Awful despair took hold upon the people when they saw the English go, but the King's party rejoiced, for now, they thought, the town must yield. Little they knew the stern courage of the people they had to deal with.

John Guiton was the mayor. He was a wiry little man who had been a merchant and a sailor. He had led a wild, rough life, hardly better than a pirate's. Used to all sorts of hardships, he was almost savage in his courage. He had become mayor since the siege began. When he was chosen he threw his dagger on the council table. "I accept," he said, "the honor you do me, but only on condition that with the point of this blade I pierce the heart of any one who talks of yielding. If I myself stoop to such cowardice may my blood wipe out my crime."

Now none dared to whisper of surrender, but the horror of hunger was awful. There was neither meat nor bread left. The people ate chopped straw and hay, soup made from parchments and skins, and a horrible paste made of bones ground to powder.

The women and children, who could not fight, were sent out of the town. But the pitiless King sent them back again. Guiton, more pitiless still in his turn, refused to open the gates to them. So many perished miserably between the royal camp and the walls of the town.

At length one of the counsellors dared to speak of yielding. Guiton did not use his dagger as he had threatened, but he boxed this counsellor's ears, and the people rose in fury against him, so that he was obliged to hide from them.

"We shall all die of hunger, " said one to the mayor.

"What matters that," he answered, "as long as one man remains to keep fast the gates?"

At length once again a British fleet arrived. But after a useless attempt to break through the dyke the British gave up the fight. La

Rochelle was left to its fate. There was no more hope, and the town yielded to the King.

When next day the King and Cardinal rode into the town they saw an awful sight. Streets and houses were full of dried up corpses which no one had had strength to bury. Those who still lived were like moving shadows, wan spectres with scarce a breath of life left in them. Even the rough soldiers were filled with pity, and tears blinded the King's eyes as he saw the gaunt creatures fall on their knees, and in hollow hoarse voices whisper, "God save the King and have mercy upon us."

No massacres followed upon the taking of La Rochelle. Food was given freely to all. But its rights and liberties were taken from the town, the walls were levelled to the ground, and the Catholic religion was once more established there.

Yet in spite of the loss of their great free town the Protestants still fought on for a few months. But at length they were forced to make peace.

Richelieu had utterly crushed them. He indeed left them freedom to worship God in their own way, but they were no longer of any power in the state.

CHAPTER 69
LOUIS XIII—THE POWER OF THE CARDINAL KING

DURING the rest of his life Richelieu's chief aim was to make France great abroad. He was far more King than Cardinal. In Germany, a war called the Thirty Years' War had begun. It was a war between Catholics and Protestants. The Emperor of Germany, a Prince of the house of Austria, was upon the Catholic side, which was the stronger. Richelieu did not wish the house of Austria to become more powerful. So he who had crushed the Protestants at home took their part abroad. Besides this, the French fought in Spain and in Austria. At one time indeed French armies were fighting in Spain, Italy, Germany, and the Netherlands all at once. At first they were not always successful, but in the end they won victory after victory. Before he died Richelieu saw the power of the house of Austria curbed, and France of greater importance among the countries of Europe than it had ever been before.

But while Richelieu made France great abroad, at home he ruled as a tyrant. He did what he thought was best for France, but he did it in high-handed fashion, and his tyranny made for him many enemies. Again and again there were plots against him. When they were discovered the leaders were punished with pitiless sternness.

Queen Mary, who had once been his friend, hated him; Queen Anne, Louis's wife, hated him; the Duke of Orleans, Louis's brother, hated him, besides many more. The King himself did not like him. Yet in spite of all Richelieu was so great a man that he kept his place of power, and forced his enemies to obey him.

Once the King became so ill that it was thought he would die. At once Richelieu's enemies gathered, planning how they would get rid of their enemy. Even Richelieu himself thought his day was over, and that his work for France must cease ere it was half done.

But the King did not die, he grew better. Then Queen Mary tried all she could to poison his mind against Richelieu. He was a villain and a traitor, she said, who plotted to make himself king.

Torn with doubt Louis left his mother and shut himself up in his room. Throwing himself on his bed he tossed about trying to think, tearing at the buttons on his coat. He must choose between his mother and his minister, and he loved neither one nor other.

But at length Louis yielded to his mother, and Richelieu was sent away.

The court was in an uproar of joy. All the Cardinal's enemies crowded round Queen Mary and Queen Anne, glorying in the news. They did not trouble to go to the King, for what power had he?

But they rejoiced too soon. Richelieu was making ready to flee when a messenger arrived bidding him go to the King at once. Gladly the Cardinal obeyed. When he came Louis received him with every mark of favor. "Continue to serve me," he said, "and I will take your part against all enemies."

Too weak to resist the torrent of his mother's words Louis had only given way in seeming. But so utterly had the Cardinal's enemies been deceived that this day was ever after known as the Day of Dupes.

Once more Richelieu triumphed over all his enemies. He became more powerful than ever. The Queen mother fled away to Brussels, and after a life of adventures and troubles she died in misery and poverty in Cologne, ten years later.

But Richelieu had still many enemies, chief among them the King's brother, the Duke of Orleans. Again and again he plotted the Cardinal's ruin and death. Once the plot all but succeeded. The murderers walked close behind the Cardinal, the Duke beside him. It only remained for the Duke to give the signal for the Cardinal's death. But at the last minute his heart failed him. He could not give the signal, and the Cardinal escaped.

The last plot of all was led by the Marquis of Cinq-Mars, a splendid, proud young man, who had become a great favorite with the King. In order to amuse the King Richelieu had himself brought this young man to his notice. Louis became so fond of him that he allowed him to do what he liked, and soon Cinq-Mars's pride and insolence knew no bounds. Cinq-Mars was gay, and splendid, and eighteen; Louis was melancholy, and grave, and forty. And these two strange friends were forever quarrelling and sulking like a couple of children, forever calling in the Cardinal to make up their quarrels. Cinq-Mars began at length to be jealous of Richelieu, who had befriended him, and he did his best to turn the King against his great minister, and plotted his death.

Richelieu well knew of these plots. He watched and bided his time.

Then suddenly one day an unknown person sent him the copy of a traitorous treaty between the King of Spain and Cinq-Mars and his friends.

Richelieu at once sent the treaty to the King. Cinq-Mars was seized and imprisoned, and along with one of his friends named De Thou condemned to death. De Thou had not joined in the plot, but he had known of it and had not told. "Ah, sir," he said, turning to Cinq-Mars upon the scaffold, "I have some right to complain of you, for you are the cause of my death. But God knows how I love you. Let us die together, let us die bravely and win heaven together."

And so these two magnificent young men died for plotting against the life of a sick old man who had not many months to live. For Richelieu was by this time so ill that he could not walk or even sit. He was carried about in a sumptuous litter which was like a room. In it were his bed and his work table, and a chair for his secretary. It was hung with crimson silk curtains and carried by eighteen soldiers of the Guard. It was so large that the gates of the towns and villages through which he journeyed were too narrow to let it pass. But all through his life Richelieu had swept men and things out of his way when they opposed him.

"I go to my end," he said. "I overturn all, I mow down all. Nothing stops me and, in short, I cover all with my red Cardinal's robe."

Now the walls of towns and cities were battered down to let his sickbed through.

He met death bravely. To the very end he was busy with affairs of state. "Do you forgive your enemies?" asked the priest as for the last time the Cardinal received the sacrament.

"I have never had any but those of the King and the state," proudly replied the dying Cardinal-King.

So, proud and hard to the end, he died.

Richelieu had set France high. He had made the King who was his slave the greatest King in the world.

"The minister," it was said, "made the King play the second part in the kingdom, and the first in Europe. He lowered the King, but he exalted the reign."

He was feared by all, loved by hardly any. When the people of France knew that the terrible Cardinal with the unbending will was dead, really dead this time, after so many attempts to kill him, there was an outburst of joy. Bonfires were lit, people danced and feasted as for a wedding or a coronation.

The King, too, eased from the yoke which had borne him down all these years, was glad. Yet he altered nothing; he obeyed Richelieu even now that he was dead.

Little more than six months after the Cardinal's death his royal slave died too. He was a sad, world-weary man who seemed glad to be done with life.

"Thank Heaven!" he said quietly when he was told he had only a few more hours to live.

He died on the 14th of May, 1643, having reigned thirty-three years exactly.

CHAPTER 70

LOUIS XIV—HOW A GREAT LADY BESIEGED ORLEANS

A few weeks before Louis XIII died his little son, who was scarcely five years old, was baptized.

"Can you tell me your name now?" asked his father, the next day.

"I am called Louis XIV," said the little boy.

"Not yet, not yet, my son," murmured his father sadly, hurt by the answer.

But the little boy did not know what he said, and did not mean to hurt his father, for when some one asked him if he would like to be King he answered, "No."

"Not even if your father died?':

"If my father dies," said the little Dauphin, "I will throw myself into the grave too."

But now his father was dead, and little five-year-old Louis was King. Of course he could not rule, and so his mother, Queen Anne, became Regent.

To the surprise of every one she took for her chief adviser Cardinal Mazarin, an Italian, the friend and follower of the great Richelieu. The Queen herself was a Spaniard. Thus strange to say France was ruled by two foreigners, the one an Italian and the other a Spaniard.

Mazarin was very different from Richelieu. Instead of being proud and imperious he was humble and gentle. Richelieu went straight to his end, overturning and sweeping away whatever stood in his path. Mazarin went round about, and tried to gain his end by flattery and smooth words. He slid into power almost before people knew it. "He found himself at the head of all the world," said one who lived in those days, "when all the world thought he was beneath their feet."

When Louis XIII died France was still at war with Spain and with the Empire. But France had now two splendid generals. One was Conde, a descendant of that Conde of whom we have already heard. He was at this time only twenty-two. But he gained so many battles that he is known as the Great Conde. He was dashing and eager, loved danger, and fought his battles with careless courage.

The other was Turenne. He was ten years older, no less brilliant than Conde, but more calm, and more careful of his soldiers' lives. He did not love danger as Conde did. It is even said that before a battle he always felt nervous and trembled. Then he would speak to his body. "You tremble, carcase," he would say, "but if you knew where I am about to lead you, you would tremble still more." But indeed Turenne did his body an injustice. For when danger was there he neither trembled nor was afraid.

These two generals, sometimes together, sometimes apart, won so many victories that at length the German Emperor was glad to make peace. This peace was called the Peace of Westphalia because it was signed at Munster and Osnabruck, two towns in Westphalia. By it France gained the whole of Alsace except Strasburg, which remained a free town. The Protestant provinces of Germany also gained much freedom, and became almost independent of the Emperor. His power was thus so much lessened that he was no longer a great danger to France.

But hardly was the war with Germany at an end when civil war began in France. This was brought on by Mazarin's misrule.

The misery of the people had been great in the time of Richelieu, for they had to pay for all his wars. Their misery was greater still under Mazarin, for although Mazarin loved money he was not clever in managing it. He loved money and he stooped to the lowest means in order to win it for himself. But while he grew rich the people starved, and at last they burst into rebellion.

This civil war was called the Fronde. It was so called from the name of the slings with which the boys used to play in the streets of Paris, and which had been forbidden by the police. It was given the name almost in scorn, for although all the great people of the time joined in the strife it seemed as if no one knew very well what he was fighting for. They were all like children quarrelling for they knew not what, and they constantly changed sides, now fighting with, now against, each other.

Even the great ladies of the time took part. The King's cousin, the Duchess of Montpensier, a very splendid princess, led her own army and was surrounded by other ladies as her officers. She was so gay, and beautiful, and masterful that she was called *La Grande Mademoiselle*, or the Great Lady. And, it was said, that although she was more than ten years older than the King she meant to marry him and become Queen.

Meanwhile she fought against him. It is told how once she arrived at Orleans to find the gates shut against her. It was her father's own city, the place from which he took his title of Duke of Orleans, and the haughty lady was much enraged that she was not allowed to enter freely.

For three hours she marched up and down in front of the gates. From the walls the people shouted at her, "Hurrah for the King! None of your Mazarin!" The Governor was more polite. He sent her sweetmeats, but he would not open the gates.

At length the boatmen on the Loire offered to break open for the Princess a gate which led to the river. Greatly delighted, she told them to be quick, and meanwhile scrambled up a mound to look on and encourage them in their work. The mound was covered with briars and thorns and beset with hedges. But this great lady thought nothing of such difficulties. She jumped the hedges and scrambled through the thorns and briars till she reached the top.

The stalwart boatmen meanwhile hammered away at the stout planks of which the gate was made, and at length smashed a hole in it. But to reach the gate from the river was not easy. The men made a bridge of boats. In the second was placed a shaky old ladder with a broken rung. But nothing daunted, the Great Lady climbed up. At the top just outside the gate there was a great deal of mud. So one of the men lifted her up, carried her across the mud, and pushed her through the hole in the gate. She was quickly followed by her lady officers, breathless, excited, muddy.

As soon as the Great Lady's head appeared in the opening, drums began to beat and the French people cheered. They were delighted with the plucky, pretty lady who had thus stormed their town. Lifting her up they carried her shoulder high through the streets, while the people crow y ded round cheering, and kissing her hands. At length with great difficulty Mademoiselle persuaded them to set her down. "I assure you I can walk quite well," she said. Thus without firing a shot Orleans was taken.

But the war was not all bloodless. There was a good deal of fighting. Several times peace was made, and as many times the war burst forth again.

Mazarin was forced to flee, not only from Paris, but from France. The Queen and the little King also fled from Paris to the Palace of St. Germain. Here they had to suffer much from cold and even from hunger. They, who had been used to every luxury, and to be cared for and waited on at every turn, had now to suffer many hardships. Here there was no state and little comfort. They had not even beds, and were obliged to sleep on the floor on bundles of straw. They had no money with which to buy food for their servants, less still to pay their wages. So many of them had to be sent away. The Queen pawned even the crown jewels in order to buy food and clothes for herself and the little King.

But at length the Fronde, after lasting about four years, really came to an end. The Queen and the little King returned to Paris and to luxury. Mazarin, about whom all the disturbance had been, returned, too, more powerful than ever.

The Fronde was the last attempt of the people of France to lessen the power of the King. Charles the Fat had begun the work of making the King absolute, Louis XIV finished it. He was an absolute monarch. He did as he liked, and neither nobles, clergy, nor people could gainsay his word.

Meanwhile it was still Mazarin who ruled in the King's name. Now that the Fronde was over he turned his attention to the war with Spain, which was still going on.

During the Fronde the great Conde had fought first on one side and then on another. At length, thinking himself ill-used at home, he proved traitor to his country France and went over to Spain. Now he led a Spanish army against his own countrymen and his old comrades in arms. Turenne was sent to fight him.

Conde well knew what a splendid general he had to face. "Have you ever seen a battle?" he asked an English prince who was with the Spanish army.

"No," replied the prince.

"Then you are going to see how one is lost," said Conde. And in fact Conde did lose the battle and others after it. Still the war went on for several years. But the King of Spain at length asked for peace, and the Peace of the Pyrenees was signed.

By this France gained some more land, and a marriage was arranged between the Spanish Princess Maria Theresa and Louis XIV. Many of the Spaniards were not pleased with this marriage. For the King of Spain had only one son, and he was very sickly and not likely to live. The Spaniards were afraid that if he died Louis might claim the Spanish throne for his wife and thus unite Spain to France. They hated the thought of this. So they made him promise never to claim the Spanish throne.

This Louis promised. But Mazarin arranged that if the Spaniards failed to pay Maria Theresa's wedding dowry this promise was to be of no avail. Now Mazarin knew very well that the King of Spain had no money, for he had used it all in his many wars. It was very likely then that the wedding dowry would never be paid, and Louis would thus be freed from his promise.

France was now at peace. The great Conde came back as if he had never been away. The King received him and talked kindly to him as if he had never done anything against his country. And when next there was fighting Conde and Turenne fought side by side and not against each other.

Mazarin was now at the height of his glory, having triumphed over all enemies both at home and abroad. He did not live long, however, to enjoy his triumph, but died less than a year after the King's marriage to the Spanish Princess.

CHAPTER 71

LOUIS XIV—THE MAN IN THE IRON MASK

LOUIS was now twenty-two, and for some years had been of an age to rule. But he had not really ruled, for all the power had been in Mazarin's hands. Yet although Louis had submitted to Mazarin he had submitted unwillingly. He had an over-powering sense of his own importance. He believed that he had been chosen by heaven to rule over France, and that to heaven alone he must answer for his deeds. "The state is myself," he used to say.

But the nobles and the people had up to this time no knowledge of the lofty ideas their King held about his office. So every one about the court asked himself who should succeed Mazarin, who should be prime minister.

They were greatly astounded when Louis announced to them that henceforth he meant to have no prime minister.

As soon as Mazarin was dead Louis called his counsellors together. "I have gathered you together," he said, "to tell you that up to the present it has been my desire that the Cardinal should manage my affairs. In future I shall be my own prime minister. You will aid me with your advice when I ask for it. I beg you therefore to seal nothing but by my orders, to sign nothing without my commands.

"The State is myself!"

"I will settle this matter with your Majesty's ministers," said an ambassador, one day.

"I have no ministers, Mr. Ambassador," replied Louis; "you mean, I suppose, my men of business."

Although Louis had no prime minister he was surrounded by great men. For the age of Louis XIV, as it is called, was the age of great men. There were great soldiers, statesmen, writers, thinkers, painters, and sculptors. Never was there a more brilliant court.

It would be impossible in this book to tell of even all the great soldiers and statesmen. But there is one statesman, Colbert, whose name must always be linked with that of Louis XIV. He was minister of finance—that is, he looked after the money matters of the kingdom, and, like Sully, he was so clever that he was able to lessen the taxes for the poor people and yet manage to find more money for the King.

Colbert took an interest in everything, in agriculture, in commerce, and in manufactures, which since the days of Sully and Henry IV had been much neglected. He took an interest too in the navy, and in the Colonies, in the making of roads and bridges, in the framing of new laws, in art and letters. There was no end to his energy, and he worked as never man worked. He worked at least sixteen hours a day, and wore himself out in the service of his King.

France grew greater in peace than she had ever done in war. "Everything in the state flourished," says a writer of the time; "everywhere there were riches. Colbert raised everything, finance, trade, manufactures, and even letters to the highest rank."

Colbert really loved Louis, but Louis simply made use of Colbert. And few people loved Colbert, for in his own way he was as much a tyrant as his master. He expected to be obeyed at once and without question. He was so cold and hard that he was called the man of marble, and one clever lady called him the North because of his chilling manners. He went his own way without listening to any one, and it was useless to try to turn him from it. One day a lady came to ask a favor. She fell on her knees before him, begging him to listen to her. Colbert rose, and fell on his knees in front of her. "I implore you to leave me in peace," he said, and she was obliged to go away unsatisfied.

Before Colbert came to power a man named Nicholas Fouquet looked after the money matters. He was clever, but he stole and wasted the people's money, and Fouquet made himself rich while the country was poor. So Louis caused him to be seized, and after a trial he was sent to prison.

He was sent to the dark and gloomy prison of Pignerol among the Alps. Here he remained until he died. And perhaps before Fouquet died there came to this gloomy fortress the mysterious prisoner who is known as the Man with the Iron Mask.

Who was this man in the mask? Perhaps we shall never know. But for some reason Louis had given orders that no one should see him, no one should even hear his name, no one should know what he had done, or why he was imprisoned. He was to be lodged in a cell, the windows of which could not be seen by any one. He was to be cut off from all sound by several doors. The Governor himself was to carry to him, once a day only, food enough to last him all day. But even he was commanded to listen to nothing the prisoner might say except about the most necessary things. If the prisoner insisted on talking the Governor was told to threaten him with death. Such were the harsh rules laid down for the treatment of this mysterious prisoner.

For many years the Man in the Mask lived in the prison of Pignerol. He was then moved from one prison to another and at last brought to the Bastille in Paris. When he travelled the greatest care was taken that no one should see him. He travelled in a sort of sedan chair made of oiled cloth. No one could see him, it is true, but neither could the poor man get any air, and so he travelled in great discomfort.

When they stopped at an inn for a meal the Governor sat opposite his masked prisoner with a pair of pistols beside his plate. And through all the long journey from the south of France to the Bastille the peasants followed the unknown one with wonder and awe. Who was he? What dreadful sin had he committed that he should thus be cut off from all his fellow creatures?

When this mysterious prisoner reached the Bastille his very name seemed to be lost. He was known to the jailers there only as "the prisoner from Provence."

For five more years his dreary, lonely life dragged out, then one day very suddenly he became ill. The next he died. In the dark of a November afternoon his body was carried out, and by the dim light of a lantern was hurriedly buried by two jailers in a graveyard near. To the end the unknown prisoner was masked with a black velvet mask. And it was not until after his death, almost as dark and mysterious as his life, that people began to make tales about him.

It was told then how he wore an iron mask with steel springs at the mouth so that he could eat. But the mask was really of back velvet.

It was said, although no one had ever seen his face, that when first imprisoned he was young and beautiful, that he always wore fine clothes and loved fine linen and beautiful lace, and that he used to amuse himself by playing on a guitar.

Even the Governor of the prison, it was said, treated him as a great person and never sat down in his presence. His table, too, was served with silver and fine linen.

One day, so the story goes, the Man in the Mask wrote something with a knife on a silver plate and threw it out of his window, toward a boat on the water just below the tower where he was shut up. For at this time he was imprisoned on an island in the Mediterranean. A fisherman picked up the plate and brought it to the Governor, who was greatly alarmed when he saw it.

"Have you read what is written on this plate," he asked. "Has any one else seen it?"

"I cannot read," said the fisherman. "And I have only just found it, so no one else has seen it."

The Governor was greatly relieved when he heard that. But he kept the fisherman prisoner until he made sure that he really could not read.

"Go," he then said; "it is well for you that you cannot read."

What was written on the silver plate? Why was the Governor so frightened?

We shall never know. Perhaps it is all a fairy tale and there was no plate and no writing.

But soon among other things people began to whisper abroad strange stories of who the Man in the Mask was. Some said that he was a brother of King Louis, an elder brother who ought to have been upon the throne, an elder brother so like himself that Louis dared not let his face be seen lest all the world should know his baseness. Others said that he was a son of Louis or that he was merely Fouquet.

They made many strange guesses. But no one was satisfied with them. So for more than two hundred years people have gone on asking questions about the Man in the Mask. They are still unanswered, although lately some people think they have proved that he was only an Italian who played traitor to Louis. Perhaps he was and perhaps not.

Others are just as sure that they have proved him to be a son of our King Charles II. Perhaps he was, perhaps not.

But although we cannot be sure who this Man in the Mask really was it gives us some idea of the terrible and absolute power of the King, when we remember that he was able to put a man in prison, and keep him there year after year without bringing him to trial. This he did too without any one daring to call his right in question. It was the King's will. That was enough.

CHAPTER 72

LOUIS XIV—THE GRAND MONARCH AT THE HEIGHT OF HIS POWER

AFTER the peace of Westphalia and the Peace of the Pyrenees Louis had no more to fear from any power in Europe. So for the first few years after he began to rule for himself there was peace in Europe. But all the time Louis was planning and scheming how to make France great, and chiefly how still more to lessen the power of Spain, in spite of the fact that the King of Spain was now his father-in-law.

So when in 1665 the King of Spain died leaving his throne to his little son Charles, Louis claimed Flanders, Franche-Comte, and all the Spanish possessions in the Netherlands for his wife Maria Theresa.

The new King of Spain reminded Louis that the Queen of France had given up all her rights to Spain or to any Spanish possessions when she married. But Louis replied that the Queen's dowry had never been paid, so that promise was of no account. And he marched into Flanders with an army and soon had possession of the chief towns. Franche-Comte too yielded to him almost at once.

But now the Dutch began to be alarmed for their own country. They had won their freedom from Spain and were now a republic. They had no wish to fall into the hands of France. So to prevent Louis becoming too powerful they made friends with Britain and with Sweden. Holland was at this time becoming very important. It had a fine navy and great colonies. Louis did not want to fight this Triple Alliance, so he made peace.

But he was very angry with the Dutch for having stopped him in his triumphal career. He made up his mind to punish them. So he plotted with Charles II of Britain to break up the Triple Alliance. Charles was in need of money, and when Louis offered him a large sum he easily consented to give up his new friends. Louis persuaded Sweden also to leave the Dutch alone. Then, with Conde and Turenne as leaders, he marched into Holland with a great army.

Although Holland had a splendid navy and great colonies it had a very poor army, and was in no way fit to stand against Louis. Added to this the Dutch were quarrelling amongst themselves. Now town after town fell before Louis until he believed himself master of the whole land. The Dutch were in despair. They thought of forsaking their country, of going aboard their ships, and sailing away to their colonies with their wives and children and all that they possessed, and leaving Holland to the French conquerors.

Then suddenly in Holland itself there was a revolution. The Dutch chose a grave young prince of twenty-two, William of Orange, to be their leader. It was a wasted and half-conquered country they offered him. But their new leader was a man of quiet, dogged determination. He had, it was said, no need of hope to make him dare, no need of success to make him persevere. He gave new courage to the Dutch, and their fortunes began to change.

Rather than yield to the French the Dutch now broke open the sluices and cut through the dykes which kept back the sea, and let it flow over their land.

Thus, although flocks and herds and crops were ruined, Holland was saved. The French could not besiege cities which rose like islands from the surrounding waters.

For two years Holland remained under water. The war, however, went on. But only in winter when the fresh water froze could the towns be attacked. Where the water was salt and did not freeze the towns were safe. But soon the war became, not one between Holland and France, but an European war.

Things, however, were changed. At the beginning of the war little Holland had stood alone against great France. Now it was France that stood alone against all Europe, for all the other kingdoms had joined with Holland. Even Spain, strange to say, now fought against France, and for her old and bitter enemy.

By land and sea the fight went on. At sea the French fought the Dutch and Spanish navies. On land they fought Dutch, German, Austrian, and Spanish armies. But in spite of the great combination against them the French were almost everywhere victorious.

All this time Charles II had helped Louis. But the British people had really been on the side of Holland, and William of Orange had married Princess Mary, the Duke of York's daughter, Now the British forced Charles to break with France and sign a treaty with Holland. Both Dutch and French were tired of the war. On the one side Holland was nearly ruined, on the other Turenne had been killed and Conde, too old and worn to fight any longer, had left the army and gone away to live quietly in the country.

Louis was not unwilling to make peace, but he made his own terms, and the other countries were powerless to do aught but submit to them. "My will alone," said Louis grandly, "concluded this peace, so much desired by those on whom it did not depend." It was called the Peace of Nimeguen and was signed in 1678. But the Dutch against whom the war had been begun did not lose an inch of land. It was Spain that was made to pay for all.

Louis now stood at the very height of his greatness and power. Alone he had fought against the powers of Europe and had been victorious. But France suffered for his greatness. Twenty years before many of the rulers in Europe had been the friends of France. At the Peace of Nimeguen France had only enemies among them.

Louis gloried in standing alone against all enemies. His pride knew no bounds, the court and the people of Paris bowed down to him, and worshipped him almost as a god. Louis received it as his right. The absolute King of France, the dictator of Europe, he was the Great Monarch. He made his court the most gorgeous in the world, and gathered to it all the wit and beauty of the kingdom. He built the splendid palace of Versailles, spending thousands and thousands of pounds upon it in order to make it a fitting home for so great a king. He built other palaces too; indeed, he must always be building, and the enormous sums he spent on these palaces helped in no small way to beggar the people. But what of that? Were they not there for his use?

Louis ruled his people as a despot. His will was law. Now he wanted to rule his people's conscience. He ordered that there should be only one religion in his land—the Roman Catholic religion. There must be no religion in the land but the King's religion. So in every sort of way Protestants were forced or persuaded to become Catholic. Some were bribed with money; those who would not take money were robbed, beaten, imprisoned, and ill-treated in many cruel ways.

Colbert did his best to protect the Protestants, for he knew that among them were the best workers and the cleverest merchants, who brought much wealth to the country. But Louis had long ceased to care for the advice of Colbert. For the great minister was anxious and troubled over the King's reckless waste of money. "A useless feast at the cost of a thousand crowns causes me more pain than you can think," he said. Yet he wanted France to be great, and Louis to be glorious. "The right thing to do, Sire," he said, "is to grudge five ha'pence for needless things, and to throw millions about when it is for your glory."

But now Colbert lay dying. He was followed to the grave by the hatred and the curses of the people. For they saw in him only the man who ground them down with taxes too heavy to be borne. They gloried in their magnificent King, and almost worshipped him. They forgot that it was to make him magnificent that they were ground down with taxes.

In the end Louis, who had treated his great adviser with gross ingratitude, sent him a kind letter. But Colbert would not even open it. "I want to hear no more of him," he said. "He might at least let me die in peace." Then in words very like those of our own great Cardinal he sighed, "If I had done for God all that I have done for that man I should be saved ten times over. But now I know not what will become of me."

The Queen too had died little more than a month before Colbert. She had never been more than a shade among the gay crowds who surrounded Louis. She had been meek and quiet without a shadow of power.

And now the King did a strange thing. He married a lady of the court named Madame de Maintenon. She was the poor widow of a poor poet some years older than the King. But Louis found her so beautiful and fascinating that he married her.

One night in the chapel at Versailles two priests waited. The great palace was silent, the long cold corridors were dark and still. But suddenly there was a flicker of light and the sound of quiet footsteps. And presently four people had gathered in the chapel. They were the King with a servant and one of his gentlemen, and a lady dressed in black. In the silence of night, beneath the trembling light of a few candles, the strange marriage took place, and the poor poet's widow became the wife of the King of France.

CHAPTER 73

LOUIS XIV—THE REVOCATION OF THE EDICT OF NANTES

THIS strange marriage of the King was never made public, and Madame de Maintenon was never looked upon as Queen. But she had far more power than the Queen had ever had. She was often with the King when he consulted with his ministers, and sometimes when matters were hard to settle he would turn to her and ask, "What does your Solidity think?"

As a rule she gave good advice, but in one thing at least her advice was bad. For she urged the King to root out utterly the Protestants.

By bribery and cruelty many were persuaded to become, or to pretend to become, Catholics. Thousands in this way were converted. "I can quite believe," wrote Madame Maintenon, "that all these conversions are not sincere. But God makes use of all ways of bringing back heretics. Their children at least will be true Catholics."

Thousands thus gave way, but thousands more resisted, and soldiers were sent over all the country to enforce the King's commandment. Many of these soldiers were dragoons. They were sent to live in the houses of those who would not obey. They plundered and wrecked the houses and tortured the people in most brutal ways, and from their name this persecution is often called the Dragonade.

Thousands to escape the misery pretended to be converted. Still Louis and his advisers were not satisfied. And on October 17, 1685, he signed the famous paper known as the Revocation of the Edict of Nantes.

This took away from the Protestants all the privileges which Henry IV had granted to them. They were ordered once and for all to give up their religion. Their churches were to be pulled down, their ministers were banished and were given only a fortnight in which to leave France. At the same time the people themselves were forbidden to leave the country.

Louis revoked the Edict of Nantes because he said there was no longer need of it. He believed, or pretended to believe, that nearly every one in France had become Catholic. If there were no Protestants a law to protect them was useless.

But Louis was wrong. There were thousands of Protestants still in France, and terrible persecutions followed, for hundreds refused to obey the new law.

The adviser who had taken the place of Colbert was named Louvois. He was minister of war and his advice was always for war. He was harsh and cruel also. It was the King's will, he said, that those who would not accept his religion should be punished with the greatest sternness: "Those who have the stupid vanity to hold out to the last shall be pursued to the bitter end."

And this was done until life became so unbearable that in spite of the fact that they were forbidden to go thousands fled from the country. They disguised themselves in every sort of way, for all the great routes and all the ports were watched. Rich merchants, and gentlemen and their wives dressed themselves as beggars in dirty old rags. With children in their arms, and leading others by the hand, they begged their bread from door to door. Many people, sorry for the poor wretches with such large families, gave them food, and in this way many children were taken safely out of the country.

And strangely enough the children themselves seemed to understand the danger. They behaved like beggar children, and never once betrayed their parents or friends who were taking charge of them.

Many ladies who had never walked a mile in their lives trudged along league after league carrying heavy loads, pretending to be travelling tinkers. Some dressed themselves as men and boys, and plodded along in the mud like footmen and pages, while their guide, who was perhaps a poor peasant, rode on a fine horse and pretended to be a great gentleman.

Others as peasant women drove cattle and pigs before them as if they were going to market. Others again who had money enough bribed the officers and soldiers to let them pass. In a hundred ways they fled the country.

Many escaped safely, but many also were caught. Then their fate was worse than ever, for the men were sold as slaves, or sent to work in the galleys, while the women were put into convents, where they suffered many torments until they changed their religion.

The French Protestants fled chiefly to England, Holland, Germany, and Switzerland, where the people received them kindly. These countries were all the richer for their coming, France was all the poorer for their going. France lost thousands of good soldiers and sailors, and above all skilled workmen. For among those who fled were men and women who knew how to spin and weave the fine silks, woolen stuffs and beautiful laces for which France was famous.

Many towns in England owe the rise of their spinning and weaving industries to these French refugees. One whole district of London (Spitalfields) was peopled by silk-weavers from Lyons and Touraine, and to this day is peopled by their descendants.

In Germany, Berlin was a dirty little town with badly built houses and narrow dark streets surrounded by a sandy desert. There the French crowded, for the Elector was a Protestant and received them kindly. The nobles who came built beautiful houses, the workmen planted market gardens, and the dirty little town began to grow into a beautiful city, the sandy desert became a blooming garden.

Louis was astonished and disgusted that his people should dare to resist his will. But even among the courtiers, even among the great soldiers and sailors, there were Protestants. They who were ready to shed their blood, to lay down their lives in the service of their King, yet demanded freedom to worship God in their own way.

Among them was the old Admiral Duquesne. He it was who had beaten Ruyter, the famous Dutch admiral. He was so bold that the pirates of the Mediterranean said his bride was the sea. He lived so long that they said the Angel of Death had forgotten him.

Yet for all his service to his country Duquesne remained unrewarded. "I cannot reward a Protestant," said the King.

"Sire," replied the old sailor proudly, "I am a Protestant, but I have always thought that my services were catholic."

"For sixty years I have rendered to Caesar that which was Caesar's" said Duquesne at another time. "It is time to render unto God that which is God's," and he begged leave to quit France. He was forbidden to do so, but he was allowed to live in peace and follow his own religion until he died.

His children, however, fled to Switzerland, and when their father died they begged to be allowed to bury him there, but the request was refused. So they raised an empty tomb and carved upon it: "This Tomb awaits the body of Duquesne. Passer, if you ask why the Dutch have raised a splendid monument to Ruyter vanquished, and why the French have refused a tomb to Ruyter's vanquisher, the fear and respect with which a king whose power extends afar inspire me, do not allow me to reply."

The Revocation of the Edict of Nantes was Louis XIV's grand mistake. It is the great blot on his reign. But the flatterers who surrounded him saw no mistake. They praised and glorified him for the deed. "It is the grandest and finest thing that he has done," was the cry. Statues were raised to the destroyer of heresy, medals were struck showing Louis crowning Religion.

But while at home Louis was being flattered and praised, the Revocation of the Edict of Nantes was arousing hatred against him in every Protestant country of Europe. These countries formed themselves into a league against him called the League of Augsburg. Then at the Revolution of 1688 William of Orange, who was Louis's bitter enemy, became King of Great Britain and Ireland, and the British joined the League of Augsburg. Louis looked upon the British Revolution as an insolent revolt of the people against kingly power. So he gladly welcomed to his court James II and his Queen and treated them with magnificent kindness.

Soon another great war began between the states of Europe and this mighty over-weening tyrant of France.

But in spite of the odds against him Louis was almost everywhere victorious. Turenne and the great Conde were indeed gone, but their places were taken by Vauban and Luxembourg, generals almost as famous. Vauban especially was famous as a great engineer as well as general. So the French were victorious everywhere in Germany, in Spain, in Italy, on sea as well as on land. William III alone seemed able to make a stand against them.

But although France was everywhere victorious the land was utterly exhausted. No one since Colbert died had known how to manage the money matters. So the taxes grew heavier, the people poorer and poorer, till they were little better than beggars. The people who lived in misery grew tired of the glory of their King. They were dying of want to the sound of *Te Deums* it was said. Men who were dying of hunger cared little for glory. Women who wept for their dear dead ones cared little for the sound of *Te Deums*, sung in honor of victories which brought to them only sorrow and mourning. So the hearts of the people turned from their King. Yet the King heeded not. He went his own vainglorious way.

A great priest and writer of the time was at length brave enough to warn Louis, but he dared not sign his name to the letter he wrote.

"The whole of France," he said, "has become nothing but a vast desolated hospital. The people who have loved you so much begin to lose their friendship, their confidence, and even their respect. Every day they die from the evils caused by famine. And while they lack bread you lack money. And you will not see the awful danger which threatens you. Every one knows it, and none dares tell you. It is time to humble yourself beneath the mighty hand of God. You must ask for peace and expiate by this shame all the glory which you have made your idol. God has held His arm raised over you for a long time past. But He is slow to strike because He has pity on a prince who all his life has been surrounded by flatterers."

At length in spite of his blind passion for glory Louis made peace. This was the Peace of Ryswick, signed in 1697. The war had brought France nothing but "glory" too dearly bought.

CHAPTER 74

LOUIS XIV—THE WAR OF THE SPANISH SUCCESSION

SOME years after the Peace of Ryswick Charles II, King of Spain, died. He had no children to succeed him, so he made a will leaving the throne to Philip Duke of Anjou. Philip of Anjou was the second son of the Dauphin of France, and grandson of Louis XIV. Louis, you remember, had married the Spanish Princess Maria Theresa, so her children were really the nearest heirs to the Spanish throne. But, you remember, she had given up all claim to the throne for herself and her children when she married.

Charles of Spain disliked France, he did not wish the King of France to be King of Spain also, so he left the throne to Philip of Anjou on condition that he should give up all claim to the throne of France. Louis had hoped always to be able to unite the two kingdoms. And when he heard upon what condition the King of Spain had made Philip his heir he was very uncertain about allowing him to accept the throne.

For before this, knowing Charles to be very ill, Louis had entered into a secret treaty with his old enemy, William III. This treaty was meant to settle the question of who should succeed to the throne of Spain in a friendly way, and so prevent another war in Europe. If Louis broke this treaty and accepted the throne for his grandson there was sure to be war. On the other hand, if he refused, was peace certain.

For three days Louis hesitated. Then he decided. He made known his will in the grand and ceremonious way in which he did everything. First he called the Spanish Ambassador into his private room, and pointing to the Duke said, "You may salute him as your king."

The Ambassador with Spanish fervor threw himself on his knees, and greeted his new King with rapture. Then Louis ordered the great folding doors to be thrown open so that all the nobles might be admitted. The Court was all agog with excitement and curiosity, wondering what the King would do. Now they crowded in, impatient to hear the news.

Louis drew himself up majestically, swept a proud glance round the eager throng and, pointing to the Duke of Anjou, said, "Gentlemen, here is the King of Spain. Birth calls him to the crown, the late King bequeathed it to him, all the nation wishes it. It is the command of heaven, and I consent to it."

Then turning to his grandson, "Be a good Spaniard," he said. "That is now your first duty. But remember that you were born a Frenchman so that you may maintain union between the two nations. That is the way to make them happy and keep peace in Europe."

The Duke of Anjou was delighted to find himself thus a King. His father, the Dauphin, hardly knew how to contain himself for joy. He made his son go before him everywhere and called him "Your Majesty.' 5 "The King my father, the King my son," he kept repeating, and he was never tired of reminding others that few people were in the proud position of having a father and a son both at the same time reigning kings.

In Spain Philip was quietly accepted as King. And although the other states of Europe were ill-pleased at this "strengthening of the power of France they were unwilling to go to war.

Peace then might have been kept had Louis been wise. But he did many things to arouse the anger of the other rulers.

Among these he announced that the King of Spain would not give up his right to the throne of France. Then when James II died he recognized the Pretender as King of Great Britain. This was as good as a declaration of war. So once more a league was formed against France. This was called the Grand Alliance. The war which followed is called the War of the Spanish Succession, and Britain took a great part in it.

Before war began William III died. He was succeeded by Anne and she carried it on. It was the greatest of all Louis's wars. Yet by this time all his most brilliant generals were dead. The British army, on the other hand, was led by one of our greatest soldiers, Marlborough. He gained victory after victory. Blenheim, Ramillies, Oudenarde, are names of which the British are proud. They meant ruin and misery to France. Never before had Louis's armies been so often and so badly beaten, and France was full of despair.

Then upon the miseries of war followed a terrible winter. The frost was cruel. Even the Rhone, the most rapid of French rivers, was frozen over. Vines and fruit trees were killed by frosts, the people starved and were found dead of cold and hunger in their cottages. Shopkeepers, peasants, gentlemen, all alike were ruined. The land was full of beggars. At the royal table even bread was lacking more than once. At length even

"GENTLEMEN, HERE IS THE KING OF SPAIN."

Louis could hold out no longer. He bowed his proud head to the storm of misfortune and asked for peace.

The allies were willing to listen, but they demanded a great deal. They demanded among other things that Louis should drive his grandson from the throne of Spain. That meant war with Spain and Louis refused. "If I must fight," he said, "I would rather fight against my enemies than against my own children."

So the war went on. But after a time a new party came into power in Great Britain. They wished to put an end to the war. So Marlborough was recalled and at length peace was made, and the treaties of Utrecht and Rastadt were signed.

These treaties were very different from those which Louis had been used to sign. For France lost much land, yielding to Great Britain the colonies of Hudson Bay and Newfoundland, and other vast possessions in the New World. France itself was left in a state of ruin and woe. And after all the misery and bloodshed Philip V still kept the throne of Spain.

The brilliant reign of Louis XIV now closed in gloom and sadness. The country was plunged in poverty, the royal household was plunged in mourning. For the Dauphin died and his eldest son died. When at length Louis himself, grown old and gray, and bent with sorrow and years, died, he left his great-grandson, a child of five, to succeed to the throne.

When Louis felt that his last hour had come he called for little Louis, his great-grandson. "My child, " he said, "you will soon be King of a great kingdom. Never forget the duty you owe to God. Remember that you owe to Him all that you are. Try to keep peace with your neighbors. I have loved war too much. Do not copy me in that nor in my great extravagance. Take counsel in all things. Try to relieve your people in every way you can. Do for them all that it has been my misfortune not to do."

Too late Louis knew his mistakes.

The magnificent King was weary of life. "I have always heard that it was hard to die," he said. "I do not find it so hard."

"Why do you weep!" he said to his servants at another time. "Did you think I was immortal?"

Louis was seventy-seven when he died, having reigned seventy-two years. It is the longest reign known in history. He had lived magnificently. He had been like a sun of splendor shedding light upon his adoring subjects. His slightest action was applauded. Even his getting out of bed and dressing in the morning, his going to bed at night, were turned into great court ceremonies at which the nobles were eager to be present. They deemed it an honor to be allowed to help him on with his coat, or to hold a candle while he undressed.

But magnificently as he had lived he died a forsaken, lonely old man. Even his wife, Madame de Maintenon, forsook him at the end, and he was left to die surrounded by servants. And although they wept around his deathbed, no one was really sorry. For his pride and his tyranny had robbed him of all love.

CHAPTER 75

LOUIS XV—BUBBLE WEALTH

WHEN it was known that Louis XIV was dead a sigh of relief and joy passed through France. Even at his funeral the people burst forth into unseemly rejoicing. The terrible, brilliant old man who had cowed them and enslaved them for more than half a century was gone, and now every one hoped for freedom and better days.

Louis's little great-grandson was also called Louis. He was scarcely five when he came to the throne, and of course could not rule. His mother as well as his father was dead. So his cousin Philip, Duke of Orleans, became Regent.

The Duke of Orleans was a clever man. But at the court of Louis XIV he had led an idle, wicked life. He had a mad love of pleasure, a deep thirst for power, but cared little for the troubles of ruling. So although he had great opportunities he did little good with his life.

His mother used to say that he was like the princess in the fairy tale. At his birth she had called all the fairies together and each one had given him some good quality or talent, until at length he had them all. But, unfortunately, there was one fairy who had disappeared for so long that every one had forgotten her. She had not been invited. She was very angry at being forgotten, and to avenge herself came to the birthday party. She too would give a gift, she said, and raising her wand, "My gift," she cried, "is that all other gifts will be of no use to you." And so it happened that with all his talents and cleverness the Duke of Orleans never became a great man. He had all the gifts, yet none were of any use to him.

As Prime Minister, the Duke chose a man named Dubois. He was a mean little man, as thin as a pitchfork, and as bad as he was thin. Every wickedness struggled in his bad little heart for the upper hand. "He fairly reeked of falseness," it was said.

Yet this bad little man was an abbot, and he wanted to be an archbishop. When he asked for the post even his friend the Duke laughed him to scorn. "If I were to give an archbishopric to such a rogue as you, where could we find another rogue enough to consecrate you?" he asked.

But Dubois was not the first bad man who had been made a priest, and another was willing to go through the ceremony. So he became archbishop. Later on, not content with being an archbishop, Dubois by bribery and persuasion got himself made a Cardinal. Yet in spite of the fact that neither the Duke of Orleans nor Dubois were good men their rule was better than any France had had for many years.

Louis XIV and all his plans were now utterly forgotten. The Regent quarrelled with the King of Spain, to put whom on the throne so many French lives had been lost. But he made friends with Britain and with Holland. Thus France no longer stood alone against all Europe.

But the chief difficulty which the new government had to face was want of money. Louis XIV had spent such a lot that the country was beggared.

It was now that a Scottish adventurer, named John Law, came to the Regent and explained to him a new idea of his of making paper money. The Regent listened to him, believed in him, and decided to follow his advice.

Then began a mad time in France. People scrambled for the paper money. They brought their gold and silver in exchange for it, and the value of it rose and rose until it became twenty times more than at first. It was a mad race for wealth. Nobles, servants, priests, shopkeepers, fine ladies, all jostled each other in their eagerness to get some of the wonderful paper, which in some wonderful way was to make them rich beyond their wildest dreams.

The great bubble swelled and swelled. Fortunes were made and lost in one day. Law himself was carried off his feet amid the general excitement. Once begun he was powerless to stop the stream of paper money which flowed out of the bank as fast as the workmen could make it.

Then the bubble was pricked. People began to lose faith in the paper money. They began to ask themselves of what real value these bits of paper were, for which they had given their gold and silver, for which they had sold their lands and goods. Having lost faith in the paper money, people tried to sell it again for gold. Every one wanted to sell it. So the value of the paper money went down and down. Soon it became utterly worthless. No one wanted notes, they wanted their gold and silver back again. But in all France there was not one tenth of the money needed.

Then arose a cry of rage and despair. Law was almost torn to pieces by the angry multitude, and barely escaped with his life. He fled to Italy, and died there in want and misery a few years later.

When the excitement of this mad race for wealth was over the people sank into a slough of dull despair. Many who but a few days before thought themselves millionaires found themselves beggars. Many found themselves homeless and perishing of hunger.

The state of France was worse than ever.

For eight years the Duke of Orleans and Dubois ruled. Then they died within three months of each other. By this time Louis was declared of age, but he was so idle and selfish that he could not be bothered to rule and let others govern for him. When he went to a State Council he never spoke, hardly listened even to what was being said, and generally played with a kitten all the time.

The Duke of Bourbon now became prime minister. He was little better than those who had gone before him. Louis himself grew tired of him and resolved to get rid of him.

One morning as the King was setting off for a ride he turned to the Duke with a smile.

"Cousin," he said, "do not keep me waiting for supper." Then he rode off.

It was a jest.

A few hours later the Duke received a letter from Louis in which he was ordered to leave the court, and go away to his own castle in the country.

The next prime minister was Cardinal Fleury, an old man of seventy-three. He had been the King's tutor, and perhaps he was the only man Louis really loved.

He ruled France quietly and tried to keep peace. But he was obliged to fight. Louis had by this time married Mary, the daughter of Stanislas. Stanislas had been at one time King of Poland, but had been driven from the throne. Now in 1733 he was once more called back. But the Austrians and Russians wanted to put some one else on the throne. So Louis felt obliged to fight for his father-in-law.

For nearly two years the war lasted, sometimes one side winning, sometimes the other. At length peace was made. Stanislas gave up the throne of Poland, and received instead the Duchy of Lorraine, which was to be added to France at his death. Thus France gained another fine province.

CHAPTER 76

LOUIS XV—THE WELL BELOVED

ABOUT two years after the Polish war another war broke out. This was the war of the Austrian Succession. When the Emperor Charles VI died, having no son, he left the throne of Austria to his daughter, Maria Theresa. Nearly all the states in Europe had promised to leave her in peace, but no sooner was her father dead than most of the rulers began to fight for parts of her kingdom.

Attacked on all sides by greedy robbers, the whole of Austria and Bohemia already in their power, Maria Theresa appealed to the Hungarians. At a meeting of the parliament at Presburg she appeared before them. Dressed in deepest mourning, she wore her crown on her head and a sword by her side. And in her arms she carried her baby son, scarcely more than six months old.

Maria Theresa was young and beautiful. Her grief and beauty and her splendid courage touched the hearts of the rough Hungarian nobles.

"I am forsaken by my friends," she said, "pursued by my enemies, attacked by my relatives. I have no hope but in your faith and courage. I put into your hands the daughter and the grandson of your King. We look to you for our safety.'

Scarcely had the Queen ceased to speak when a mighty shout rang out. Hundreds of swords flashed in the wintry sunlight, and as the nobles held them above their heads they cried, "Let us die for our King, Maria Theresa."

Yet, although the Hungarians were ready to fight for her, France and all Europe besides were against the young and lovely Queen. Britain was her only friend.

Many battles were fought and the French won a great victory against the British at Fontenoy. It was a terrible battle, and even the French who won lost seven thousand men. It is one of the greatest victories ever won by the French over the British. Louis himself was present and the Dauphin also. Never since Poitiers had the King of France fought with his son beside him. Never since the days of St. Louis had a French King won a great victory over the British, and it is strange to think that it was left to one of the least gallant of French kings to win this one.

Yet at Fontenoy the French were commanded by an invalid, Marshal Saxe. He was so ill that he could not sit on his horse, but was carried in a litter.

At five o'clock on a May morning the fight began. For four or five hours the cannon thundered. The British fire was terrible, yet the French withstood it.

Then the British leader ordered the infantry to advance. On they marched, in spite of a murderous cross fire which mowed them down whole ranks at a time, until they almost reached the French lines.

The English officers saluted. "Gentlemen of the French Guard," they cried, "Fire!"

" Fire yourselves, gentlemen of England; we never fire first," replied the French. So the British fired. Almost the whole first rank of Frenchmen fell. Again the British advanced. Again they fired with such deadly effect that the French gave way before them.

For one terrible hour it seemed as if the battle was lost. The French lines were in confusion. Marshal Saxe begged the King and Dauphin to leave the field. "I will do my best yet to win the battle," he said.

"I know that well enough," replied Louis. "But here I remain."

Then the French, gathering all their forces, made a last terrific attack. The British gave way and the battle was won by the French, at the very moment when it seemed lost. Utterly exhausted, Marshal Saxe had still strength to make his way to the King.

"I have lived long enough Sire," he said, "now that I have seen your Majesty victorious."

But the brave general's life was not yet done. He won another victory and yet another until the war came to an end, with the Peace of Aix-la-Chapelle in 1748.

By this treaty France received nothing at all in spite of having won many victories. For Louis said he wanted to treat "as a King and not as a merchant." So France gained only an enormous debt, ruined trade, and "glory."

Almost at the beginning of the war Fleury, the prime minister, had died. Although toward the end of his life his rule had been feeble he had greatly improved the money matters of the kingdom. Now they once more fell into a terrible state. For the King was recklessly extravagant, he took no interest in the affairs of the kingdom, and spent huge sums of money on his favourites.

During the war Louis had been very ill. Indeed at one time it was thought that he would die. Then although the people had really no cause to love him, they were seized with sorrow. Night and day the churches were open and thronged with people praying for their King's life. As the priest said the prayer for the King's health his voice was broken with sobs, with sobs the people answered. "If he dies," they cried, "he will have died fighting for us."

But Louis did not die. When the messenger bearing the news of his recovery reached Paris he was mobbed by the people. They crowded round him, kissing the horse he rode, the boots he wore. From street to street went the joyful cry, "The King is well, the King is well." Once again the churches were thronged and Te Deums were sung. Paris went mad with joy.

When Louis himself returned to Paris, his entry was a triumph like that of some ancient Roman Emperor. The people crowded round him, cheering, rejoicing, blessing him. They called him the Well-beloved. With tears in his eyes Louis cried, "Ah, how sweet it is to be loved. What have I done that they should love me so?"

Indeed he might well ask. What had he done? No King perhaps had ever done less to earn the name of " Well-beloved." But the French had always been eager on the least excuse to love and honour their King. They were ready to suffer much to make him glorious and great.

But these transports of joy died away. The people learned to curse the King they had blessed and cheered.

Meanwhile, however, for eight years there was peace, and France once more became prosperous in trade and commerce.

Then the Seven Years' War broke out. In this war Louis joined with his old enemy, Maria Theresa, against the King of Prussia, who had been one of her chief enemies in the War of the Austrian Succession, while Britain, on the other hand, joined with Prussia against France and Austria,

But the war between France and Britain was fought, not in Europe, but in India and Canada and upon the sea. So that while at home Louis had to fight Frederick II of Prussia, one of the greatest of soldiers, in Canada Wolfe was defeating Montcalm and winning Quebec. The French were also being driven out of India, and were losing one after another their West Indian colonies.

At length, in 1763, the Peace of Paris was signed, by which France lost Canada and the West Indies, while in Europe the lands of Prussia, Austria, and France remained exactly as they were before the war.

During the last years of Louis XV the state of France grew worse and worse. But Louis was sunk in selfish ease. He cared nothing about it. "The monarchy is growing very old," he said, "but it will last my time. After me the Deluge!" He spent more and more money, often in shameful ways. Each year he sank deeper and deeper in debt. To get money he used every means possible, many of them bad. He sold titles, and when a wealthy citizen had bought a title often after a year it would be taken away from him. So if he still wished to be a noble he was forced to buy his title again. All posts were sold. By paying, any one could become a judge or an officer in the army, so that there were far too many judges and far too many officers. In some regiments it is said that there were not more than three soldiers to each officer.

Other posts were created just on purpose to be sold. They were often absolutely useless and silly. There was an inspector of wigs, a comptroller for piling wood, and many other posts quite as empty and useless. But in spite of all these ways of getting money, Louis sank always deeper and deeper in debt. At last he became bankrupt—that is he refused to pay his debts. And when the people cried out against this, Louis's minister was indignant. "The King is master," he said. "Necessity justifies all." It was the same minister who said, "The people is a sponge which one must know how to squeeze." At length, in 1774, Louis fell ill. Then, as once before, the people waited for news of their King's death. Now, however, they shed no tears, they prayed no prayers. Their only fear was that he might not die. But this time he did die. He was sixty-four, having reigned fifty-eight years.

CHAPTER 77

LOUIS XVI—THE OATH OF THE TENNIS COURT

LOUIS XV's son the Dauphin had died in 1765. So after his long reign Louis XV was succeeded by his grandson, Louis XVI, a young man of twenty. He had already been married for about four years to Marie Antoinette, a daughter of the beautiful Empress Maria Theresa.

On the day that Louis XV lay dying the Prince and Princess sat together awaiting the news. Suddenly there was a noise like thunder. It seemed to rumble through the palace to the door of the room in which they sat. Louder and louder, near and nearer, it came. It was the noise made by the crowd of courtiers who, forsaking the dead, came to salute the new King.

When the Prince and Princess heard the noise they knew what it meant. Together they threw themselves on their knees, and with tears running down their cheeks cried, "O God, guide us, protect us; we are too young to rule.." Then utterly overcome with the thought of his coming duties and difficulties, the new King fainted. When he came to himself again he cried out, "Oh! what a burden. And no one has taught me anything about it. It seems as if the heavens were falling upon me."

Louis XVI was a clumsy, vulgar-looking, stout young man. He was modest, kindly intentioned, and good, but timid and yielding, and very far from being the strong ruler needed for France at this time. He did not really want to be a King. He was much more clever with his hands than with his head. He was happier when he was helping the workmen about the palace of Versailles than when he was talking business. He was happiest of all when he was shut up in his own workshop making locks.

Marie Antoinette was beautiful, charming, and clever, but frivolous and ignorant. When she came to France she could hardly write, and in spite of the great position she was to fill she never read anything but novels. She ruled her good-natured, stout husband, and made fun of him. She never understood or loved the French people. She had no sympathy with their sorrows and misery, and in return the people hated her with a bitter hatred.

Louis XVI, on the other hand, really loved his people, he really wanted to do right. He began his reign by putting an end to much of the useless extravagance of the King's household. But it would have needed a much stronger man than he to cure the evils which the misrule of ages had brought upon the people.

At first Louis was helped by a clever man named Turgot. He brought some order into the money matters of the kingdom. But he taxed the nobles and the clergy to do it. Now the nobles and the clergy were called in France the privileged classes. They did not pay taxes. That was left to the peasants and such people, to Jacques Bonhomme whose back was broad. So now when Turgot wished to tax the nobles and clergy they grew angry. They grew so angry that Louis was afraid and sent Turgot away. Yet but a short time before he had said, "It is only Turgot and myself who love the people.'

When the fall of Turgot became known the whole Court rejoiced. The clergy held special services of thanksgiving and prayers in the churches. Only the wise and far-seeing grieved. "Since Turgot has lost his place," said a great man, "I see nothing but death before me. I am crushed heart and brain."

Turgot was followed by another clever man, a Swiss banker named Necker. He was not so great as Turgot or so bold. But he too wanted reforms. He did away with at least six hundred useless, silly posts such as the inspector of wigs and the comptroller of piled wood. But he too met with the same anger on the part of the privileged classes. He too was sent away.

About this time the British colonies in America rebelled against King George and the War of Independence began. France helped the Americans, and both in America and in India there was fighting between French and British. But at length, in 1783, the war came to an end. The independence of America was acknowledged and France not only had the joy of seeing the side she had helped win, but was able to make good terms for herself.

Thus the humiliation of twenty years before, when she had to give up Canada and many another rich colony, was blotted out. France once more it seemed was to take a great place in Europe.

But the war had cost a great deal of money. The Royal treasury was empty. The minister of finance began again to talk of reforms, of taxing the privileged classes. The idea was scornfully and proudly rejected, and the minister was sent away. Another was appointed. He fared no better, and, giving up his post, he fled to Italy, leaving the money matters in utter confusion.

The people had now grown restless and angry. It was plain to the wisest among them that the money matters could never be made better until new laws were made. They began to say that the only way to improve things was to call the States-General together and let the people decide what reforms were needed.

Then, seeing no way out of the difficulty, Louis called back Necker, the clever Swiss banker. He also called together the States-General.

The last States-General had been called early in the reign of Louis XIII. So for more than one hundred and fifty years the French Kings had ruled without a Parliament. They had become absolute monarchs, doing as they would, acknowledging no will but their own. They had brought the country to the very edge of ruin. Now as a last hope they were forced to ask the will of the people they had so long despised. So on May 5, 1789, the States-General met—Nobles, Clergy, and the Third Estate.

This day we may look upon really as the last day of the old French Monarchy. The deluge had come.

The day before the States-General met there was a procession through the streets of Paris. The King and Queen were there in all the splendour of their royal robes. The nobles followed gaily dressed with gold-embroidered cloaks, feathered hats, and jewelled swords, the clergy scarcely less brilliant in their robes of office. But it was not upon them that all eyes were turned, but upon the crowd of commoners, upon the people. They were all dressed in black with short black cloaks and black felt hats such as they were bound to wear by law. It was not for common folk to dress in gay colours, to wear feathers and jewels. Those were for the privileged classes.

Through the streets the long procession passed until they reached the church, where mass was said.

The next day the three Estates were gathered in a large hall at Versailles. The King opened the parliament. He made a short speech, and when he had finished he put on his hat. The Nobles, as was the custom, did the same. Some of the Third Estate followed their example. At once a murmur ran through the hall. Not daring to deny to the Third Estate the right they took, the King again took off his hat, so both Nobles and Commons were obliged to do the same.

Thus almost at once it became plain that the parliament was divided into two parties. On the one side were the Nobles and the Clergy, the privileged classes, who would yield none of their privileges. On the other was the Third Estate, who were bent on gaining some privileges.

The first question to be settled was whether the Estates should sit together in one hall, or should sit in three separate halls. Or whether, as it was said, they should vote by heads or by orders. The Nobles and Clergy insisted that they should each sit in separate halls, and that the voting should be by orders. That is, if a measure passed two of the Estates, it was carried and became law.

But the Third Estate well knew that if the voting was by orders they would have no power whatever. For whenever they pleased the Clergy and Nobles would vote together and thus would be two to one. So they insisted that they should all sit in one hall, and that the voting should be by heads, for in numbers they were equal to the Clergy and Nobles together.

The Nobles and Clergy paid no heed to what the Third Estate said. They were determined to have their own way, so they left the Third Estate to sit alone in their hall while they in their own halls elected presidents, formed committees, and generally set the work of a parliament going. The Third Estate with dogged patience did nothing. They knew their own strength. They invited the other two Estates to join them, and when they refused they still waited.

At length the Third Estate sent a last invitation to the others to join them. This being refused, they declared themselves the National Assembly, and the only real representatives of the French people.

This bold action filled the King and the court with dismay. They determined to crush this revolt at once, and the National Assembly was forbidden to meet for three days. The National Assembly paid no heed. But when the members arrived at the door of the hall they found it shut and guarded by soldiers.

In greater and greater numbers the angry crowd gathered about the closed doors. Some proposed one thing, some another. Then in a tumultuous crowd they ran to the great empty tennis court which was the only, large building near. There they solemnly swore never to separate until France had been given a constitution— that is, a Government by which the country might be ruled wisely, and without tyranny or oppression, and in which the people should have some voice. This is called the Oath of the Tennis Court.

CHAPTER 78

LOUIS XVI—NOT REVOLT, BUT REVOLUTION

EVEN after the Oath of the Tennis Court neither King nor Nobles realized how determined the people were. They had no idea of giving in to them. Three days later the King held a Royal Session at which all three Estates were present. Louis made a long speech. Then at the end of it he said: "Gentlemen, I command you to separate at once. To-morrow you will resume your sitting, each in the hall appointed for you." The King then went out. The Nobles and a great part of the Clergy followed. The Commons remained in their seats.

They looked at each other with pale and anxious faces. How would it end?

Then the Grand Master of Ceremonies re-entered the hall. "Gentlemen, you have heard the orders of the King," he said.

"Yes," answered the president, "and I am now about to take the orders of the Assembly."

Then Mirabeau rose. Mirabeau was of noble family, but he took the part of the Commons, and had been chosen as one of their members. He was a great writer and speaker, and soon showed himself a leader of men. Now he spoke for the president. "Yes, sir," he said, turning fiercely upon the Master of Ceremonies with flashing eyes, "yes, sir, we have heard the King's intentions. But you have neither place, nor voice, nor right of speech here. You are no fit person to be his messenger to us. Go, tell those who sent you that we are here by the will of the people, and that we shall never be driven hence but at the point of the bayonet." Then all the members cried, "It is the will of the Assembly. It is our resolution!" And the Grand Master of Ceremonies, terrified at the storm of anger he had called forth, withdrew in silence and haste.

Meanwhile Louis returned to his palace. As he passed through the streets there was not a single cheer. It was the first time in his life that he had appeared among his people without receiving a sign of affection and love. He was hurt and depressed, and when the Grand Master came to tell him that the Third Estate refused to move he replied wearily, "Ah, well, if they will not leave their hall let them stay."

So at length the Nobles and the Clergy, finding they could not move the Commons, gave way. Very unwillingly they went to join the Third Estate.

The Court was conquered for the time being. But they did not mean to give in, and hoping yet to avenge themselves, they gathered the troops together. The Commons asked the King to disband them again. He refused.

Then the people of Paris rose in revolt. They armed themselves with every kind of weapon they could lay hands on. Swords and guns were seized from Government stores, every smith and armourer was busy, and fifty thousand pikes were made in one day. The whole city was soon in unutterable uproar and confusion.

The mob needed some outlet for its fury. Soon everywhere cries were heard, "To the Bastille! To the Bastille!" The prison called the Bastille was looked upon as a sign of tyranny. In it many and many a prisoner had been shut up for long years merely on the caprice of the King. The people hated it, and now they vowed it should no longer stand.

With shouts and yells the maddened crowd rushed through the streets until they reached the Bastille. But round the solid stone walls the mob howled and raged in vain. They had no cannon strong enough to batter them down. Their shot blazed and rattled and fell harmless. They could not hope to take it by storm.

Had the Governor chosen to hold out hunger alone could have made him yield. But after an hour or two the Governor gave way. The doors were thrown open and the furious mob burst into the prison. The prisoners were at once set free. There were only seven of them. One had been there thirty years, for what crime he knew not. Another had gone mad.

The leaders of the attack had promised the Governor his life and safe conduct to a place of safety. But they promised more than they could perform. The fury of the mob was not yet spent. They seized upon the Governor and slew him along with some of his soldiers. Then setting their heads upon pikes they carried them in triumph through the streets.

Late at night the news was brought to Louis at Versailles. "Why," he cried when he heard it, "this is a revolt!"

"Nay, Sire," replied the noble who had brought the news, "it is a revolution."

The taking of the Bastille seems but a small affair. Yet it is from that day that the French date their new national life. It is their great national holiday. On the 14th of July there are rejoicings throughout the length and breadth of France. Every village is gay with the national flag; every town has its fireworks, feasting and dancing.

The day after the fall of the Bastille the King yielded. He went to the

"TO THE BASTILLE! TO THE BASTILLE!"

Assembly. This time he went without pomp and splendour, without court or guards, but on foot, accompanied by two of his brothers only. He told the gathered members that he had sent away the soldiers as they wished, and bade them believe that he had only the welfare of the kingdom at heart.

At first he was received in sullen silence, but when he called the Assembly the National Assembly instead of the States-General the members cheered loudly. After all the King was really with them! In a body they rose and accompanied him back to his palace, while the crowds shouted and cheered.

Good-natured Louis was swept along by the force he could do nothing to stem. He had no power over the revolted people of Paris. Yet he thought it well to seem to approve of what they did. So two days later he set out from Versailles to visit Paris. All the way his carriage was followed and accompanied by a wild rabble of men and women. They were ragged and excited, almost all carried weapons of some kind, guns and swords, scythes and sticks. They were a hungry, miserable mob and few among them knew what they wanted. They only knew themselves to be wretched and starving.

The King reached the Hotel de Ville, or Town Hall, in safety. Around him everywhere he saw a surging mass of people shouting, not "God save the King!" but "God save the Nation!" Everywhere instead of the white cockade of the Bourbons men and women were wearing cockades of red, white, and blue. They were the colours the people had chosen as their own, and since then they have become the national colours of France.

Louis saw himself surrounded by new soldiers. They, too, wore cockades of red, white, and blue. For, to keep some sort of order amid the terrible disorder, the men of Paris had formed themselves into a new army which they called the National Guard. As general they chose a young noble named La Fayette. He had fought as a volunteer on the side of the Americans in their War of Independence, and was one of the few nobles who joined the people of France in their revolt.

Standing upon the balcony of the Town Hall Louis knew himself to be alone among a revolted people. Yet he still clung to the belief that this terrible storm would die down. He still believed in the people's love of a King. So when La Fayette handed him a tri-coloured cockade he fastened it into his own hat with a smiling face.

Then for the first time that day the air rang with shouts of "Long live the King!"

CHAPTER 79

LOUIS XVI—HOW THE KING AND QUEEN WENT TO PARIS

LOUIS returned to Versailles with a lightened heart. The people had cheered him, he had seen smiling faces around him. He believed still in his people's love. All would yet be well.

But the spirit of revolution spread. Men were seized and hanged in the streets of Paris without trial or shrift. In the country the peasants rose, plundering the castles and slaying the nobles. In the Assembly on the night of the 4th of August a law was passed doing away with all privileges.

The sitting began at eight o'clock in the evening and by two o'clock in the morning the whole order of things was overturned. Every title and privilege was done away with. Every man was declared equal before the law. No man had any rights but as a citizen of France.

But nevertheless these same free and equal citizens were starving. It seemed to the hungry, excited people that if only the King and Queen were in Paris they would somehow have bread enough to eat. So a famished crowd of women set out for Versailles. It rained and in the afternoon a wet and draggled multitude reached the town. Some went to the palace, others stormed the hall where the Assembly sat. What did they want? they were asked.

"Bread, and to speak with the King," was the answer. "Bread, and to speak with the King."

But with all his good-natured willingness what could the King do? Nothing. So the crowd remained about the palace, hungry, wet, and unsatisfied. Night came on, fires were lit, a horse which had been killed was roasted and eaten by the famished mob.

It was a wild and restless night. Then toward five in the morning the crowd burst into the palace. They swarmed into the marble court, up the grand staircase, and nearly reached the Queen's rooms, having killed two of her bodyguard. Rushing to the Queen, one of her ladies roused her. "Madame," she cried, "get up! Do not stop to dress! Run to the King's room!"

She flung a petticoat round Marie Antoinette, and without stopping to fasten it the Queen fled in terror to the King. One of her ladies followed, carrying the little Dauphin. They reached the King's rooms. Oh! horror! the door was locked! It was an awful moment. The Queen knocked and knocked again wildly, while the howls of the maddened mob came nearer and nearer and nearer. At length the door was opened from within, and sobbing with terror the Queen stumbled over the threshold. For the moment the danger was over.

The rioters were soon driven out of the palace. La Fayette, the captain of the National Guard, arrived and swore to protect the King and his family. But without the palace there swayed and surged a sea of maddened men and women. Their voices rose and fell in angry shrieks. "The King!" they cried, "the King!"

At length Louis showed himself upon the balcony. A mighty shout rent the air. "Long live the King!

To Paris! The King must come to Paris!" Then there were cries of "The Queen! the Queen!"

Marie Antoinette hesitated. She dared not face that yelling crowd, for did not the people hate her?

"Madame," said La Fayette, "come with me."

"What! alone on to the balcony?" The Queen shrank back.

"Yes, Madame, come."

"Ah well, if I must go to death I will go," replied the Queen proudly.

Then taking the Dauphin by one hand and her little daughter by the other, Marie Antoinette stepped out on to the balcony, followed by La Fayette.

"No children!" yelled the crowd; "no children!" so the Queen sent back the Dauphin and Princess, and stood alone.

The scene in the court below was terrible. It was a tossing sea of fury, of white faces, streaming hair, waving arms.

As the Queen stood alone upon the balcony the roar of the crowd redoubled. The whole air rocked and trembled with harsh sound. La Fayette said nothing. It would have been useless in the deafening noise, but he bent and kissed the Queen's hand, as if to show that he, the general of the people's soldiers, was yet the humble subject of the Queen. Then once more the mood of the crowd changed. The air was rent with cheers, "Long live the General! Long live the Queen! To Paris! to Paris!"

"My children," cried the King at length, "you wish me to follow you to Paris. I will come."

At one o'clock the procession set out. What a march it was! A steady drizzling rain was falling: in front, beside, behind the royal carriage the yelling, hurrahing mob splashed and tramped along the muddy roads. The air was filled with mingled noises, guns were fired, drums were beaten. The women danced, and sang, and shouted. Pointing to the royal carriage, "We shall not want for bread now," they cried, "for we are bringing the baker, and his wife, and the little baker's boy with us."

The march was slow. For six hours the royal carriages moved onward through increasing uproar. At length in the wet, dark October evening they reached the Tuileries.

The palace had been unused for a long time. Nothing was ready to receive the royal family; there were not even beds enough. But at length everything was settled. The noise without ceased, lights went out one by one, and the long weary day closed at length in silence.

The King was now little more than a prisoner. But nearly a year passed in comparative quiet. The National Assembly followed the King to Paris and held its sittings in an old riding school. It busied itself by making a Constitution, or set of laws, for France.

Many changes were made, titles were done away with. France was no longer divided in provinces, but into eighty-three departments of nearly equal size, and each named after some mountain, river, or other natural feature. The church estates were declared to be the property of the nation, and the money from them was rearranged so that the great prelates got less and the poor clergy more.

The King resigned himself to the new state of affairs, but many of the nobles fled from the country. They were called "emigrants" and they found a refuge in all the countries round, in Germany, Switzerland, Italy, and England.

On the 14th of July, the anniversary of the taking of the Bastille, a great national fete was held. In a vast open space called the Champs de Mars, or Field of Mars, a huge altar was built. It was called the Altar of the Fatherland, and was a hundred feet high, and decorated with flags from each of the eighty-three departments.

In front of this altar the King sat upon a throne; beside him with equal state sat the president of the Assembly; behind were the Queen and royal children, and the whole great space was crowded with men, women, and children in holiday dress. A bishop, surrounded by a hundred other bishops, all wearing sashes of red, white, and blue, said mass.

Then La Fayette advanced to the altar. He drew his sword and in the name of the National Guard took the oath of fealty to the new Constitution, to King, to Law, to Nation. Cannon roared and from a hundred thousand throats the cry went up, "Long live the Nation!"

The King, too, swore, "I, King of the French, swear to keep the Constitution decreed by the Assembly and accepted by me," he said. Then the Queen stood up, raising the Dauphin in her arms. It was if she would say, "See my son! He too joins in the oath."

It seemed as if the revolution was at an end, as if peace had come. It was not so. The passions of the people were far too deeply roused to be so easily quieted. Men gathered themselves into clubs, where great speakers made violent and bitter speeches attacking everybody and everything, teaching people to distrust and suspect each other. Several parties were formed. Some, though wishing for reform, wanted still to have a king, others wanted to have no king. These were called republicans, as they wanted to set up a republic instead of a monarchy. But some even of these were far more extreme than others.

Mirabeau was among those who wanted to have a king. He defended Louis so much that his own party began to murmur against him and talk of the great treason of the Count of Mirabeau. But Mirabeau had ruined his health with the wild life he had lived when young. Now it could not stand the tremendous strain of work and excitement. He became very ill and died. "I carry with me the ruins of the monarchy," he said as he lay dying.

And indeed with Mirabeau Louis lost all hope of being a king again in truth. He knew that in Mirabeau he had lost a friend, although the Queen had always hated and distrusted him, and was not sorry when he died. "Do not rejoice," said Louis; "we have suffered a greater loss than you can imagine."

CHAPTER 80

LOUIS XVI—FLIGHT

THE King's position grew now worse and worse. He was a King only in name, and an imprisoned one at that. At length he resolved to flee from Paris. He hoped to be able then to gather an army and reconquer his kingdom. So the royal family began to make preparations for flight. But these preparations were slow, too much fuss was made, too many people knew of the plans.

The King's friends tried to persuade him to travel in one carriage with his daughter while the Queen followed in another with the Dauphin. But the King refused. He would be saved with all his family, he said, or not at all. So a fine new travelling carriage was built large enough to hold them all. But from its size and newness it was far more likely to be noticed on the road than a small old carriage would have been.

The King also insisted that troops of soldiers should be stationed in every town and village along the road. In vain his friends told him that these soldiers would only attract attention, and make people wonder what was happening. Louis was one of those unhappy people who generally give in to others, but who are now and again obstinate at the wrong time. Now he was obstinate, and the soldiers were sent to guard the route as he commanded.

The Queen too had new dresses made in which to travel, so the ladies of the court could not fail to know that something was about to happen. It is said that even La Fayette knew what was intended, and that he spoke of it to the King. The King, however, swore so solemnly to him that he had no intention of running away that La Fayette believed him.

At length all was ready. It was now the middle of June, and all through the long summer day the King and Queen followed their usual quiet life. Toward evening the Queen took the children for a walk. Then they had supper and went to bed. The Queen too went to bed. But almost as soon as she was left alone she rose again. She slipped quietly to the Dauphin's room and awakened him.

The poor little boy was very sleepy and did not want to get up. But when the Queen told him that he was going to war, and that he should have a regiment of his own to command, he jumped up at once. "Quick, quick," he cried, "give me my boots and my sword, and let us go." Henry IV was his hero, and he longed to lead his troops as he did at Ivry.

But it was very disappointing to begin with, for the Dauphin found that instead of wearing a sword he was dressed like a little girl. Then through the dark, silent palace he and his sister were hurried to a door which was seldom used, where now a carriage was waiting. The children and their governess were put in, and it drove off quickly into the night.

After driving a little way the carriage stopped in a quiet street at a place appointed, and waited for the King and Queen. A long time passed, and no one came. To the governess and the frightened children it seemed never-ending. Suddenly the street was lighted up with a flare of torches, and the clank of swords, the tramp of heavy feet, were heard. "It is La Fayette," cried the little Princess in terror.

The governess hid the Dauphin in the folds of her dress, and told him to keep still as a mouse. Then with beating hearts they waited. The glare of the torches fell upon the carriage and passed. The sound of clanking footsteps died away in the distance. The danger was over. They had not been recognized.

More anxiously than ever they waited. At last the King came. He was dressed like a servant, and wore a little plain wig, and had passed the sentinels at the great gate of the Tuileries quite easily. He had even stopped to tie up his shoestring under their very noses.

Last of all came the Queen. She had left the palace last, and both she and her guide had lost the way in the dark and wandered about for half an hour not knowing where they were. Now just as she crossed the street La Fayette passed again. But he did not recognize her. He went on his way, and the Queen hastily sprang into the carriage, which drove off at once.

"Oh, how glad I am," cried the King as she sprang in; "here you are at last." And they all kissed each other with laughter and tears, for the first, and it might seem the most dangerous, part of their adventure was safely over.

Swiftly they drove through the streets until they reached the outskirts of the town, where the great travelling carriage awaited them. As quickly as possible they all got into it and set off as fast as horses could carry them, leaving the old carriage and horses on the road to go where they would.

"At last," cried Louis, drawing a great breath of relief, "I am out of Paris, where I have drunk deep of so much bitterness."

As hour after hour the heavy carriage rumbled on, the King's heart grew lighter and lighter. "Once we are past Chalons," he said, "we shall have nothing to fear." Hardly had he spoken when the harness broke. It was an hour before it was mended.

Even apart from such mishaps the progress of the heavy carriage was very slow. Again and again there were delays, and everywhere the King arrived later than he was expected. Meanwhile the presence of the soldiers made the people in the towns through which they passed more and more curious and uneasy. But all day long the carriage rumbled on mile after mile, no one trying to stop it.

At length at a village where horses were changed the travellers paid with a new piece of money. The postmaster looked at it. He looked at the face of the servant who sat in the carriage. It was the same face, there was no mistaking it. This plainly dressed traveller then was the King and no mere serving-man! The postmaster was a republican, but he said nothing and let the carriage go on its way. As soon as it was gone, however, he mounted his horse and rode after it.

Night came on once more. The carriage rumbled along the dark and silent road until the town of Varennes was reached. Here all was in uproar. For the postmaster had reached the town first and warned the people that the King was coming. The alarm bell was rung and the streets were full of excited folk. Where the road crossed the river a laden cart was drawn across the bridge to prevent the royal carriage from passing. The mayor of the town, who was a little grocer, put on his scarf of red, white, and blue, and with a lantern in his hand awaited the King's coming.

The heavy carriage reached the bridge. The rattle of a drum was heard, and a voice cried, "Halt there! show your passports."

The passport was shown. It was in order. The lady, it seemed, was the Baroness Korff, who was going to Frankfort with her children and servants.

"I have come from Paris," said the supposed Baroness, "and am going to Frankfort.'

"In that case," replied the grocer, "you have come out of your way a good deal."

The make-believe Baroness begged to be allowed to go on her way. But the mayor did not believe the passport. He was troubled and doubtful. He made all sorts of difficulties. It was too late to countersign the passport that night; the country was full of wild, lawless people. It would be dangerous to go on, the Baroness had better wait till morning, he said. His house was close by, and he offered it to her and her party.

At first the King and Queen refused to leave their carriage. But at length they saw that it was useless to resist. So they all got out, and entered the grocer's house. Still Louis refused to own that he was King.

And no one could be certain, for no one in the little town had ever seen him. Now it seemed hard to believe that this stout, little man in plain wig and common gray clothes could really be their King. But at length an officer who had often seen the King entered the little room in the grocer's house where the royal family was gathered. He had no doubt at all. "Ah, Sire," he said, as he saluted.

Then at length Louis acknowledged that he was King.

"Yes," he cried, "I am your King. Placed in the capital amidst daggers and bayonets I come to seek in the country, among my faithful subjects, the liberty and peace which you all enjoy. I cannot rest in Paris unless I die, both I and my family."

The mayor was touched by the King's words. He pitied the Queen too, who looked frozen with fear, utterly worn out by sorrow and anxiety. The grocer's wife seemed a kindly woman. With tears and prayers and promises the Queen tried to touch her heart, tried to make her persuade the mayor to let them go. The Queen pointed to the tired children who lay together sleeping peacefully upon the bed belonging to the grocer's children. Surely for love of them they might win freedom. But the mayor was deaf to all entreaties, he refused to let them go. All pleading was in vain.

The long miserable night passed at length, and in the morning the royal party once more entered their carriage. Once more they set out, this time for Paris.

Before they went an old, old woman came into the room. She was the grocer's grandmother, who lived in a village near. She had been born when the Grand Monarch was on the throne, and in her heart she kept a deep reverence for royalty. When in the night she heard that the King and Queen were at her grandson's house she got up and dressed in haste, and taking her stick hobbled the long miles to see them.

It was a wonderful thing to her to think that the King and Queen were really and truly beneath her grandson's roof. Now she gazed at them in awe, curtsying shyly and awkwardly. Then she went to the bed where the little Prince and Princess still slept. They were the children of France. The pretty little boy would one day be King.

She wished to bless them, but she could not speak. She fell on her knees beside the bed, and hiding her worn, wrinkled face in the counterpane she wept long and bitterly.

It was not easy for France to say farewell to the splendours of royalty. When the royal family reached Paris they found an immense crowd gathered. But it was a silent crowd, for the order had gone forth, "Keep silence and remain covered." Upon the walls everywhere might be seen the notice, "Whoever applauds the King shall be beaten; whoever insults him shall be hanged." So in silence the royal family once more entered the palace of the Tuileries, and the door was locked upon them.

This time they were real prisoners. They were watched with the greatest care. Night and day sentinels stood at the doors of their rooms, upon the stairs, and in the passage. To escape again was impossible.

The party who wanted to depose the King and have a republic in name as well as in deed were stronger now than ever. In Paris men had formed themselves into clubs, where they discussed everything, often with much bitterness and violence. One was called the Jacobin Club because it met in the old convent of St. James. Another was called the Cordeliers from the name of another old convent where they met. These clubs began to have members, not only in Paris, but all over France. Both of them were violently republican. The Jacobins especially believed that kings were bad and useless, and that the sooner France had done with them the better.

Now a petition asking that the King might be deposed was placed on the altar on the Champs de Mars. Thereupon the Mayor of Paris proclaimed that no crowd would be allowed to gather, that if one did gather it would be scattered by force. The people, however, did not believe him, and men, women, and children crowded in thousands to sign the petition, or to see the show. They were ordered to disperse, and when they would not La Fayette commanded his soldiers to fire. A few people were killed and wounded by the shots, and many more were killed in the flight for safety which followed.

This was called the Massacre of the Champs de Mars. It did much to widen the breach between those who wished to reform the monarchy, and those who wished to overturn it altogether.

But in the meantime the poor captive King still kept some empty show of royalty. The Assembly had by this time finished making the new Constitution. The King was asked to give his consent to it. This he did. Amid loud cheers of "God save the King" he went to the Assembly, and solemnly swore to keep the new Constitution. Then, its work being finished, the Assembly broke up. It had been called the Constituent Assembly, its work being to form a new Constitution.

CHAPTER 81

LOUIS XVI—DEATH

A new Assembly was now formed which was called the Legislative Assembly. Before it separated the old Assembly had forbidden any of its members to be elected to the new one. This was done out of a sense of fairness, but it lost the King his last friend. In the New Assembly the members were nearly all republican, although they belonged to different parties, some more violent than others.

The most powerful party was called the Girondins. They were so called from the department of the Gironde from which many of them came. They were republicans, but they were not violent enough to please the Jacobins or the Cordeliers. More extreme than the Girondins was a small party called the Mountain. They were so called because they sat upon the highest seats in the Assembly Hall. They were the most violent of the republicans who had sworn to overthrow the monarchy.

But now, while France was still full of unrest and trouble within, troubles began to threaten from without. The rulers of the surrounding states began to look with terror on the doings of the French people. They began to be afraid that their own people might follow the example set them. The emigrant nobles too had roused sympathy, and had already gathered an army of foreign troops under the leadership of one of Louis's brothers. And now other princes gathered their armies and made ready to fight France.

France was in no fit state for war. The army was small, it was in disorder, the generals had little experience, and there was no discipline. Still war was declared against Austria. The French were at first defeated. The Prussians then joined with the Austrians against them, and their leader, the Duke of Brunswick, published what was known as the Manifesto of Brunswick. In this he declared that he had been given the right by the other rulers of Europe to help the King of France, and that he was resolved to punish those who rebelled against him and utterly destroy Paris. This made the people of Paris furious. Once more they rose in rebellion. "To the Tuileries! To the Tuileries!" was the cry.

A furious crowd soon surrounded the palace. The King had his Swiss Guard about him, but it was impossible for them to defend the palace against the maddened, excited mob.

"Sire," said a member of the Assembly, "your Majesty has not five minutes to lose. There is no safety but in the National Assembly. You must go there."

The King was ready to go, not so the Queen. She wanted to fight to the last. "But, sir," she cried, "we have soldiers-"

"Madame," he answered quietly, "all Paris is on the march. Time presses."

So in a sad procession the King and Queen and the children left the palace, which they were never again to enter. They crossed the garden and entered the Assembly.

The fugitives were then led to a little room behind the president's chair. It was a little room used by the reporters, and was not more than twelve feet square. There they remained for a whole day.

Meanwhile the rioters forced the doors of the palace, which the Swiss Guard vainly tried to defend. They were overcome and nearly all killed. When the King in his hiding place heard the firing he was grieved to think of his faithful Guards being thus uselessly slain. So he sent them orders not to fight any more. But though they tried to obey his commands very few of them escaped.

The mob now rushed into the palace, plundering and destroying. Finding no one to resist them they killed every one they came across — cooks, porters, and servants of every kind. From cellar to garret they were hunted and slain without mercy. Only the women were saved. "Let the women go," they cried. "Do not dishonour the nation."

In a few hours the palace was empty and deserted. Crowds then besieged the Assembly Hall. They demanded that the King should be deposed at once. To this the Assembly would not consent But they decreed that in the meantime his power should be suspended and that a new Assembly should be chosen which should decide what should be done with him. In the meantime the King and his family were imprisoned in a gloomy fortress called the Temple.

But all the violence and wrath against the King in Paris did not stop the disasters and defeats in the army. Still news of fresh losses reached Paris. It seemed as if there was nothing to stop the Duke of Brunswick from carrying out his threat and marching on the capital. The news of these constant and strange disasters threw

Paris still further into wild disorder. Each party blamed the other. All spoke of treachery.

Then Danton rose in his place and spoke. He was one of the leaders of the Cordeliers Club, a stern man, a republican, yet a lover of France, as so many were who seem to us in this time of blood and terror only to have been filled with violence and hate. It was needful, he said, to strike terror to the hearts of the Royalists.

So one night all the gates of Paris were closed. Then men went from house to house taking prisoner any who were thought to have kindly feelings toward the King. Such a number were taken prisoner that all the prisons in Paris were not enough to hold them, and many large convents were also turned into prisons.

For a few days the wretched people were kept in prison. Then one morning the alarm bell sounded. It was rumoured that the Royalists had betrayed the city to the Prussians. Louder and louder grew the cry. Then a horrible massacre began. Whether it was prepared beforehand like the massacre of St. Bartholomew, or whether it was merely the outcome of wild panic, has never been found out. But whether prepared or not no one tried to stop it. Those who might have done so looked calmly on while armed murderers rushed into the prisons and put the helpless prisoners to death without mercy.

The Assembly, even, made no attempt to stop the murders. While the prisons ran red with the blood of his countrymen Danton made a great speech about saving the fatherland from a foreign foe. "We must have courage," he said, "and again courage, and still again courage, and the fatherland is saved."

For three days the slaughter lasted. How many were killed is not known. This is called the Massacre of September as it began on Sunday, September 2, 1792.

On the 21st of September the new Assembly which had been agreed upon met. It was called the National Convention.

In the Constituent Assembly the party which wanted to reform the monarchy had been strongest. In the Legislative Assembly the Girondists or moderate republicans had been strongest. Now in the National Convention the Mountain or violent republicans were strongest. With steady steps the King had been swept toward his fate.

The Mountain at once proposed that Louis should be deposed. This was done, and the Republic was proclaimed.

To this all parties in the Assembly were agreed. But agreement stopped there. The Girondists were content that the King should be merely deposed. The Mountain desired his death.

"Louis must die because the fatherland must live," said Robespierre, one of the leaders of the Jacobin Club, a man of extreme opinion.

And so at length the last sad chapter of Louis's long, sad story was reached. He was accused of being a tyrant and an enemy of his people, and was Condémned to death. He was Condémned to have his head cut off by the guillotine. This was a new machine invented by a Doctor Guillotin, after whom it was called.

Louis heard his sentence with noble calmness. At first in the Temple the royal family had been allowed to live together, and although they were carefully watched were allowed some amount of freedom. But when it was found out that plans for their escape were still afoot,

Louis was separated from his family, and they were no longer allowed to see each other. This was a great cruelty, for Louis loved his wife and children dearly.

Now he begged to be allowed to see them once again. This was granted to him, and together they spent a last sad hour. They clung to him with tears and kisses. At length gently he bade them go.

"But we shall see you again," sobbed the Queen. "Yes, to-morrow morning," answered the King, and tore himself away.

But they never saw each other again. Next morning, calling his faithful servant to him, Louis bade him take some little remembrance to his family. "Say to the Queen," he said, "to my dear children, to my sister, that, although I promised to see them this morning, I wish to spare them pain. How much it costs me to go without receiving their last embraces!"

Through the crowded, silent streets Louis drove for the last time. He kept his eyes fixed on a book of prayers and seemed to see nothing else.

He reached the foot of the guillotine. Here his hands were tied, and as he mounted the steps his confessor cried, "Son of St. Louis ascend to Heaven!"

The King tried to say a few last words to his people. But that was not allowed, and the drummers began to beat so loudly that his words were drowned. Then Louis bent his head, and in a moment his troubled life was over.

The executioner held up the head that all might see it, and the air was rent with shouts, "Long live the Nation! Long live the Republic! Long live Liberty!" In the register of the Republic it was written, "Louis Capet died on the 21st January, 1793, at twenty-two minutes past ten in the morning. Profession: Last King of the French."

Louis was thirty-nine and had ruled for eighteen years. Throughout his reign he had done little to earn respect. But at the end, when we see him a humbled, broken man, shorn of every sign of grandeur, we must give him both respect and pity. He died bravely, and he died, not for his own sins, but for the sins of those who had gone before him. Louis himself had not been a tyrant, he was well meaning and forbearing, he but reaped what others had sown. In happier times he might have reigned peacefully, and been followed to his grave by the tears of a loving, sorrowing people.

CHAPTER 82

THE REPUBLIC—THE RED TERROR

THE news that the French had killed their King was received by all the other Kings of Europe with horror and anger. They resolved to punish the French. Great Britain joined with the rulers of the continent, and five armies attacked the boundaries of France.

Even in France itself the King's death won many friends for royalty, and civil war began. The people of the district called La Vendee rose against the Convention, and in the army of the Emigrants the little Dauphin, who was still a prisoner in the Temple, was proclaimed King under the title of Louis XVII.

To meet all these troubles strong measures were needed. The men of the Mountain were the most ruthless, and they succeeded in getting the power. Now they formed a body called the Committee of Public Safety. Its meetings were held in secret, and it was given power to do whatever it thought best for the good of the Republic, both at home and abroad.

The Girondins protested against this Committee in the name of Liberty. But the Mountain raised the people of Paris against the Girondins. Many of them were taken prisoner, others fled to the country.

Then began what is known as the Reign of Terror. The prisons were soon filled with "suspects"—that is, with men and women of whose love for the Republic there was the slightest suspicion. Friends of the royal family and friends of the Girondins alike were suspected, tried, and found guilty. Day by day these poor people were led out to die. At first some sort of trial was gone through. Soon there was no time to waste on such forms, and crowds were Condémned at once.

The people went mad for blood. They crowded daily to the Revolution Square, where the guillotine was always ready. To see the aristocrats die was the horrible entertainment of the day. Women sat knitting as they watched the victims fall, glorying in the agonies of their last moments. They wore ornaments in the shape of guillotines, and children played with toy ones. The very prisoners amused themselves with mock trials and executions, casting lots for who should play the parts of prisoner, judge, and executioner.

All life was unhinged. The knowledge of what was right and wrong grew confused, for men and women saw through a mist of blood and horror.

Their struggle for freedom had at first raised up for the French people many friends in generous and sympathetic hearts. Their horrible excesses now raised for them many enemies. The Revolution, it was thought, would begin a new time of peace and justice and freedom. It had brought only fresh bloodshed and tyranny under new names. Many who at first had wished them well, now turned from them in sad disappointment.

Many of the Girondins who fled from Paris to escape the Red Terror fled to Caen. There lived there a young and beautiful lady named Charlotte Corday. She had lived a lonely life, for her mother was dead, and her father more taken up with his books than with his daughter. So the love that might have been given to father and mother she gave to France. And her love of France was great. She believed that the Revolution was right, but all the horrors of which she now heard made her sad. She longed for peace to come again to the poor unhappy country. "Peace, peace," she kept saying to herself, and more and more she longed to do something to bring it back.

The Girondins who had fled blamed Marat for the evils of the Terror. Marat was one of the leaders of the Jacobin Club. He taught men to distrust each other, to believe in no one. When Charlotte Corday heard the Girondins blame Marat for the horrors of the Terror she made up her mind to rid the world of this monster. Had she but known it, Marat had already little power. He was ill, and not likely to live long. But this Charlotte did not know, so she set out for Paris full of her great purpose.

But although she tried time after time to meet Marat, something always came in the way. At length she wrote to him saying that she had things of importance to say to him. But when she went to his house the woman who opened the door would not let her come in. Marat, however, heard her voice, and although he was having a bath he called to her to come in.

So Charlotte Corday was shown into a little dim-lit room where Marat sat in his bath. Even there he was at work. With a great coarse cloth wrapped round him and a board across his knees he sat busily writing.

"Citizen," said Charlotte, "I have come from Caen and wish to speak with you."

"Ah," replied Marat fiercely, "what are the traitors doing at Caen? Which of them are there?"

Charlotte named one and then another, and Marat wrote the names down as she spoke.

Then as she finished, "That is good!" he exclaimed. "In a week they shall be guillotined."

The words gave Charlotte Corday courage. She quickly drew the knife which she had hidden in her bodice, and bending down struck Marat full on the heart.

"Ah, help! my dear," he cried, and lay still. He was quite dead.

The woman of the house rushed in uttering loud shrieks. In a few minutes the room was full of people. With cries of grief and rage they surrounded the dead man and his murderess. Charlotte Corday did not try to escape. She stood there as if frozen, making no effort to flee. Her work was done. She had killed the monster, she had brought peace to her unhappy country, and she gloried in her deed. "I killed one man," she said, "to save a hundred thousand. I killed a savage beast to give peace to my country."

Very calmly she went to prison, calmly she heard her sentence, the sentence of death. Her beautiful hair was cut off, she was dressed in the scarlet robe of a murderess and so was led through the streets to the dreadful guillotine, followed by the mingled curses and blessings of the crowd.

Splendid and beautiful she looked as she mounted the scaffold, the bright evening sun shining strangely on the blazing scarlet robe, lighting up her dark eyes and brown-gold hair.

So Charlotte Corday died for the Revolution. She was neither a saint nor a martyr. She was merely mistaken. Swept away from the knowledge of what was beautiful and true by the horror of the times, she died in vain.

Her deed of violence was not only useless, it was harmful. For it was thought that she had been in league with the Girondins. The hatred against them and against the aristocrats grew more bitter than ever, and the slaughter of them went on worse than before, not only in Paris but throughout France.

The poor Queen, who had been left in the Temple! after Louis's death, was executed, as well as many other great people. She had been hard-hearted and proud, understanding little, and perhaps caring little, about the misery of her people. But she met death bravely and like a Queen. On the scaffold we can feel only pity for her.

The poor little Dauphin died in prison, perhaps partly because of the ill treatment he received there. His sister was set free at the age of seventeen, but she spent a sad and wandering life until she died at the age of seventy-three.

The Revolution now made many other violent changes. The Christian religion was forbidden, churches were desecrated and robbed, Sunday was done away with, and a day of rest arranged every ten days. An entire new calendar was arranged and the year I was said to begin on September 22, 1792, the day on which the Republic was proclaimed. The year was still divided into twelve months, but each month had thirty days and so five extra days had to be added at the end of the year.

The months were also given new names. Vendemiaire, the first month, beginning on September 22nd, was Vintage month; then followed Foggy month, Frosty month, Snowy month, Rainy month, Windy month, Budding month, Flowering month, Meadow month, Harvest month, Heat month, Fruit month.

At length some even of the men who had set up the Terror began to wish to stop it. Then they in their turn were suspected, seized, and Condémned to death by those who were still more violent than themselves. Thus Danton and many others perished. It was Robespierre who had them seized and Condémned, but he in his turn was also accused and put to death. At last each party having tom the other to pieces the Red Terror came to an end.

CHAPTER 83

THE REPUBLIC—THE DIRECTORY AND THE "LITTLE CORPORAL"

WHILE these terrible struggles were going on at home, France had been making a brave fight abroad. Badly fed and badly clothed though they were, the French soldiers once more began to win battle after battle. For from the ranks clever soldiers arose who knew how to lead. Only upon the sea were they defeated by the British. In Belgium, on the Rhine, in Italy, in Spain, victories were won, and at length in 1795 all the allies except Austria, Britain, and Sardinia made peace with France.

The Convention then separated, and a new government named the Directory was called together. Under the Convention many bad things had been done. But France at least had been saved from being conquered by foreign nations.

Still Britain and Austria continued to fight against France, and in the Spring of 1796 three great armies set forth. One marched into Germany, another into Austria, and the third into Italy.

This third army was commanded by a young Corsican officer named Napoleon Bonaparte, who a short time before had been wandering about the streets of Paris, a penniless adventurer. He had, however, made himself useful to the government by helping to put down riots in Paris, and by driving the allies out of Toulon, and he rapidly rose in rank from lieutenant to general.

Now in Italy Bonaparte swept all before him. He turned the ragged, hungry rabble given him to command into a disciplined army, with which he won battle after battle, and took town after town until almost the whole of Italy was at his feet. His soldiers soon grew to love him, and were ready to follow him anywhere. He had risen rapidly from being a nobody to being a famous general, but his men, out of the love and admiration they had for his daring, gave him the name of the "Little Corporal."

But Bonaparte did not only fight and win battles, he signed treaties and made peace with the various princes as he chose without consulting the Directors in Paris. Whatever happened to the Republic he meant to make Napoleon Bonaparte great. "Do you suppose," he said, "that I triumph in Italy for the glory of the lawyers of the Directory? Do you suppose I mean to found a Republic? What an idea! The nation wants a chief, a chief covered with glory."

At first the Directory had been delighted with his skill and success. Soon they began to fear him, and be jealous of him. The people, on the other hand, adored him. When from Italy Bonaparte returned to Paris they crowded to see him and cheer him. And not a few were heard to declare that it was time to be done with the Directory and have a King once more. And who should be King but the "Little Corporal?"

Britain was the last foreign foe which stood out against France. Now it seemed to Bonaparte that the best way to get the better of Britain was not to attack the country directly, but through its trade and commerce with India. To do this he decided to get possession of Egypt and of the routes through the Mediterranean.

At first the Directory were very much against this plan. But at length they gave way, not so much because they believed in it, but because it would keep this dangerous, restless soldier occupied far from France.

So with a great army and twenty ships of war General Bonaparte set sail for Egypt. On his way he took Malta, for he knew that it was one of the keys of the Mediterranean, the command of which he desired for the French.

The island was held by the Knights of St. John, an order founded in the far-off Crusading times. And had they been filled with the courage and daring of those days they could easily have held their fortress, for the walls were strong and thick. But French gold did what Bonaparte's cannon could not have done, and after a mere pretence of fighting the gates were opened. "I took Malta when I was at Mantua," said Bonaparte. By that he meant that the Knights had agreed with him to betray their fortress. But if this was so they must soon have regretted their treachery. For Bonaparte put an end to their knighthood and expelled them from Malta. Then taking with him all the gold and silver and treasure that he could find the general sailed on to Egypt.

A storm was brewing and it was growing dark when at length Alexandria came in sight. But in spite of deepening night, wind and waves, General Bonaparte landed, for he well knew that Nelson and a British fleet were scouring the Mediterranean in search of him. Then as the day dawned his famished—weary men marched against the town of Alexandria. The crumbling walls gave way before them, and in a few hours the tricolour, the red, white, and blue of the French Republic, was waving on the ramparts'.

Egypt at this time was supposed to be under the Turks. But the real power was in the hands of the Mamelukes. They were a fiery, lawless people, famous for long ages for their skill in fighting, and for their superb horsemen. Their chief, who was called a Bey, now gathered his forces to defend Cairo, and Bonaparte marched to meet him there.

It was a terrible march. The men who had trudged merrily through the heat of Italy drooped beneath the misery of it. Italy had been hot, but not with the burning, barren heat of the desert. The sky blazed above their heads. The sand burned beneath their feet. The Arabs flung stones into the few wells along the route, so that to get even a cupful of water needed long toil. Without shade, without water, bitten by scorpions, tortured by clouds of insects, the men lost courage. Loud and deep were their murmurs. They saw nothing but death before them. Too feeble and disheartened to keep up, many dropped out of the ranks.

Then indeed swift death overtook them. Somewhere from out the desert dust white-robed horsemen dashed. For a few minutes the desert rang with shouts, and cries, and musket shots, then silence and stillness once more fell upon the glowing stretch of sand, the blue sky was flecked with black where dark birds of prey hung above the spot where Frenchmen lay forever still.

It was only Bonaparte who seemed to feel neither heat nor fatigue. He rode among the soldiers encouraging them, cheering them. Other officers too did their best, and through their misery the men could still jest. "It is all very well for you," said a soldier one day to his officer who was scolding him, "it is all very well for you, General, you have always one foot in France." The General had a wooden leg.

At length the army reached Cairo, and beneath the shadow of the mighty Pyramids a battle was fought. For here the Mamelukes awaited their foe.

"Soldiers," said Bonaparte pointing to the Pyramids, "forty centuries look down upon you," and the battle began.

From out the haze and dust of the desert, riding swift and fiery Arab steeds, the Mamelukes dashed upon the Frenchmen. White-robed, their weapons gleaming with gold and jewels, the rich trappings of their horses glowing in the brilliant sunshine, they sped onward, uttering wild war cries.

Unshaken, the glittering line of bayonets met the shock. Again and again the Mamelukes returned to the charge. Again and again they were broken against the awful wall of steel, and thrown back in disorder. At length, swept down by the steady fire of the French, they scattered and fled. They disappeared into the desert, leaving men and horses dead and dying on the field.

A few days after the battle of the Pyramids Bonaparte rode in triumph into Cairo. But here amid his triumphs he got bad news, news which made his victories worthless. He heard that the French fleet had been utterly destroyed by Nelson in the battle of the Nile, and that all the treasure taken from Malta was sunk in Aboukir Bay. The news filled Bonaparte with sorrow and anger, for the British, whom he had set out to overthrow, had once more got the best of it; and by destroying the French fleet they had imprisoned Bonaparte and his soldiers in their newly conquered land.

The army was in utter despair. Even the officers lost hope; their leader alone seemed cheerfully to face whatever fate might bring, and he calmly set himself to the task of governing Egypt.

But by this time the Turks, freed from the fear of the French fleet, had declared war with France, and a Turkish army set out to assail Bonaparte in Egypt.

Bonaparte on his side determined not to wait to be attacked, but to march to meet the foe. So again the dreary, painful march through desert lands began.

Fighting battles and taking towns on the way, Bonaparte at length reached St. Jean d'Acre. But St. Jean d'Acre did not fall before the conqueror as other towns had fallen. For now he had against him not only Turkish but British soldiers. Sir Sidney Smith was anchored before the town with a couple of British ships, and his big guns were of far more use than all the Turkish soldiers put together. The guns indeed were many of them French. For Sir Sidney had captured Bonaparte's as they were coming from Alexandria, and so the very guns with which he had hoped to break down the walls of St. Jean d'Acre were used to defend them.

Still these walls were weak and crumbling, and in spite of the loss of his guns, Bonaparte hoped to take the town. Assault after assault was made, but all in vain. For the British were just as determined to hold the town as Bonaparte was to take it. "This town is not defensible according to the rules of war," said Sidney Smith, "but according to every other rule it must and shall be defended."

Soon Bonaparte had to fight another enemy. Plague broke out in his camp. At length, in great disgust, he gave up the siege and marched back to Egypt. "That man has made me miss my future," he said, speaking of Sir Sidney Smith. "Had St. Jean d'Acre fallen I would have been Emperor of all the East."

The march to Cairo had been a new and dreadful experience. It was as nothing to the retreat from St. Jean d'Acre. All the old misery of thirst and heat had to be borne, and now the soldiers were exhausted and discouraged; they were laden too with the heavy burden of their sick and dying comrades. It was an agony hardly to be endured. Yet Bonaparte would not own defeat, and he entered Egypt like a conqueror in triumph, with the banners taken from the Turks flying before him.

CHAPTER 84

THE REPUBLIC—THE CONSUALTE, AND GENERAL BONAPARTE

BUT while these things had been happening in Syria and Egypt the Directory had been ruling badly. In Europe a new league had been formed against France. France was threatened on all sides by British, Austrian, and Russian forces. In Italy almost all that Napoleon had won was lost again. All France was full of discontent and anger against the Five Majesties of the Luxembourg, as the Directors were called.

While in Syria Bonaparte had heard nothing of all this. Now he received a letter from his brother and a lot of old newspapers which were full of bad news. At once he made up his mind to return home.

But the French fleet had been destroyed. Without ships it was impossible to take the army back to France. So Napoleon made up his mind to leave it behind. Very secretly he laid his plans. He let it be known that he was going on a journey into Upper Egypt. Then quietly one August night he rode away toward Alexandria, taking his best generals with him. There he set sail for France, deserting the army which had suffered so much in the cause of his mad ambition.

The expedition into Egypt had been nothing but a wild goose chase. But in spite of that the French people were dazzled with it, and Bonaparte's journey from the coast to Paris was a triumphal progress. Towns were illuminated, joybells were rung, bonfires were lit, everywhere he was received with cheers and delight.

All this pleased General Bonaparte greatly. For he had never meant to be a mere soldier. He meant to rule France. So he was not ill-pleased to see the Directors make mistake after mistake. He was not ill-pleased to know that they had lost the confidence of the nation.

At length one day Bonaparte entered the Assembly, followed by his soldiers. A scene of utter confusion followed, drums beat loudly, shouts and cries of "Long Live the Republic! Long live Bonaparte!" were heard, and the Directors fled before the glittering bayonets of the conqueror.

That was the end of the Directory. This is called the Revolution of Brumaire or Foggymonth. It took place on November 9, 1799. It was greeted with joy, for all over France men had come to hate the Directory.

A new government was at once formed called the Consulate. There were three Consuls, one of which was Napoleon Bonaparte. He took the title of First Consul, and his power was almost equal to that of a king.

Many of General Bonaparte's first acts as Consul were wise and good. The people were weary of the storms that had swept over France for so many years. So although he had gained his power unlawfully and by force they yielded willingly to the rule of this imperious soldier.

One of the first things Bonaparte now did was to try to make peace with Britain. He wrote to King George. "Must the war be eternal?" he asked. Could France and Britain not believe that "Peace was the first of all needs, the brightest of all glories?"

But in spite of his fine speeches the British did not believe that Bonaparte was sincere. He wanted peace only on his own conditions and for his own ends, and the war went on.

After Great Britain Austria was the greatest enemy France still had to fight. And the war was still being carried on in the north of Italy, which was then in the possession of Austria. So now Bonaparte decided to march into Italy with another great army.

For months he made his preparations, gathering an army in secret, and quietly sending it by various routes into Switzerland. For Bonaparte meant to take his enemy by surprise and while they were preparing for a front attack suddenly swoop down upon them from behind. The great barrier of the Alps had to be crossed. But what then? No difficulties daunted Bonaparte. It was barely possible to cross, he was told. Then it could be done!

Bonaparte's march through the St. Bernard Pass into Italy is one of his most famous feats. It was a tremendous undertaking, for in those days there were no fine roads across the Alps, as there are to-day. It was impossible for the heavy gun carriages to pass along the rough uneven ground. So the guns were taken from their carriages and placed on pine trunks hollowed out for the purpose. A hundred men or more were yoked to each one of these and thus, panting and struggling, they dragged the heavy cannon up the steep mountain pass. The gun carriages were taken to bits. Some parts were slung on poles, and carried by the men. The rest, along with the ammunition, was laden on mules, which were strong and nimble and well used to the mountain paths.

To the heavily laden men the march was hard and wearisome and to cheer them onward bands played and drums beat. At some of the worst places the bugles sounded the charge, so as to fill the men with courage, and make them fight the difficulties of the road as they would fight a foreign foe.

Day after day in an unending train foot and horse poured through the pass. Sometimes the road wound along between towering snow mountains which seemed ready to fall and crush the adventurous army. Sometimes it led along a narrow ledge on the edge of a giddy precipice. Sometimes it led through snow drifts into which the foremost men sank knee deep. But ever they pressed onward, not daring to halt for fear that those coming after should be thrown into disorder.

At length they gained the top. Here stands the Hospice of St. Bernard and here the kindly monks served a meal of bread and cheese and wine to the jaded men. Then the descent into Italy began.

All went well until the little Fort Bard was reached. It was held by the Austrians and completely blocked the way, for it commanded the whole pass, which is very narrow. It was in a very strong position, but held only by a few hundred soldiers. With time it could be taken. But Bonaparte had no time to lose. For his chance of success was in surprising the enemy. And to surprise them he must move quickly.

It was an anxious moment. "The Consul took many pinches of snuff," said one of his soldiers. "Here he had need of all his great genius."

But this last difficulty was soon overcome. The foot-soldiers found a narrow goat-track which led round the fort out of the range of its guns. By this they scrambled along till they had safely passed the fort. It was not possible, however, to carry the cannon along such a narrow path, and without artillery the whole expedition would have been useless. So one dark night French soldiers stole into the little town above which frowned the fort. They littered the streets thickly with straw. The guns were once more mounted upon their carnages, the wheels of which were bound with straw, everything that might rattle or jangle was carefully muffled. Then the guns were quietly drawn through the straw-strewn streets, not a pistol-shot away from the all too confident Austrians.

Now at length the difficulties were over, and without further hindrance the French army streamed down into the plains of Italy.

The French who had already been fighting in Italy, under the brave General Massena, were now shut up in Genoa, which was besieged by both British and Austrians. Both people and soldiers were starving. Everything had been eaten, even to cats and dogs. There was nothing left but boots and knapsacks, grass and nettles. Still, though day by day their courage sank, they held out. Now when the news of Bonaparte's splendid march across the Alps reached them their sinking courage rose. They would soon be relieved.

But General Bonaparte had no thought of marching to Genoa. For he had a great plan in his head by which he meant utterly to crush the Austrians, and he could spare no soldiers to relieve the starving town. So leaving Massena and his brave men to their fate, Bonaparte marched toward Milan. Everywhere the people who were friendly to the French greeted him with delight. It seemed to them that he had come down from the clouds with an army to crush the hated Austrians, to free them from a hated rule.

Near the town of Alessandria the great battle of Marengo was fought. It was now June, and in the early dawn the fight began and all day it raged terribly. By five o'clock the battle seemed lost for the French. In many places they fled. The Austrian leader, a brave old man of eighty, was both wounded and weary of the fight. And believing that he had won the battle, he went back to Alessandria to send the news of his victory to his Emperor.

But suddenly a change came. A French officer with fresh troops rode up. The French who had fled now rallied, and two hours later the Austrian victory was turned into a French victory.

But it was dearly bought, for almost as many of the French as of their foes lay dead. Yet it was complete, and next day the Austrian leader asked for peace. That day a treaty was signed which gave back to France all that Bonaparte had won in his earlier wars. Thus in one battle he had regained all that had been lost.

It was scarcely two months since Bonaparte had left Paris. During that time he had filled Europe with dismay and delighted the French. "The nation wants a chief covered with glory," he had said. Now he returned to them covered with glory, the second time conqueror of Italy. The people received him with wild delight. Night after night the streets of Paris were illuminated, and crowds stood for hours patiently in the hope of seeing the hero of Marengo if but for a moment.

Still the war with Austria went on. At length in December the French General Moreau won a great victory at Hohenlinden. After this Austria was glad to make peace. France was thus at peace with all Europe,

Great Britain alone continuing to fight, winning again and again.

Bonaparte had induced some of the powers of Europe to unite against Britain in a league called the Armed Neutrality. But in the Battle of the Baltic Nelson shattered this Armed Neutrality. After two years' blockade Malta surrendered to the British. Sir Ralph Abercromby attacked the French who were still in Egypt, where Bonaparte had forsaken them, and utterly defeated them. Thus Britain had nothing more to fear from France and at length, both sides being weary of fighting, peace was signed in March, 1802.

It now seemed that the wars of the Revolution were really at an end, and Bonaparte turned all his attention to governing France and to bringing some order out of wild disorder. In these few years of peace he did much for France. Everything was in confusion and the First Consul attended to everything. For as Wellington once said, "Nothing was too great or too small for his proboscis."

The French went back to the old way of counting days and months. The Roman Catholic religion was once more established, and with it came again Sunday and the week of seven days. A general amnesty or peace was proclaimed to the emigrants, so that many gentlemen and nobles who had fled returned with their families. Titles were once more used. People were once more addressed as Madame and Monsieur instead of merely as citizen and citizeness. In every way life seemed to turn back into old familiar ways.

But Bonaparte was not content with merely returning to old ways. Many new things were founded, among them new schools and a new university. The Bank of

France was opened, museums were built, roads were made.

But perhaps the best thing Bonaparte did was to frame anew the laws. These laws were given the name of Code Napoleon and they are to this day the laws by which France is ruled.

CHAPTER 85

THE EMPIRE—NAPOLEAN EMPORER AND KING

ALL this time Bonaparte's power was increasing. But still he was only General Bonaparte, only Consul for ten years. It was now proposed that he should be made Consul for twenty years. But with growing power Bonaparte's ambitions had grown too. To be Consul for twenty years no longer seemed to him a great thing. He wanted to be the first man in France now and always. He wanted power, but he wanted the people to believe that in taking it he was doing them a great favour.

"You think I owe a fresh sacrifice to the people," he said. "I will make it, if the will of the people commands it."

He refused therefore to be Consul for more than ten years until the will of the people had been heard. So all through the land papers were sent to which the people might put "Yes" or "No." But the question asked was not "Shall Napoleon Bonaparte be Consul for twenty years?" but "Shall Napoleon Bonaparte be Consul for life?"

To such a length was the First Consul willing to sacrifice himself for the people.

Although a great many people did not vote at all, three million and a half said "Yes," only a few thousand said "No." Bonaparte, delighted with the result, was proclaimed Consul for life. "Senators," he said grandly, "the life of a citizen belongs to his country. The French people wish mine to be wholly dedicated to it. I obey their will."

Henceforth the First Consul was no longer Bonaparte. He was now really King of France although in name he was still only Consul. And like other kings, he used his Christian name, and now called himself Napoleon.

Napoleon had many enemies. There were the stern Republicans, who hated to see the hopes of the Republic utterly overthrown. There were the Royalists, who still hoped to see the Bourbons on the throne again. So there was almost constantly a plot brewing to kill or overthrow Napoleon.

When these plots were discovered those who took part in them were sternly punished. Some were put to death, others imprisoned or banished.

The last prince of the great house of Condé was the Duke d'Enghien.

He was living quietly in the Black Forest beyond the borders of France when a plot against Napoleon was discovered. There was no reason to believe that he had anything to do with the plot. But Napoleon persuaded himself that he had. So one night a regiment of French soldiers crossed the Rhine and surrounded the Duke's house.

The Duke at first wanted to fight. But he was almost alone. He could not have held out long against hundreds of soldiers. So to avoid a useless loss of life he gave himself up. He was taken prisoner to France, and the next night was shut up in the Castle of Vincennes.

Here in the middle of the night he was awakened and led out to be tried. But his trial was a hollow sham, for his sentence was already passed, his grave already dug.

The Duke answered the questions put to him bravely and truthfully. But as he looked at the cold, gloomy faces of the judges he knew that no justice awaited him there. He begged to be allowed to see the Consul. His request was refused. His doom was fixed.

Before the gray March dawn had come he was led out to the moat of the castle, where the flickering light of a few torches lit up the pale faces and dark uniforms of a line of soldiers, and showed the grave already dug. For a minute the Duke bent his head in prayer. Then drawing himself up he bade the soldiers shoot straight. A moment later he fell dead, shot through the heart.

The news of this murder, for it could be called nothing less, filled all Europe with loathing. Many who had been ready to make friends with Napoleon fell away from him. His own mother reproached him for having by this deed stained his name with a blot that could never be wiped out. But others saw in the plot a means to win something for Napoleon he had long desired. This something was nothing less than the crown. For Napoleon was no longer content to be an uncrowned king.

It was now time, said his friends, to make the power hereditary in Napoleon's family. That is, that it should be decreed that his children should reign after him. Only in this way, they said, would the plots against Napoleon cease. For there would not be any good of killing one Bonaparte if it were certain that another Bonaparte would reign after him.

It was Napoleon's own idea, it was his desire. But once more he made it seem as if the wish came from the people, as if in accepting the honour he yielded to the will of the people.

So but a few days after the murder of the Duke d'Enghien the Senate begged Napoleon to take the title of Emperor. "You are founding," they said, "a new era, but you must make it last forever. Splendour is nothing without duration. Do not delay, great Man! finish your work. You have delivered us from the confusion of the past, you bless for us our present good; make us also sure of the future. Citizen First Consul, be well assured that the Senate speaks thus to you in the name of all the citizens."

There were many more fine speeches. But once more Napoleon insisted on an appeal to the people. Once again they answered "Yes," and so on May 18, 1804, Napoleon was proclaimed Emperor of the French.

"I accept," he said, "the title which you too believe to be useful to the glory of the nation. I hope that France will never repent of the honour with which she loads my family. At least my spirit will no longer be with my descendants on that day when they shall cease to be worthy of the love and confidence of this great nation."

What changes! It was but a few years since Napoleon Bonaparte had wandered about the streets of Paris hungry and penniless, hardly knowing where he would get his next meal, or how he could procure a clean shirt. Now, he was Emperor. Now, richly dressed, he drove through these same streets in a splendid carriage, while the people thronged to see and cheer him.

A few years before the French people had risen in revolt against tyranny, they had stained their hands in blood, they had filled the land with war and terror to rid themselves of a privileged class, and fulfil their dream of making every one equal. Now they brought back all that they had fought against. For as soon as Napoleon became Emperor he surrounded himself with a new nobility. He gave his brothers thrones. He made his sisters princesses. He showered titles on his generals and friends. He brought into use again all the old forms and ceremonies of court life. The Republic, which ever since Napoleon had become Consul had been a mere name, was now completely at an end.

But Napoleon felt that there was still something lacking to make his glory complete. No crown had been set upon his head. Only the Pope could crown an Emperor. So he made up his mind to be crowned by the Pope like Charlemagne the great Emperor whose Empire he hoped to rival.

Napoleon's pride and vanity were so great, however, that he could not bring himself to go to Rome to be crowned. He wanted the Pope to come to Paris to crown him there.

Never before had such a thing been done. The Pope at first was very much surprised at Napoleon's request. He was very unwilling to crown him. For how, he asked, could he crown the murderer of the Duke d'Enghien?

But at length he consented, half in fear, half in hope. He feared Napoleon's mighty conquering hand if he refused. He hoped to win something for the Church by consenting.

Napoleon's pride was so great that he would not go to Rome to be crowned. It was so great that the idea of greeting the Pope humbly as one more august than himself was hateful to him. Therefore to avoid a formal greeting he made up his mind to pretend to meet the Pope unexpectedly while he was hunting in the forest of Fontainbleau.

So as the Pope's carriage drove along, the Emperor came riding to meet him clad in hunting dress and surrounded by hounds and horsemen.

The Pope's carriage stopped in the muddy road. The Pope, clad in beautiful white robes and wearing fine white silk shoes, was unwilling to get out. But at a little distance Napoleon waited, so the old man was forced to get out and walk a step or two toward the proud young Emperor.

The two great rulers kissed each other. Then the Emperor's carriage was driven up, the servants opening both doors at once. The Emperor immediately took the right side or place of honour, and an officer led the Pope to the left side. Thus without any words Napoleon showed the Pope that he claimed the higher place. Indeed the poor Pope soon found out that he had gained nothing by yielding to Napoleon's will. He was treated as a mere chaplain as the reward of his Condéscension.

All that could be done to make the Coronation splendid was done. Money was poured out right and left. And when at length the chilly December morning dawned the streets of Paris were thronged with people all anxious to catch a glimpse of Napoleon and his beautiful Empress Josephine as they drove through the streets in their glittering carriage. And as Napoleon entered the great church of Notre Dame, wearing a gorgeous robe of purple velvet and crowned like a Caesar with a wreath of golden bay leaves, he was greeted with shouts of "Long Live the Emperor! Long live the Emperor!"

It was a great moment, one for which Napoleon had long schemed and struggled. But soon he grew tired of the ceremony; he grew impatient for it to be over. To him the prayers and thanksgiving to God meant nothing. It was little to him that his crown and sword should be blessed, that his head should be anointed with holy oil. He believed that it was useful to him, that the splendid show would increase his power, but he found it wearisome.

At length the moment came when the Pope raised the crown to set it upon the Emperor's head. But instead of allowing him to do so Napoleon himself took the crown and set it upon his own head. It was as if he would show that he owed his power to himself alone.

About six months after Napoleon was crowned in Paris he went to Italy. He was already an Emperor. Now he took to himself the title of King of Italy, also crowning himself with the famous and ancient iron crown of Lombardy. "God has given it to me. Let him who touches it beware!" he cried as he set it upon his head.

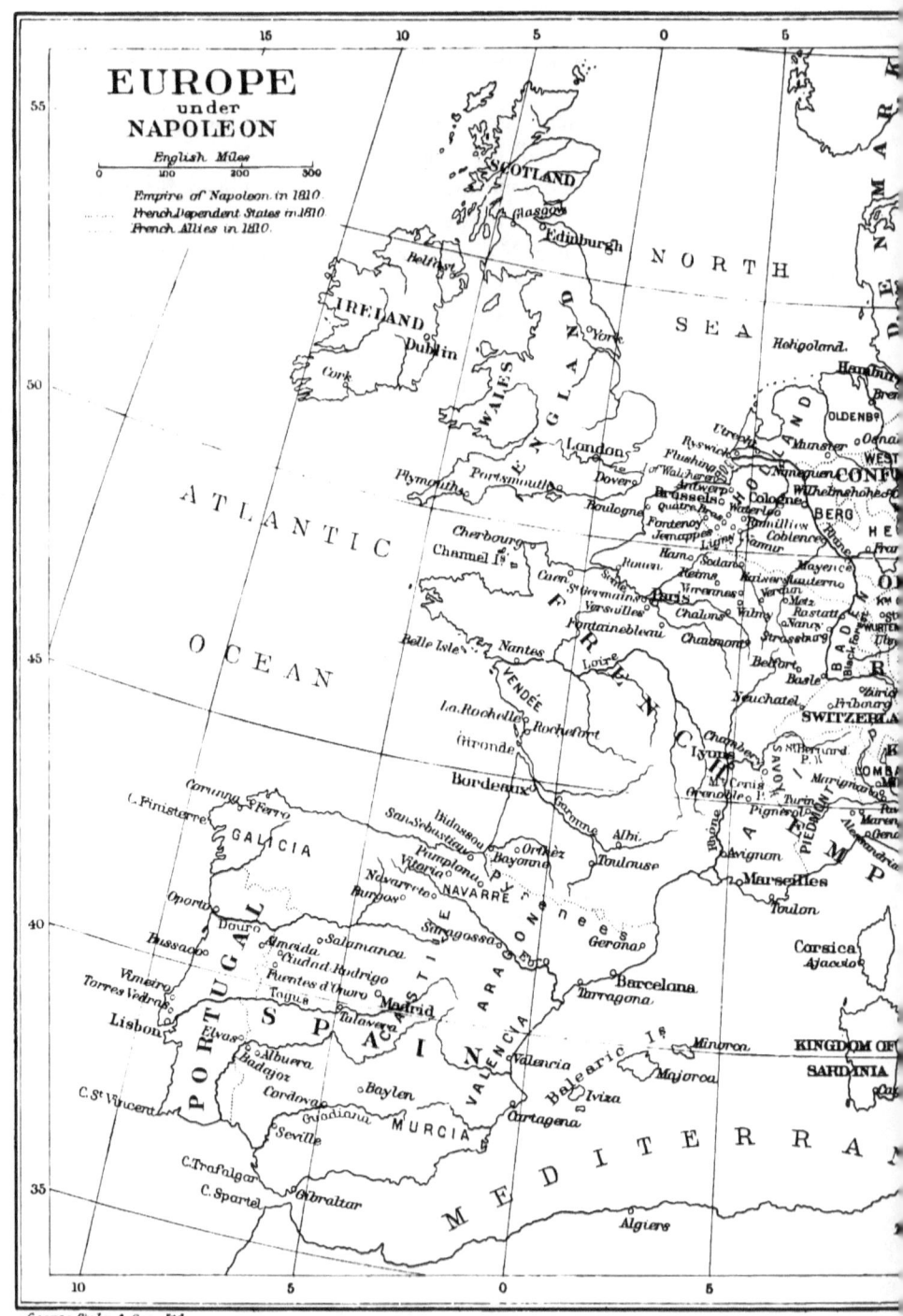

CHAPTER 86

NAPOLEON I—THE SUN OF AUSTERLITZ

BUT while these things had been happening in France, the kings and rulers of Europe had again been uniting against Napoleon. Already two years before this Britain had declared war, and Napoleon was full of an idea of invading England.

He now gathered an army which he called the "Army of England," and built a whole fleet of flat-bottomed boats in which to carry his soldiers across the channel. His preparations were great and long, but at last everything was ready, even to the medals which were to celebrate Napoleon's victories and which were marked "Struck at London, 1804."

Napoleon was sure of success. His plans were well laid if only the British and the winds and tides had fallen in with them. But somehow neither the British nor the weather played the parts he planned they should. So his great invasion never took place.

Meanwhile all over Europe war was once more kindling. Russia, Austria, and Sweden joined with Britain against France. So for the time Napoleon gave up the invasion of England, and marched his Army of England, as it was called, into Germany to fight the Austrians and the Russians.

Napoleon moved so quickly that he defeated the Austrians again and again before the Russians could come to help them, and at length drove them to take refuge in the town of Ulm.

The Austrian leader, General Mack, was old. He lost heart, and with hardly a show of fighting he now yielded to Napoleon.

On the 20th of October, Napoleon took his stand upon some rising ground near the town of Ulm, there to receive the submission of the conquered Austrians. Dressed like a simple soldier in an old gray overcoat and a plain hat, the Emperor stood warming himself beside a fire. He was surrounded by a brilliant staff, and behind him his army stretched rank upon rank in glittering parade array. The day was cold and gloomy and dark rain clouds hung over hill and valley. But now as if to make the spectacle of Napoleon's triumph more brilliant still the sun shone out, and its splendour was reflected from a thousand glittering points of steel.

Drums beat, bands played, the gates of Ulm opened. Slowly and in silence the Austrian army advanced, regiment after regiment. First of all came the general. "Here is the unfortunate Mack," he said, as bowed down with shame and grief he gave up his sword.

After him, hour by hour, the long line of soldiers filed before the conqueror. Some threw down their arms in sullen gloom, others in helpless anger, bitterly ruing in their hearts that they had lived to surrender, while a few seemed glad to have done with fighting.

On this day more than twenty-three thousand men yielded themselves prisoners, and the Austrian army was almost wiped out. Yet there had been little fighting. "I have destroyed the Austrian army by simple marches," wrote Napoleon to the Empress. "Our Emperor has found a new way of making war," said his soldiers.

"He no longer makes it with our arms, but with our legs."

Napoleon had begun his career of conquest. But, although he did not yet know it, on the very day after his triumph over Austria he had received a great check. For on the 21st of October, Nelson had shattered the French fleet in the Battle of Trafalgar.

When Napoleon did hear the news he was bitterly angry. It spoilt for him all his success in Austria. To wipe out the disgrace of defeat by sea he felt that he must win new victories on land. And it was against the Russians that he now turned his sword.

At Austerlitz a terrible battle was fought. It has received the name of the Battle of the Three Emperors. For the Emperor of Germany, the Emperor of Russia, and the Emperor of the French were all upon the field.

When the day of battle dawned a dense mist hid the hostile armies from each other. Unbroken silence reigned, and it was hard to believe that beneath that white pall thousands of men were waiting, ready to fly at each other's throats as soon as they could see.

Gradually the mist grew lighter. Then suddenly the sun broke through the veil and shone redly forth in wintry majesty. It shone upon the two armies face to face ready to fight. It shone upon the little gray-coated figure of the soldiers' hero. With cheer upon cheer the soldiers greeted him as he rode along the lines, for they remembered that exactly a year ago he had been crowned, and they meant to give him a coronation present of a victory. "I promise you," an old soldier had said the night before, "I promise you the standards and the cannon of the enemy with which to celebrate the anniversary of your coronation."

As Napoleon listened to the cheers his heart swelled with pride. "Ah,"

THE LITTLE GREY-COATED FIGURE OF THE SOLDIERS' HERO.

he cried, in delight, "the sun of Austerlitz has risen." He took it as a good omen, and ever after when the sun shone upon one of his great feats he would say, "It is the sun of Austerlitz."

Napoleon's victory was complete. But the struggle was fierce. At length, however, in the early dusk of the winter afternoon, the allies fled before the French. They fled across two frozen lakes. The ice gave way beneath their weight, it was shattered by the cannon balls of the French, and thousands sank in the chilly waters, or were crushed to death between the broken masses of ice.

Austerlitz was one of the greatest victories ever won by the French. And Napoleon, who well knew how to please his men and win their hearts, praised them for it. "Soldiers, I am well pleased with you," he said. "You have this day justified all that I expected of your daring. You have decorated your eagles with undying glory. Soldiers, when the French people placed the imperial crown upon my head I trusted to you to keep it ever bright with glory, which alone made it of value in my eyes. When you have done all that is necessary for the happiness and welfare of your country, I will lead you back to France. There you will be the objects of my tenderest care. My people will receive you with joy, and it will be enough to say, 'I was at the Battle of Austerlitz' for them to reply, 'Here is a brave man.'"

By the treaty of Presburg, Austria now made peace with Napoleon. He as conqueror disposed of many of the states of Germany as he chose. He took away from some, and added to others. The states along the Rhine he united into a Confederation, under the protection of France. He formed new kingdoms, and gave them as gifts to his brothers and sisters.

By all these acts Napoleon had despoiled the German Emperor of the last vestige of power. So feeling himself utterly beaten, feeling his claim over Germany to be now but an empty one, the Emperor gave up his title so far as Germany was concerned, set free all the German princes from their oath of fealty to him, and henceforth called himself only Emperor of Austria.

Thus at last the Empire which had been founded by Charlemagne was shattered forever. It was shattered by the man who had dreams of himself building up an Empire to which that of Charlemagne would be as nothing.

While the German Emperor had been fighting, however, Prussia, the largest of all the German states, had remained at peace. But Napoleon had determined to conquer Prussia too, and at length he almost forced the King of Prussia to declare war.

In this new war Napoleon was as fortunate as in the last. On one day two battles were fought, one at Jena, where Napoleon himself led the French, one at Auerstadt, where they were led by General Davoust. In both the Prussians were beaten. Then Napoleon's armies swept through Prussia, taking fortress after fortress until he marched in triumph into the capital, Berlin.

But even with his capital in the hands of the enemy the King of Prussia did not yield and the Czar of Russia now marched to help him. The war was continued all winter, battles being fought in bitter frost and snow. But still fortune was ever on the side of the French. Victory was ever theirs. At last the war ended with the battle of Friedland, in which the allies were utterly defeated. It was fought upon the same day as Marengo had been, and Napoleon, who well knew how to encourage his men, as he rode among them on the morning of the battle bade them remember it. "It is a lucky day!" he cried. "It is the anniversary of Marengo."

Again the French won the victory. Again the great General was pleased. "My children have worthily celebrated the anniversary of Marengo," he wrote, to the Empress Josephine. "All the Russian army is routed. The Battle of Friedland is a worthy sister of Marengo, of Austerlitz, of Jena."

After the Battle of Friedland the Czar begged for peace. Napoleon admired the dash and courage of the Russian soldiers, and wanted to have them for his allies; he had, besides, other motives for wishing for peace, and so a meeting was arranged between the two Emperors.

A magnificent tent of crimson velvet was set up upon a barge on the river Nieman not far from the town of Tilsit. It was decorated with the flags of Russia and of France. Beneath them the two great rulers met.

It is said that as the Czar embraced Napoleon he cried out, "I hate Britain as much as you do."

"If that is so," answered Napoleon, "then peace is made."

The two rulers entered alone into the tent. They remained together there for some time, and when their conference was over they appeared to be the best of friends.

The Czar was young, he was dazzled and fascinated by the brilliant genius of Napoleon, he was beguiled by his flattery. So he yielded to Napoleon's proposals, and made peace with little regard to his old ally the King of Prussia.

The King of Prussia was not asked to the conference, but was treated with harshness and insult. For Napoleon, knowing that he could not be flattered and beguiled like the Czar, felt that he must be crushed. So he was scolded, and bullied, and despoiled of half of his kingdom.

Then having as he thought made a firm friend of the Czar, and utterly crushed the King of Prussia, Napoleon returned to Paris.

CHAPTER 87

NAPOLEON I—A KING OF KINGS

IN all his wars Napoleon's chief and final aim was the conquest of Britain. The battle of Trafalgar had forever shattered his hopes of invading Britain directly. It made him all the more determined to conquer Britain by conquering Europe. He meant to bring all Europe under his sway, so that at length Britain would stand utterly alone without a friend, and thus be forced to yield to him. To gain his end he fought not only with sword and bayonet. He fought with trade.

While at Berlin Napoleon issued what is called the Berlin Decree. By this decree he ordered Europe to cease to trade with Britain. No British goods were to be allowed to come to any port in Europe. No country in Europe was to be allowed to send goods to Britain, and every British subject found on the Continent was to be seized as a prisoner of war.

In his eagerness to crush Britain Napoleon was blind to the fact that he was bringing great suffering, not only upon the other countries of Europe, but upon France itself. Trade was hampered and throttled, and the common things of everyday life grew dearer and dearer. Such things as coffee and sugar, boots and shoes, cotton and woollen goods, rose so high in price that poor people had to go hungry and in rags.

The Decree brought want and misery into every poor man's house. It raised up in the hearts of the people, not so much hatred against Britain, as hatred against the tyrant whose proud will brought the suffering.

Even then Napoleon's orders were not obeyed, for smuggling was carried on to an enormous extent. Every one smuggled, even the officers in the French army. Napoleon's own soldiers were shod with British-made boots, and dressed in cloth made on British looms.

Yet Napoleon clung to his Continental System, as it was called. At the Treaty of Tilsit he had forced both Russia and Prussia to agree to it. Both countries, however, soon found that it pressed heavily upon them.

But while most of Europe thus bent to Napoleon's will, one country resisted. That country was Portugal. So now Napoleon made up his mind to make war on Portugal and force it to yield. "The fall of the House of Braganza will be a new proof that ruin is certain to overtake any country which attaches itself to Britain," said Napoleon.

Now in order to reach Portugal Napoleon had to pass through Spain. So he made secretly a bargain with the Spanish King, promising when Portugal was conquered to share it with him.

At this time the Queen of Portugal was mad, and her son John ruled as Regent. When he learned that a French army was marching to attack him, he determined to flee to Brazil. For it seemed impossible for little Portugal to stand alone against the might of France.

So when after a hurried and toilsome march across the snowy Pyrenees the French army arrived at Lisbon; they found the Queen and Prince Regent gone, and the people too hopeless to resist.

Soon the whole of Portugal was overrun by French soldiers, and everywhere the tricolour of France replaced the flag of Portugal. "The House of Braganza," said Napoleon, "has ceased to reign."

But although Portugal was making little or no resistance French soldiers continued to stream into Spain. Instead, however, of making their way toward Portugal, they spread through Spain; they closed round Madrid.

At the same time the Spanish royal family was torn asunder by quarrels. The King was old and feeble, the Queen ruled by her favourite, Godoy. The King had given up his throne in favour of his son Ferdinand. But almost at once he repented of the deed. Ferdinand, however, refused again to give back the throne. So the quarrel grew bitter. Then, hearing that Napoleon was coming, both father and son resolved to appeal to him for advice.

It was at Bayonne that father and son met Napoleon. Here on French territory, beset on every side by a hostile army, they found themselves little better than prisoners. It soon became plain to both that it did not suit Napoleon's plans for either of them to reign in Spain. Indeed a month before, had they but known it, he had written to his brother Louis, "I have decided on placing a French Prince on the Spanish throne. If I make you King of Spain will you accept it? Can I reckon on you?"

Powerless in the hands of the great schemer, the old King gave way at once. For a little time the young Prince held out, sullenly refusing to listen to Napoleon's arguments. But at length, cowed by the Emperor's threats, fearing even for his life, he gave in. Father and son signed away their rights to the throne of Spain and all her colonies.

Thus without fighting a single battle Napoleon had brought another great kingdom under his sway. But he had done it by trickery unworthy of a great ruler. Even Napoleon himself felt the need of justifying the act. "From some points of view, I know, my action is not good," he said. "But my policy requires that I should not leave behind me so near to Paris a kingdom hostile to mine." Yet at the time Spain was not hostile. For France and Spain were allies.

Napoleon now sent for his brother Joseph and made him King of Spain. And thus he thought the matter was settled. "I consider the most troublesome part of the business is over," he said. But he was mistaken. The most troublesome part was about to begin. For the Spanish people utterly refused to have an upstart Corsican for their king, and all through the country they rose in rebellion against French rule.

It was in vain that Napoleon made good laws, and reformed the oppressive backward laws of Spain. The Spaniards were not grateful. They preferred to be ruled badly by their own King to receiving favours from an usurper.

All over the country the Spaniards rose, forming themselves into companies, often under the leadership of monks. Walled towns held out fiercely, the country people attacked the French soldiers on the march, dashing down upon them unawares among the mountains and valleys. They harassed their march, refusing them food and supplies of any kind.

All differences among themselves were forgotten. Peasants, nobles, priests, and soldiers all fought together for the same end.

The Spaniards also sent to Britain asking for help.

Spain and Britain had been at war, for Spain was the one country which had joined with France against the allies. At the Battle of Trafalgar Spanish ships had fought against us side by side with those of France.

But now the British decided to help Spain. "The kingdom thus nobly struggling against the usurpation and the tyranny of France can no longer be considered as the enemy of Great Britain," said King George in Parliament. So an army was sent to Spain, under Sir Arthur Wellesley, that great soldier who afterward became the Duke of Wellington.

"In war men are nothing," once said Napoleon. "It is a man who is everything." And Napoleon was to find to his cost that he had now to fight a man whose genius was scarcely less than his own.

But in all the Peninsular War Napoleon and Wellington never met. For Napoleon had so many schemes in hand that he had little time to give to Spain. He left the war very much to his generals. But it was while he was in Spain that bad news came to him. He heard that Austria was getting ready to fight him. And in spite of the fact that he had quite lately had another meeting with his friend the Czar, so as to make sure of Russia, he heard that he, too, was ready to join with Austria. So giving his generals orders to "drive the British into the sea," Napoleon dashed away to Austria to fight there.

This second campaign against Austria was short, and it was one of the most deadly ever fought by Napoleon. It lasted scarcely three months and never had the great general's genius seemed more brilliant. In five days he won five victories, then for a second time he entered Vienna in triumph.

The war came to an end with the Battle of Wagram.

It was a terrible slaughter. It was, too, one of the least certain of Napoleon's victories, the loss on both sides being nearly equal. The old vigour and dash of Napoleon's army had vanished, for it was no longer a truly French army. It was filled with recruits from every land and people he had conquered. They no longer fought for freedom, or for country. They fought for the love of fighting, or because they were forced to it by the great conqueror who led them.

But although Wagram was barely a victory it was enough to make the Austrians yield once more. In October the treaty of Schönbrunn was signed. By it the Emperor lost still more of his land, and Napoleon once more returned to Paris in triumph.

Napoleon had by this time extended his Empire still farther. He fought with the Pope, took and held him prisoner for three years. Then the Papal States were added to France.

A little later Napoleon also dethroned his brother Louis, whom he had made King of Holland. For Louis was not obedient enough, and had dared to set at naught Napoleon's Continental System. Holland too was then added to France.

The Empire had now reached its greatest extent. Never since the days of Charlemagne had one man ruled over so many lands. The borders of France itself now reached eastward as far as the Rhine, northward to the borders of Denmark. The kings of Spain, Naples, and Westphalia were the Emperor's brothers. The whole of Italy, Portugal, and Switzerland were under his sway. The kings of Bavaria, Nuremberg, and Saxony, and many other lesser princes were his vassals.

Napoleon was an emperor, a maker and unmaker of kings. But he was, after all, in spite of all his pride, only an upstart, the son of a poor Corsican lawyer.

Napoleon wanted to forget that, he wanted to take his place among the kings and queens of ancient family, to be one of them, and unite his family with theirs. He wanted a royal princess to be his wife, he wanted to have children who could claim kinship with kings and queens of ancient lineage.

He already had a wife, the beautiful Josephine, to whom he had been married long, long ago, when he was only a poor soldier. But she was no princess, she was not even a great lady, and she had no children. And so Napoleon put her away. His duty to the nation demanded it he said.

Then, strange to say, Napoleon married the Duchess Marie Louise, the daughter of his enemy, the Emperor of Austria. Marie Louise was very young, very ignorant. She had no love for Napoleon, and looked upon him as the worst enemy of her country. She married him now in the hope of saving Austria. "I am ready to sacrifice my own happiness," she wrote to a friend, "for the good of the state, sure that one only finds true joy in doing one's duty."

So this timid and frivolous girl of eighteen became the Empress of the French, the wife of the most famous soldier and conqueror in all the world.

A year later a little son was born to Napoleon, who was overjoyed. He at once called him the King of Rome. For that was the title always given to the eldest son of the Emperor of the Holy Roman Empire.

CHAPTER 88
NAPOLEON I—THE HEART OF RUSSIA

MARIE Louise had wanted to do something for her country, and she did. The Russian people had as time went on been growing more and more angry with Napoleon's Continental System. Now Napoleon's marriage with Marie Louise made the Czar still more angry, and at last war between France and Russia broke out. And this war was the beginning of Napoleon's downfall. And thus, not only Austria, but all the other countries of Europe were delivered from his tyranny.

War was at this time still going on in Spain, and if Napoleon had been wise he would not have begun another until that was finished. But his eyes were blinded and dazzled with his own glory. He had never forgotten his dreams of conquering India and the East. Russia was one step toward that, so the Russian campaign began.

It was June when Napoleon marched into Russia with the Grand Army, as it was called. At first he found no enemy to fight, but only mile after mile of barren, deserted country. For the Russians had laid waste their land so that the enemy might find no food. The burning summer sun blazed down upon the men, who trudged along wretched roads ankle deep in dust, which rose in clouds as they passed.

They were choked with dust, they were hungry and thirsty, too. For many of the horses fell ill and died, and the immense wagon loads of food which Napoleon had ordered to accompany the army were left behind. There was no food to be found in the country except after long search. Both bread and salt soon failed. Then the men were reduced to eating meat without salt, with a paste of flour and water for bread. So from the very beginning the difficulties and the hardships of the campaign were great.

At length the two armies met. There were several fights, and after each the Russian army retired before the French, farther and farther toward the heart of Russia. They left desolation in their train. For they burned their towns and villages, destroyed the crops and stores rather than let them fall into the hands of the French.

As the Russians retreated the French toiled after them. For Napoleon was eager for a great victory. He knew already that he played a losing game, that the Russian campaign was a mistake. But his pride demanded a victory before he made peace.

"We must make up for lost time," he said. "We must have an immense victory before Moscow, a taking of Moscow which will astonish the world."

Those around Napoleon tried to turn him from his folly. "The Emperor will not find peace at Smolensk or even at Moscow," said one of his generals. "He will only be farther from France. Peace flies before us even as does a battle; only it flies farther."

But all persuasion was in vain. Napoleon would not yield. "The die is cast," he said, and the army marched onward.

At Borodino Napoleon had his wish. For there a great battle was fought. It was the most deadly battle of modern times. But although the victory rested with the French, they paid dearly for it, for almost as many French as Russians lay dead upon the field.

After Borodino the Russians again retreated. Again the French followed. Scorched by the heat of the blazing sun, choked by the dust of the sandy roads, and with the smoke from the burning towns and villages through which they passed, they still struggled on. At length about a week after the Battle of Borodino the Grand Army came in sight of Moscow.

It was the city of rest and plenty to which the wornout men had been looking forward for many a weary day. It was the paradise of ease for which they longed after their long toil and hardship. Whenever they gained a height they searched eagerly through the mist of dust and smoke for a glimpse of the long-desired city. So when from the height above the town they saw at length the great city stretched out beneath them, its golden domes and many coloured roofs resplendent in the morning sunshine, a great cry of joy ran through the ranks. "Moscow! Moscow at last!" they shouted, as long before the Crusaders had cried, "Jerusalem! Jerusalem!" at the sight of the Holy City.

Forgetting their past miseries in the thought of coming rest and plenty, the French marched joyfully into the town. It was hushed and empty. To the tramp of their feet the streets resounded strangely. Silent, deserted houses gazed down upon them from either side.

The Russians had fled, leaving their Holy City a prey to the foe. For the first time on entering a conquered capital Napoleon found no one to witness his triumph. For the first time in all his triumphant career there was no submissive people to beg humbly for his mercy. It was a bitter disappointment.

All the vast army supplies of food and clothing had been carried away or destroyed. But still much was left. And at first the French revelled in food and drink such as they had not tasted for many a long day.

The paradise of rest and plenty was reached. But it was not long to be enjoyed. For almost at once fire broke forth, and soon flames were raging far and near. Whether the fire was first caused by carelessness or by intention, whether it was set alight by Frenchmen or by Russians, is not certain. But the Russians had broken the fire engines before they left, and all efforts to put out the flames were vain. Even when they were put out in one place they started mysteriously in another. A strong wind sprang up which fanned the flames to fury. Many of the buildings were of wood, so whole streets were soon alight. Palaces and churches were seen one moment wrapped in flame and smoke, the next they crashed together and fell in glowing ruin.

The heat grew intolerable. The constant roar of the flames was now and then broken by frightful explosions, and burning fragments were scattered wide, each brand as it fell lighting fresh fires. The whole city seemed doomed to destruction.

Napoleon had taken up his quarters in the Kremlin, the palace-fortress of the Czars. And from there for two days he watched the frightful devastation in gloomy thought. His officers begged him to move to a place of safety. He sullenly refused. At length, almost too late, he yielded to their prayers and fled. But now the way to safety lay through a lane of fire, through torrents of sparks and smoke, and the flames, whipped to fury by the wind, scorched the hands and faces of his officers as they hurried after him.

For five days and nights the fire raged. By night the sky glared like a huge furnace with the reflected light, by day it was overcast with rolling clouds of dense smoke, through which the sun glowed like a blood-red ball.

By the light of the burning city Napoleon at length saw things as they really were. He wrote to the Czar asking for peace. But the Czar made no reply.

Day by day Napoleon waited, and day by day food grew scarcer and scarcer. In wider and wider circles the foraging parties swept the country round in a vain search for food. In vain Napoleon offered rewards to the Russian peasants if they would but bring supplies. There was no pity in their hearts for the famished invaders; they would rather have seen them all perish than sell them one sack of flour.

It was now October, and winter was not far off, that winter which in

Russia comes with icy blasts, with bitter frost and snow. Without food, without proper clothing, it was impossible for the French army to pass the winter in Russia.

So Napoleon at length made up his mind to leave Moscow and reach some warmer climate before the coming of the cold weather, and the retreat began.

At first the men marched forth gaily enough, laden with the plunder of Moscow, with jewels and gold and silken stuffs which they were taking back to France. The weather was fine, and they were on their way home. They were fairly well supplied with food, which had been gathered by a last effort from all around Moscow.

But soon all the food brought from Moscow was done, and the pains of hunger made themselves felt. The fight for food grew fierce and bitter. If a horse fell, men rushed upon it like hungry animals. Human kindliness seemed forgotten. Comrades would cheat each other for a loaf of bread, quarrel over a handful of potatoes. Each day they grew weaker. Each day they fell by the way, dying in hundreds.

And still, although hardly able to crawl along, the wretched men had to defend themselves, had to fight. For pursuing Russians everywhere hung upon the march, shooting down all within range of their guns. Soon discipline was at an end, and the retreat became a headlong flight. Many threw away their weapons and refused to fight, for they saw that those who were wounded were left to perish where they fell. For men dying themselves of hunger could not carry wounded comrades. Others left the ranks, and straying away either died of hunger or were shot or taken prisoner by the Russians.

Then the cold came. Snow fell white and blinding. It turned the country into a pathless waste from which every landmark was wiped out. Men lost their way, wandering they knew not whither until they lay down to die, and the snow covered them gently in their last sleep.

And so through ever-growing misery and disaster the men staggered on, and day by day the Grand Army grew less and less. At length twenty thousand haggard, ragged, hungry men reached and crossed the Nieman. They were all that were left of the half million gallant soldiers who had gone so gaily forth to conquer the Russians. Without winning a battle the Russians had conquered Napoleon. Or, rather, Russia had conquered him.

CHAPTER 89

NAPOLEON I—FAREWELL TO FRANCE

BUT long before the shattered army reached the Nieman, Napoleon had left it, and was speeding back to France. He wanted to reach Paris before the news of his disaster. He wanted to raise a new army as speedily as possible. For he had heard that there was a plot against him in Paris. The Prussians, too, encouraged by the example of Spain, were ready to rise and fight for their liberty.

Napoleon quickly raised a new army, many of whom it is true were mere boys. To them he added the remnant of the Grand Army among whom, happily for him, there were some of his best officers and most tried soldiers. Only a few months after the. Russian disaster he marched into Germany.

The Czar had again joined with the King of Prussia, for he had now sworn utterly to defeat Napoleon. "No more peace with Napoleon," he had said, after the taking of Moscow. "We cannot reign together. It must be he or I, I or he." With tears running down his face the King welcomed the Czar, who had forsaken his friendship for that of Napoleon at Tilsit. That was forgiven now "Wipe your tears," said the Czar, "they are the last Napoleon will ever cause you to shed."

The war began, and although the French were still victorious their victories were dearly bought. Then Austria joined with Russia and Prussia, and at Leipsig, the final struggle took place. This battle has been called the Battle of the Nations, for soldiers of nearly every country in Europe fought on one side or another.

For three days the fight lasted, and in the end the French were beaten. Napoleon and his army fled toward the Rhine, hotly pursued by the victorious allies.

Everywhere behind him the conquered nations threw off the yoke of France, and demanded freedom once more. But Napoleon would not yet yield to their demands. Then the allies invaded France, and continued the war on French territory.

Seeing their country thus invaded, the people of France rose in wrath against the invaders. Napoleon placed himself once more at the head of his army, and marched to meet the foe. Never perhaps had his genius shown itself greater than in this war fought upon French soil. Very many of his soldiers were untrained boys. They were so youthful looking that they were called Marie Louises in honour of the Empress. Many of them did not know how to use a gun, and a peaked cap was their only sign of uniform. They were often without officers.

"Where is your lieutenant?" asked a general one day, as he rode past a company.

"We never had one," replied a young soldier.

"Where is your sergeant then?" said the general.

"We have no sergeant either," replied the boy. "But it does not matter. Do not be afraid, we will fight all the same."

Yet with such an army Napoleon kept the foe at bay. But even his genius could not for long hold back a force ten times as great as his own.

At length the allies reached Paris. It was the first time since the days of Joan of Arc that a foreign foe had come within sight of its walls. Now for one day it held out, then it surrendered.

Side by side the King of Prussia and the Czar rode into the town. The streets were crowded with people. Some watched the procession with sad and frowning faces. Some exulted that at length they had been relieved from the awful tyranny of the Emperor.

For Napoleon's reign was at an end. The Senate which in the days of his glory had overwhelmed him with flattery now turned from him. By a declaration of the Senate he was deposed on April 2, 1814.

But still Napoleon would not yield. He wanted to march to Paris, to fight again for his Empire. France, however, was tired of war. "We have had enough," said one of his officers. "Let us not begin a civil war."

"Do you want to live under the Bourbons then?" cried Napoleon in wrath.

"No," was the answer, "we want the King of Rome."

"Do you think then that if I abdicate you will have my son? Never! The Regency of my wife is impossible," replied the Emperor.

But to resist was useless. Napoleon at length saw that it was so, and he abdicated in favour of his little son. A day or two after this the Battle of Toulouse was fought. With it the Peninsular War, which had lasted five years, was brought to an end. Had what was passing in France been known in Spain that battle need never have been fought.

And now Napoleon had to leave France and go to the island of Elba in the Mediterranean, which was all the Empire left to him. The day of his departure the Old Guard was drawn up the palace of Fontainbleau. There Napoleon said good-bye to them. "Soldiers of my Old Guard," he said, "for twenty years I have found you ever constant on the road to honour and glory. In these last days, as in the days of my prosperity, you have been patterns of bravery and fidelity. I go, but you, my friends, must continue to serve France. Do not pity my fate. Adieu, my children I would I could embrace you all."

They brought the standard to him. He kissed it with tear-dimmed eyes. And as the men watched, tears coursed down their bronzed cheeks. With sobs they murmured brokenly, "What a leader we have lost."

Himself shaken with sobs, Napoleon turned from them quickly, entered his carriage and was driven away southward.

On the first part of his journey Napoleon was greeted with cheers. For he was passing through land that had been overrun by the enemy. Here the people cared little, for what Napoleon had done in battles far away. They knew that he had at least fought skilfully and bravely against the enemy who now invaded their land. So they cheered him.

But as he passed still farther southward, and came to people who knew nothing of the invasion, but who only knew that he was the monster who had tom from them their sons and brothers, and left them to die in far off lands, he was no longer cheered, but cursed. Here the people crowded round his carriage, threatening to hang him on the nearest tree, or drown him in the Rhone. At length to escape the fury of the mob Napoleon was forced to dress himself in the uniform of an Austrian officer. Thus disguised he fled until he came to the sea, and there set sail for his new Empire of Elba.

CHAPTER 90

THE HUNDRED DAYS

THE allies now set aside Napoleon's little son, and the Bourbons were restored. Louis XVI's little son had died in prison, so the brother of Louis XVI was now proclaimed King under the title of Louis XVIII, the little prince who died in prison being looked upon as Louis XVII.

And thus the Bourbons, to drive whom from the throne all the blood of the Revolution had been shed, returned once more. Yet it could hardly be said that it was by the will of the people. Many of them would rather have had a Republic. But the country was too worn out with wars to fight any longer. What most people wanted was peace. And hoping to gain it they took the King offered to them.

The new King was already old. He was fat and lazy. He was ill too and could scarcely walk or move without help. It was a great change from the restless, untiring Emperor who bestrode Europe. "We who have just come from him who passed over Europe with the stride of a giant must get used to seeing a King lying in his armchair," said one of his courtiers.

Like his people the new King wanted peace. In twenty-five years of exile he had learned much. He knew that it was no longer possible to rule France as a despot, and he was quite willing that the people should have some power.

Napoleon had been a despot. He had done as he liked, and the people had grown weary of his tyranny. Now Louis XVIII granted to the people a new Charter of Freedom, and France became a constitutional monarchy like Great Britain. The Charter gave the ruling power to the King and to two houses of Parliament something like ours, one a house of peers, and one a house of deputies chosen by the people.

But among the nobles who now returned, even among the princes of the royal family, there were many who had forgotten nothing of their old pride, and learned nothing by the Revolution. They disliked the Charter, or any appearance of liberty for the people, and they urged the King to many acts which soon made the people restless and discontented.

Then when the French soldiers who had been kept prisoner by the Russians and Germans were set free and returned home, the discontent increased. For the soldiers still loved the general who so many times had led them to victory. The army still loved Napoleon, and neither people nor army loved Louis XVIII.

And so it began to be whispered abroad that after all the Emperor was not far away, after all he would return. With the spring flowers he would come, it was said. People began to wear violets, and to talk about a mysterious "Corporal Violet." Pictures and medals too were everywhere sold, some showing a sleeping eagle with the words underneath, "He will waken again." Others showed a sleeping lion with the words, "The waking will be terrible."

Napoleon was soon weary of his little island empire. He too grew restless and discontented. And when from France letters came telling of the discontent and unrest there he grew more and more restless. At length he resolved to fight and win his crown once more. He set out from Elba, and on March 2, 1815, less than a year after his abdication, he once more landed in France.

And the people who but a few months before wanted to hang him or drown him in the Rhone now received him with joy. "Down with the nobles! Down with the priests! Long live the Emperor!" was the cry as Napoleon marched onward to Paris. Everywhere the people crowded to catch a glimpse of the big gray coat and cocked hat of the little man who had such a strange power over the hearts of men.

At Grenoble the Royalist army stopped the way. "There he is," said their leader. "Shoot him!"

The soldiers turned white. Their knees trembled beneath them, their guns shook in their hands. Not a shot was fired.

Alone Napoleon advanced. "Soldiers," he said, in his strong, calm voice, "you know me."

Again he advanced a few steps. Throwing open his coat, he cried, "If there is a soldier amongst you who wants to kill his Emperor he can do it. I come to offer you my body."

Still not a shot was fired. Instead, a great cry burst forth, " Long live the Emperor!" The ranks were broken, and in a fury of joy the soldiers rushed over to the returned Emperor's side. They crowded round him, kneeling at his feet, reverently touching his coat, cheering and weeping.

Once more Napoleon had an army and an empire. "Never before," said a great writer, "has a man taken an empire by merely showing his hat." His march to Paris was a long triumph. Towns and villages were gay with the tricolour, the air echoed with cries of "Long live the Emperor!" The white cockade of the Bourbons disappeared, the tricolour reappeared as if by magic.

Louis XVIII fled to Belgium. At Vienna the allies were gathered, struggling to rearrange the states of Europe which had been turned upside down by Napoleon's wars and conquests. It was a difficult matter, and they had found it hard to agree over it. Now the news that Napoleon had landed in France and had marched in triumph to Paris and that Louis XVIII had fled put an end to their squabbles.

At once they proclaimed Napoleon an outlaw and began to prepare for war. It was in vain that Napoleon assured them that he had no wish to fight and conquer any other country. He only wished to be allowed to rule France in peace. No one believed him. From every country of Europe soldiers gathered to invade France.

But Napoleon, making up his mind to strike first, marched to meet the allies. And it was in Belgium on the field of Waterloo that his last battle was fought.

Napoleon staked his all on this last battle. He staked his all and lost. Through the long summer day the battle raged, and when evening came Napoleon's army was fleeing from the field, carrying Napoleon himself along with it.

The people of Paris were filled with horror and grief at the news of the defeat. They were filled with anger against the Emperor. Now that he was no longer victorious they would have none of him. The very people who had welcomed him tumultuously a few months before now demanded his abdication for a second time.

Napoleon made a last effort to regain his power. He sent his brother Lucien to plead for him in Parliament. "France," he said, "yesterday acclaimed Napoleon as her liberator. If for one battle lost she forsakes him today, to what a grave reproach of inconstancy and lightness does she not expose herself to history."

"Prince," said one of the members, rising to answer him, "you missay the nation. It is not for having abandoned the Emperor Napoleon that history will accuse France. It is for having followed him too far. She has followed him in the sands of Egypt, and in the deserts of Russia, on fifty battlefields, in misfortune and in success. It is because they followed him that three million Frenchmen lie dead. We have done enough for him. Our duty now is to save our country."

The struggle was vain. The glory and splendour of empire were to be his no longer, and Napoleon yielded. For a second time he abdicated. "I offer myself a sacrifice," he said, "to the hate of the enemies of France. I proclaim my son Emperor of the French."

But the proclamation of his son was a mere form, and Napoleon well knew it. "It is for the Bourbons that I abdicate," he said bitterly. From the height of glory to which he had climbed he could not bear that both he and his family should fall again to nothing. He was only forty-five, and what had he not done in those few years? What might he not yet do? In ten years from being a penniless unknown soldier he had risen to be an Emperor. For another ten years he had ruled Europe, playing with kings and kingdoms, setting them up or pulling them down as it pleased him. Then came his fall. Now for a hundred days he had believed himself as powerful as of old. But the hundred days were over and all his might and his power were fallen from him.

No one wanted him. There was no room for him anywhere, not even in France. He was told to leave the country. But that was hard to do, for every port was watched by British ships. So not knowing what else to do Napoleon gave himself up to the British.

On board the Bellerophon he was brought to England. He was not, however, allowed to land, but remained on board until it was decided what should be done with him.

At length it was decided to send him to St. Helena, a little island in the South Atlantic, as there he could be allowed a larger amount of freedom with less chance of his escaping than anywhere else. There he lived for nearly six years, and died on May 5, 1821.

CHAPTER 91

THE STORY OF THE EMPEROR WHO NEVER REIGNED

WHEN Napoleon abdicated he lost not only his Empire. He lost, too, his home and his family. For Marie Louise was easily persuaded to forsake the fallen Emperor. She returned home to her father, taking her little son with her.

And now that Napoleon was an exile and a prisoner, the Emperor of Austria tried in every way to make his little grandson forget all about his father, and all about his life in France. For the French people had no thought of taking the King of Rome for their ruler.

So he was no longer called the King of Rome, but merely Duke of Reichstadt, which was an Austrian title. All the books and toys which had been brought from France were taken away from him. He was made to speak German, and to learn his lessons in German. But the poor little boy hated it. "I will not be a German," he would cry. "I will be a Frenchman."

In the end, however, he came to speak and write German like his native language, and although he always spoke French well, too, he found it difficult to write correctly.

But even if outwardly the young Duke seemed to be growing into a little German, in his heart he remained fiercely French. And young though he was, he could not be made to forget about his father. He thought about him all day, dreamt about him at night, and never forgot him in his prayers. Yet the Duke did not know what had become of his father. He was always trying to find out. "My father is in the West Indies, I think," he would say, or, "I have always heard my father was in Africa." But those around him constantly tried to turn the talk aside, for they thought it was best that he should know as little as possible about his father.

One day the Duke said to his tutor, "Who is reigning in France now?"

"A King," was the reply.

"But I know an Emperor once ruled there," said the Duke. "Who was it?"

"That was your father," answered the tutor, "who, because of his unhappy love of war, lost his crown and Empire."

"Is my dear father wicked then, since he did so much mischief?" asked the little boy.

"It is not for us to judge him," quickly replied his tutor. "You must continue to love your father and pray for him."

The Duke's tutors had a hard time. For the Duke not only asked them difficult questions, he was a naughty boy, too, and gave them much trouble. But then he was a sad boy, for he was always longing for something he could not have. Kept apart from the one person he loved and admired, not allowed even to hear about him, or know what had become of him, it was little wonder that he was unhappy. And his unhappiness often made him naughty.

Then too he was very lonely. He was one little boy among a lot of grown-up men. For even his mother soon left him. She went away to live in Italy. There after a time she married an Austrian gentleman. She seemed to forget all about Napoleon, and to think very little about her poor, lonely son.

The little Duke, however, did not long for his mother and miss her as he longed for and missed his father. He did not cry when she left him. But when at length he was told that the father, whom he had not seen since he was a tiny boy, was dead, he wept bitter tears.

Yet the Duke of Reichstadt was not always unhappy. His grandfather and grandmother loved him dearly, and in their own way tried to make him happy. His great delight was soldiers. He liked better than anything to talk of battles and war. He loved to play at soldiers, and he would stand at the window clapping his hands in delight while the guard of the palace was being changed. When he grew up he meant to be a great general.

But he liked adventures too. One of his favourite books was Robinson Crusoe. And with the help of one of his tutors he built a log hut in the garden of the palace which was called the Robinson Cave.

The Duke was only ten when his father died. But even then there were many plots to set him upon the throne of France. And as he grew older, and at length learned something of the history of his father's greatness, his thoughts, too, turned more and more to France. He hoped more and more one day to sit upon the throne.

But all these hopes were doomed to disappointment, all these conspiracies were fated to fail. For as the Duke grew up he became very ill. It was soon plain that he could not live long. At the age of twenty-one he died. With him died the chief hopes of the Bonapartists, as the friends of Napoleon were called.

I have told you a little about this only son of Napoleon, not because he was great, but because he was one of the saddest figures in history. Born to a high place, he lived all his life in the shadow of his father's downfall. Acclaimed in the cradle as a King, he lived at his grandfather's court an exile, without a kingdom, without a country, almost without a name. He could never hope to regain them but by bloodshed. Perhaps it was best for himself, and best for France, that he died.

He never reigned, yet he has been given the empty title of Napoleon II. When in after years another Napoleon seized the throne of France he took the title of Napoleon III.

CHAPTER 92

LOUIS XVIII—THE WHITE TERROR AND THE HOLY ALLIANCE

AFTER the downfall of Napoleon, once again Louis XVIII returned to Paris. There was little joy at his return. Few of the French really wanted a King, above all a Bourbon. But he was, they said, smuggled in in the baggage wagons of the enemy, and they were obliged to accept him.

For France had now to do many things at the bidding of the allies. The country was treated by them as a conquered country. The French were made to pay enormous sums of money to make up for all the damage done to the countries Napoleon had invaded. All his conquests were taken away, as well as some French territory. And it was arranged that for five years all the fortresses along the borders of France should be garrisoned by foreign soldiers.

Thus Napoleon after all his wars and conquests left France smaller and poorer than he found her. He left her too a prisoner, as it were, in foreign hands until it was seen how she would behave.

Louis XVIII had no easy task. On the one hand was the bulk of the nation who were resolved to defend the rights for which they had fought at the Revolution. On the other hand were the returned nobles who had not forgotten their old rights and privileges, and who wanted to bring them back again as they had been before the Revolution. Louis could not please both; if he pleased the one party he made the other angry.

At first the nobles and the extreme royalists did many violent deeds. In different parts of the country royalist mobs rose and massacred the Bonapartists. Several of Napoleon's generals were put to death. Catholics rose against the Protestants, and so many dreadful deeds were done that this time is known as the White Terror.

While these things were going on in the country the royalists in Parliament were trying to do away with the Charter framed at the Restoration. But Louis saw how dangerous and unwise this was. He dissolved Parliament, and announced that he meant to keep the Charter, and by degrees the White Terror died away.

For nine years Louis lived through a troubled reign. More than half the people were discontented with his rule, they were always ready to rise, and there were many plots against him. Still France remained at peace within her own borders.

But beyond her own borders France was soon once more at war. The rulers of Russia, Austria, and Prussia had formed a league which they called the Holy Alliance. By this league all three agreed to reign as Christians should, and to help each other in a kindly, brotherly spirit whenever there was need. This league seemed very right and good. But the real meaning of it was that these three monarchs joined to ensure absolute power to the rulers, and to crush out all efforts after freedom on the part of the people.

The Spanish people now rebelled against their King, Ferdinand VII, and drove him from the throne. He, as a prince, had signed away his crown, you remember, at the bidding of Napoleon. Now he wanted to rule as a despot, and his people rebelled.

The Holy Alliance resolved that Ferdinand should be set upon his throne again. They persuaded Louis XVIII to declare war with Spain and send an army to fight the rebels. So a French army, led by the King's nephew, the Duke of Angoulême, marched into Spain once more.

Many of the people of France were against this war, for their hearts were with the Spaniards in their struggle for freedom. But when the Duke of Angoulême returned victorious the people greeted him with joy. For the French army had once more recovered its lost glory in Spain. The soldiers once more looked proudly at the white flag of the Bourbons. Until then it had seemed to them only a sign of mourning and of disgrace. Now it had led them to victory.

The army began to forget Napoleon a little, having found a leader in the Duke of Angoulême

Louis XVIII was by this time growing very old and feeble. But to the end he tried to do his work and hide his illness from his people. He tried, as he said, himself to "show a good face to the enemy." So although he could not move without help, and although he was so wearied that he constantly fell asleep over his business, he insisted on trying to do it.

On his birthday he used always to hold a reception. Now his doctors urged him to give it up. But he would not. "A King should never be ill where his people are concerned," he said. So he dressed himself up in his royal robes, and sat upon the throne while the people passed before him.

For a long time he sat bowing and smiling as usual to the people as they passed. But before the ceremony was over his strength was utterly gone. His head fell forward on his breast, it sank lower and lower until he was fast asleep.

The last of the courtiers slipped quietly past the throne in awed, uneasy silence, feeling rather as if they were passing through a chamber of death than as if they were taking part in a great court function. Then, still sleeping, the tired old man was carried to his room.

Even after this the King still struggled on. But not much longer could his feebleness be hidden, and about three weeks later he died.

"Gentlemen, the King is dead," said the court physician on the morning of September 16, 1824. Then turning to Louis's brother, and bowing low, he added, "Long live the King."

It was the last time that the old form was heard in France. Louis XVIII was the last king of France to die on the throne, the last King of France to be buried among his ancestors at St. Denis.

With a salute of a hundred and one guns he was borne to the abbey. There he was laid to rest with all the ancient form and ceremony of a King's funeral, which had not been seen in France since the death of Louis XV.

Louis XVIII was not a great King, but he was sensible and did his best. He had to rule at a very difficult time, and his own family made his task harder for him. He himself was willing to be a liberal King, but his own family and the nobles urged him on to despotic acts which did no good, but merely raised up anger against the Bourbons. Yet through all his troubles he steered safely. He died a King, leaving France at peace.

CHAPTER 93

CHARLES X—THE REVOLUTION OF JULY

LOUIS XVIII was succeeded by his brother, Charles X. Charles was already sixty-seven when he came to the throne. Unlike Louis, he had learned nothing by his exile, and he had no intention of being a liberal King. ' "I would rather hew wood," he said, "than be a King like the King of England."

"The Charter is the best inheritance I can give you," said Louis before he died. "Observe it, my brother, for my sake, for the sake of your subjects, and for your own." But at once it became plain that Charles X cared nothing for the Charter.

Soon discontent grew great. Then one day when the King was reviewing the soldiers of the National Guard they broke out into cries of "Hurrah for the Charter! Down with the ministers!"

As the King heard these cries his face grew dark with anger. Seeing him look so angry a soldier approached him. "Sire," he said, "do you think it an insult that the troops should cry 'Hurrah for the Charter?' Is it not a good thing?"

At this the King grew still more angry. "I have come here to receive homage," he said hotly, "not lessons." Then next day, half in anger and half in fear, he disbanded the National Guard.

Charles X was bent on being an autocrat, and, in spite of all warnings, he went on his own way. At length on July 20, 1830, he published what are known as the Five Ordinances. In these Five Ordinances he made many changes in the government, giving more power to the King, and less freedom to the people.

Charles X had, of course, no right to do this. For according to the Charter he could only make laws by the consent of Parliament. But Charles had set the Charter at naught.

Next day all Paris was in an uproar. The people rose in defence of their rights and liberties, for which they had fought so hard and paid so dearly. The three days which followed — that is, July 27th, 28th, and 29th — are known as the Three Glorious Days of July.

Barricades were thrown across the streets. They were made of paving stones, of wagons, of heavy furniture dragged from the houses, of anything that came to hand. Shops and factories were closed, and people of all classes swarmed in the streets.

Shouts of "Long live the Charter! Down with the Bourbons! Hurrah for Liberty! To arms, to arms!" were heard everywhere. Amid indescribable confusion the white flag of the Bourbons was torn down, the royal arms with the golden fleur-de-lis were broken in pieces and trodden under foot. Once more the red, white, and blue was seen everywhere, once more the tricolour floated from the Townhall.

Marshal Marmont, who was in charge of the troops round Paris, wrote to the King, begging him to give way, and so quiet the revolt. "Sire," he wrote, "it is no longer a riot; it is a revolution. It is very necessary that Your Majesty should take some means of quieting it.

The honour of the crown can still be saved. To-morrow perhaps it will be too late."

But Charles X was blind and deaf to all but his own pride. He told the General to fight and stop the riot. But that was no easy order to carry out. For every man in Paris had suddenly become a soldier, every house was turned into a fortress. Tiles, logs, broken bottles, and every sort of missile were thrown in showers from the roofs and windows, wounding and killing the soldiers as they passed.

All over Paris there was fighting. Every barricade, every bridge, every street was fought for, and many deeds of bravery were done. At one bridge an unknown young man, eager to make a passage across it for his comrades, rushed upon it with a tricolour flag in his hand. The bridge was swept with grape shot, and he fell riddled with wounds, his flag about him.

"My friends," he, cried, as he died, "remember my name is Arcole." And his name has been remembered. For the people gave his name to the bridge, and it is called so to this day.

But the soldiers did not want to fight. They did not want to kill their brothers in the cause of tyranny. Many of the officers broke their swords rather than turn them against their countrymen. Many of the soldiers simply stood still, and did nothing. Others went over to the insurgents.

Again Marmont wrote to the King. "I ought not to hide from you," he said, "that the situation grows more and more grave."

Again the King replied that he would not give way an inch. He would not believe that his crown was in any danger from the mob. "It is not the mob," said an aide-de-camp. " it is the whole population that has risen." But Charles did not believe it. He calmly spent the evening playing whist, while the thunder of cannon shook the walls of his palace, and the bivouac fires of his revolted subjects could be seen from the windows. "Paris is in anarchy," he said. "Anarchy will bring Paris back to my feet."

But Charles was wrong. A few hours later, dusty, and wearied, and downcast, Marmont entered the King's room. "Sire," he said, "it is with grief I have to tell you that I have not been able to keep your authority in Paris."

Then, too late, Charles yielded. He revoked the Ordinances he reinstated the National Guard, he recalled the Parliament. "It is to late, " said one of the leaders of the people, when the news was brought to them "it is too late, the throne of Charles X has melted in blood. "

Charles at length saw that it was indeed too late, and he abdicated in favour of his grandson, a child of ten. Then he set out for England. He felt sadly that his day was over, but he was resolved never to return to France by foreign help, as his brother Louis XVIII had done. "My grandson," he said, "will never return to France by the aid of foreign bayonets. He will be recalled by the French themselves, or he will die in exile."

Charles X was kindly received in England. And as once before when he had fled from the Red Terror, he was again, by the British Government, given Holy-rood Palace at Edinburgh in which to live. After a time he removed to Austria, where he died in 1836.

CHAPTER 94

LOUIS PHILIPPE—THE ADVENTURES OF A REBEL PRINCESS

CHARLES X had abdicated in favour of his grandson, the Duke of Bordeaux. But those who had resisted his acts of tyranny had no mind to live under the rule of a child, or of the Regency of that child's mother.

No, they had determined to have a king, but one of their own choosing. And their choice fell upon the Duke of Orleans. He was descended from that Duke of Orleans who was Regent in the time of Louis XV. His father had made himself notorious at the time of the Revolution. When titles were done away with he called himself Philip Egalité or Philip Equality. He had taken part with the Revolutionists, had voted for Louis XVI's death, and was himself put to death during the Terror.

Philip Egalité's son, who was now Duke of Orleans, had always been friendly with the party of freedom. The people believed that he would be a liberal king, and so the crown was offered to him.

Upon the walls of Paris a placard appeared. " Charles X," it said, "can not again enter Paris; he has shed the blood of the people.

"A Republic would expose us to frightful divisions; it would embroil us with Europe.

"The Duke of Orleans is a prince devoted to the cause of the Revolution.

"The Duke of Orleans has never fought against us.

"The Duke of Orleans is a citizen king.

"The Duke of Orleans has worn the tricolour under fire; he will wear it again; we want no other.

"The Duke of Orleans will accept the Charter as we have always wished it and understood it.

"He will accept the crown from the French people."

At first, however, the Duke seemed unwilling to accept the crown. But in reality he was pleased, and he at length consented to become King.

The Duke of Orleans was already a man of fifty-seven when he came to the throne, and he took the title of Louis Philippe I. Some wished him to appear to continue the old line of kings and call himself Philip VII. But others were strongly against this. "The Duke of Orleans," they said, "has been chosen not because he is a Bourbon, but in spite of being a Bourbon." He was not called King of France, but King of the French, because the throne was not his by descent, but by choice of the people.

Louis Philippe's reign is often called the monarchy of July, as it was the result of the Revolution of July, 1830. From the very beginning he had many troubles to face. For there were three parties against him. There were the Legitimists, those who wanted Charles to be restored, or who wanted his grandson Henry, in whose favour he had abdicated, to be King. There were the Bonapartists, those who wanted Napoleon's son to be made Emperor. There were the Republicans, who wanted neither king nor emperor, but a Republic. So during the first ten years of his reign Louis Philippe's crown was threatened again and again. There were plots to kill him and frequent risings.

Less than two years after Louis Philippe came to the throne there was a royalist rising in the south of France. But the leader was not Charles X, who was spending dull days in Holyrood, but the beautiful and gay Duchess of Berry. She was the mother of the young Duke of Bordeaux, or Henry V as the Legitimists loved to call him.

She delighted to think that a woman could reconquer the crown which men had lost. Her head was full of the stories of Sir Walter Scott, and she wanted to do something gallant and adventurous like some of his heroines. From the very beginning she had little chance of success, and the wiser heads among her own party looked upon her revolt as a mad prank. They pointed out the difficulties, and tried to turn her from her project. "You ought to hang Walter Scott," said one of them in despair, "he is the real culprit." For the Duchess refused to see any difficulties. She would only listen to those who shared her hopes, and by her smiles, and her charm, won over many to her side against their better judgement.

So this fascinating, laughter-loving lady landed one April day at Marseilles. The next day there was an attempt at a rising. But from the very beginning it was a piteous failure. It began at eight o'clock in the morning. By twelve it was over.

By four o'clock the Duchess received a letter from one of the leaders. "We have lost," it said. "You must leave France."

But the Duchess would not thus lightly give in. "To come so easily," she said, "and return having done nothing would be worse than defeat, it would be a new and still more fatal abdication."

So she resolved to march into La Vendee, where the Royalists were strong, and try her fortune there.

Disguised sometimes as a peasant boy called Little Peter, sometimes as a servant, sometimes as "Mr. Charles," she journeyed from village to village, from farmhouse to farmhouse. Sometimes she walked, sometimes she rode on horseback. In spite of the dangers, the fatigue, the dreadful roads, and the rough fare, she was always cheerful and cool, enjoying the disguises, making light of the hardships and dangers. And although many knew her secret not one man was ready to betray her to the government.

But arrived in La Vendee the Duchess found little to encourage her. The people there told her that they had neither guns nor ammunition. They knew the attempt was desperate, they had no hope of succeeding, and they begged her to give it up. But in spite of all prayers the Duchess was bent on going on. She believed that when it was known that she was ready to fight, the whole of the west of France would rise to a man. So she issued proclamations in her own name calling herself Regent of France. "I call upon every man of courage," she said, "God will aid us to save our country. No danger, no fatigue, will discourage me. You will see me in the front of battle."

Meanwhile when the leaders of the Legitimist party in Paris heard what was happening in La Vendee they were very much alarmed. They too knew that the revolt would be a hopeless one, and they sent a gentleman to try to persuade the Duchess to leave France. After long search by moors, and fens, and lonely country ways he found the farm in which the Duchess was living. He asked to see "Mr. Charles," and was shown into a miserable little room. Here upon a rickety bed for a throne, with a pair of pistols beside her for a sceptre, sat this strange Regent of France.

The gentleman tried every argument he could think of to persuade the Duchess to leave France. It was all in vain.

At length the date of the rising was fixed. On the night of June 3rd alarm bells were heard throughout the country and the peasants rose and armed themselves. But they were in small and scattered companies, there was no union among them, they obeyed no leader, and in a few hours they were defeated and scattered in flight.

The insurrection was at an end, and the Duchess fled for refuge to Nantes. With only one lady as companion she walked the long miles from the village in which she was hiding. Several times they met the King's soldiers, but each time they escaped, for the soldiers never suspected that this merry peasant boy, trudging cheerily along the country roads, was the great Princess for whom they were searching.

The Duchess reached Nantes in safety, and for several months she remained there safely hidden. But at length she was betrayed to the Government by a man named Duetz, who had pretended to be her friend. She was taken and kept prisoner for several months.

It was then discovered that she had been secretly married to an Italian gentleman. After that she was no longer a danger to the King. For the Legitimists considered that by marrying a foreigner she had lost the right to be looked upon as Regent. So the Duchess was set free. She soon joined her new husband, and lived quietly in Switzerland until she died.

CHAPTER 95

LOUIS PHILIPPE—THE ADVENTURES OF A REBEL PRINCE

ALMOST at the same time as the Duchess of Berry's insurrection the Republicans rose in Paris. It was the worst of all the Republican risings during the reign, but it, too, was soon put down.

The Bonapartists also rose more than once, and their leader was Louis Napoleon, son of the great Napoleon's brother Louis. He considered himself the head of the family and rightful heir to Napoleon's greatness. For in 1832 Napoleon's only son, after a sad life at the Court of Vienna, had died at the age of twenty-one.

For a long time Louis Napoleon had turned his thoughts to the throne of France. Now he believed that the time for taking it had come. He issued proclamations calling on the men of France to rise and follow him in the name of Liberty. "My name is a flag," he said, "which ought to bring back memories of greatness to you."

At length the Prince left Switzerland, where he had been living, and marched toward France. At Fribourg he expected to meet many generals ready to take up his cause. But he was mistaken. "Tell the Prince," said one old general, "that if he believes he has a party in France he deceives himself. We have a great veneration for the memory of the Emperor. That is all."

For three days Louis Napoleon waited in vain. Then he marched on to Strasburg. A colonel of one of the regiments stationed here had promised to help him. So early one morning the soldiers were called together, and the Prince suddenly appeared before them. With drawn sword in hand their colonel advanced.

"Soldiers," he cried, "a revolution has burst forth in France. Louis Philippe is no longer on the throne. Napoleon II, Emperor of the French, comes to take the reins of government. He is before you, and comes to put himself at your head. Soldiers, your colonel has answered for you. Then cry with him, 'Long live Napoleon! Long live the Emperor!'"

As he ceased speaking the soldiers burst forth into loud cheers.

Then the Prince spoke. He seized a standard and looking up at it he cried, "Soldiers! behold the sign of French glory, destined now to become the sign of liberty. Let us march together against the traitors and oppressors of our country to the shouts of 'Long live France! Long live Liberty.'"

Once more cheers burst forth, and Louis Napoleon believed that his cause was gained. He thought that now he had only to march quickly toward Paris, and that the people would rise in his favour, and the garrisons yield to him as he passed. He never doubted but that when the nephew of the great Napoleon appeared before the walls of Paris with a large army at his back all France would welcome and support him.

But before an hour had gone Louis Napoleon found his castles in the air come tumbling about his ears. Almost at once cries of "Long live the King!" mingled with those of "Long live the Emperor!" One regiment refused to join the revolt. Their colonel ordered the soldiers to arrest the Prince, and after a short struggle he was taken prisoner.

The revolt was at an end without a drop of blood being shed.

Louis Napoleon was sent to Paris. But the King did not wish to keep him prisoner. He thought it best to make as little of the rising as possible. So he merely ordered the Prince to leave France, and go to live in America, where he would be far enough away not to do much mischief.

But Louis Napoleon did not stay long in America. He soon returned, and about four years after his attempt at Strasburghe landed at Boulogne. He had with him only about thirty soldiers, and a few friends and officers. And with this little company he hoped to conquer the crown of France.

In the middle of an August night they disembarked a little to the north of Boulogne, and marched to the town. Here at the barracks in the dawning of the day much the same scene was gone through as four years before at Strasburg. A lieutenant who had joined the conspirators roused the soldiers out of their sleep. Only half awake they were drawn up in the courtyard, and told that Louis Philippe had ceased to reign, and that Louis Napoleon was their Emperor.

Then the Prince spoke to them in burning, stirring words, reminding them of the great deeds of his uncle. The sleepy soldiers hardly knew what to think of it all. But because they were commanded to do so they cried "God save the Emperor!"

Their captain, however, soon heard of what was going on. He rushed to the barracks. The conspirators tried hard to keep him from reaching his men, but he shouted to them, "You are being deceived! Cry 'God save the King!'"

As soon as the men heard the voice of their captain the Prince's cause was lost. In a few minutes the barracks were in an uproar. In the confusion the Prince raised a pistol which he held in his hand. It went off and hit a man in the face, wounding him badly. At the sound of the shot the conspirators fled.

Having failed with the soldiers they tried to raise the people of the town. But not a man would join them. In a very short time Louis Napoleon and his followers were fleeing toward the seashore.

They gained their boat, and pushed off, but the soldiers pursued them, and fired upon the boat. It was overturned, and Louis Napoleon was brought back a prisoner.

The news of this attempt at revolt was received with a sort of pitying disdain rather than with anger. But the "Imperial little fool," as some one called him, was not allowed to go free this time. He was sentenced to be imprisoned for life in the fortress of Ham, in the north of France. There he remained for six years, when he escaped. He did not, however, attempt to lead another revolt.

Besides all these risings there were at least seven attempts to murder Louis Philippe. "But I have a strong breastplate," he said once. "I have my five sons." By which he meant that even if he were killed the monarchy would not cease, for he had five sons to succeed him.

CHAPTER 96
LOUIS PHILIPPE—THE REVOLUTION OF FEBRUARY

LOUIS Philippe had a very disturbed reign at home. But he did his best to keep peace abroad. During his reign, however, France had one great war. This was with Algiers. It lasted during his whole reign, but in the end the French conquered Algeria. It is now one of the greatest colonial possessions of France.

Besides gaining this large colony the state of France was improved in many ways under Louis Philippe. Great railways were built, factories sprang up, trade increased. It was now, too, that the telegraph was discovered, and the power of steam, all of which helped to make life easier and happier for many people. Schools were founded, and much was done especially for the education of girls. For under Napoleon girls were hardly taught at all, for he did not see the use of their being taught anything, as they could not fight.

But now with wider education, more money, and happier, more peaceful fives, many of the people of France began to ask to be allowed to have more say in the ruling of the land.

At the first Restoration, France had been given a Constitutional Government and the people had been allowed to vote for members of Parliament. But the amount of rent which a man had to pay before he was allowed to vote was placed so high that only the very rich could vote. In Great Britain at the present day every man (and perhaps soon every woman) over twenty-one who pays £10 rent is allowed to vote. But in France in those days only men who were twenty-five and who paid more than £8 in taxes were allowed to vote. The result was that many of the thinking people were shut out from all share in the government. Lawyers, doctors, professors, schoolmasters, were all too poor.

Now the people began to clamour for a wider franchise, as it was called. They said that it should not be wealth alone that should give a man power to vote, but that every one who had enough education to understand something of public matters should be given the right. The King, however, who had been quite willing to give the people freedom so far as the Charter went, was not willing that they should have more. Neither he nor his ministers would listen to the ever-increasing clamour for reform, neither he nor his ministers would pay any attention to the ever-growing discontent.

Added to this discontent there now came a time of distress. Several bad harvests followed one after the other, work became scarce, wages fell. The poor people were hungry and miserable, and they blamed the King and his ministers for all their misery.

Then those who were eager for reform went about the country giving great banquets in different towns. Hundreds of people were entertained at these banquets and speeches were made, always in favour of reform, often very violent against the Government. These banquets did much to spread the ideas about reform, and the King and his ministers grew more and more disturbed by them.

At length it was proposed to hold a great banquet in Paris. The Government, afraid of what this might lead to, forbade it. Still the reformers decided that it should take place, and they fixed the date for February 22, 1848. Again the banquet was forbidden. Then the reformers yielded, and the day before it ought to have taken place the banquet was given up.

The King was delighted. He thought that the trouble was over. "They have seen, rather late it is true, that they were playing too high a game," he said.

But after all the banquet was only a small thing. The real discontent which lay behind it was just as great or even greater than before. The King, however, was happy and confident. But when the fateful day of February 22nd dawned it was seen that Paris was in a ferment. All day long the streets were filled with crowds of idle, excited people who shouted, "Hurrah for reform! Down with the ministers!"

Nothing very serious happened that day. But as the days passed the excitement grew wilder and wilder, the troops were called out, blood was shed.

Too late Louis Philippe realized that this was revolution once more.

Sunk in an armchair he sat in his beautiful palace of the Tuileries surrounded by his sons and a few of his advisers. Through the windows came the ever-increasing roar of the maddened crowd. In the room it was very still. "The flood rises! The flood rises," murmured some one.

Messengers came and went. The King was advised now this way, now that. And ever the news that was brought to him became more and more alarming, the sounds of firing could be heard more and more distinctly.

Suddenly a man, dusty and excited, shouldered his way through the crowd which now thronged the doorway. He went straight to the King.

"What is it?" asked he.

"There is not a minute to lose," replied the man. "You must abdicate."

From without came harsh shouts, "Abdicate! Abdicate!"

The poor old King bowed his head. "I abdicate," he murmured.

Then rising, he opened the door leading to the room in which sat the Queen.

"I abdicate," he repeated in a louder voice. Then slowly and brokenly he returned to his armchair.

The Queen ran to him. "You shall not! Oh, you shall not!" she cried, her voice broken with sobs.

Throwing her arms about him she drew his head upon her breast, kissing him again and again.

"Rather let us die here," she sobbed. "Mount your horse, go out and fight. The army will follow you." "Ah!" she said, turning passionately to those around, "how can you forsake your King at such a time? You do not deserve so good a King!'

But the roar of the mob, the crack of musket shots, grew nearer and nearer, louder and louder.

"There is not a minute to lose," said one of the King's sons. "The balls are whizzing through the courtyard."

"Is it true?"asked the King. "Is no defence possible?"

"None! None!" cried many.

Then in deep silence the King rose. "I am a peaceful King," he said. "Since all defence is impossible, I do not wish to shed French blood uselessly, and I abdicate." Going to his desk he slowly began to write: "I abdicate this crown, which the will of the nation called me to wear, in favour of my grandson, the Count of Paris. May he succeed in the great task which falls to him to-day."

Less than an hour after signing his abdication the poor old King of seventy-five walked quietly through the garden of the Tuileries leaning on the arm of the Queen. They entered a carriage which waited for them at the gates, and were driven quickly away.

So ended the reign of the last King of France. It had begun with a revolution. It ended with a revolution.

Louis Philippe fled to England. There he lived very quietly, and a little more than two years later there he died.

CHAPTER 97

HOW A PRINCESS MADE A LAST STAND FOR THE BOURBONS

THE Count of Paris, in whose favour Louis Philippe abdicated, was only ten years old. He was the son of Louis Philippe's eldest son, the Duke of Orleans, who had been killed two or three years before by being thrown out of his carriage. He was therefore the direct heir to the throne. But in these excited times it was hardly to be expected that the French would accept as King a child of ten, or submit to be ruled by his mother as Regent.

This the Duchess of Orleans well knew. When the King and Queen had fled she felt very lonely and helpless. But she had to think of her little son, and she made up her mind to make one attempt to win the throne for him. Holding her two little sons by the hand she went to the Houses of Parliament. As she stood before the Assembly, dressed in mourning, her cheeks pale and her eyes red with weeping, every heart was touched. Loud cries rang out, "Long live the King Long live the Regent!"

As the Princess listened a faint colour came into her pale cheeks, a light of hope shone in her blue eyes. But alas! it was only the pity of moment for a woman in trouble. It soon became plain that the feeling of the Parliament was against a King. As the Princess looked at the hot, excited faces of the men who surrounded her, she knew there was little hope for her or for her son.

One of the King's friends rose to speak. "The King has abdicated," he said, "and left the crown to his grandson, the Regency to the Duchess of Orleans." He then asked the Assembly to acclaim the young King.

But at his words violent protests burst forth from every side. First one spoke, then another, and the angry argument was tossed from this side to that. Soon the noise and confusion in the hall became intense. Friends fearing for the safety of the Princess begged her to go. She shook her head with a sad smile. "If I go," she said, "my son will never enter here again."

So, gentle and calm amid the swaying, shouting crowd she sat. At length she stood up to speak. Her voice was lost in the hubbub and tumult of noise.

In vain some members cried, "Let the Duchess speak!" They but increased the tumult.

For a moment the Princess stood resolute. Then feeling the hopelessness of it she sank back on her seat in helpless silence.

Presently the doors of the hall were burst open, and a crowd of men, students, soldiers, workmen of all kinds, rushed in. Wild-eyed, drunk with violence and with wine, the rabble surged into the hall, brandishing firearms, yelling hoarsely. "Down with the Regency!" they cried. "Down with the Parliament! Show the traitors out! Hurrah for the Republic!"

The members fled in all directions. With difficulty a path for the Duchess and her two little sons was forced through the crowd. In spite of the efforts of her friends she was nearly stifled, she was separated from her children, but at length they all reached her carriage, and were driven away to a place of safety.

The last hope of the Bourbons was gone. That night the Republic was once more proclaimed.

CHAPTER 98

THE SECOND REPUBLIC—LOUIS NAPOLEON BECOMES PRESIDENT OF THE FRENCH

THIS revolution of February, 1848, was a revolution of chance and of surprise. It is sometimes called the "Revolution of Contempt." It was brought about by a mere handful of Republicans in Paris. The news was received with astonishment, almost with consternation, in the country. Still the Republic was accepted quietly enough. A provisional government— that is, a government for the time being—was at once established, and one of its first acts was to make a law that every Frenchman over twenty-one, whether he was rich or whether he was poor, should have a vote. This is called Manhood Suffrage and it is still the law in France.

A new Parliament was elected by Manhood Suffrage. The members for the most part were moderate Republicans who were quite content to replace the King by a President, and otherwise make few changes. But there were some members who were extreme Republicans, others who were socialists, and they wanted much greater reforms. So very quickly quarrels arose.

Paris continued in a state of wild unrest, and people began to dread a return of the terrible days of the First Revolution. In June there was a general rising of the workingmen in Paris. Once more barricades were thrown up, and for four days a deadly battle raged in the streets. Eleven generals were killed or wounded, besides thousands of the citizens.

The old Archbishop of Paris was also killed. He was a timid man, and when the insurrection first broke out had been overcome by fear. But he felt that it was his duty to do what he could to quiet the people. So putting his fear behind him he went to the general who commanded the troops, to tell him that he was going to speak to the people, and beg them to put an end to this fearful civil strife.

Vainly the general told the Archbishop that what he meant to do was full of danger. "My life is but a small thing," he answered steadfastly. So together they set out.

At the Place de la Bastille, as the square where the Bastille had once stood is now named, a truce was called. There the old Bishop, clad in his beautiful robes, stepped forward to speak to the people. He had only gone a few paces when a shot rang out, and he fell. It was a chance shot, and not meant in treachery, but the Archbishop was mortally wounded.

The news of this disaster spread from barricade to barricade. It filled the rioters with shame and horror. Little by little the firing ceased. When night came the city was once more quiet.

Next day the Archbishop died. "God grant," he said, "that my blood be the last to be shed."

But the strife was not yet over. It was not until many weeks had passed that the rioters were at last thoroughly overcome.

And now the French people were asked to choose a President to be head of the Republic. There were five men to choose from. One of them, strange to say, was Prince Louis Napoleon, who had already twice attempted to make himself King. Surely the men who wanted a Republic were not likely to choose such a man as President. But Louis Napoleon was the man who was chosen. He was chosen by more than five and a half million votes, four million more than any other.

There were many causes to help toward this strange result. The wild riots of June had made many of the people of France afraid of the Republic, yet they hated the old kingly family, and were equally afraid that they might return. And, greatest of all, there was magic in the name Napoleon. It filled the country with enthusiasm. Crowds marched to the polling booths with flags waving and drums beating, and cries of "Long live Napoleon!"

On December 20, 1848, at the age of forty, Louis Napoleon was proclaimed President of the French. He solemnly swore to respect the liberties of the people, and never to use the power given to him for his own glory. "Between you and me, fellow citizens," he said, "there can be no quarrelling. Our wills, our wishes, are the same.

"We have a great mission to fulfil. It is to found a Republic in the interests of all, and a just and firm government filled with a true love of country.

"Let us be men of country, not men of party, and God helping us we will at least do good things if we cannot do great things."

But for Louis Napoleon to be President was only one step toward something greater. Whatever he might say he did not mean to rest there.

He had only been chosen President for four years, and the same man could not be chosen President twice. So now Louis Napoleon tried to make the Parliament pass a new law allowing him to be elected a second time. But Parliament refused.

CHAPTER 99

THE SECOND EMPIRE—NAPOLEON III AND "THE CRIME OF DECEMBER"

"WHEN Louis Napoleon found that he could not get what he wanted by peaceful, lawful means he made up his mind that he would get it by unlawful means.

He made his arrangements quickly and quietly. He laid his plans well. Few people were in his confidence, but the chief of the police was one of them.

Then suddenly before day dawned one cold December morning sixteen of the chief members of Parliament were arrested in their beds, and with about sixty other leading Republicans were marched off to prison.

When it was light, men on their way to work saw upon the walls of Paris, a proclamation that the Parliament was dissolved. "Frenchmen!" said Louis Napoleon "the present situation cannot last much longer. Instead of framing laws for the good of the nation the Assembly arms for civil war. It attacks the power I hold directly from the nation, it encourages every evil passion. I have dissolved it, and I call upon the whole of the people to judge between us."

Then he asked the people to make him President for ten years. This they did by seven and a half million votes.

This is called Louis Napoleon's Coup d'Etat or Stroke of State. It was the act of a great statesman, said his admirers. It was a crime, said others, and they spoke of it as the Crime of December. In any case it was simply a breaking of the law. But it was so carefully planned, so well carried out, that no one resisted, and it succeeded perfectly. "The Empire is made," said a Republican bitterly when it was all over.

He was right. For Louis Napoleon was no more content with being President for ten years than his great uncle had been with being Consul for ten years.

He now did many things as if he were a King. His head was engraved on the money, his name was added to the church prayers. Yet for a little time longer he tried to keep people's eyes shut to the fact. He tried to delude the French people with the idea that France was still a Republic.

But Louis Napoleon was a dreamer as well as a conspirator, and he kept steadily to his dreams of greatness. He worked quietly and well. When a few months later he made a journey through the country, he made speeches everywhere, turning people's thoughts toward the idea of an empire. Everywhere he was greeted with cries of, "Long live the Emperor!"

At last he felt the time had come. The people were asked once more to vote whether Louis Napoleon should be Emperor or not. More than seven millions said "Yes," only a few thousands said "No."

So on December 2, 1852, Louis Napoleon was proclaimed Emperor of the French. He took the title of Napoleon III, the great Napoleon's son, who died in Austria, being looked upon as Napoleon II.

After he became Emperor, Napoleon III married a beautiful Spanish lady who thus became the Empress Eugenie.

He lived in great magnificence, and tried to make his court as dazzling and splendid as in the days of the Bourbons or of his great uncle. He made Paris splendid too, pulling down many old houses and building them up again as magnificent palaces.

Napoleon III promised the French peace. In a famous speech he had said, "Some people say 'The Empire means war.' I say, 'The Empire means peace.' And it does mean peace. For France wants it, and when France is satisfied, the world is at rest."

But although Napoleon III promised peace he was almost constantly at war. During his reign one war followed upon another almost without pause.

The greatest of these was the Crimean war. In this the French joined with the British to help Turkey against Russia.

Now the British and the French, who had been such deadly and bitter enemies for so many hundreds of years, fought side by side as comrades. Side by side they fought in the burning heat of summer, and the terrible cold of a Russian winter. It was a strange sight. It was strange, too, to find them fighting for the Turks, whom the Christians, and especially the French, in far-off days, had done their best to drive out of Europe. At length after two years' fighting the war ended in victory for the allies, and peace was signed in March 1856.

After the Russian war came an Italian war. Italy at this time was still divided into many states, of which Lombardy and Venetia were still under the rule of Austria. Now many Italians longed for a free and united

Italy. Chief among these were Victor Emmanuel, King of Sardinia, and his minister, Cavour. They persuaded

Napoleon III to help them, and in 1859 he declared war against Austria.

Once more the French were victorious, and the war came to an end with the great victory of Solferino, by which the Austrians were driven out of Lombardy.

Although Italy was by no means free "from the Alps of the Adriatic," as Napoleon had said he would make it, he thought he had done enough. He made peace with Austria and left the Italians to fight out their own freedom.

Other wars followed which for the most part had some just cause. But at length Napoleon began a foolish and unjust war with Mexico. He tried to force the Mexicans to accept Maximilian, the brother of the Emperor of Austria, as their ruler.

The Mexicans did not want Maximilian, and they fought desperately against him. Then having spent a great deal of money, and lost a great many men in vain, Napoleon called his soldiers back to France, leaving Maximilian to his fate.

Thus forsaken Maximilian could do little. He was soon defeated, taken prisoner, and shot.

This sad ending to the Mexican expedition did a great deal of harm to Napoleon III. He alone was to blame for it. France as a country had been against the expedition, and after its miserable failure much discontent against the Emperor began to show itself.

CHAPTER 100

THE SECOND EMPIRE— NAPOLEON III A PRISONER

YET while France had been carrying on all these wars abroad there had been peace at home, and the country prospered. At first after he became Emperor, Napoleon III did as he liked, and the people had little part in ruling the land. But as discontent against him grew he found himself forced more and more to give way to the demands of the Republicans. Still Napoleon believed that the hearts of the people were yet with him when a great war broke out between France and Germany.

In 1870 the Spanish people offered the throne of Spain to Leopold of Hohenzollern, a nephew of the King of Prussia. The French immediately declared that they would not allow this Prince to become King of Spain. For Prussia was now the most powerful state in Germany, and they feared what might happen if Prussia and Spain were united.

Prince Leopold said at once that he would not accept the throne. But the French were not content with that, they insisted that the King of Prussia should promise never to give his nephew leave to accept the Spanish crown. This the King refused to do, and war broke out.

This is called the Franco-Prussian War. France was not ready to fight. The Prussian army was far larger and far better drilled than the French. The King of Prussia had the great statesman Count Bismarck to advise him, the great soldier von Moltke to lead his armies. Napoleon himself was no soldier, he had neither statesmen nor generals who could compete with the Germans, and from first to last the war went against the French.

The Prussians won every great battle, they took every town they besieged except Belfort. This town held out gallantly for more than three months, and only yielded at length when the war was over, and the Germans victorious.

But long before the war was over Napoleon III's Empire had vanished. It was at the battle of Sedan that he lost his crown.

In the narrow valley of the Meuse, near the town of Sedan, the battle was fought on September 1, 1870. On the hills around lay the Germans, in the valley lay the French, utterly at their mercy. Yet for a long day the desperate fight lasted.

The morning dawned still and misty, but as soon as it was light enough the battle began. Hour after hour Napoleon rode aimlessly about the army. Then hopeless and downcast, sunk in gloomy thought, he went back to Sedan, and looked no more at the battle.

As the day went on Napoleon's thoughts grew more and more gloomy. At length he determined that the useless fight must cease, and ordered a white flag to be hoisted over Sedan. Even then some of his officers refused to yield. The Emperor was not leading the battle, and they did not see that he had any right to interfere, but in the end they too saw the hopelessness of the struggle and gave way. Then Napoleon surrendered himself to the King of Prussia.

"Sire, my brother," he wrote, "not having been able to die in the midst of my troops nothing remains to me but to put my sword into your Majesty's hands."

The King of Prussia accepted Napoleon's surrender, but his terms were hard. He demanded the surrender of the whole army as prisoners of war together with all arms and baggage.

Crushed though he was, Napoleon could not at first make up his mind to submit to these conditions, and he resolved to see the King to try and get better terms. So at five o'clock next morning he set out. But as the Emperor drove along he was met by Bismarck. Together they turned aside into a little weaver's cottage which stood by the road to talk.

At first the talk began in a tiny room upstairs, but it was dirty and close, so after a time, as the morning was clear and sunny, Bismarck ordered two chairs to be brought out to the front of the cottage. And there the fallen emperor and the triumphant statesman finished their talk.

It was of no avail, and the terms remained the same. The King sent his royal prisoner to Germany to the castle of Wilhelmshohe where once, his uncle, Jerome, had played at being King of Westphalia. So the last Emperor of the French passed out of his country forever, a captive.

Napoleon went sadly on his way. But he was not yet without hope. He was still Emperor, he was still a dreamer. The Empress would make peace, he thought, and he would return once more to France. But these dreams were soon at an end. As the train stopped at a station on the way to Wilhelmshohe the newspaper boys were excitedly yelling the news, "Fall of the Empire! Flight of the Empress!"

It was in this way that Napoleon III learned that the Empire for which he had schemed and plotted had gone from him forever.

THE FALLEN EMPEROR AND TRIUMPHANT STATESMAN TALKED TOGETHER.

CHAPTER 101
THE THIRD REPUBLIC

> "The tumult and the shouting dies;
> The captains and the Kings depart."

BEFORE the King left France he had been allowed to send a telegram to the Empress. It was very short. "The whole army is defeated and captive," it ran, "and I am a prisoner."

This was the first news of the awful disaster to reach Paris. Shortly before, some one came to the Empress with the rumour that the Emperor was a captive. The Empress had a warlike spirit. She had urged her husband to the war, never doubting of success. She would not now believe in the disgrace of surrender.

The Emperor a captive! With flashing eyes she turned upon the speaker. "You lie!" she cried. "He is dead!"

A little later the telegram was handed to her.

When the news became known throughout the city the grief and wrath were terrible. Once more angry, excited mobs surged through the streets, and shouts of "Down with the Emperor! Long live the Republic!" were heard.

The mob at length burst into the Parliament. There amid unutterable noise and confusion they insisted that the Republic should be at once proclaimed.

So on September 4, 1870, the Third Republic was proclaimed.

Unnoticed in the general excitement the Empress, accompanied only by one lady, quietly left the great palace of the Tuileries on foot. She took refuge for the night in a dentist's house, and from there she fled to England. There when his captivity in Germany came to an end the Emperor joined her. There two years later he died.

"Were you at Sedan?" he murmured to the doctor who stood beside his deathbed. Then he lay still and spoke no more.

So ended his eventful life.

He had been a fugitive and outlaw for more than half his days. He had been adventurer, pretender and prisoner. He had been President and Emperor, and for fifteen years one of the foremost men in Europe. And through all, through obscurity or greatness, he had been a dreamer and conspirator. To the last he was a dreamer, to the last he believed that he would one day return to France, and rule there once more.

But that was not to be either for himself, or for his only son, the Prince Imperial. He joined the British army, and was killed in the Zulu War in 1879, when he was only twenty-three.

The Empress Eugenie, now a very old lady, still lives in England.

After the Republic was proclaimed a new Government was framed which was called the Government of National Defence. They decided to go on with the war rather than yield to the very hard terms which were the only ones the Germans were willing to accept.

"We will give," they said, "as much money as we have, but not an inch of our territory, not a stone of our fortresses."

But under the Republic the war went no better for the French than it had done under the Empire. The Prussian army marched on victoriously. And little more than a fortnight after Sedan the Germans appeared before Paris and the siege of the capital began.

The King of Prussia took up his quarters at the palace of Versailles. And while Paris starved he held great state there. There it was that with great pomp and splendour he was proclaimed Emperor of Germany. This first Emperor of modern Germany was the grandfather of the present Emperor.

For more than four months Paris held out, the people suffering terribly from hunger and cold. During the long winter days it was a city of darkness, for coal and gas gave out. The city of light and gaiety was changed into a city of sadness and silence, the silence only broken by the scream of shells, the roar of cannon. No more carriages drove about the streets with rattle of wheels and clatter of horses' hoofs. For the horses were all eaten for food. To keep themselves from starving the people gladly ate even cats and dogs. Only very bad bread was to be had, and little enough of that. Not for years had such a cold winter been known. The people cut down the trees in the boulevards and gardens for firewood.

In spite of all their sufferings the people held out with dogged patience, with heroic hopefulness. They hoped against hope that relief would come from the armies still fighting beyond the walls. But only news of fresh defeats and losses came to them. At length on January 29, 1871, Paris yielded.

The terms of peace were almost the same as those the Germans had offered months before. France had to give up the provinces of Alsace and Lorraine, and had also to pay an enormous sum of money. Many of the French fortresses too were to be garrisoned with German soldiers until all the money was paid.

France was vanquished and humbled. As the leader of the government read the conditions in Parliament the tears ran down his cheeks. Since the Hundred Years' War, no war had been so disastrous to France.

But the troubled land was not yet to have peace, and under the very eyes of the conquering Germans a civil war broke out.

Some of the people of Paris revolted against the government. They got possession of the cannon, and pointed them against the city. They elected a new government which was called the Commune.

Then a second siege of Paris began. This time it was Frenchman against Frenchman, the government being the besiegers, the rebels the besieged.

For weeks the rebels held out. But at length the government army succeeded in entering Paris. Then a dreadful fight followed, for Paris was only won street by street. And as from one after another the Communists were driven back with dreadful slaughter they set fire to all the chief buildings.

What Prussian cannon failed to do, the madness of revolted Frenchmen did. One after another the splendid palaces of Paris were wrapped in flame. They were piled with everything that would burn easily, strewn with gunpowder, soaked in oil, and then set ablaze.

Night after night the sky was red with the flames, day by day rolling clouds of smoke darkened the spring sunshine. But at length the dreadful week drew to an end. The Communists were vanquished, and driven out of their last strongholds. So at last came to a close one of the most terrible revolts in all French history.

To the victors was left a desolated capital. The splendid palace of the Tuileries, where so many scenes of French history had been enacted, was a blackened ruin. Never more would King or Emperor tread its noble halls. The Hotel de Ville or Townhall, the old building which had seen so many governments rise and fall, had now itself fallen, together with many another building round which French history centred.

Yet from this disastrous war and cruel civil strife France recovered quickly. In a few years the ruins in Paris disappeared, noble buildings rose in their place and a garden blooms where once the palace of the Tuileries stood. By 1873 all the money which the Germans exacted had been paid, and the last German soldier marched back again to his own country. From that release the Third Republic may truly be said to date.

Since then France has remained a Republic and at peace with Europe. Although she still sorrows for the loss of Alsace and Lorraine, the country has gradually regained its place among the great powers, and has in every way grown more prosperous. And last, but for us perhaps not least, the old bitterness which lay for so many hundreds of years between France and Britain has vanished. The rivalry is now a friendly one, and John Bull looks upon Jacques Bonhomme as his very good friend.

VIVE L'ENTENTE CORDIALE!

www.ingramcontent.com/pod-product-compliance
Lightning Source LLC
Chambersburg PA
CBHW030252100526
44590CB00012B/373